THE WORKS OF SRI CHINMOY

QUESTIONS & ANSWERS

VOLUME IV

THE WORKS OF SRI CHINMOY

QUESTIONS & ANSWERS

VOLUME IV

★

EARTH'S CRY MEETS HEAVEN'S SMILE

LYON · OXFORD

GANAPATI PRESS

LXXXIX

© 2019 THE SRI CHINMOY CENTRE

ISBN 978-1-911319-12-2

See appendix for notice regarding this edition.

FIRST EDITION WENT TO PRESS ON 16 JUNE 2019

QUESTIONS & ANSWERS

VOLUME IV

EARTH'S CRY MEETS HEAVEN'S SMILE

BOOK 1

I – QUESTIONS AND ANSWERS

1. When one sees through the light of the soul, does he see through hundreds of lifetimes?

Sri Chinmoy: When one sees through the light of the soul, one can see the future possibilities of one's present incarnation, and at the most, one or two future incarnations, not hundreds of lifetimes. This statement applies to past incarnations as well. These glimpses need not be in any chronological order. However, in the cases of great spiritual Masters like Krishna and Buddha, this principle is not applicable, for the remotest past and the farthest future, in exact chronological order, is at their command.

2. When we see through the light of the soul, is it always with the feeling of joy?

Sri Chinmoy: Yes. It is always with a feeling of inner joy and this joy may often be expressed by the shedding of tears. This shedding of tears is the outer expression of the soul's delight and has nothing to do with human sorrow, grief or frustration. It is like a mother shedding tears when she sees her son returning home from abroad. Her tears are the expression of her inner joy.

3. When the soul chooses a new body, does it have a blueprint laid out as to its mission, or does the soul's mission evolve during one's lifetime, depending on circumstances and environment?

Sri Chinmoy: The soul always comes down to earth with a certain mission. However, the earthly environment can help or hinder this mission. It also happens that the soul, at times willingly, makes an adjustment to its surroundings. Then it gradually tries to fulfil its mission with the full recognition and co-operation of the environment.

4. Does the soul have many missions, or just one, in a lifetime?

Sri Chinmoy: There is only one mission, but there are many aims. One soul may wish to become a poet, an artist or an engineer in a lifetime. Each soul may aim at various creativities, but these are aims. They are not to be confused with the soul's mission. The soul's mission is always first and foremost: God-realisation; then comes the manifestation of God-realisation on earth. However, one's aim may help him in his God-realisation or it may delay him, depending on the individual's approach to Truth.

For example, if one is a writer, it is well and good. If he goes on writing without aspiration for God-realisation through his writings, he may one day become a very great writer, but he has not necessarily progressed in his self-discovery. On the other hand, if one writes to express the Divine in his writings, if one's outer expression is the result of one's inner aspiration, and if one has taken to writing as a self-dedicated service to the Supreme in humanity, then certainly the aspirant in the writer is leading him to the realisation of God. To come back to your question, from the standpoint of absolute Truth, there is only one mission and that is nothing but Self-realisation.

5. *Does the vital have a mission separate from the soul's or is it related to the soul's mission?*

Sri Chinmoy: The vital and the body do not have a separate mission. But when they collaborate with the soul's mission, it becomes theirs, too. The vital hungers for name and fame, which are only aims. When the vital identifies itself with the soul and willingly accepts the soul's mission, then the soul's mission undoubtedly becomes the mission of the vital.

6. *How does one know if he is attending to his soul's mission or simply satisfying his vanity?*

Sri Chinmoy: One can distinguish between the two only when one works without being motivated by desire and without being affected by the results of his actions. When one is in that state of consciousness, one can easily know whether one is attending to one's soul's mission or just satisfying one's vanity. Work done in self-dedication leads the aspirant towards the fulfilment of his soul's mission. Work done for self-gratification drives man towards the pleasures that end in self-annihilation.

7. *It is often said that the soul needs certain experiences even though they may seem adverse at the time. How are we to distinguish between the experiences the soul needs and our own desire to forge ahead through egoistic stubbornness?*

Sri Chinmoy: The soul does not have any experience which is unnecessary. Whenever the soul has an experience, there is a divine purpose behind it. But on the physical plane, we often fail to see that divine purpose. We see it as a mere incident in our journey here on earth. There are many things which our physical mind cannot comprehend while our soul is having the experiences. It is also true that through our stubbornness, we impose some insignificant experiences on the soul. But what we call "adverse experiences" are not adverse to the soul because in the soul's wide vision of light, these experiences are all possibilities to grow, to develop, to manifest a higher truth or to fulfil a greater mission on earth.

8. In this age of Kali Yuga, are more people becoming aware of their soul's mission, or is this kind of awareness for future generations?

Sri Chinmoy: One cannot give a categorical answer to this question because what the golden future will look like is uncertain and obscure, with all kinds of possibilities and impossibilities intermingled. It is very easy to appreciate the past dawns. Living in this era, we cannot judge the aspiration of the past or the aspiration of the future. But we do know that since the world is evolving, human consciousness is awakening towards a brighter light. Since the world, from the spiritual point of view at least, is progressing, there is more than a mere possibility for a higher consciousness to dawn upon earth. The achievement of the past does not and cannot satisfy the present. The present demands something higher, deeper and more fulfilling. The role of the Kali Yuga will sooner or later be over. The Golden Days will unmistakably dawn.

To come back to your question, we all know that the present-day world is more aware of scientific discoveries than it is aware of the soul's mission. The future generations will have both science and spirituality at their highest, not as two dire competitors, but as two complementary forces. Both science and spirituality will achieve the perfect perfection of matter and spirit. The gradual evolution of the earth-consciousness will grant the soul more opportunity to know why it has come and what it has to do in the great drama of the Supreme.

9. Does our soul have contact with the mind of the so-called higher planets like Venus and Saturn?

Sri Chinmoy: First of all, Saturn and Venus have no mind, either human or divine. Secondly, only the yogis can have free access to the planets Venus, Saturn, etc. Ordinary souls cannot have this capacity, but they can have a glimpse of these planets in their dreams, or in a very high state of meditation.

10. There is always talk about this world destroying itself; then people become personally alarmed. Would the end of the physical world as we know it be a threat to the soul?

Sri Chinmoy: If the physical world is destroyed, it would not be a threat to the soul, for the soul can stay in the souls' region. But if the soul wants to manifest the divine in all its aspects, then it must incarnate in a human body in the physical world.

11. I understand you to say that some spiritual figures in India claim that today you are here, tomorrow you are not here, that the world is an illusion. But aren't those so-called spiritual figures actually corrupting the pure teaching of Shankara on the question of Maya? Shankara never really disavowed the existence of this phenomenal world. Am I right in saying this?

Sri Chinmoy: Yes, you are right. But the general conception of Maya has been misinterpreted in the East. Even now ninety-nine per cent will say that Shankara advocated Maya, the doctrine that the world is an illusion.

What Shankara wanted to say, if I am correct, is: "The world is not an illusion, but we must not give importance to the transitory things. There is something eternal, perpetual, everlasting and we must try to live in the Eternal and not in the transitory."

Now at present, or very recently, you can say, about eighty years ago, some of the modern Indian thinkers came to the conclusion, after throwing considerable light on Shankara's philosophy, that he did not actually mean that – that the world is a colossal illusion.

Neti, neti, "Not this, not this", the Upanishads cried and Shankara echoed. But what is that "this"? It is something that is finite, it is something that is binding us all the time. So people thought that if we leave the world, perhaps there would be a better world somewhere else. It is just like standing on one shore and thinking that the other shore is safe and full of joy and delight. But it is not true.

Each person has his own way of understanding the truth. You are at perfect liberty to understand it in your own way. How many people can go into the deeper meaning of the Truth? Some people think that the world is an illusion while others feel that it is not an illusion. It is deplorable that we do not or cannot see the world in its totality. We look at the truth with our finite consciousness, with our limited understanding. When we do that, we see that the world is nothing but an object of ignorance. We feel that we must enter another world, the world of Bliss and Perfection.

To come back to your question, Shankara's very short earthly existence was surcharged with dynamic energy. He strode the length and breadth of India on foot, preaching his philosophy; he set up temples in key parts of the country. What he offered to the world at large was, in fact, dynamic truth and not the so-called illusion which the world so forcefully associates with his teachings.

II – SRI CHINMOY'S FIRST TELEVISION INTERVIEW

12. Interviewer: Master Chinmoy, I have just introduced you in Spanish and explained some of your works that I have read in Spanish. What is your mission now in Puerto Rico, and how long will you stay here?

Sri Chinmoy: My mission here in Puerto Rico is to help the sincere seekers in their inner life and help them realise their spiritual perfection. I shall be staying here until 6 August and then I shall leave for New York, where I have another Centre. We have two Centres, one here in Puerto Rico, the other in New York.

13. Interviewer: Master Chinmoy, is this the first time that you have been in Puerto Rico?

Sri Chinmoy: This is my fourth visit. I was here exactly a year ago, last July. That was my first visit. Then I came here twice after that. So this is my fourth visit.

14. Interviewer: How many people do you have working at your Centre in Puerto Rico?

Sri Chinmoy: We have here now fifty members, fifty sincere seekers, I must say. And there are many who are connected with the Centre but are unable to come to the meetings owing to family problems and so on.

15. Interviewer: Are your students well acquainted with philosophy? Are they students of different stages or are they all of the same level?

Sri Chinmoy: They attend the classes, they come to me to receive help and guidance in their self-realisation, but they are not of the same standard. Some of them are very well versed in both Eastern and Western philosophy, while others are not. All of them come to me and meditate with me, and ask me spiritual questions to solve their inner and outer problems. The students range from absolute beginners to the most advanced aspirants.

16. Interviewer: Well, it is a very broad problem in order to attain to realisation, is it not?

Sri Chinmoy: Yes, it is a lifelong problem. To be accurate, a lifelong process. It depends on the individual. It may even take a few incarnations to achieve realisation.

17. Interviewer: Master, I understand that in order to reach the height you have now attained, it took you a very long time. I would like you very much to tell me how you felt the inner call, how you started preparing yourself for the spiritual life.

Sri Chinmoy: When I was very young, about a year and a half old, my parents took me to a spiritual place in South India .... in Madras State. I was taken to that spiritual ashram three times more in my early childhood. And when I was twelve years old, I became a permanent member, a spiritual seeker in that ashram. I stayed there for twenty years, from the age of twelve to the age of thirty-two, practising the spiritual discipline and living the inner life.

Then the Divine within me, the Supreme, commanded me to come to the West. He said, "I want you to be my instrument.

I want you to help my sincere, spiritual children in the West. This is your Mission. Go to the West. My spiritual children there are thirsting for the spiritual life. I am in you, with you and for you."

18. Interviewer: Master Chinmoy, but – do you not think that the East is more prepared, more inclined to understand the spiritual life and practise it than the West?

Sri Chinmoy: According to my own understanding of the Truth, the West has also abundant possibility to realise God. As the East has ample opportunity, so also has the West. True, formerly the East was more inclined to the inner life and the spiritual life. But now those days are gone. Even in the West there are many sincere seekers who can stand on the same level as the most advanced aspirants in the East. God-realisation is not the sole monopoly of the East. God is Omnipresent. The West also has infinite divine qualities. For example, the West has dynamism and the West is extremely fortunate in giving importance to time. Time is a great factor in the spiritual life. The West knows the value of time, whereas in the East, in the name of Eternal Time, we have become very lazy. We wallow in the pleasure of idleness.

19. Interviewer: I just wondered, Master Chinmoy, if by creating the high materialistic form of life we have now, whether we have put too many barriers between ourselves and the Divine.

Sri Chinmoy: This is, to some extent, true, but at the same time, in the West, you have been aspiring for material perfection, which will help you hold the Divine most solidly. The Western soil is spiritually fertile. The West can easily and effectively express the Divine through the most advanced material development in the physical world. The East does not have that material development. The sense of material development is absolutely necessary for the East.

Here in the West, your material development need not stand as a barrier. On the contrary, it can be of great advantage. You have both dynamism and material development. Like the East, if the West is ready to accept and feel the Truth that the Divine is not only in Heaven, but here on earth, and if the West cultivates, develops and adds Eastern silence to its matchless dynamism and material development, then God's all-transforming Smile will dawn on the West.

20. *Interviewer: Master Chinmoy, in Puerto Rico do you find great spiritual possibility?*

Sri Chinmoy: I must say in all sincerity that there is a great possibility for the spiritual life here in Puerto Rico, and many people are practising it. Unfortunately some of them are doing this unconsciously. They are eating something but they do not know what they are actually eating. The Puerto Rican soil is extremely fertile. The seeker in Puerto Rico is spiritually genuine. Hence the spiritual fulfilment in Puerto Rico is inevitable.

21. *Interviewer: And will it be your task and the task of your Centre to make them realise their spiritual Goal?*

Sri Chinmoy: That is my sole aim. They are ready, they are fit, and they are able to enter into the inner life. Some of them are actually moving fast across the path of the spiritual life. To my sorrow, there are some who are not aware of their inner aspiration. So I wish to make them conscious of what they are truly doing.

22. Interviewer: Master Chinmoy, I am curious about the meaning of these three letters which you pronounce, "AUM".

Sri Chinmoy: AUM is a Sanskrit syllable, or you can say, a complete word. We have, in India, the Trinity: Brahma, Vishnu and Shiva – the Creator, Preserver and Transformer. *A* represents Brahma the Creator, *U* represents Vishnu the Preserver and *M* represents Shiva the Transformer. And this AUM is the breath of the Supreme. The Indian sages, seers and yogis of yore chanted this AUM and they got their souls' illumination and liberation. Even now, most of the seekers in India chant AUM most devotedly. They will have their realisation by chanting AUM, the Power Infinite.

III – QUESTIONS AND ANSWERS

23. How can one reach God in one's lifetime?

Let us change the word "reach" and instead let us use the word "realise". When we use the term "reach", we feel that we have to come to a certain place. Now you are sitting over there and if you want to reach me, you have to come to me by either walking or jumping or flying. But when we use the term "realise", there is no separation. Where is God? God is deep within us. But God-realisation in one life, in one short span of time, by one's own personal effort, is next to impossible. But along with one's personal effort, if the aspirant has absolute aspiration, one-pointed dedication, if he has the blessings, grace and concern of a very great spiritual Master who represents God to his disciples, and if he has been assured by his spiritual Master on this point, then, in one life, he can realise God.

If one does not have a fully realised Master, a Guru, but if his aspiration is most intense, then God's Grace showers on him and God Himself plays the part of the human teacher, that is to say, the spiritual Master. If God sees that the particular aspirant is absolutely sincere and he deserves self-realisation in this life, then, as I have said, God plays the part of a human Guru. Otherwise it is a spiritual Master who becomes a pilot and takes you across the ocean of ignorance to Light, Wisdom, Peace, Bliss and Plenitude.

You have got a Guru, Agni, so your problem is over, and your aspiration is most intense. I say it with the very depth of my heart that this Guru of yours will never fail you. You will always be in the inmost recesses of his heart. He will carry you, carry you to the Golden Shore of the Beyond.

24. God could have made man perfect to begin with. What was His reason for putting us to all the trouble that we are going through to attain perfection?

Good. God could have started His creation with perfection. But fortunately or unfortunately, that was not His intention. What God wanted was to go through ignorance to Knowledge, through limitation to Plenitude, through death to Immortality.

In the outer world, we see limitations, imperfections, doubts, fear and death. But in the inner world we see Light, Peace, Bliss and Perfection. When we live in God's Consciousness, there is no imperfection. It is all Perfection.

God is a divine Player. He is playing His divine Game and He knows the Ultimate End. At each moment He is revealing Himself in us and through us, in spite of the very fact that we see, nay create, a vast gulf between ourselves and God. In addition to this, we feel that God is in Heaven and we are on earth. In the physical world, the miseries, troubles, frustrations and despair that we are going through are nothing but experiences on our way to the Ultimate Goal. Who is, after all, having all these experiences? It is God and God alone. And when we consciously identify ourselves with God's Consciousness, we observe that there is no imperfection because God is perfect Perfection. But if we do not live in the Divine Consciousness, and if we feel that we are the doers, naturally we will be yoked to the imperfection of the outer world. What actually is happening is the self-revelation of God in His manifested creation. A seeker of the Supreme, living in the Supreme, being one with the Consciousness of the Supreme, sees and feels that his consciousness, his life, both inner and outer, are the projections of God's ever-transcending Perfection growing into perfect Perfection.

IV – QUESTIONS AND ANSWERS AT THE PUERTO RICO CENTRE

25. Sometimes in my meditations, I come to think about the feeling of Eternity, you know. I come to feel that human beings have lived forever and will live forever. This feeling, instead of causing me pleasure and a good sensation, on the contrary causes me great anguish and pain. I feel then that I am all alone, that I am living a life of my own, different from everything. I feel that I have no world left, that by the power of my mind, I have destroyed the world and am alone by myself. This thought causes me a great deal of pain and I have wanted to mention this state of mind. I want to know if I am taking a wrong path.

When, in your meditation, you feel that you are lonely, alone, it is not actually the loneliness of the human being. At that time you get a glimpse of the Sole One. This One pervades all. We call it Brahman, the One without a second. When you feel that you are lonely, it is really the feeling of your unconscious oneness with that Absolute Oneness. But when the physical, the vital and the mental beings are not transformed to a considerable degree, they are afraid of this super-loneliness. It is not actually loneliness, as I have said, it is the sense of the Oneness. You see the reality; you feel the One pervading everything.

Now, what is actually happening in your meditation is that at times your aspiration, before it reaches its Goal or before it finds its abode in the Goal, ceases. Your heart's mounting flame rises upward, but there are a few stops and breaks. If there were a gradual and continuous flight and if it were uninterrupted, then you would not feel the loneliness at the lower levels of your consciousness. Please try to keep your aspiration uninterrupted at all times. The inner runner must complete his race divine.

The infinite Eternity and the Eternity that you are speaking of is in the motto of our Centres: "Man is Infinity's Heart, Man is Eternity's Breath, Man is Immortality's Life." The breath which Eternity possesses is man. Most of us have had countless lives and some of us will have countless more. In your case, it is the divine realisation or the spiritual realisation that you need. One can attain the achievements of twenty incarnations in one lifetime provided one takes to spirituality in all sincerity and dedication and listens to one's spiritual guide most devotedly. Since you have the intense aspiration, you are accomplishing it successfully. That is why the spiritual Masters say, "Take to the spiritual life and enter into the divine. This divine is your own infinite Self. The sooner you start your journey, the better for you."

When you live the spiritual life, you live in Eternity. This Eternity does not present itself as a problem, but as an inspiration, encouragement, aspiration and illumination. It is Eternity that is constantly carrying us into the immortal Self and that immortal Self is our real Self.

26. I have been reading the minor Upanishads and I want to ask you something about them. If they are "minor", why are they so profound in the script and in the meaning?

Sri Chinmoy: I believe that we are living in a world of economy! If we say that the "minor" Upanishads are profound, then you will agree, I hope, with those that feel that the "major" Upanishads are more profound.

The thing is – in India, many great scholars accept sixteen or eighteen Upanishads as authentic and original. Some accept only twelve which they take as "major" and others accept only eight; the rest they consider "minor". These people feel that not all but some of the Upanishads are momentous in their depths and in their embodiment of Truth. But you yourself will be the best judge. You kindly read the major ones first. According to me, the most significant ones are: Katha, Isha, Kena, Prashna, Mundaka,

Mandukya, Taittiriya, Aitareya, Chandogya, Brihadaranyaka, Svetasvatara and Kaivalya.

I am sure, Gauri, that you know that there are only one hundred and eight Upanishads! If you have the time, patience, inspiration and aspiration to study all the one hundred and eight Upanishads, then it is simply wonderful. But do not come and tell me that some of the later Upanishads are not only insignificant, but a mere repetition of the former significant ones. To be frank with you, I have just studied sixteen. They have given me what I sought and at the same time, what they stand for: lofty aspiration and mystical revelations.

27. Another question about the Upanishads: why was the King of Death, Yama, not there when Nachiketa arrived?

So you are carrying us into the lore of the Katha Upanishad! Wonderful. That was not the fault of the King of Death. If I come to your house without making a previous appointment or without your knowledge and do not find you at home, I can't blame you, can I?

Nachiketa's father, Vajasravasa, said, "Thee I give to Death." But the King of Death did not say, "O Nachiketa, I am waiting for thee, for thee alone." Yama was busy at that time with someone else.

28. When the soul is going to reincarnate, is it forced to do so or does the soul have the privilege of making this decision?

When the soul leaves the body, it gradually goes back to its own region, after leaving the physical, vital and mental and psychic sheaths. Nobody can compel the soul to reincarnate, save the Supreme. The Supreme has the power to compel the soul, but He does not do it. The Supreme does not compel anybody to do anything. The soul has an inner urge to fulfil the Divine here on earth. Some souls want to take rest for a few years, say ten, twenty, forty or sixty years, while others who are not developed and are full of earthly desires and want to fulfil their countless unfulfilled desires, come back to the physical world sooner. To be sure, they are not going to fulfil anything spiritual here on earth. They just come back to the world of manifestation to fulfil their countless human desires.

The soul, as I have already said, is not compelled to reincarnate; but if a soul wants to descend, before doing so, it investigates the family, the environment, the circumstances and a few other things. Before actually entering into the family, the soul has to have an interview with the Supreme. Then the Supreme either approves of the soul's decision or He may merely tolerate it. There is a great difference between approval and tolerance. I am sure you know this.

Then there are some souls who have had enough of earthly experiences, that is to say, sufferings and frustrations. These particular souls usually take the oath of Nirvana. They do not come down again. They remain in the Void. But there are aspiring souls who will not accept any defeat. They will come down to have the Divine Victory in spite of their repeated defeats. These souls will come and go until the Divine Victory has been fully established on earth. Truly you are one of these divine warriors.

Something more I wish to add. The soul is not compelled. The human father says to his son, "You are my son. You have to listen to me." But the Supreme Father does not do that. It is only the ignorant human being who commands. The higher we go, the clearer this becomes to us. Normally the Supreme puts into our consciousness what he actually wants us to do in order to fulfil Himself in infinite ways in us and through us. Compulsion is only in this world, not in the higher worlds. Earlier I said something about the inner urge. It is the inner urge that compels the soul to reincarnate and not any outer force. My Father, the Infinite, is the most compassionate Being here on earth as well as in Heaven. It is my bounden duty to fulfil Him here on earth, there in Heaven. Finally I must realise that by fulfilling Him, I am fulfilling myself unmistakably, totally, divinely and supremely.

29. I wish to ask something further, regarding the previous question. Religion has told us that we have come from the Spirit and we go back to the Spirit at the end of our present incarnation. Now if we go back to our Father, then what is the use of reincarnation, realisation and so forth?

There are many religions on earth that do believe in reincarnation. Reincarnation is an undeniable fact. Now let me explain to you briefly what we mean by reincarnation. You play a game, but you cannot play it forever. You cannot play it twenty-four hours at a stretch. You have to rest from time to time. Similarly in the process of evolution through a long series of reincarnations, we are trying to complete the game. This divine game that we are all playing is called the Lila. We cannot complete the game in its fulness during one span of life. Also we are not playing the game in a divine way. We have not reached the Goal. Our Goal is still a far cry. Now if you want to embody your Father's infinite consciousness on earth, and want to reveal and manifest your Father, who, you feel, is in Heaven, then you have to play His divine game of reincarnation. There is no other way. When we go to Him after each lifetime, it is only for a rest.

V – INTERVIEW ON WHOA RADIO STATION

30. Interviewer: This morning we have Sri Chinmoy here in the studio. He will give us an example of a prayer chant in Sanskrit to start the program.

[Sri Chinmoy sings a *Shloka* from the *Brihadaranyaka Upanishad.*]

Mr Jim Knight: Ladies and gentlemen, you have been listening to Sri Chinmoy Ghose chanting a prayer, which, to those of us in the Western world, was quite foreign. We are going to get into that and find out what that was about, and we have many questions to ask Sri Chinmoy this morning.

With us in our studio we have Miss Dorothy Eisaman, Mr and Mrs José L. Casanova, Miss Carmen Suro, Mr Ramon Torres Peañ, Mr Ed Belville, and acting with me this morning in the process of asking the questions, is Mr George Riddell.
Mr George Riddell: One of the first questions that comes to us: there is evidently a very sacred note in that chant and I was wondering if you might interpret it for us in English, to know what it was about.
Sri Chinmoy: Thank you. This chant is one of the most famous chants in India. From time immemorial, this chant has been sung, chanted by the seekers of Truth. The seers, the sages of the Upanishads sang this chant. The significance, the meaning of this prayer is:

> Lead me from the untruth to the Truth.
> Lead me from darkness to Light.
> Lead me from death to Immortality.

The firmament of India still resounds with this soul-stirring chant of the Vedic and the Upanishadic seers of India.

31. Mr George Riddell: Typical themes like that seem to run through all religious hymns and chants, and now that you mention "Vedic", I wonder if Yoga itself is a part of another religion of India or is it a religion in itself?

Sri Chinmoy: Yoga is no religion. Yoga transcends all varieties of religion. It is something infinitely deeper than the so-called "religions". Yoga is the Living Breath that makes us feel that God is within us, of us and for us. Yoga is the direct communion with God. It is our union with God that Yoga teaches us. And at the same time, it is the language of our inner and spiritual life. Right now, I am speaking in English in order to convey my feelings, thoughts and ideas. Similarly, if I want to speak to God, commune with God, then the language that is required is called Yoga.

32. Mr George Riddell: Do you meditate or do you pray? In Yoga, how do you communicate with God?

Sri Chinmoy: In Yoga we pray, we concentrate and we meditate. When we pray, we get an inner feeling of going upwards, that is to say, with our hearts we feel that we are crying for something from Above. When we concentrate, we focus all our intense attention on something, it may be an object or it may be a person, in order to identify ourselves with it. And when we meditate, we enter into the deeper regions, deeper planes of consciousness.

By prayer, we enter into the Kingdom of God, by concentration we can also enter into the Kingdom of God and also, of course, by meditation. These three ways, prayer, concentration and meditation, are the most effective ways to commune with God.

33. Mr George Riddell: Some of the other members here may have some questions that they wish to ask, and I think we should start with the ladies first. Miss Carmen Suro may have a question.

Miss Suro: Yes, I would like to ask the Master what is the difference between experience and realisation in the spiritual life?
Sri Chinmoy: The difference between experience and realisation in the spiritual life is this: a realised person can say, "I and my Father are one; I and God are one"; whereas an aspirant having many spiritual experiences, or even one, can say and feel that he is slowly but inevitably growing into the realisation of God.

Experience shows and tells us what we will eventually become, the possessor of God-Consciousness. But in realisation, we come to know what we truly are: absolute oneness with God forever and through Eternity. This is the difference between experience and realisation.

34. Mr Jim Knight: One question has interested me. Everybody in all religions tries to relate himself to God, and I wonder, Sri Chinmoy, if you could give us a short explanation of what Yoga says of God. What is God and what is the relationship between God and man?

Sri Chinmoy: God and man – this is the eternal question and the eternal answer. God is the living Breath and that living Breath is in man. Man has a goal and the name of that goal is God. In God is man's satisfaction, achievement and fulfilment. Through man is God's Satisfaction, Achievement and Fulfilment. Man needs God to realise his true Self. God needs man to manifest Himself on earth.

35. Mr Jim Knight: Are you saying that God and man are one and the same?

Sri Chinmoy: Yes. God and man are one and the same. God is man yet to be fulfilled in His Infinity and man is God but he has yet to realise it.

I have to grow and God has to flow. I grow as a human being into His highest Consciousness and God flows into me and through me with His Infinite Compassion.

36. Mr George Riddell: Now, according to Yoga, when your physical being ceases to exist or when you do what we call "die", what happens to your spiritual self?

Sri Chinmoy: When we die, our physical body, the physical sheath enters into the physical world and is disintegrated by burial or cremation. The vital sheath enters into the vital world. The mind enters into the mental world. Then slowly the soul goes back to its own region. There, usually, it stays for a few years – it depends on the individual soul – according to its necessity and according to its preparation. Now after taking rest for some time, the soul feels that the time is ripe for it to enter into the world once again to fulfil its divine mission. God-realisation takes a good many incarnations.

Before the soul enters into creation, it tries to observe the environment, the situation and the family from above; which family it is going to accept. Then the soul goes to the Supreme for approval. Sometimes it gets this approval; sometimes the soul comes into creation merely with the knowledge of the Supreme. Again it starts its journey, it tries to unveil the inner Divinity and at the same time, it tries to manifest the Divine in the field of creation. So this is how the process of reincarnation continues.

We believe in reincarnation. We know that we have millions of desires to be fulfilled. At the age of four I had many desires; at the ages of ten, twenty, thirty, forty, sixty, these desires are not yet fulfilled. Neither we nor God will be satisfied unless we are fulfilled. First we get our fulfilment in satisfying our desires in the ordinary human life. Then we have our fulfilment in achieving our higher aspiration. Right now, we want money, name, fame and all this. Later we try to achieve Light, Peace and Bliss with our spiritual aspiration. In one incarnation, in one short span of life, we cannot do all that. We need many incarnations. That is why, according to our Indian philosophy, reincarnation is a positive fact and a positive truth.

37. Mr George Riddell: Speaking of reincarnation, this brings to mind the idea of the wheel of karma. Now on the wheel of karma, a person or a soul is reincarnated in human form. Or can he be reincarnated in other forms?

Sri Chinmoy: Let me say as a preface to my answer that a soul is in this table, a soul is in the chair, a soul is in the plant, a soul is in everything. A soul, of course, is in all human beings. It is all a matter of the degree of manifestation. The Christ had a soul, I have a soul, we all have a soul. In the case of the Christ, He had the Supreme's all-pervading Consciousness. In the ordinary person's case, his degree of manifestation is not anywhere near that. Similarly, the soul that is in this table, this chair, is nowhere near our soul in degree of manifestation.

But, in answer to your question, once the soul has come into human incarnation, once it has accepted human life, it does not, as a rule, accept animal life. Once upon a time, we were all in the animal kingdom, but as a general rule, the soul does not enter into animal incarnation from the human state. But very rarely it happens that people are still in the animal consciousness although they have a human body. They are in the animal kingdom with their passions and lust, their lowest vital desires. In such cases the Supreme allows the particular human being, the human soul, to enter into a particular animal to enjoy itself, to work out and throw away all these lowest vital movements. There the soul remains, say for six or eight months or a year. But it does not mean that the soul has to remain perpetually in the animal kingdom. No. And only in very rare cases does the soul go into the animal world. We have got a human body and from here we grow – from man we grow into the superman.

38. Miss Dorothy Eisaman: Master, am I correct in saying that we who are believers in God must grow in Grace daily?

Sri Chinmoy: You are absolutely correct in saying that the believers of God must grow in God's Grace daily. A true believer of God feels that his very existence on earth, his inner and outer achievements and fulfilments are entirely due to God's Grace; also he is truly fortunate to see that his so-called personal efforts, too, are an act of God's Grace. At every moment he feels that without God's Grace he is nothing and with God's Grace, he is everything.

39. Mr George Riddell: Listen, that last one is definitely in line with much of Christian preaching and I find that what you say is very similar to the pronouncements of the Christian churches. I am not familiar with the Moslem or the Hebrew religion, but it seems to go through all religion and probably through the Hindu religion in India and various other religions throughout the East.

Now, this Grace, I was wondering if, according to Yoga, will this Grace be flowing from God all the time, or would this Grace flow directly to a particular man from God, or does it flow through other mediums between God and man? When a man feels that he is receiving Grace, does he know that he gets it directly from God, or does he get it through these other mediums? I think I have made myself clear.

Sri Chinmoy: If the aspirant is of a very high calibre, he can get this Grace directly from God. Otherwise, the beginner needs a helper, a teacher or a guide in order to bring down God's Grace into him. The Grace of God is all the time descending in a constant shower, but the beginner is not conscious of this fact. And ordinary human beings are totally ignorant of the fact that there is such a thing as Grace. They think, "As you sow, so you reap." This is true to some extent, but there is also God's Grace which can expedite our life's journey and at the same time negate, nullify our wrong actions.

So to come back to the question, it depends on the individual, where he stands. But again, we have to know that God's Grace is something which we badly need in our day-to-day life, in our outer life as well as in our inner life. God's Grace is our real meal, the energising, fulfilling meal. The Bible has taught us that man does not live by bread alone, and we, the seekers of Truth, add to it that man can live and does live by God's Grace alone.

40. *Mr George Riddell: Does anyone else have a question? Mr Casanova!*

Mr Jose L. Casanova: It seems that modern man has made quite a mess of the world with constant wars, riots, rebellions, strikes, delinquency, etc. And ordinary corrective methods seem to be a total failure. Do you think, Master Chinmoy, that this is a natural order of things or is there any way for modern man to live in peace and have universal love and order?

Sri Chinmoy: You are right. We have made a mess of the world. Now, from the spiritual standpoint, this is not the natural order of things. Far from it. The most natural order in our human existence would be the life of peace, with universal love obeying faithfully a universal law. *Now* your question is, "How can man do that?" Man can do that by thinking God's thoughts and by living God's Truth. Impossible it might seem today, but tomorrow it will be not only possible, but inevitable. United, let us raise our consciousness into that Golden Tomorrow.

41. Mr George Riddell: In Yoga, do you have a Scripture, as we have the Bible?

Sri Chinmoy: We have many scriptures in India. Among these are the Vedas, the Upanishads and the Gita. Just as your Bible is a collection of writings and not one particular piece of writing, so are our scriptures a collection of religious and spiritual books. The most loved and revered scripture of India is a book that I have mentioned, the Bhagavad-Gita. This book, by the way, is often called the Bible of India.
Mr George Riddell: The Gita is also used in Islam?
Sri Chinmoy: They have their Koran. The Koran is the sacred book of the Moslems as we have the Gita and you have the Bible.

42. Mr Jim Knight: One of the great, perhaps the greatest Indian political leader of all time was the Mahatma Gandhi. How did he relate to Yoga?

Sri Chinmoy: Mahatma Gandhi – what was his position?
Mr Jim Knight: What was his position in relation to Yoga?
Sri Chinmoy: "Mahatma" means "Great Soul" and so he was. But from the strictly spiritual point of view, Mahatma Gandhi

was not a yogi. He was a patriot, political leader, martyr. But he was not a self-realised soul like Ramakrishna, the Buddha and others. You can say he was a religious saint. Self-realisation he did not have, but he had boundless love for humanity and his interpretation of God is unique. He said, "Truth is God. Denial of God we have known. Denial of Truth we have not known." For him, religion was nothing but Truth. He lived the life of a saint. God gave him boundless love and compassion. This was Mahatma Gandhi. But when the question of self-realisation, self-discovery comes in, he cannot be placed on the same footing as the Christ, Ramakrishna, Buddha and so on.

43. Mr Ed Belville: Sri Chinmoy, the question in my mind is: why do we need a teacher or guru? Or is it important to have a teacher to follow the spiritual path?

Sri Chinmoy: In this world we cannot do anything without the help of a teacher. The teacher may be necessary for a second or for a year or for many years. If I want to learn music, at the beginning I have to go to a musician. If I want to learn how to dance, I have to go to a dancer. If I want to learn about the sciences, I have to go to a scientist. In order to learn anything in this world, we need a teacher at the beginning. Then how is it that we do not need a teacher to help us in our inner, spiritual life?

A soul enters into a human frame, a human body and then the human being grows and completes his first year of existence, his second year, third year and so on. What has the mother done during these years? The mother or the parents? They have taught him how to speak, how to eat, how to dress, how to behave. He learns everything from his parents. Without their guidance, he would grow up a human animal, an abnormal being. The parents played their part in the formative years of the child.

Similarly, in the spiritual life the necessity of a teacher is inevitable because the spiritual teacher has to teach the student how to pray, how to meditate, how to concentrate. Then, when the student learns and he goes deep within, he can do all this by himself.

Right now I am here in Puerto Rico. I know that New York exists and that I have to go back to New York. What do I need to get me there? An aeroplane and a pilot. So in spite of the fact that I know that New York exists, I cannot get there alone. I need help. Similarly, we all know that God exists. You want to reach God, but someone has to help you, carry you. As the plane takes me, carries me to New York, someone has to carry you to the Consciousness of God which is deep within you. Someone has to show the path in order to enable you to enter into your own divinity, which is God. So this is the answer – that at the beginning, we need a teacher.

44. Mr Ramon Torres Peña: Master Chinmoy, what do you mean by "concentration"?

Sri Chinmoy: Concentration is the open secret of focussing all one's attention on a particular object or person in order to enter into and have one's identification with that object or person. The final stage of concentration is to discover and reveal the hidden ultimate truth in the object of concentration. What concentration can do in our day-to-day life is unimaginable. It most easily separates our heart's Heaven from our mind's hell so that we can live in the constant delight and joy of Heaven and not in the perpetual worries, anxieties and tortures of hell while we are here on earth.

45. *Mr Jim Knight: I have another question deviating just a little bit from what we have been talking about. Most of us in the Western world who are ignorant of Yoga have a tendency to think of a Yogi as someone, let us say, sitting with his legs crossed, or someone standing on his head, someone doing particular exercises or things that seem strange to us. How or why does a Yogi perform these feats? How does it relate to his religion?*

Sri Chinmoy: Some people take these exercises to keep the body fit, free from physical ailments and so forth; while others take them in order to get realisation. But realisation can never be had by merely doing hatha yoga exercises. What these exercises actually do is to help the seeker enter into the true spiritual life.

In the beginning a child, when he reads, he reads aloud in order to convince his parents that he is reading. But a grown-up person does not do that. He reads silently. Now in the physical world, there is a similarity. Right now most of us are physically very restless, no better than monkeys. We cannot stay more than a second without getting restless. But there are aspirants who can just sit down and make their minds calm and quiet and then they enter into the deeper regions of the being. It is these physical exercises and postures, when we do them, which relax our body and give us peace of mind for a short period of time.

But these exercises will never give us realisation – never! These are the preliminary stages. We say in our true spiritual system that the beginners in hatha yoga are like kindergarten students. And one can easily skip kindergarten. But we have to go from kindergarten to elementary school, high school, college and then to university. Concentration, meditation and contemplation are taught in the higher courses. Otherwise just by taking physical exercises and making the body strong, the athletes, the boxers, the wrestlers would all have realised God by this time. All the sportsmen would be God-realised souls!

I must emphasise the fact that hatha yoga exercises are far superior to the Western system of exercises which are often done abruptly, vigorously and, to some extent, violently. The hatha yoga exercises are done calmly, quietly, in a meditative mood. They strengthen the nerves and calm the mind, unlike most of the Western exercises.

The body is necessary. We must have a sound and solid body so that the soul can act in and through the body in the field of manifestation. But if we expect something more from the body, then we are being foolish.

46. Mr George Riddell: Are you a vegetarian?

Sri Chinmoy: I am a strict vegetarian. Sorry, I take eggs, so I cannot say that I am a strict vegetarian. But I take no meat or fish. I stopped eating meat and fish when I was twelve years old, the age that I entered seriously into the spiritual life.
Mr George Riddell: Are you married?
Sri Chinmoy: No, I am not married.
Mr George Riddell: Do you practise celibacy?
Sri Chinmoy: Of course. Without celibacy, there can be no true spiritual life, not to speak of God-realisation.

47. Mr George Riddell: We have one question from our radio audience. Someone has called in with a question. Her question is, "What do you think of the communication between the living and the dead? Do you think there is a communication?"

Sri Chinmoy: There is a way to communicate with the dead. As a matter of fact, there are various ways. If one has occult powers or spiritual powers, one can easily communicate with anybody living or departed. What we call "death" is not the extinction of consciousness. It is only a transition. Today I am here; tomorrow

I will be in New York. Similarly, now I am here on this earth; after some years, I will be somewhere else in one of the other worlds. On the strength of our self-realisation, we can enter into the soul of a person who is either here or elsewhere; either in Heaven or in hell.

On earth we can make either a short distance call or a long-distance call to any part of the world. The telephone is the medium. Similarly, our conscious oneness with God or, we can say, our self-realisation, enables us to commune with anybody, whether here on earth or there in Heaven.

48. Mr George Riddell: In your answer you have mentioned something that has disturbed my mind. You said something about "Heaven and hell". How does Yoga relate to Heaven and hell?

Sri Chinmoy: Heaven and hell are two planes of consciousness. With our human mind we feel that Heaven is elsewhere and that it is full of joy; whereas hell, we feel, is full of torture. This is not the case. Heaven and hell are two planes of consciousness into which we daily enter. When we do good things, we are in joy, we are in Heaven. When we do wrong things, we are in hell. Each moment we are experiencing Heaven and hell. Heaven is right here, deep inside us. It is up to us whether to live in our inner Heaven or in our outer hell.

49. Mrs Sarah Casanova: Some persons are disturbed by the problems surrounding them. They think they can find escape in suicide. Do you think this is a door that we can open at our sweet will to escape from responsibility and suffering?

Sri Chinmoy: I have been hearing for the past few years, from many people, about this idea of committing suicide. Suicide is by no means an escape. There is no escape; there can be no escape. We can escape from this room, but we will be caught in another room. We think that we can escape from this world by killing ourselves.

Unfortunately, this is not the only world. There are other worlds as well. In this world I can take my life, but in another world I will have to continue my existence. Nay, I will be caught. God's Consciousness is All-pervading and He will be able to catch me, the thief.

To come back to your question, suicide can never be an escape. Why do people commit suicide? They commit suicide because they feel that they are miserable, frustrated; others do not understand them. They feel that by committing suicide, they will be freed from countless responsibilities, inner turmoil and pain. Or they feel that as they have committed many wrong actions, they will be mercilessly punished, and they prefer to take their life first. So they need an escape. Now who escapes? Not a divine hero. A hero fights; a thief escapes. A coward escapes. But not he who is on the right path. If I am on the right path, I will not try to escape. He who wants to commit suicide is a coward. He does not face the world.

First of all you have to face the world, live in the world in order to establish your divine qualities on earth. We have to accept. If we do not accept the world, what are we going to face? When we face the world, if there is anything wrong with the world, we can rectify it. So those who are committing suicide are committing the worst possible mistake. To be sure, there is no escape for them either in this world or in any other world. They are not only killing themselves, but are also killing the fruitful possibilities of their future incarnations.

50. Mr George Riddell: There are many people in the United States who claim that with the use of certain drugs they are able to get closer to God. Of course the Chinese have been using opium for centuries and centuries. How do you feel about using stimulants, drugs, etc., to stimulate the mind in order to get closer to God?

Sri Chinmoy: Let me start out by saying that there are two ways of approaching the Truth. One way is that by meditation and prayer, we know the real Truth, we feel the real ecstasy, we see the real Light, we experience Existence, Consciousness, Bliss. These last three go together and we can come into that state only through meditation and oneness with God. But those who are taking drugs are putting the cart before the horse. They are deceiving themselves into thinking that they already know the Truth. At the same time, they are not aware of the fact that by taking drugs, they are damaging their inner, spiritual faculties which are of paramount importance in order to enter into God's kingdom. Let me make it clear to you.

If you throw me into a sea and plunge me, immerse me forcibly in the water, not allowing me to come to the surface, then what shall I see? All blank, all white. And that is what actually happens to those who have taken to drugs. Through the effect of chemicals, a violent change of consciousness is effected. They get an experience – all white! Even if it is a higher experience, they cannot sustain it unless they take another dose of chemicals. But when I pray, when I concentrate, when I meditate, I enter into the Living Consciousness of God and I can learn to remain there. This is the positive and natural way of entering into God. God is natural and I am His son, you are His son; we have to follow the natural process. But by taking to drugs and using these artificial means, people are unconsciously, if not deliberately, negating the real Truth.

I have two or three students who used to take drugs. They have had first-hand "experiences". They tell me now that when they were taking drugs, it was nothing but self-delusion and self-annihilation. Now what they experience is self-acceptance and self-fulfilment. So this is the difference that they have now discovered. Needless to say that I am proud of their present spiritual achievements.

To come back to your question: no man can come closer to God by taking drugs or stimulants. He can come closer to God only by loving God and meditating on God.

51. Mr George Riddell: We are just about coming to the end of our time now. We have time for one more question.

Mr Ed Belville: I would like to ask one more question before we sign off. Can a Westerner become a real yogi?
Sri Chinmoy: Your name is Mr Ed Belville. We are greatly honoured to be here at this Radio Station WHOA, where you have brought us, Mr Belville, and made all the arrangements. At this hour you are asking me this particular question. I wish you to remember this question some day either in this incarnation or in your immediate future incarnations.

You are a Westerner; you are an aspirant, a sincere aspirant. You are bound to realise God; you are bound to become a yogi in one of your forthcoming incarnations. Then you will see whether a Westerner can become a yogi or not. A yogi is he who is in union with God's Consciousness. Yoga is not the sole monopoly of India and a yogi is not the sole product of India. I am God's son, you are God's son. We have the equal right, the equal privilege to go to our Father, to enter into our Father's Consciousness. Many Western spiritual masters have entered into God's Consciousness and received what the Indian yogis have received. You too, can do it. For God-realisation, geographical boundaries do not exist. God's Consciousness pervades the length and breadth of the world and beyond. So, being a Westerner, a human being, you are caught by God's all-pervading Embrace. You cannot escape; you also have to have self-realisation. Then only will God leave you.

Westerner, Easterner, Northerner or Southerner, all must needs have this union with God; all can and all must become a yogi or a yogini. It is a matter of time, either today or tomorrow. God will not allow anyone to remain unrealised or unfulfilled.

Mr George Riddell: Well, that is all the time we have now. We thank you very much, Sri Chinmoy Ghose, for the privilege of having you here and for accepting our invitation to come here and explain Yoga to us.

VI – QUESTIONS ASKED AT THE UNIVERSITY OF PUERTO RICO

52. Please explain what will be the first step for an ordinary person who has not been in contact with spiritual teachings and wants to enter into the path of self-realisation.

Sri Chinmoy: The important thing is the ultimate Goal. If a person wants to have self-realisation, then the first step, the very first step, should be the acceptance of the spiritual life. Without accepting the spiritual life, one cannot realise God. It is simply impossible. The spiritual life, of course, is a very vast field – one has to know where one actually stands right now. If, as the first step in the spiritual life, one wants to have a better life, a more harmonious life, a more peaceful life, and if he feels that the Peace, Joy and Harmony that he seeks are still beyond his reach, then he has to start by reading from a few Scriptures; he should get some illumination from religious and spiritual books. These books will inspire him to some extent to enter into the inner life. Then when the person has studied the books and is getting some inspiration, but is unable to go farther, at that time he has to put into practice what he has studied in the books. When he is practising these new principles, if he is not satisfied with his achievements, then he has to search for a teacher, a spiritual teacher. It is the teacher who can help him in his spiritual life, who can tell him what kind of spiritual discipline is needed for him.

I must emphasise again that at the very outset he has to determine that he needs the spiritual life. There is no other life that can give him self-illumination. When he is sure that it is the spiritual life that can give him that, then he has to enter into his deeper part. Through his inner cry, through prayer, through aspiration, through concentration and meditation, he has to start on the very first lap of his divine journey.

53. The body is mortal while the soul is eternal. What is the importance of having a body?

Sri Chinmoy: The soul is eternal and the body is perishable, true. But we have to know the supreme importance of three things: first, the embodiment of Truth, second, the revelation of Truth, third, the manifestation of Truth. It is on earth and through the physical body that the soul can manifest its own Divinity which is the infinite Peace, infinite Light, infinite Bliss. It is here on earth that the soul can manifest this. This earth is the field of manifestation and at the same time, this earth is the field of realisation. God-realisation can be achieved only here on earth and not in other spheres, not in other planets, not in other worlds. So those who care for God-realisation have to come into the world; and the soul has to accept the body because the body is absolutely necessary here on earth for the manifestation of the soul's Divinity.

On the one hand, when the soul leaves the body, the body cannot function; the body dies. On the other hand, when the soul wants to manifest, it has to be done in the body, with the body. So we have to know what we actually want. If we want to negate the body, destroy the body, what can the soul do? It has to leave the body. But if we want to achieve something here on earth and if we feel the necessity of establishing the Kingdom of Heaven here on earth, then it has to be done with the conscious help of the body. The body is the instrument of the soul. In the *Katha Upanishad* it says: "The soul is the master, the body is the chariot, the reason or intellect is the charioteer and the mind, the reins." The body needs the soul, the soul needs the body. For the realisation of the highest and deepest Truth, the body needs the soul; for the manifestation of the highest and deepest Truth, the soul needs the body.

54. What results would we have in our society if a large number of persons in the society accepted Yoga?

Sri Chinmoy: If a large number of people accepted Yoga, then the face of society would be completely changed. Society would not suffer. On the contrary, society would undergo a radical change for the better. Why? Because Yoga can tell society what the actual Truth is in man's day-to-day life. Yoga can show us how Truth can be seen, felt and realised. Yoga can teach society what true love is, what true human relationships and feelings should be. If society is ruled by ordinary human minds, by emotional feelings and so forth, society can never achieve perfection. But if society, at least a larger number in society, can feel the need for God who is All-Love, who is All-Perfection, who is All-Compassion, then only will society discover its true meaning. Society will gain abundant truth from the very acceptance of Yoga.

Yoga is not something unnatural; it is something absolutely natural, it is something practical, it is more practical than the ordinary human life can conceive. It wants to prove in a practical way that God is not only in Heaven, but here on earth. So the greater the number in society to accept the spiritual life, the inner life, the quicker, the easier will be the transformation of the life of society.

55. What happens if a person wants to enter the spiritual life but has to adjust himself to the material life?

Sri Chinmoy: As I said before, Yoga and life must go together. We have to go deep within to discover the spiritual life, but without negating the material life. From inside we have to come outside; we cannot go inside while holding on to the values of the outer life. We need the inner life and in the inner life is to be found infinite Joy, Peace and Bliss. From the inner life, we bring to the fore our inner, divine qualities. The material life can then be easily adjusted. The material life, in fact, has its true significance only when it is supported by the inner life. Now at present what is actually happening is that we are trying to separate the material life from the spiritual life. Actually there is no such division, but unfortunately people think that either one has to accept the material life and wallow in its pleasures or else one has to be a complete ascetic; that there can be no compromise. This is not true. Life has to be accepted – the material life – but not in a sense of total indulgence. The material life is to be accepted for the manifestation of our divine, inner qualities. Through the material life, we shall have to fulfil the message of our inner life. Now how can we do this?

One should try to aspire in one's day-to-day life to combine both the material and the spiritual life. One can do this through the remembrance of something higher or deeper. What is that higher and deeper thing? It is God, the Divine. If God comes to one's mind before anything else, then only will God flow through, from the spiritual life into the material life. God has to be placed first in one's life, without negating the material life or the outer world. If we place God first, then God enters, on our behalf, into the outer world, into the material world. But if we place the material world first, then we cannot reach God because the process is wrong. It is from God that we have to enter into the material life. God looms large in the inner life and from the inner life we can and must bring Him into the outer life. This is how we can adjust ourselves to the material life and make it one with the spiritual life.

56. *You explained that the soul needs the body. I understand that the soul is the one that is in union with God. Will we retain our individuality or shall we lose our individuality when we realise that union with God?*

Sri Chinmoy: God does not want us to discard our individuality, but ordinary individuality and real, divine individuality are two different things. God Himself is, at the same time, One and Many. He has produced infinite human beings, human souls. He is One, but in the field of manifestation He has become Many. He has selected each person as His chosen instrument, that is to say, each human soul is His chosen instrument. This kind of divine individuality which God has given to us is not the ordinary individuality which is determined by the ego: "I am this, you are that." God's individuality is a unique manifestation of His Reality. There is no clash, there is no jealousy, there is no fight, no battle. God Himself is manifesting Himself in a unique manner in you, in me and in others. That kind of individuality, different from the individuality of the ego, God retains for humanity. It is a unique expression of the Divine in His multiplicity. Each one is a chosen instrument of God, but without ego, without pride, without vanity. It is just like the petals of the lotus; each petal has its own beauty and its own uniqueness.

57. *If a person practises Yoga, what kind of life will be led in his daily activities?*

Sri Chinmoy: In his daily activities he has to be, first of all, sincere, honest and pure. He has to have purity in his mind, in his body, in his speech and in his ideas. Anyone can practise sincerity, honesty and purity. Then if he really wants to practise Yoga, the deeper Yoga, each day for about fifteen minutes, he must devote himself to his inner search, to his self-discovery. These fifteen minutes of meditation have to be learned from someone who can teach him. He needs a teacher for meditation, for his inner illumination. The individual has to know how sincere he is or how far he wants to go, how deeply he wants to accept Yoga. If he feels that he has to go up to the end of the road, that he wants to reach the goal, then he has to follow some strict, inner discipline and he has to meditate, concentrate and so forth. But if he wants to remain satisfied with obtaining a little peace, joy and light, then what I said at the beginning, in answering your question applies here. Let him be perfectly sincere in all his activities.

58. Does a person who has not practised Yoga have the same grade of unity with God after death as one who practises Yoga?

Sri Chinmoy: No. One who has practised Yoga will alone have eventually the conscious oneness with God. He will see God here on earth and there in Heaven. My dear friend, just by leaving the body, one does not immediately go to God. For God-realisation, one has to be here on earth. It is mere foolishness to think that when we leave the body, we immediately fly to God. No! It is not like that. One has to realise Him here on earth. It is by listening to the dictates of the soul that one realises God here on earth. Otherwise people only need commit suicide in order to realise God after death. Anyone would be able to leave the world and fly to God.

VII – QUESTIONS ASKED AT THE INTER-AMERICAN UNIVERSITY, SAN JUAN, PUERTO RICO

59. What is the best point we can use to fix our gaze for concentration?

Sri Chinmoy: It depends on the individual. Some people find it easier to look at the flame of a candle and concentrate, while others find it easier to look at a beautiful flower. Still others prefer to look at the rising sun and concentrate. So if the individual gets a kind of inner joy when concentrating on a particular object, he should concentrate on that object in order to achieve his goal.

60. Is Yoga considered a religion or a philosophy?

Sri Chinmoy: Yoga is neither a philosophy nor a religion. Yoga transcends both philosophy and religion; at the same time, it houses both religion and philosophy. Religion and philosophy can lead a human being up to God's Palace, while Yoga, which means union with God, man's conscious union with God, leads an aspirant right up to God's Throne.

61. When you speak, you close your eyes. Is this a kind of concentration or what is it?

Sri Chinmoy: When I was speaking, you observed me closing my eyes. It is not that I was concentrating; it was only that I was entering into various worlds. There are seven higher worlds and seven lower worlds. When I close my eyes and then open them, this blinking that you see indicates that I am moving, my soul is moving from one region to another. During my talk, I was in a very high consciousness. Hence my soul got the opportunity to move from one plane of consciousness to another.

62. Is there any difference between one religion and another religion? Does Yoga demand renunciation of all religions?

Sri Chinmoy: There is no fundamental difference between one religion and another because each religion embodies the ultimate Truth. So Yoga does not interfere with any religion. Anybody can practise Yoga. I have disciples who are Catholics, Protestants, Jews and so forth. One can practise Yoga irrespective of religion. Now if one has been taught Hinduism, he may be afraid of accepting Catholicism and vice-versa. But the real aspirant who has launched into spirituality and Yoga will find no difficulty in remaining in his own religion. I tell my disciples not to give up their own religion. If they remain in their own religion and practise the spiritual life and the inner discipline, they will go faster because their own religion will give them constant confidence in what they are doing and confirm what they are actually practising in their life. So I always tell my students to stick to their own religion, for Yoga does not demand renunciation of any religion.

63. Is it easier for you to concentrate while you are standing?

Sri Chinmoy: For a spiritual person like me, concentration can be done at any moment, at any place and in any position. I can concentrate even while I am running. About fifteen years ago, I was a very good sportsman – an athlete in India. Even while running the fastest hundred meter dash, I used to concentrate. While I was pole vaulting – in the air – I was able to concentrate. So concentration can be done at any moment, at any place, in any position; it need not be done only while sitting.

When the inner being compels us to concentrate, we concentrate. There is no hard and fast rule that one has to concentrate only while standing or while seated in the lotus position. When the inner being inspires us, we aspire and this aspiration can be expressed either in the form of concentration or meditation.

64. Is reincarnation an entity in itself or is it a religious belief of Hinduism?

Sri Chinmoy: There are religions which accept the belief in reincarnation whereas there are other religions which do not. The Hindu religion, Hinduism, believes in reincarnation. But reincarnation in itself has very little to do with Hinduism or any other religion. Now what is reincarnation?

It means that the soul comes into the world with a new garment. Now we are wearing clothes, garments. At any moment we can throw them off. They are at our disposal. Similarly, when the soul finds the body to be no longer capable of receiving the highest Truth or when the soul finds that the body needs rest or when the soul feels that God wants it to leave the body, it leaves; and again, when God wants the soul to enter into a new human body, the soul enters. And I wish to add that this concept of reincarnation is not only the Hindu idea or the Hindu philosophy or the Hindu way of approaching life, but it is a truth to which many, many people in the West adhere.

In the Gita, one of our most sacred books, and sometimes called the Bible of India, we find a beautiful verse on reincarnation. I wish to cite it. [Sri Chinmoy chants Verse 22, Chapter 2 of the Bhagavad-Gita in Sanskrit.]

> "As a man discards his old and worn-out clothes and takes on new ones, so does the embodied soul discard this body and migrate from body to body."

This is what we call reincarnation from the Hindu spiritual point of view.

65. What is meditation?

Sri Chinmoy: There are three stages in our spiritual practice. It starts with concentration, then meditation, then contemplation. Someone here asked me about concentration and I have answered. Now meditation is the second stage. When you meditate, what you actually do is to enter into a calm or still, silent mind. We have to be fully aware of the arrival and attack of thoughts. That is to say, we shall not allow any thought, divine or undivine, good or bad, to enter into our mind. Our mind should be absolutely silent. Then we have to go deep within; there we have to observe our real existence. When we speak of our outer existence, we see our limbs and our body, the gross body, that is all; but when we go deep within, we approach our true existence and that existence is in our soul, in the inmost recesses of our soul. When we live in the soul, we feel that we are actually, spontaneously doing meditation.

So if you want to know what meditation is, I wish to say that meditation is that very state of our consciousness where the inner being, instead of cherishing millions of thoughts, wants only to commune with God. Meditation is God's language as well as man's language. Now I am speaking in English and you are able to understand me because you know English well. Similarly, when one knows how to meditate well, one will be able to commune with God. Thus meditation is the language we use to speak to God.

66. Is life after death a reality or just a belief?

Sri Chinmoy: There are two lives: one is the life that we are seeing here. We have a short span of life, say forty, sixty or eighty years; then we pass behind the curtain of Eternity. There is an eternal Life. This Life existed before the creation, it exists now in the creation, then it passes through death and it goes beyond death and enters again into its own realm. So when we speak of life here, we think of the short span of life that we are seeing: sixty years or eighty years. But eternal Life is not like that. It had no beginning and it has no end. It existed, it exists and it will forever exist. Through our meditation, when we realise God, when we stay in God, we become the possessor of that eternal Life. Consciously we go beyond the veil of death and we remain in the eternal Life, which has neither beginning nor end.

67. Is life after death a sort of consolation?

Sri Chinmoy: Obviously it is not. I have just explained that life after death is the highest affirmation of Truth. In this life, you have not fulfilled even all your desires, let alone your aspirations. How can you do all this in one lifetime? Desire fulfilled today is bound to be followed by frustration tomorrow. Then man throws away desire like a dirty cloth; man enters into the field of aspiration. He wants to grow, he wants to have infinite Joy, infinite Light, infinite Bliss. These infinite gifts cannot be possessed by an individual in the course of one short span of life. For that we have to come back into this world. The soul comes back again and again in order to fully manifest its divinity here on earth. Because we cannot do all this in one short lifetime, the soul comes back and enters into various successive bodies in order to embody, fulfil and manifest the Divine.

68. That humming that I heard from you – I want to know if it is a kind of meditation.

Sri Chinmoy: Chanting is not, strictly speaking, a form of meditation. It is an invocation. You invoke God to enter into you, into your inmost self, into your inner existence. Meditation is different. While in chanting you usually invoke God to permeate your whole existence, in meditation you try, in a broader way, to enter into God's Infinity, Eternity and Immortality.

69. Recently I read about a person who was buried alive for eighteen days and then he was able to come back alive. Is there any relation between this sort of thing and what you are doing?

Sri Chinmoy: My teaching is not a kind of miracle-mongering. My business is to help the aspirant to reach God. When one wants to reach God, realise God, I try to help the person. But by being buried underground for eighteen days or by performing other feats, I can not lead my students to God nor are the students helped in their spiritual search. What leads us to God is our aspiration, our inner, mounting cry. So I do not advocate this kind of miracle.

What I want from my students is this inner cry. A child cries for his mother's love; a spiritual child needs and wants to have infinite love from God. And how can he get it? Only by reaching and realising God. My philosophy and spirituality are different from those who are meant only for displaying and teaching their supernatural capacities, their miracles.

70. So what that person did has nothing to do with Yoga?

Sri Chinmoy: It has very little to do with true Yoga. Yoga means "union with God". If somebody does miracles, he is not helping you directly or indirectly to realise God. At most we learn from him that there is no end to human capacity. If one enters into the secret domains where the inherent powers of the cosmic realities exist, one can get the capacity to do anything.

I know an amusing incident in connection with a fakir in India who used to perform this very feat you mention. He could remain buried for long periods of time and often lay underground for as long as twenty-one days. Once it happened that when he was dug up from his long burial, the moment he regained consciousness, he looked around frantically for his girlfriend who was standing amidst his relatives, friends and admirers. Having found his paramour, he left the spot immediately with her.

Now did his unusual achievement help the audience in any way in their aspiration for God-realisation? You tell me. By performing these miracles, we in no way inspire others to unite themselves with God, whereas in helping someone in his aspiration, his concentration and his meditation, we do help the person to realise God.

VIII – QUESTIONS ASKED AT YALE UNIVERSITY

71. What role does the vegetarian diet play in your teachings?

Sri Chinmoy: In my teachings the vegetarian diet plays a most important role. In order to become pure, a vegetarian diet helps us considerably. Purity is of paramount importance in our spiritual life. This purity we must establish in the physical, the vital and the mental. When we eat meat, fish and so forth, the aggressive, animal consciousness enters into us. Our nerves become agitated; we unconsciously become restless and aggressive. The mild qualities of vegetables, on the other hand, help us to establish in our inner life as well as in our outer life, the qualities of sweetness, softness, simplicity and purity.

But again, if you ask me whether by becoming a strict vegetarian you can realise God or not, then I would say "No", a definite "No". There are millions and millions of people on earth who are strict vegetarians, but I don't think there are millions and millions of God-realised souls on earth. For God-realisation we need aspiration. But in answering your question, I wish to say that it is always advisable, if possible, to have a vegetarian diet in order to further one's progress in the inner discipline, so that one can feel that even the body, with its purity, can help one's inner aspiration to become more intense and more soulful.

72. It seems to me that it takes a certain amount of energy and desire to follow the path of your teachings. And what about the rank beginner on it? Sometimes you can't muster enough energy to get yourself going!

Sri Chinmoy: You are right. Not only to follow my path, but to follow any spiritual path, one has to have some energy, some spiritual energy and aspiration. But I think that if one has to wait for this dynamic and spiritual energy, then one will never start one's journey. So if you really want the spiritual life, I say: throw yourself into the inner life. Don't look either backwards or sideways. Look ahead and jump into the Sea of Spirituality. Start from where you are. If you have limited energy, if your aspiration is insignificant, then I wish to say something to you. Go deep within. You will get to the Inner Well, the Source of aspiration.

You cannot become a multimillionaire overnight. You have to start with a penny. Similarly if you have a little aspiration, if you really care for God, then start uttering God's name once a day, early in the morning. Gradually you can transform the whole day, into a repetition of God's name and make real headway towards your self-discovery. If you have a sincere cry for God, then you can start your spiritual journey, no matter where you are or what you have.

73. *My mind wanders and I would like to know how I can better my concentration so that I can keep my mind focussed on one point or on one thought without lower thought-structures wandering around.*

Sri Chinmoy: Before you actually start your concentration, I wish you to repeat the name of God at least twenty times as fast as possible. "God, God, God ...." In one breath, please try to repeat the word "God" as many times as you can. First try to purify your breath by repeating God's name. The breath has to be purified. Unless and until our breath is purified, our mind will wander; thoughts will attack the mind mercilessly. After you have repeated God's name, I wish you to focus all your attention on a particular picture. You are a university student and at the same time you are a disciple of mine. You can focus your attention on my picture or look at your own picture. Look at your reflection in the mirror. Do not feel that you are experiencing two bodies with one consciousness, but feel that you are feeling one body with one consciousness, even though the body in the mirror is a reflection of yourself. There should be no other thought besides this one, "God wants me; I need God. He will illumine me, my life; I shall fulfil Him, His mission." Then you will see that slowly and steadily God's divine thoughts are entering into you and permeating your whole inner and outer existence.

74. I am studying to be an actor at the Drama School here at Yale. Is it possible to follow the spiritual path and also have this earthly value, or must I totally devote myself to the spiritual path and be devoid of everything else?

Sri Chinmoy: This is a very wrong conception of spirituality. True spirituality never, never negates our earthly life and our significant earthly values. True spirituality only simplifies our earthly life; it purifies and illumines our human existence. We are now in ignorance. We know that we are caught in the meshes of ignorance, but spirituality shows us how we can come out of ignorance, how we can free ourselves from the bondage that we have consciously or unconsciously created. If you want to be an actor, spirituality will never prevent you from being one. On the contrary, spirituality will inspire you in your acting line. Spirituality never negates. It is like your private tutor. It will teach you privately and secretly to be successful and meaningful in your outer as well as your inner life. Nothing has to be given up. Everything has to be changed and transformed. If you give up, then what are you going to achieve? If you give up this world, what are you going to do? It is here on earth that you have to realise God, reveal God and fulfil God.

75. There are many books on reincarnation on the market that you can buy. But is it something that can be understood by the intellect, the laws of reincarnation?

Sri Chinmoy: The laws of reincarnation can never be understood by the intellect. After one has realised the Ultimate Truth, one can not only understand the laws of reincarnation, but seize the entire picture of the whole system of reincarnation from the beginning to the end. In order to understand the law of reincarnation, one has to enter into the region of the soul and abide therein. One has to go far beyond the domain of the intellect. By studying books, even if you study millions of books on reincarnation, you cannot enter into the region of the soul. To enter into the region of the soul, you have to aspire and meditate. All you can understand by the intellect are certain very insignificant principles in the boundless realm of reincarnation.

IX – QUESTIONS ASKED AT YOGA OF WESTCHESTER, NEW ROCHELLE, NEW YORK

76. Could you tell us what an aspirant's duty to society is, if he has one, and how he should relate to his total society? Should he be withdrawn or should he contribute, and if so, what should be the nature of his contribution?

Sri Chinmoy: This same question was asked by a university student at the Inter-American University in Puerto Rico recently and I shall be happy to answer it again for you. It depends. First of all, we have to know the standard of the aspirant. If the aspirant feels that the inner life, the spiritual life, is of paramount importance, that he cannot do without it – if he is of that calibre – then he has to devote most of his time to the inner life, the spiritual life, to God-realisation; his inner being will tell him to what extent he can contribute to society. But if the aspirant is just learning the ABC of the spiritual life, then I wish the aspirant to accept society as something important, needful and significant in his life, something that goes with the inner life and something that should be accepted along with the inner life.

Again, I wish to say that if he is a true aspirant, he has to go deep within in order to know *how* to help society. To help society is a wonderful thing. To be a philanthropist is a wonderful thing, and if that particular philanthropist goes deep within and gets the direct message from the inner being, from God, then I think that only at that time will his help to society be really meaningful. Otherwise, the so-called help or contribution to society by an aspirant will be an act of self-aggrandisement, self-nourishment, a feeding of his ego.

So we have to know where the individual aspirant stands. In order to realise God, one does not have to leave society altogether for good. If one leaves society, or in the larger sense, humanity, then how can one establish and manifest divinity here on earth?

But one has to be wise in his spiritual search. He has to know that God comes first and then humanity. If one goes to humanity first and serves humanity according to his limited capacity or just to feed his ego, then he is not fulfilling God in society or in humanity. So to serve humanity properly, divinely, one has first to go to divinity and from there, one has to approach humanity. At that time, the help will be most beneficial.

77. Do you feel it is important for the aspirant to follow the vegetarian diet?

Sri Chinmoy: The answer will be yes and no. It depends on the individual aspirant. We all know that we have come from the animal kingdom. We believe in reincarnation. So once upon a time, we were all animals. Now, we have come into the human creation and we are progressing and evolving and all of us will realise God on the strength of our aspiration.

For an aspirant, it is advisable to be a vegetarian precisely because when he eats meat, the aggressive quality of the animal enters into him. We are trying to live a life of peace and tranquillity. If we sincerely want that kind of life, then it is foolishness on our part to eat something that would diminish our peace and tranquillity and stand in the way of our meditation, concentration, etc. So it is always advisable to accept the vegetarian life. But, again, there are some countries or some parts of the world where it is exceptionally cold and there it is impossible for those particular people, to live on vegetables alone. What are they going to do then? There only if they eat meat can they remain on earth. Then, again, there are some sincere seekers whose physical constitution is very weak. Some children, for example, who are very ill require meat for a short time to regain their strength. Others from the beginning of their lives have been eating meat and now they have formed such a habit, such a bad habit, you can say, that they cannot manage without it even for a day. What are they going to do? On the one hand, they have sincere aspiration, genuine aspiration, but their body revolts. I feel, in such rare cases, that they should eat meat.

But as a general rule, it is always advisable to be a vegetarian because we are trying to throw away the animal qualities and propensities from our nature. Already when we go deep within, we see that we have two different qualities or natures; the divine and the undivine. The undivine is the animal in us and the animal within us will always be aggressive and destructive. The divine in us will always be progressive and illumined. So if we want to march and run towards our Goal, then we have to do away with our animal life. To do that, whatever animal qualities we take into us in the form of meat or in some other form have to be discontinued.

Now to come back to your question, if one says that one has to be a vegetarian in order to realise God or that one cannot achieve God-realisation unless he is a vegetarian, then I say that it is pure foolishness. There are many meat-eaters who have realised God: Christ, Vivekananda and many others who realised God, but ate meat as others do. There are many. A few months ago someone told me that in order to have purity in abundance, he stopped eating meat, but he also felt that just by becoming a vegetarian, he would be able to realise God. He would not have to meditate, he would not have to concentrate; only by becoming a vegetarian, he could achieve union with the Absolute. So I told him that in India, all widows without exception are forbidden to take meat. When their husbands die, on that very day, they have to stop taking meat. Now in spite of my deepest love and respect for Indian widows, I don't think that they are all God-realised souls. That kind of feeling towards the vegetarian life is absurd. Yet we have to strike a balance. For a sincere aspirant, it is certainly advisable and helpful to be a vegetarian.

78. My question concerns karma. I would like to know what is the best way to get rid of bad karma.

Sri Chinmoy: The best way to get rid of bad karma is to enter into the field of meditation, concentration and aspiration. If you want to get rid of your bad karma, the first thing you have to do is to forget about it. If you think of it, unconsciously you are cherishing it, but if you think of good karma, that is to say, aspiration, meditation and concentration, then you are walking along the right path. What you did yesterday, what you ate yesterday or ten years ago is now not at all important. What you want to do now and be now is of paramount importance. We have to know that we are not the children of the past, but of the golden future. Yesterday did not give you realisation. Yesterday did not give you fulfilment. You are going to get it either today or in the distant future or in the near future. You have to know that if you look forward, one day you will reach your Goal, but if you look backward, you will remain where you were and where you are. So in order to get rid of bad karma, the only medicine is meditation in the form of aspiration, or concentration in the form of aspiration.

79. Do you think that the aspirant needs a living Guru for realisation?

Sri Chinmoy: To be very frank with you, the necessity of a living Guru in order to realise God is not absolutely indispensable. The first person who realised God on earth, the very first realised soul had no human Guru. The poor fellow who first realised God had only God as his Guru.

If you have a Guru, what happens? It facilitates your inner spiritual progress. A Guru is a private tutor. At every moment in life's journey, ignorance tries to test you, examine you and torture you, but this private tutor will teach you how to pass the examination. If you have a private tutor you know how much help you can get in order to pass the examination. Moreover, if you get a Guru, once you get him and once you are in his boat, he takes you to the Golden Shore. You on your part do not have to work as hard as you would have done without a Guru.

The Guru is approached by his disciple at any time, any hour of the day or night, in his suffering, in his joy. The necessity of a Guru for a sincere disciple is certainly of paramount importance. But at the same time, it is not indispensable. However if someone is wise enough to want to run towards his Goal instead of stumbling or merely walking, then certainly the help of the Guru at that time is considerable.

Again a true disciple feels that the Guru and the disciple are not two totally different beings; that is to say, he does not feel that the Guru is at the top of the tree and he is at the foot of the tree, that he is all the time washing the feet of the Guru. No, he feels that the Guru is his own highest part. If he has the feet, he has also the head. He feels that he and the Guru are one, the Guru is his own highest and most developed part. Therefore he does not find any difficulty in surrendering his lowest part to his highest part. It is not beneath his dignity to offer his lowest to his highest because he knows that both the highest and the lowest are his.

So to come back to your question: the need for a teacher. It is absurd to feel that for everything else in life we need a teacher but not for God-realisation. But again, God is in everybody and if you feel that you don't need human help, you are most welcome to do it alone. But why does one go to the university when he can study at home? He need not go to university, but he feels that there he will get expert instruction. In this world, if you want to make fast, faster and fastest progress in the inner life, spiritual life, then I must say that the necessity of a Guru is almost indispensable.

80. What you said before about denying the animal in man troubles me. I feel that as the inner life and the outer life are two sides of the same truth, that the animal and the pure wisdom in man are also two sides of the same truth and two sides of God and I can't understand why one must run away from one side of oneself.

Sri Chinmoy: Actually one is not running away. When I say that one has to get rid of it, I mean that one has to illumine one's own consciousness. My philosophy is the philosophy of acceptance. After accepting life as it is, one has to try to transform and illumine it. If night is illumined into light, you will see the total extinction of night because it becomes all light. Now in the field of manifestation, yes, God is in the animal. God is everywhere. God is in pure water. God is in filthy water. Why do you drink pure water and not filthy water in which God is also present? Because you know you will get sick and perhaps even die. Similarly in this world, we have to know what is necessary to reach our Goal, what things are required. God is in everything, but what we cannot utilise in our journey has no place in our aspiring consciousness. If the animal quality is obstructing our way, we have either to illumine it or destroy it. We simply try to illumine it and when night is transformed into day, you can no longer call the night "night". It is "day". So with the animal in us, either we have to throw it aside or we have to illumine it.

In our yoga, the yoga of acceptance, we do not actually destroy anything; we transform it. When we transform something, it loses its original unlit or destructive quality. Now about your simile of the obverse and the reverse, the inner life and the outer life. The outer life is the expression of the inner life. It should be. But the outer life cannot be dark and undivine, while the inner life is bright and divinely illumined. We are in a process of evolution. Once upon a time we were in the plant life, then we came to the animal life and now we are in the human life. We are evolving, transcending. The inner and the outer life must be united because God is inside, God is outside. The inner life has to inspire, energise and permeate the outer life; the outer life has to be the perfect expression of the inner life. It must catch up with the inner life and be a worthy embodiment of it.

81. *What is self-realisation?*

Sri Chinmoy: Self-realisation means self-discovery in the highest sense of the term. One realises one's oneness with God – consciously. Now you have studied books and people have also told you that God is in everybody. But you have not realised God in your conscious life. When one is self-realised, one consciously knows what God is, what He looks like, what He wills. Those who have not realised God will say, "God may be like this, God may be like that" – it is all mental speculation. But when one achieves self-realisation, one remains in God's Consciousness and one speaks to God face-to-face. He sees God both in the finite and in the Infinite; he sees God as Personal and Impersonal. In this case, it is not mental hallucination or imagination;

it is direct reality. This reality is more authentic than my seeing you right now in front of me.

82. You spoke of a Guru as someone to help make a short cut in the search for realisation. I find it hard in myself to channel myself in the search. Could you recommend or direct me somehow in a channelling of my energies towards self-realisation, because I find it hard to direct myself in that way.

Sri Chinmoy: Have you studied spiritual books? No? Then to start with, I wish you to study some sacred spiritual books. Please do this and then ask Sarama about the inner life. She will help you and guide you. Only one thing: right now do not think of realisation, liberation and salvation and all that. Those who, at the very beginning of their journey, use the terms "self-realisation", "liberation", "transformation" all the time are just fooling themselves, to be very frank with you. Please do not think I am criticising you or blaming you, but I wish to say in front of you all that these are big words. Some spiritual Masters say that one should not utter these words at all at the beginning, words like "realisation", "divinisation", etc. These are all big, big words. Only when one is on the threshold of true liberation, one can use them, or when one is far advanced in the spiritual life. Otherwise, people just entering into the spiritual life who have not learned the ABC of the spiritual life, say, "I want God-realisation, I want liberation." Very often I hear this from people and I feel so sad. Before they have actually started climbing the tree, they want the fruit from the topmost branch.

So please launch into the spiritual path, learn the ABC of the inner life. For that, discipline is required. Just as you take exercises every day or almost every day, to develop your muscles, you should likewise meditate regularly without fail, for five minutes, ten minutes, according to your capacity and according to the instructions given to you by some teacher. Then you have to know the necessity of feeding the child within you. When the child cries, immediately the mother runs to feed the child. Similarly we have, all of us, a child within us, a divine child, the soul. This soul has to be fed, developed, if we want spiritual fulfilment, if we want the manifestation of God here on earth. So if we feed our outer body thrice a day, it is only sensible that we feed the inner child within us at least once a day. If we do that, we shall eventually feel the Divine and realise God.

83. Should we understand that the extent of self-realisation that we can achieve is subject to our effort and our will, which is what I did understand from your last response, or is it ultimately determined in some way by something beyond our own will?

Sri Chinmoy: Two things go together – individual effort plus the Divine Grace. If I sleep all the time, God is not going to liberate me, but at the same time if I feel that on the strength of my personal will, by hook or by crook, I will be able to realise God by exerting all my power, it is foolishness. So we have to know that God is on the third floor and I am on the first floor. There should be a rendezvous, a meeting place. I have to go to God; I have to go to the second floor with my personal effort, that is to say, with my tears, my soulful cry. And then God will come down from the third floor to the second floor with his infinite Grace, Compassion, and there we meet together. He has to give what He has, His Compassion, the flood of Compassion, and I have to give my little personal effort and my tears, the flood of my tears. Then if we come together, there we meet together.

Here I wish to say something. A woman spiritual Master once was asked by her disciples how much personal effort she made in order to realise God. She said before she had realised God she thought that her personal effort was ninety-nine per cent and God's help, God's Grace, was only one per cent. She was working so hard in order to realise God. But when she realised God, then she found that it had been just the reverse; that God's Grace was ninety-nine per cent and her personal effort was only one per cent. There she did not stop. Then she said, "My children, this one per cent of personal effort was also God's Grace. It was the divine Grace which I got and others did not get. And this Grace of God allowed me to make that most insignificant personal effort."

X – QUESTIONS ASKED IN 1969

84. How can we teach ourselves to love humanity, not just as a collective whole, but also specifically, when a person's defects and bad qualities are so obvious?

Sri Chinmoy: When you see that a person's defects and bad qualities are so obvious, try to feel immediately that his defects and bad qualities do not represent him totally. His real self is infinitely better than what you see now. On the other hand, if you really want to love humanity, then you have to love humanity as it stands now and not expect it to come to a specific standard. If humanity has to become perfect before it can be accepted by you, then it would not need your love, affection and concern. Right now, in its imperfect state of consciousness, humanity needs your help. Give humanity unreservedly even the most insignificant and limited help that you have at your disposal. This is the golden opportunity. Once you miss this opportunity, your future suffering will be beyond your endurance. Because a day will come when you will realise that humanity's imperfection is your own imperfection. You are God's creation; so is humanity. Humanity is only an expression of your universal heart. You can and must love humanity, not just as a whole, but also individually if you realise the fact that until humanity has realised its supreme Goal, your own divine perfection will not be complete.

85. How can we tell if our love is vital or pure?

Sri Chinmoy: You can easily tell whether your love is vital or pure. When your love is vital, there is a conscious demand, or at least an unconscious expectation from the love you offer to others. When your love is pure or spiritual, there is no demand, no expectation. There is only the sweetest feeling of spontaneous oneness with the human being or beings concerned.

86. Is it possible to prevent oneself from giving off impure vital love and to substitute the heart's pure love for it? How can we consciously give pure love?

Sri Chinmoy: It is not only possible, but absolutely necessary, to prevent oneself from giving off impure vital love. Otherwise one will have to constantly wrestle with the gigantic forces of ignorance. One has to use love, not to bind or possess the world, but to free and widen one's own consciousness and the consciousness of the world. One must not try to *substitute* the heart's pure love for the impure vital love. What one must do is to bring the heart's purifying and transforming love into the impure vital. The vital as such is not bad at all. When the vital is controlled, purified and transformed, it becomes a most significant instrument of God.

Now you want to know how you can consciously give pure love to others. You can consciously give pure love to others if you feel that you are giving a portion of your life-breath when you talk to others or think of others. And this life-breath you are offering just because you feel that you and the rest of the world are totally and inseparably one. Where there is oneness, it is all pure love.

87. In what way does love for one's Guru differ from devotion to him? Is it possible to have one without the other?

Sri Chinmoy: To have love for one's Guru is to take the first step into the spiritual domain. The second step is devotion. One cannot take the second step unless one has taken the first step. Moreover, true love and pure devotion cannot be separated.

They breathe together. Love sees the Truth. Devotion feels the Truth. Surrender becomes the Truth.

88. When we concentrate on love and devotion, should we direct it mainly to the Supreme or to our Guru?

Sri Chinmoy: It entirely depends on the disciple's conscious awareness of the Guru's spiritual status. If the disciple's ignorance compels him to feel that the Guru stands only ten inches higher than he himself stands in the spiritual domain, then naturally he will direct his love and devotion to the Supreme. But if he sincerely and consciously and spontaneously feels that the Guru is a God-realised soul and that there is a yawning gap between him and his Guru in their inner achievements, if he feels that the Guru has achieved and established his conscious and constant oneness with the Supreme, and that the Guru is the representative of the Supreme for the disciples and that he is the direct channel streaming downward from the Ultimate Source to cultivate the soil of human aspiration, *then* the disciple with the least possible hesitation, can direct his love and devotion to the Guru. To be sure, neither the Supreme nor the Guru is hurt when you approach *one* leaving aside the *other*. As a matter of fact, just because they know that they are absolutely *one*, they are equally and supremely pleased with you when you offer your love and devotion to *one* of them.

89. Do the words "psychic" and "spiritual" mean the same thing?

Sri Chinmoy: No, the word "psychic" and the word "spiritual" are not the same. Let us better use the term "the psychic being" instead of "psychic". It then simplifies the matter. The psychic being is the conscious representative of the soul. It is the aspiring, divine spark in us. It is supremely beautiful and is the fondest child of the Supreme. The psychic being is an entity which only humans have. The animals and plants and material objects, etc., do not have a psychic being. However each object, animate or inanimate, does have a soul.

Anything that concerns this divine being or pertains to it is described as "psychic". But the word "spiritual" is something general and all-pervading. It includes and envelops everything, including the psychic being. You can liken the word "spiritual" to a garden and "psychic" to a most beautiful mango tree bearing countless, delicious, energising mangoes.

90. What is devotion? Just a desire to do everything possible for one's Guru?

Sri Chinmoy: For a disciple, devotion means his purified, simplified, intensified, devoted, consecrated, conscious and constant oneness with his Guru. The disciple must feel that the Guru is the spiritual magnet constantly pulling him towards the Infinite Light of the Supreme. Devotion does not mean just a desire to do everything possible for one's Guru. Devotion is something infinitely deeper than desire. Devotion is the conscious awareness of Light in operation. In this Light the aspirant will discover that when he does something for the Guru or the Guru asks him to do something for him, he has already been given more than the necessary capacity by the Guru.

91. What are the manifestations of devotion?

Sri Chinmoy: The manifestations of devotion are simplicity, sincerity, spontaneity, beauty and purity. The manifestations of devotion are also one's intense, devoted feeling for the object of one's adoration and the feeling of one's consecrated oneness with the Inner Pilot.

92. If we feel that we are not devoted enough, how can we increase our devotion?

Sri Chinmoy: If the aspirant feels that he is not devoted enough, then he can do four things to increase his devotion. (1) He should try to love the Master more than he already does. (2) He should try to feel that the Master loves him infinitely more than he thinks. (3) He should try to develop more purity in his outer life. (4) He should try to feel that the highest Truth can and will come to him from the Master and through the Master alone.

93. If one has aspiration, but not devotion, does this hinder his spiritual progress?

Sri Chinmoy: If the aspirant has aspiration and not devotion for the Master, certainly it hinders – I must say it hinders considerably – the aspirant's spiritual progress. If the aspirant does not care for a Master and wants to aspire all by himself, then it is a different matter. He is not expected to show devotion to anyone. But here also I want to say that if he *really* aspires, then he has to feel that one day he has to reach his far-distant Goal through devotion. Now in order to reach the Goal, even without a Guru, he still needs conscious devotion to the Goal Itself, and if the aspirant feels that he has no need for this devotion, then he is hopelessly mistaken.

There comes a time in the spiritual life when one is bound to feel that devotion and aspiration can never be separated. Devotion is the candle, aspiration is the flame. No matter which path one follows, if his aspiration is not founded on one-pointed and surrendered devotion towards his highest Goal, then the realisation of the ultimate Truth will always remain impossible.

94. What is the difference between spiritual strength and spiritual power?

Sri Chinmoy: When we use the word "strength", we usually refer to the physical strength, the vital strength, the mental strength or even we go as far as the inner strength. When we use the word "power", we try to indicate a divine power which is the night-chasing capacity and the soul-fulfilling capacity of one's inner being. In the spiritual life, it is always better to use the word "power" instead of "strength". For power, unlike strength, immediately gives us the feeling of an essential aspect of God. Strength is bound in the physical and it can be used only in the physical world. Power too can be used *in* the physical, *for* the physical, but it is not bound there. Its home is high, very high, in the loftiest regions of the Infinite Consciousness.

95. In the spiritual life, the importance of purity is always stressed. Are pure actions worthwhile if thoughts are impure? How can we purify our thoughts?

Sri Chinmoy: Yes, in the spiritual life the importance of purity is always stressed. It is not only unavoidable but supremely necessary, for without the soulful purity, in the true spiritual life, the aspirant's life, will have to dance with futility. It is true that when you act, your thoughts must be pure. That is why the spiritual Masters say that it is not so much *what* you do but *how* you do it. Since I am one of them, I wish to add that at the beginning, even if your thoughts are impure and motives conditional, do not be upset. Start your inner journey from where you are right now. If you wait for purity to flood your outer consciousness before you start your inner and outer workings, then I tell you that you are doing something absurd. If you stick to the spiritual path, then the divine purity is bound to dawn on your inner life and your outer life in the course of time. You want to know how you can purify your thoughts. You can purify them just by feeling that your thoughts are coming out of your devoted and consecrated inner life and not from your doubting, suspecting, scrutinising, reasoning, fault-finding and correcting mind.

96. Should husband and wife try to feel the same kind of love and devotion for one another as they try to feel for their Guru or should it be of a different kind?

Sri Chinmoy: Dear Lucy, God bless you! I hope you understand the fact that there is a slight difference between a couple and a great spiritual Master in their spiritual attainments. The love and devotion that you will show to Savyasachi [Mr Carl Brown] and the love and devotion that he will show his better half will no doubt make you two inseparably one in your inner life and outer life. But if you two expect realisation, illumination and liberation from each other on the strength of your mutual love and devotion, I think you have to wait until the Eternal Time enters into infinite ignorance. The love and devotion that you must necessarily have for the spiritual Master in order to realise the transcendental Truth should spring from the inmost recesses of your crying, searching and aspiring heart. The kind of love and devotion you offer to your spiritual Father is infinitely purer, deeper, higher, more surrendered and more illumined than the kind of love and devotion that the husband and the wife can possibly offer to each other.

The husband and the wife can truly, soulfully, unmistakably and unreservedly become *one* if and when they discover their oneness with their Master *first*. One partner has to feel the living presence of the other partner in the heart of the Master. Then only will the divinity of the *one* be reflected in the life of the *other*. Let the husband and wife together, combined, show their love and devotion to their Guru. The Guru, in no time, will show them what he has for them, the Infinite Flood of Liberation.

XI – QUESTIONS ON SURRENDER

97. Is there any relationship between surrender to God and progress in the opening of the chakras?

Sri Chinmoy: There is no direct relationship between one's surrender to God and one's progress in the opening of the chakras. One may totally surrender to God, but God may not or need not open that person's chakras. The full opening of the chakras may give the aspirant some occult powers, but that does not indicate that his surrender to God is stronger or going to be stronger as the result of the opening of the chakras. Far from it. If the surrender to God's Will is not complete, the occult powers that you get from the opening of the chakras is a veritable curse, instead of a covetous boon. One's misuse of occult power can and does lead one astray. To be sure, if he uses the occult power to draw the attention and admiration from the world and not in conformity with God's Will, for him, the realisation of the highest Absolute will always remain a far cry.

98. Does the achievement of complete surrender assure that one will have the possibility of accomplishing self-realisation in this lifetime, or are there other factors that enter the picture?

Sri Chinmoy: Mere achievement of complete surrender does not assure self-realisation in this lifetime. There are other factors that must enter into the picture; God's choice hour and the aspirant's receptivity in its fullest measure and the full readiness of the entire being, to name only a few, are required for realisation to dawn on the aspirant. Again, I wish you to know what complete surrender means. It means that the aspirant's surrender is joyful, soulful, spontaneous, unconditional, constant, forever and forever.

99. Am I correct in assuming that surrender necessarily precedes realisation, or may it occur at the time of the first realisation experience or later?

Sri Chinmoy: You are correct in assuming that surrender precedes realisation. It is inevitable. Now as for realisation and experience, they are two totally different things. Realisation is oneness with *Oneness Itself.* Experience is, at the most, a momentary or limited feeling of oneness with the highest Truth. So you cannot speak of "the experience of realisation". Realisation is not an experience; it is Reality itself. You can correctly say "the *oneness* of realisation in the realisation-consciousness".

100. Having once surrendered completely, is there any possibility of backsliding, or will the strength of the disciple's aspiration and oneness with the Guru's consciousness prevent this?

Sri Chinmoy: In one of my previous answers, I have told you what complete surrender means. If surrender has already achieved that kind of perfect perfection, then there can be no possibility of backsliding on the part of the disciple. A disciple who achieves perfect perfection in his or her surrender will undoubtedly be the highest pride of the Guru.

101. Realising that the ability to surrender is ninety-nine per cent dependent upon Grace, I have been using part of each meditation time to pray for the Grace of God and my Guru. In view of the fact that you have said that prayer is a lesser form of devotion than meditation, I wonder whether what I am doing is a worthwhile effort.

Sri Chinmoy: I am extremely glad to learn that you have realised the fact that the ability to surrender is ninety-nine per cent dependent on the Divine Grace. That you are praying for Grace is an excellent thing. Unfortunately however, there has been a slight misunderstanding. I have not said that prayer is a lesser form of devotion than meditation. What I stated was that prayer is a lesser form of aspiration and that the rung of meditation is by far the highest in the spiritual life. Since you are meditating devotedly, you are undoubtedly doing the right thing in also praying. Needless to say that your effort is entirely worthwhile.

102. At times, when praying and meditating on surrender, I am moved to copious tears. I feel these tears as different from those tears of soul's joy which I have experienced at times. The anguish which accompanies them, makes me feel that these are not even tears of aspiration, but merely of frustration, and this disturbs me. How can I aspire for, and concentrate on surrender without becoming so emotional? Even writing this question, I find myself moved to tears.

Sri Chinmoy: I am sure you know that when the soul expresses its joy with tears it means that the soul is expressing its deepest gratitude through the physical being. As you know, in the soul's joy, there can be no frustration. There you get only the feeling of a vast and total oneness with the Highest on the strength of your surrender.

During your meditation and prayer, at times what you feel is the uncertain drive of your yet-uncontrolled emotional vital. Since you have, a few times, experienced the tears of your soul's joy, which are a kind of divine light, the frustration that lies in your unlit emotional vital cannot last for long. Again if your prayer is flooded with purity and your meditation is surcharged with luminosity, even in the domain of gross vital, instead of frustration you will have a partial sense of psychic realisation, of Truth in the form of heart's spontaneous joy. The spontaneous joy of the heart can easily enable you to meditate on total and integral surrender. Please try to illumine your emotional vital through your soul's light. Once the limited emotional vital is illumined, it enters into the boundless sea of all-achieving and all-fulfilling surrender.

103. What is involved in the surrender of the vital and of the physical body? Having surrendered with the heart and the soul, how can we best help the other recalcitrant members of our being to surrender?

Sri Chinmoy: After surrendering the heart and the soul, if you want your recalcitrant members, the vital and the physical body, to surrender to God, you can do two things. The first thing is to make them feel that they are as important as the heart and soul in the fulfilment of your mission on earth. The second thing is to threaten them, saying that you will remain in the soul's region and not care for their limited happiness, achievement and fulfilment on earth. Your inspiration, aspiration and your threat and withdrawal will compel them to make a decision and very often it is seen that they do care for boundless joy, achievement and fulfilment and that they identify themselves consciously and sincerely with the heart and the soul and become part and parcel of the integral surrender.

104. I have the feeling that when our heart and our soul have surrendered, we can know it ourselves, in fact do know it in our heart, but, other than being told by the Guru, are there any ways in which we can know positively that our vital and physical being have surrendered?

Sri Chinmoy: It is not always inevitable that one knows definitely when the heart and the soul have surrendered to the Will Divine. There are many cases where we have seen that in spite of the heart's surrender and the soul's surrender to the Divine, the aspirant still gropes in the dark, playing with uncertainty. Here is the need of a Guru. If the Guru says that your heart and soul have both surrendered, then rest assured that they have certainly done so.

There is one positive way of knowing that one's vital and physical being have surrendered and that is through widest expansion and enlargement of one's vital and physical being. In the constant flow of inner delight and outer dynamic, confident urge, one invokes the Highest to descend into the lowest, thus bringing the Supreme atmosphere into the earth atmosphere.

105. As one may consciously feel that one deeply wishes to surrender and may in fact do so intellectually, without yet ridding oneself of the fear within the physical mind, this would seem to indicate that the different levels of mind each have an independent relationship to surrender. Would you please explain what the relationship is?

Sri Chinmoy: You know well that there are the physical mind, vital mind, subtle mind, intellectual mind, intuitive mind apart from the infinitely higher ranges of the mind, the Overmind and Supermind, etc. If you want to offer the different levels of the human mind proper, then you have to give due importance to each, individually and collectively, with your aspiration. You have to create a basic and fundamental union amongst them. You have to feel that these are petals of a lotus and the lotus is your own aspiring life. Unless and until the lotus is offered totally, and fully bloomed, the realisation cannot be complete and the acceptance of the Inner Pilot will not be for Eternity.

106. When fear holds back the physical mind from surrender, it operates like an invisible enemy. This fear, being subconscious, is something of which we may be totally unaware, and even when told that it exists and is holding us back, it remains a fear that we do not feel. I daily offer my fear to the Supreme, but this offering has a feeling of unreality. How may we overcome an invisible obstacle such as this?

Sri Chinmoy: I am glad that you feel that fear acts like an invisible enemy. If you become more aware of your inner life and deeper existence, you will realise that fear is not only a visible, naked enemy but your worst possible foe. It is absolutely true that fear holds back the physical mind from total surrender. If a spiritual Master tells the disciple that he has inner fear, then he should have perfect faith in the Master, although he may not feel the existence of this fear. The Master's Vision is always faultless. The Master has no need to tell a lie. He gains nothing by telling a certain disciple that deep down in his being there is real fear. If the aspirant is not aware of fear, the culprit, that means that either in the subconscious or unconscious part of his being, he gets some joy when he identifies himself with fear. Here at this point, the Master can say if he wants to, that the unaspiring and insincere part of the disciple is unconsciously in collusion with fear to prevent the Light from descending from above.

You say that you offer your fear to the Supreme daily. This is something absolutely necessary, wonderful and praiseworthy. But to my surprise, you say that this offering of yours has a feeling of unreality. If only once you cared to believe that the Supreme does exist on earth to accept your offer and your unconsciously cherished fear, then your feeling of unreality would disappear. The Supreme will make you feel, on the strength of your implicit sincerity, that you do have fear.

You want to know how you can overcome this invisible obstacle. I wish to tell you that you can overcome all obstacles, visible and invisible, on the way towards your God-realisation if you have genuine faith in the Master's inner inspiration, outer dispensation, higher guidance and deeper wisdom.

107. How does surrender affect rebirth into our next incarnation? Does it in any way assure that we will be able to pick up where we left off without the loss of time which often occurs?

Sri Chinmoy: If one's surrender is complete and constant, then the result of surrender, which we call conscious oneness with the Divine, will bring the aspirant into a first-class spiritual family in his next incarnation. From the very beginning, he will be inspired and nurtured spiritually by the parents. He will not have to wait for seventeen or eighteen years to convince his physical mind about his inner spiritual thirst. His will be the life of conscious awareness in the field of spirituality right from the dawn of his birth.

I just said that the parents would inspire the child. It is equally true that the child, the very divine face of the child will inspire the parents to dive deep into the sea of spirituality.

Sarama, our path is the path of love, devotion and surrender. I am sure by this time all the members of our family have come to realise it.

NOTES TO BOOK I

1–11. *(p.3)* Questions answered on 20 August 1966, New York City. Twenty-nine questions also answered on that same day are not reprinted here, they are part of *Yoga and the Spiritual Life*.

11. *(p.7)* Kalipada (Mr Harold Wong), Waterville, Maine. Concluding question asked on 20 August 1966 at the second class of the summer series on yoga.

12–22. *(p.9)* On 20 July 1967, Sri Chinmoy appeared on television for the first time. He was interviewed on the Government Station, WIPR (Channel 6), in San Juan, Puerto Rico. The interviewer was Señor Hector Campos Parsi, a well-known musician and composer who has a weekly TV program in which he interviews persons prominent in the arts and sciences.

23. *(p.14)* Agni (Mr José Luis Casanova), San Juan Centre, Puerto Rico, 15 January 1968.

24. *(p.15)* Dulal (Mr Sol Montlack), Manhattan Centre, 1 October 1967.

25–29. *(p.16)* These questions were asked on 12 July 1967 during a question period at the Puerto Rican Centre.

25. *(p.16)* Agni (José L. Casanova).

26. *(p.17)* Gauri.

28. *(p.18)* Sudha (Miss Carmen Suro).

29. *(p.20)* Usha (Mrs Daisy Mattern).

30–51. *(p.21)* Sri Chinmoy was interviewed on radio station WHOA, San Juan, Puerto Rico, on 10 December 1967 by Mr Jim Knight and Mr George Riddell.

52–58. *(p.38)* These questions were asked at the University of Puerto Rico on 26 August 1968.

59–70. *(p.44)* These questions were asked at the Inter-American University, San Juan, Puerto Rico, on 17 October 1968.

71–75. *(p. 51)* These questions were asked at Yale University on 4 December 1968, following the talk "God's Dream-Boat and Man's Life-Boat".

76–83. *(p. 55)* These questions were asked after the lecture "Is Spirituality Man's Birthright?" at Yoga of Westchester, New Rochelle, New York, on 13 November 1968.

76. *(p. 55)* Chiranta (David Serlin), Pleasantville, New York.

77. *(p. 56)* Faye Hammil Levey, New York City.

78. *(p. 58)* Alan Faskowitz, Bronx, New York.

79. *(p. 59)* Anna Maria Nicholson, New York City.

80. *(p. 60)* Gary Jabobs, Flushing, New York.

81. *(p. 61)* Janice Carmichael, Cos Cob, Connetticut.

82. *(p. 62)* Arun (Richard Hein), Thornwood, New York.

83. *(p. 63)* Lillian Steinfeld, Pleasantville, New York.

84–96. *(p. 65)* These questions were asked by Mrs Lucy Brown in the summer of 1969.

97–107. *(p. 73)* These questions on surrender were asked by Sarama (Mrs Linda Smiler) in late 1969.

EARTH'S CRY MEETS HEAVEN'S SMILE

BOOK 2

I – QUESTIONS AND ANSWERS, UNITED KINGDOM AND CONTINENTAL EUROPE

108. The soul is without beginning and without end. Then is there any limit to its progress?

Sri Chinmoy: It is absolutely correct that the soul has neither beginning nor end. It is constantly progressing and moving towards its Goal. It has infinite potentialities because it is part of the Self. In our Gita, we have the most sublime description of the soul: "The soul is ancient, permanent, eternal, immutable and all-pervading. Weapons cannot cleave it. Fire cannot burn it. Water cannot drench it. The wind cannot dry it." This is the description of the soul given by the Lord, Sri Krishna.

You can easily see the difference between a human body and the soul. The body lasts for seventy or eighty years and then it has to die. The soul, however, is imperishable.

Everybody can see the soul. Not only can you see it, but you can talk to it.

109. How can I talk to the soul, Guru?

Sri Chinmoy: How? Only one word: aspiration. A-S-P-I-R-A-T-I-O-N. Aspiration and nothing else. No other medicine is required; only aspiration. You know about Mrs X. I was telling you about her the other day. She started coming to our meetings last November and now she has become a student at our New York Centre. She is under my spiritual guidance. Last May, the 5th of May, it was her birthday. She saw her own soul and had a talk with it.

For the preceding few months, she had been constantly trying to see her soul and to see if all that I had said about it was really possible. She asked me many, many questions about the soul.

[We are going to publish these questions and answers.] Then I said, "Questions won't do. You have to meditate on the soul and see it for yourself."

She did meditate on the soul. On the 5th of May, her birthday, early, in the small hours of the morning, she saw her soul. While she was seeing her soul, I saw it at the same time. We live in the same building. I live on the fourth floor and she lives on the first floor. She told me everything in detail and I concentrated on her to see if it was correct. It was all true.

If she can do it, I do not see any reason why you, Akuti, cannot see and talk to your own soul. Try. I shall be glad to help you.

110. The population of the earth is constantly increasing in number. Are they new souls that are coming to the earth? Do they come from other worlds?

Sri Chinmoy: No, the souls do not come from other worlds. They come down from the soul's world proper. They are souls that have been on earth before. After they have left the body, the ordinary souls usually take between six and twenty years to come back. The souls that take the Nirvanic Path, the path of blissful extinction, do not come back at all. But the souls that are progressive and want to fulfil the Divine here on earth, will naturally come back to achieve their own realisation and to participate in God's full and complete manifestation.

Now you are asking about the new souls coming to earth. Certainly the Divine is constantly creating new souls who come to earth for the first time along with the older souls that have been here time and time again. Souls that have left the body for a rest in the soul's world are coming back and new souls are also coming to earth.

Many of the new souls are not developed at all. They have just left the animal level and they are most undeveloped. I have seen many people in New York who are in their very first human incarnation. The other day I saw the photograph of a model who was in her very first human incarnation. I even have a few disciples, among my hundreds, who are in their first two or three incarnations. These young souls, if they are fortunate enough to become connected with a spiritual Master at the very beginning of their journey, can make very fast progress and be spared many lives of unconsciousness. Normally, however, it takes hundreds of lives before the human being consciously aspires for the life of divine realisation.

111. In the human vocabulary, there are two words, attachment *and* detachment. *But when the disciple aspires in the spiritual way and begins his unfoldment, does the meaning of attachment change? Can you explain it in the human sense and also in the spiritual sense? If he is well-grounded in the spiritual path, then that attachment won't disturb him, will it?*

Sri Chinmoy: No matter how well-grounded you are in the spiritual life, you will see that in attachment there is only frustration. In attachment, if your desires are not fulfilled, immediately frustration comes in. As soon as we take to the spiritual life, we must end all attachments. To be freed from attachment does not mean that you have to be cold, aloof and distant towards everyone. Attachment should be transformed into proper understanding and oneness. Attachment is not real oneness. Attachment exists often just for the moment; then out of sight, out of mind. Real oneness with human beings is most important. In oneness we are never frustrated because oneness implies the strongest inner understanding. And this inner understanding is illumination.

Who illumines us? God; and this illumination comes only through aspiration. Through aspiration we are going to the Beyond; the far, farther, farthest Beyond. Attachment and desire go together. They constantly bind us. In all of us, attachment is there. From our love for humanity, we come down to our love for our nation; then from the nation, we come to a particular city; then we come to a particular village; then we come to our family. Then from loving the whole family, we find, if there are five members in the family, that we are more attached to one member. This is how desire is limiting and binding us. From attachment to our country, we finally limit and attach ourselves to one person. But if we start with aspiration, then all the time we will be transcending and transcending. From the husband or the children, from the family, we will go to the city, to the province, to the country, to the earth. Finally, we shall become universal. We have to know that detachment liberates, while attachment only binds.

How can we have detachment? It is through aspiration. Detachment does not mean completely cutting off all relationships. Detachment is the proper understanding of the Truth at its own level. And in detachment, we will see that we are one with humanity on the strength of our inner life. We misunderstand and fear the word *detachment,* because we feel that we are breaking something. No, we are not breaking. We are actually connecting ourselves properly in the inner world to other people with our illumining and fulfilling souls. This we do with aspiration. The more we aspire, the larger becomes our vision. And this vision is our real reality.

When we start our journey in life, we limit, limit, limit and finally we come down to our gross body-consciousness. Even in the body we have more attachment to a particular limb or to a particular beautiful portion or feature. See how attachment manifests. This is my body, but I pay all attention to a particular limb or a particularly good feature. Attachment manifests itself in every insignificant way. But, fortunately, with our aspiration we are transforming the tiniest attachment into the mightiest oneness in the great unity of God's creation.

112. I am not very sure that I understand what you mean by inner peace *or* keeping the mind quiet. *When I am very close to nature, near the sea or beside flowers or anything that is Nature, I get a feeling of peace. I would like to enjoy this peaceful feeling everywhere, even when I am in places that are not so quiet. But I am not sure that I can ascertain if this is* inner peace *or whether it is just the atmosphere of the place that gives me this peaceful feeling.*

Sri Chinmoy: Your peaceful feeling is altogether a different experience from the inner peace I was speaking of. What is actually happening in your case is that you are identifying your outer mind with Nature. Nature has its own rhythm, its own harmony, its own peace and its own joy. When you are identified, consciously or unconsciously, with universal Nature, it is all vastness and immensity. There you lose your own outer existence, the existence of separateness, the feeling that you are separate from other persons. In that state of unified oneness, you become totally one with universal Nature; you become part and parcel of the vast and the Infinite. There you forget your ordinary life, which is your name, your physical frame and your outer existence. Indeed, this is a wonderful experience! In that state, you do not have to make your mind calm and quiet, for your mind itself is not functioning; you have already become identified with the treasure of universal Nature's consciousness.

In that state, your mind is not responding; you are not talking to anyone. No. You are seeing the trees, you are seeing the ocean; but actually you are not functioning mentally. But you have identified yourself with these natural things, and now what they represent and what they have is being mirrored in your own outer life. So this experience is entirely different from the experience that I was speaking about.

I was speaking about inner peace, which most seekers, at the beginning, do not have. When they seek, they have constant attacks of worries, anxieties, doubts, along with constant normal thoughts. Even when they are not talking to anybody, the mind is responding. But in your experience your mind is not responding to any of the disturbances of the outer world. Your soul has become one with universal Nature. The things which are encompassed by universal Nature are representing themselves before your mental vision as your very own. At the same time, you become the witness, totally detached, observing things but not responding.

This is a very good experience, a very high experience. You are trying to identify yourself with cosmic Nature. This is very good, but this experience is different from the experience that I was referring to.

113. Is it true that each person has a guardian angel?

Sri Chinmoy: Yes. It is absolutely true. In the West, you call this protecting being a guardian angel, while in India, we call it the family deity or the deity of the individual soul. Again, the protecting guardian can be one deity or many deities. Normally, however, one person is connected with only one deity, apart from God. God is all-Protection for everyone, far above and far beyond any guardian angel. But each individual soul will usually have a spiritual guardian angel. And there are some souls of whom God, so to speak, is very fond; they have more than one guardian angel. These guardian angels try their best to protect the individual soul.

Do you remember the children's opera *Hansel and Gretel* by Humperdinck, where Hansel sings, "When at night I go to sleep, fourteen angels watch do keep." Now, these deities also try to illumine the consciousness of the human being. They do not have the omnipotent power, however. Therefore, in spite of the very fact that the guardian angel tries hard to protect or to save the human being, the angel may fail. But the angel has considerable power, abundant power, and very often we see the miraculous success of an angel or angels.

It is only the Will of the Supreme, only the power of the Supreme that can protect us at every moment, no matter what kind of danger we are in. Something more, unlike all other protection, the Protection of the Supreme is always unconditional. But for our intimate, individual care and protection, it is absolutely true that each human being has at least one guardian angel who has a particular connection with him and hovers over him to protect and guide him.

114. Master, what exactly is initiation?

Sri Chinmoy: In the Western world, I hear the word *initiation* used very often in speaking about the spiritual life. "Are you initiated?" "Has he been initiated?" Constantly I hear, "initiation, initiation," from the disciples.

Now the main purpose of initiation is to bring the soul to the fore. At the time of initiation, the Guru makes a solemn promise to the individual seeker or aspirant that he will do his best to help the seeker in his spiritual life. The Guru will offer his heart and soul to take the disciple into the highest region of the Beyond.

The Guru can initiate the disciple in various ways. He can perform the initiation in India's traditional way while the disciple is meditating. He can also initiate while the disciple is sleeping or even while the disciple is in his normal consciousness, but calm and quiet. The Guru can initiate the disciple through the eyes alone. He can also do a physical initiation which is to press the head or the heart or any part of the body. That is the purely physical aspect. But along with the physical action, the Guru, when he touches the heart, can initiate the disciple in a psychic way. The Guru can feel the soul within the disciple's heart; he can see the soul and he can act upon the soul.

Yesterday, while I was initiating X, I was writing down the name of her soul on her heart. And I saw her soul very vividly while I was blessing her on the crown centre. This centre is on top of the head and it is called *Sahasrara* or the Sahasrara Chakra, the thousand-petalled lotus centre. From that centre, if the Kundalini rises up and goes beyond that spot, one enters into Nirvana, the highest bliss. One marches into the Absolute.

Now, in my case, very often with the aspirants whom I consider to be my disciples, I have initiated them through my eyes. Many times you have observed my eyes when I am in my highest consciousness. At that time, my ordinary eyes, my human eyes, become totally one with my third eye and they take the Light from my third eye. These two ordinary eyes receive and imbibe infinite Light from the third eye and then they enter into the aspirant's eyes. This way I initiate them. Many times you have observed my eyes radiating divine Light here at this Centre.

I have initiated quite a few disciples of mine. Those who are not my disciples I have no right to initiate. And whoever is my disciple need not ask me to initiate him because I know what is best for him; that is to say, whether the outer initiation will expedite his inner progress or not. The act of initiation can also be done by occult and spiritual processes. There are various ways, but I prefer the initiation through this third eye, which I feel to be the most convincing and most effective way. Immediately the Light from my eyes, having come from the third eye, enters into the aspirant's eyes and then into his whole body; it percolates there from head to foot. I see the Light, my own Light, glowing in the disciple's body. And when I do initiate, it is my Light, the Light of the Supreme, that enters into the person, the disciple.

Real initiation, as I said, is the total acceptance of the disciple by the Master. The Guru accepts the disciple unreservedly and unconditionally. And even if the disciple goes away after initiation, finding fault with the Guru, the Guru will act in and through that disciple forever. The disciple may even go to some other Guru, but the Guru who has initiated a disciple will always help that particular seeker in the inner world. If the later Guru is noble enough, then he will allow the former Guru to act in and through the disciple. Although the physical relation with the former Guru is cut off, and physically the Guru is not seeing the disciple, spiritually he has to help the disciple; he is bound to help him because he had made a promise to the Supreme. Sometimes the disciple, in fact, does not go to any other Guru; he simply falls from the path, deviates from the path of truth. But his former Guru has to keep his promise.

After accepting the spiritual life and being initiated by a spiritual Master, the disciple may drop from the spiritual path for one incarnation, two incarnations or even several incarnations. But his Guru, whether he be in the body or in the higher regions, disembodied, will constantly watch over the disciple and wait for an opportunity to help him actively when the disciple again turns to the spiritual path. But a time comes when the disciple is bound to come again to the Master's spiritual guidance. The Guru is truly detached, but just because he made a promise to the disciple and to the Supreme in the disciple, the Guru waits indefinitely for an opportunity to fulfil his own promise.

So I wish to tell you here, that some of the disciples who came to me to follow my path most sincerely, have also left me most sincerely. But, if in the inner world, they are my disciples, if I had already accepted them and they were my real disciples, if they claim even once to be my disciples, I wish to tell them I have not forgotten them. Neither shall I ever forget my soulful promise to them. They may take one, two, five or six incarnations to come back to the aspiring life; but no matter how long they take, I shall have to help them and I must, in their march towards God-realisation.

Those who have been close to me must feel the actual flowering of their initiation the moment they have wholeheartedly dedicated to me their entire life – body, mind, heart and soul. This is the flowering of the initiation. It is really more than initiation; it is their own revelation of their inner divinity. At this moment they feel that they and their Guru have become totally one. They feel that their Guru has no existence without them. Similarly, they have no existence without their Guru. Mutually the Guru and the disciple fulfil each other, and they feel that their fulfilment is coming directly from the Supreme. And the greatest secret they have learned from their Guru is this: only by fulfilling the Supreme first, can they fulfil the rest of the world. Now you may ask, "How can they fulfil the Supreme? How can the Guru fulfil the Supreme?" The Guru plays his part by taking the ignorance, imperfection, obscurity, stubbornness and unwillingness from the disciples and by carrying them faithfully and devotedly to the Supreme. The disciple fulfils the Supreme by constantly staying in the Guru's boat, in the inmost recesses of the Guru's heart, and feeling that he exists only for the fulfilment of his Master. Him to fulfil, him to manifest is the only meaning, the only purpose, the only significance of the disciple's life. This is the most important thing that one has to understand about initiation.

115. Can the Guru help the aspirant even after the Guru has left the body?

Sri Chinmoy: If the Guru is really a realised person, then he can and he has to. Now, suppose I die today, all the disciples that have accepted me as their Master, genuinely and devotedly, (and these do not include my followers, admirers and friends, but only my true disciples) would be served by me and would be taken care of by me. I am bound. I am the conscious slave of all my disciples. I shall have to be at the beck and call of all my disciples. No matter where I go. Wherever I go after I leave the earth plane, I shall have to be inside you, within you, my disciples. This is always the case if the Guru is a fully realised soul.

Otherwise, you know, there are many Gurus, like schoolteachers. If an ordinary Guru dies, he will not be able to keep any inner contact with you. In fact, even while he is in the body, the ordinary Guru does not have much inner connection with the disciples. If you are here in Puerto Rico, and the ordinary Guru is on the Continent, he will not be able to have any inner knowledge of you. Even here, if you are in this room and he is in the other room, he will not be able to maintain an inner connection. And when he leaves the body, it will be simply impossible for him to have the slightest possible connection with you.

But if the Master is a realised soul, he can easily maintain an inner contact with his disciples. And he has to do it because he has made a solemn and soulful promise to the aspirant that he will take him to God. The Master has gone back to Heaven and the disciple is still on earth. Yet the Master has to fulfil his promise.

Now there are some Gurus who are very sincere and dedicated, but at the same time, they are not fully realised. What they do sometimes, is this: when they leave the body, they feel that their disciples who are still on earth need a particular kind of help in their quest for self-realisation or God-realisation. If the Guru has no jealousy (a truly God-realised person has no jealousy), he will come to his disciples in a dream and say, "Go to that particular Guru and become his disciple. I have played my part. But you need further help and I know that So-and-so is a sincere person. He will help you in your God-realisation." But a mean and possessive Guru would say, "Wait my son, until I come back again to earth. I shall recognise you and you will recognise me. Don't go to any other Guru. You stay alone."

As I have said, there are some Gurus who, after having left the body, advise their disciples in this very incarnation to go to another Guru who is still on earth, who can teach them how they can realise God. They are undoubtedly noble and wise Gurus.

In New York, I have six or seven followers who have been asked by their own Guru to come to me. And they came. The first thing that happened was that they saw in me their own Master who had left his body three years earlier. The truly selfless Gurus let others carry on for them.

But if the original Guru made a promise to you, no matter where he lives, after leaving the earth, he has to be within you and with you to help you, even if you stay on earth for another forty or fifty years. In this case, it is just like having two rooms. Here is one room (life) and there is another room (death). Ordinary people cannot open the door. So when the Guru opens the door, he sees you, and when he goes back to his own room, he still has free access to this door. So once the Guru has made a promise, he is bound to keep it. He will not leave you until he has given you full realisation and has brought you to God.

116. Would you say something about death?

Sri Chinmoy: Yes, I will speak on death. I shall have to repeat many things that I have said before, since I have written and spoken a great deal on this subject.

The Bhagavad-Gita, India's great spiritual epic, tells us that just as we discard a worn-out garment and accept a new one, even so the embodied soul discards this body and accepts a new one. The soul is eternal and immortal; weapons cannot cleave it, fire cannot burn it, water cannot drench it, wind cannot dry it. It is invincible.

Now, in the external life, I have two rooms: a living room and a bedroom. In my living room I write, I work and I talk to people. In my bedroom, I take rest; I sleep. In my living room, I have to prove that I exist. In my sleeping room, I have only to take rest. Now in the spiritual world, the living room is life; the sleeping room is death. In the room we call death, life in the ordinary sense of the term is not there. I need no one when I am in this room, because I go there to rest. But people are afraid of this room because they feel that this room, death, is not theirs, whereas life is theirs. They feel that death is strange and alien and far away, whereas life is close and familiar. It is not true; both life and death are the soul's possessions.

Now as all of us here have accepted the spiritual life, the inner life, I wish to tell you a few things concerning spiritual death. In the spiritual life, we consider a man dead who is not aspiring and not making any progress. The man who does not aspire for a higher life, the man who does not care for progress, is more useless on earth than a dead man. The question then arises: what should a man do who wants to aspire and make progress at every moment? What should he do? He has to be conscious all the time of what he is doing and what he is not doing. He has to be conscious in the physical, in the vital, in the mental, in the psychic and in the soul. He has to place his mind and his body inside his soul, so to speak, and then he will see that his life can be turned into a constant progress. The higher and deeper reality can be easily brought forward into his physical existence. This is the first step.

Now to go back to death. Why do we die? Almost nobody wants to die, but in spite of our intense desire to stay on earth, we are compelled to leave the body and pass behind the curtain of eternity. Why? Simply because this earthly body of ours is imperfection itself. It cannot play the game of life unendingly and divinely. It is limited. After a few decades of existence on earth, it requires rest. If the physical body could play its part in the Divine *Lila* (the Divine Drama) in a divine manner, we would never have to experience death. But the body is not yet divine. Yet a day will dawn when this physical body of ours will aspire to receive higher peace, higher light, higher power and will bring them down into the physical plane itself. At that time, the necessity of death will not exist at all.

Remember that it is the body that dies and not the soul. The body dies but the soul goes back to its own home and takes rest. The soul is very, very wise. It does not forget what it did on earth; it carries with it the essence of the experiences that it had while it was in the land of the living.

When the body dies, the soul slowly and steadily, at the appointed hour, passes beyond the subtle physical plane, the vital plane, the mental plane, the psychic plane and finally enters into the soul's region, there to take rest. What does the soul do there while resting? It tries to assimilate its past experiences, the essence of thousands of experiences which it had on earth. Here it attempts to determine its new incarnation, new environment, new society, new possibilities, new aim and new vision for its earthly journey. When the determination is complete, it goes to the Supreme. The soul reveals everything to the Supreme and with His kind approval, it enters into the world again. It comes with new hope, new life, new determination and new will-power to unveil its inner potentialities and at the same time, to manifest the Divine in the most beautiful and most fulfilling way. The soul tries to bring all the gifts and achievements of its own previous evolution into play for this fullest possible manifestation.

Each birth and each death has a special significance. Through each birth and death, the sempiternal life gains a special experience in its cosmic game. They say that we die only once, but this is not true. At every moment an ardent aspirant feels that he has had a death and a new life. The soul is moving from one momentary experience to another. The moment we go beyond the barrier of ignorance, the realm of ignorance, we die. Why? Because we are born into a new world of inner wisdom. When we go beyond the realm-boundaries of ignorance, we actually enter into the realm of light and peace, and that is what we call dying at every moment and having a new birth.

When I, as an aspirant, go up, what do I do? I go towards my self-realisation. When God, the Divine within me, enters into the world, He goes towards His Self-Manifestation. Humanity is the fertile soil to grow Divinity. Divinity discovers its unique Truth only in humanity. And when humanity is transformed radically and integrally, we will have a life of perfect Perfection. This will be the integral and absolute transformation which mankind dreams of, a transformation of the body, the vital, the mind and the heart. Later will come the total transformation of society. In that Golden Hour, death is bound to leave us for good.

Immortality will breathe in us and through us perpetually. Let us all concentrate on that Golden Hour.

117. In your talk about death, you mentioned something that I would like you to elaborate on a little more. I understand that you asked yourself a question. You said, "Why does the physical body die?" And then, in answering that question, you mentioned that the time would come when the physical body would last indefinitely. Will you please explain that a little further?

Sri Chinmoy: Our span of life on earth is short. In India, it is forty or fifty years. Here in the West, it is seventy or eighty. In this span of seventy or eighty years, we do not have time to fulfil even our ordinary desires, let alone our aspirations. The physical body has to aspire for the spiritual life and it cannot do it even for a week steadily. Today I am aspiring and praying with the physical body; tomorrow I become a victim of inertia. I don't get up in the morning to meditate because the body does not want to. The body disappoints me and becomes a stumbling block. It does not aspire continuously, not to speak of aspiring divinely. As soon as the body starts praying or meditating, immediately it thinks of the office, the children, the wife, the house. I mean, of course, that the physical mind thinks of all this. But a day will come when the body will try unceasingly to bring down higher and higher Truth, Light and Peace from above. This is what an aspirant will do, not an ordinary man. This Light, Peace and Power will permeate even the physical body and the physical consciousness. When our physical bodies are surcharged with the higher Light, Peace and Power, there will be an abiding spiritual truth even in the most physical movements. At every moment, there will be a continuous flow of Light and Joy towards the Absolute, towards the Ultimate; a flow without interruptions. Right now the body does not have even an iota of Light or Bliss. But through conscious aspiration the body will have everlasting light. When the body has that everlasting Light, naturally it will be the Light that gives Life. When divine Light permeates the entire body, we will be able to stay on earth indefinitely. At that time, we will have the opportunity to conquer death consciously.

Now we have to live and sometimes we wish we didn't have to be here. But when the body is transformed, we will not feel a reluctant compulsion to live, but only that a divine opportunity has been given to us to go to the Highest. We shall also feel that this opportunity extends for a long period of time. This, you see, is the blessing that you get by invoking higher Bliss and Light. And once this Light enters into us, it gives us lasting Reality. This Reality is actually the breath of the Life Eternal, Perpetual Existence. Then the question of death does not arise because if you continue to aspire consciously and soulfully for two hundred years or so for the highest Light and highest Bliss, and also if it is done uninterruptedly, then the problem of death cannot exist. At present, we meditate for one day and then we take a holiday for ten days.

118. You see, Guru, as for me, I am not interested in remaining too long in this physical body. I am sincere in this. It is just a question of discussing the possibilities of having the body last longer than it usually lasts. Now I have read in oriental books that there are souls who have remained in the same physical body for two hundred, three hundred and more years.

Sri Chinmoy: Why only in the Orient? In the Occident also there are such souls.
Bhodananda: An old friend of mine is close to ninety years of age. We were talking about this subject and he said, "Well, I am not in a hurry to die because I know that I have to come back. So if I have to return, I would rather stay here."

Sri Chinmoy: The question is, "Is he enjoying the world or is he thinking of God and trying to realise God?" If your friend wants to remain on earth only to enjoy himself, then let him enjoy himself to his heart's content.
Bhodananda: He wants to learn; he wants to grow spiritually.
Sri Chinmoy: Then it is a different matter altogether. Then it is better for him to remain in his present body. But without aspiration, if anybody wants to stay indefinitely, then it is sheer stupidity.

119. Well, I don't know of anybody in the West. At least for the past one hundred years. But in the East, in India and other parts of the East, Tibet and so forth, I have read about souls that have remained in the same physical body for several hundred years.

Sri Chinmoy: Yes, there are some who have achieved the inner realisation, spiritual realisation. At the same time, on the strength of that inner realisation, they want to continue to live. They say that their only wish is to remain on earth. They do not take an active part in earthly activities; they stay in the Himalayan caves or in unknown or obscure places. They do not want to work for the world.

Now there are other souls who are not spiritually realised but who live for an indefinite period of time. They have somehow made friends with Nature. They do not have any high realisation, nothing of the sort. Only they have become children of Nature, Mother-Earth. All of us here are not children of Nature. Although we see Nature all around us, we are not identified with Nature. In us the mind is working unceasingly and this mind is sophisticated and unlit. This mind is the product of the outer world. But in their case, there is no mind at all. It is all Nature within them and outside them. They are like little children. Their whole existence is composed of a spontaneous oneness with Nature. So in them Nature becomes perpetual, Nature plays unceasingly. True, these people live for hundreds of years, but they are not realised persons.

120. But in connection with the average body, the physical body, is it possible for the body to renew itself indefinitely? To rejuvenate itself and thus last indefinitely?

Sri Chinmoy: Yes, it is possible and it depends upon how fast the seeker is progressing spiritually. At the same time, even if he is running at top speed, still the goal is very, very far away. And at that time, we have to have unending patience.

Another difficulty at the present time, is that our present physical bodies are not responsive enough to the inner forces which are trying to express themselves when we progress inwardly. These forces want to express themselves in the outer physical being as well as in the inner being. As our inner spiritual life develops, the body could also become more luminous, strong, beautiful and divine. But the trouble is that the body tends to become rigid and crystallised as it gets old, and while the soul is trying to express itself more powerfully through the physical, the body resists. The inner being is becoming more divinely illumined, wise and vast, but the physical vehicle, the body, does not receive the vastness, wisdom and illumination. On the contrary, its growth is cramped. It is like a plant which becomes too big for the clay pot. Finally the pot cracks. When this happens, the body ceases to serve its purpose and it dies. The soul, as it were, cannot use the outer covering and it throws it off.

The situation cannot remain like this. We do not have to die. If we can make our bodies plastic, flexible, responsive instruments, sensitive to the growth of the soul, our bodies will be divinely transformed. Both the inner life and the outer life will march hand in hand. They will be the glowing and growing embodiments of a never-ending Light, Beauty and Power. The body can be immortal just as the soul is. What happens now is that there is in almost everyone a hiatus between the progressive will of the soul and the stagnation of the physical sheath. When the outer sheath is about to be disintegrated or destroyed, it says, "I will go." And the soul says, "Go," for it knows that it cannot fulfil itself in this limited physical body. The body has become an impediment to the soul's manifestation. This is why the body dies.

But we can prolong the life of the physical body. We shall save ourselves much trouble if we do that. For our ultimate aim is to be immortal, to progress eternally in one body and work unconditionally for the Supreme.

Otherwise what happens is that at the age of seventy or eighty I die. Then after a few years when I come back into the world, I have to spend eighteen or twenty years, if not forty or fifty years, in ignorance, limitation and bondage. Moreover, during my childhood and youth, I am forced to become once more all that the ordinary ignorance-filled world is. But if I can continue in my present body and complete the game of realising the Reality, then I don't have to suffer any delay.

121. Please explain if a desire to live can keep a body alive even though the body is diseased.

Sri Chinmoy: It can, but determination must be present as well as desire. Desire is good; but behind desire there should be determination and behind determination there should be the soul's power, the soul's will. Otherwise, just by desiring, it is not possible to prolong one's life. There are many people who are suffering from diseases, and who do not want to die. They have an intense desire to live. But desire alone is only the first step. A further step is the determination to fight up to the last moment. "I won't die, I won't die, I want to stay, I want to stay on earth. I cannot die." This is to be done with determination. Now beyond determination is the soul's will-power. At this point you say, "I know I am not the body. I am the soul. How can I die?" With that soulful attitude, you can easily succeed.

But we can start with desire. Desire is the first step. The second step is determination. The last step is the soul's will-power. Normally, people do not want to die. Everybody wants to live. Then why do they die? I explained at great length why people die. The physical body is unable to make further progress. Instead of becoming a pliable instrument of the soul, the body hardens and breaks down. It is full of defects and limitations, and these defects and limitations increase as the years go by. Finally, when the body can no longer support and manifest outwardly the wishes of the soul, it dies. At the present time, we may not be able to divinise our human bodies by bringing into them the divine Light, Peace and Power. But if we draw on the soul's will-power and utilise it, we can prolong our lives. It is for the soul alone that we should and must live. When we meditate on the soul, we help our bodies with the soul's divine Energy and Will.

II – MEDITATION

122. Meditation – a talk

What is meditation?

Meditation is man's self-transcendence.

What does meditation mean?

Meditation means man's inner achievement and his outer fulfilment.

Why do I have to meditate?

You have to meditate because you need self-mastery.

Should I meditate to develop my intellect?

No, you should meditate to develop your intuition.

What is the best time for meditation?

3 a.m. is the best time for meditation. That is called the Hour of God, the *Brahma Muhurta*. At that hour, the cosmic gods and goddesses start to perform their heavenly duties at the express command of the Supreme. At that divine hour, you too can begin your inner journey.

I need Peace.
Please tell me if there is any special time for me to meditate on peace.

Early in the evening, between six and seven, is the best time to meditate on peace. Nature, as it offers its salutations to the setting sun, will inspire you, comfort you and help you in achieving peace.

I need Power.

Then meditate at twelve noon. The blazing sun and the most dynamic hour of the day will help you.

I need Joy.

Then meditate early in the morning between five and six. Mother-Earth, with her sweetest love, will help you.

I need Patience.

Then meditate in the evening. Meditate sitting at the foot of a tree. Meditate on the tree. Its sacrificing consciousness will help you.

I need Love.

Then meditate at midnight, looking at your own picture. Your Inner Pilot will help you.

I need Purity.

Then meditate on your incoming breath and your outgoing breath early in the morning before you leave your bed. Your soul will help you.

*

Now I wish all of you to meditate for five minutes. After that, I wish you to ask me any questions on meditation. Your questions should be framed in one or two short sentences, please.

123. When I meditate, there is something that holds me back so that I cannot meditate.

Sri Chinmoy: The thing that holds you back is fear and this fear has no meaning at all. If you want the wealth which the ocean holds deep inside itself, you have to dive within. Fear and wealth don't go together. Only if you have inner courage, can you receive the inner wealth. It is fear of the unknown and the unknowable that prevents you from diving deep within. But what is unknowable today becomes merely unknown tomorrow, and the day after tomorrow, it becomes known. The vastness of truth can never destroy you. It can only embrace and fulfil you.

124. When I start to go deep within, I feel sleepy.

Sri Chinmoy: It is not sleep; you are making a mistake there. While you are meditating, your mind is entering into the world of calmness and silence. There you don't have to create any movement or be dynamic. This world of silence is not the ordinary sleep where one becomes totally unconscious. On the contrary, it is a very good state. Try only to grow into that state with utmost sincerity, humility and devotion.

However, if meditation proper has not taken place, if you are merely preparing to meditate and you feel sleepy; it means that inertia and sloth are present. But if it is after a good meditation that this feeling comes, it is not sleep at all. You are entering into the world of silence and mistaking it for sleep.

125. While meditating, I feel some forces in the Ajna chakra *and in the heart centre that transform my face and my physical. What are these forces?*

Sri Chinmoy: These are the divine forces that are trying to transform your physical nature and your physical outlook. So when you meditate seriously, the *Ajna chakra* is activated by the Eye of vision. There the divine forces are working to bring into the body the vision of the luminous future, the Reality of the Beyond. And when you are concentrating on the heart centre, the *Anahata,* they are trying to make you identify yourself with the vision of reality which is knocking at your door. This reality embraces the divine luminosity, divine power and divine consciousness which is your soul's birthright.

126. How do I know that while meditating, I am entering into a higher plane and it is not just my imagination?

Sri Chinmoy: There is a very easy way to know. If you are actually entering into a higher plane, you will feel that your body is becoming very light. Although you don't have wings, you will feel that you can fly. In fact, when you have reached a very high world, you will actually see a bird inside you that can easily fly in the sky as real birds do.

But when it is your imagination, you will get a very sweet feeling for a few minutes, and then immediately dark or frustrating thoughts will come into you. You will say, "I studied so hard, but I did not do well in my examination." Or, "I worked so hard in the office today, but I could not please my boss." These negative forces in the form of frustration will immediately come in. But if it is really a high meditation, you will feel that your whole existence, like a divine bird, is going up and flying; flying high into the sky. While feeling this, there is no sad thought, no negative thought, no frustrating thought. It is all joy, all bliss, all peace. You are flying in the skies of Delight. When it is imagination, you may get joy for a few fleeting moments and then doubt enters in. You may in fact say, "How can I meditate so well? Yesterday I did so many wrong things; I told so many lies. How can God be pleased with me? How can I be having such a high meditation?" This is no meditation. But when it is truly a high meditation, it is pure joy with no questions and no doubts; only the soul-bird flying in the sky of Delight.

127. Master, during my meditation, I see a triangle of pure, white light behind you that covers your head. What does this mean?

Sri Chinmoy: When you see this light, it is a very good experience. The triangle here represents three of my inner qualities in the form of light. You are seeing my Consciousness in the form of light, my Bliss in the form of light and my Power in the form of light: Consciousness, Delight and Power in the form of a luminous triangle.

128. How can I purify my mind so that I can have a good meditation?

Sri Chinmoy: In your case, the best thing to do is to feel every day for a few minutes that you have no mind. Say, "I have no mind, I have no mind. What I have is the heart." Then after some time, say, "No I don't have the heart. What I have is the soul."

You have to know that the mind is almost always impure, bringing in dark and bad thoughts; even when it is not doing this, it is still a victim to doubt, jealousy, hypocrisy, fear and all that. All negative things first attack the mind. You may reject them for a minute, but again they knock at your door. This is the mind. But the heart is much, much purer. Even if you have fear or jealousy in the heart, the good qualities of the heart come forward. Affection, love, devotion, surrender and other divine qualities are already there in the heart. That is why the heart is much purer than the mind. But again, the heart is not totally pure because the vital being is around the heart. The lower vital, situated near the navel, tends to come up and touch the heart centre. It makes the heart impure by its influence and proximity. But at least the heart is not like the mind, which is always opening its door to impure ideas. The heart is far better than the mind. But the best is the soul. In it there is no impurity. It is all purity, light, bliss and divinity. You must say, "I have the soul."

When you say, "I have no mind," this does not mean that you are becoming an animal again. Far from it. You are only saying, "I don't care for this mind which is bringing me so much impurity and torturing me so much." When you say, "I have the heart," you feel that the heart has purity, not abundantly, but it has purity. But when you say, "I have the soul," you are flooded with purity. Then after some time, you have to go deeper and farther by saying, not only, "I have the soul," but "I am the soul." The moment you say "I *am* the soul", and you meditate on this truth, your soul's infinite purity will come up and enter into the heart. Then from the heart, the infinite purity will enter into the mind. So when you say "I am the soul," you will purify your mind and your heart and you will have a wonderful meditation every day.

129. When I am meditating, I feel my head expanding and I feel that something is pounding the top of my head.

Sri Chinmoy: You get pressure on your head? Two seemingly contradictory things are happening. On the one hand, you say that your head is expanding; this is the purified consciousness that is expanding in your mind. On the other hand, the impure thoughts, the impure consciousness wants to pull down Light from above by force. When they do so, they feel a heavy pressure. When the pure forces in us want to pull down something from above, there is no pressure. Why? Because what happens is this: when our little divinity looks up and invites the highest Divinity to enter, it sees its oneness with the Highest like a child who sees its father. The child is not afraid because he knows that it is his own father. He knows that he has very little strength, but his father is his very own. He has no fear. He calls his father and his father comes to him. But if he invites someone else's father, he may be afraid of that person, even though he is calling him. He may fear that that man will show him an angry face and say, "Why did you call me?" This fear he has because he is not the son of that father. That is to say, the father and the son are not of the same origin. The son sees someone unfamiliar, so he experiences a kind of uneasiness and fear.

Now similarly, when impure thoughts invite the highest Divinity to descend, the Divinity is ready to come, but the impure thoughts are afraid because they think they will be crushed. At best they do not get any familiar feeling. But our divine thoughts, our pure thoughts, do get a familiar feeling when they see the Divinity coming down in abundant measure. It is the undivine in us that is always afraid of the Divine even though at times it wants to see the Divine. Observing that the Divine is foreign and strange, the undivine feels uneasy and experiences a severe pressure on the head.

130. During my meditation, there is a very strong sound and within that sound, there are thousands of sounds.

Sri Chinmoy: Here you have to know that this sound you hear is the sound of the inner Divinity, and inside this Divinity, all the time, Infinity is growing. The first sound is the Source, the cosmic sound. Inside that is the infinite manifestation of sound. The first sound is the cosmic vibration, *Anahata* we call it, the soundless sound. Then inside this sound, you will hear an infinite number of sounds because from the Divine One, many have come.

God was One. He wanted to divinely divide Himself up and thus enjoy Himself in multiple forms. That is why we are now here on earth.

Now, this soundless sound that you hear within contains within itself the creation. That is why there are other sounds that you hear inside it. Those inner sounds are vibrating and offering you the manifestation inside your consciousness. The multiple sounds are the sounds of identification with the universe, with the manifestation. The first sound is the Source of Realisation, the Highest. The other ones are the sounds of the infinite manifestation.

131. When I meditate and I force myself to go deep within, something inside me accuses me of trying to reach God for myself and not for God's sake.

Sri Chinmoy: Well, you have to know that that thing inside you is absolutely right. Your soul, your purest soul, will always tell you that if you want to realise God, it has to be to please God and not to please yourself. I have been constantly telling people that if they want to realise God in their own way, it is useless. Of course that is better than not wanting to realise God at all. Millions and billions of people are sleeping and snoring, spiritually. At least the people who want God for themselves are not sleeping. But you have to know why these people want to please God. Why? Because they feel that God will then give them something to make them happier. Now they are unhappy. They feel if they please God, He will use His power to make them happy.

But the real aspirant says, "I don't want happiness, I don't want anything. I only want what God gives me. I love Him wholeheartedly; it is His business to make me happy or to make me miserable, to give me joy or to give me frustration. I want to please Him in His own Way. If He wants to give me all kinds of problems, if that is His Will, then let Him give me millions of problems. I shall shoulder them and remain happy. But if He wants me to be free of problems, so that I can think of Him and meditate on Him all the time, then I shall be equally happy."

A real seeker will try to please God in God's own Way. He will say: "If God wants me to be in perpetual hell, I will remain there because that is what He wants. But if He wants me to be in the Transcendental Heaven all the time, that is where I shall be." A real devotee, a real disciple will say: "Master, Thy Will be done and not mine; never."

132. Very frequently when I start my meditation, I feel a vibration as if I were a motor. This vibration starts going up into my head and then my head more or less falls, as though I am falling asleep. When I try to wake up, the vibration returns.

Sri Chinmoy: When you are meditating, you have to feel that energy is coming from your heart centre right into your mind. And then, when the energy comes up into your mind, you must feel that you are not falling down or falling into sleep. At that time your soul's Light is coming forward and touching the mind.

The soul urges, and indeed compels the mind to surrender to the soul's Light. In your case, when the soul enters into the mind and convinces it to surrender to the divine Light, your mind actually does surrender for a short period of time. The mind is convinced of the Light that the soul has given it. But what happens is that, unfortunately, you bring the mind forward again. That means that you don't want to keep your surrender to the soul's Light constant. First the mind bows to the soul's Light and then after a few minutes, the mind wants to regain its supremacy. If the surrender is complete, the mind remains silent in a divine way. And that is what the soul wants for the time being.

Later, when you find you are getting boundless joy, the soul will tell you to come back to the mind's original plane, but this time, because the soul has been pumping Light, Light, Light into the mind, the mind will be surcharged and flooded with the soul's Light. At that time, if the soul tells you to do something or I tell you to do something, immediately your mind will jump to do it. At the present time, the mind does not jump and run at the soul's command because it sees the higher Light for only ten minutes; then for two hours it wants its own limited knowledge. But if you remain in the soul during your meditation as long as your soul wants, then the mind will be surcharged with Light. And then the soul says to the mind: "Now you can go back to your own plane. You are now well protected, you are now illumined, you are now safe."

You drive your car to the gas station and when the tank is full immediately you drive the car away. So in the spiritual life, once the mind surrenders to the Light of the soul, it is filled with soul's boundless Light. You can then use the mind divinely whenever you want to. So allow the mind to remain in the soul's Light until the soul says, "Now, mind, you can go home because you are safe. You are safe because you feel that you are from the divine Light and for the divine Light."

133. Always when I try to go beyond the mind, it says, "No, carry me with you. I want to go there, too."

Sri Chinmoy: That is a very good thing, when the mind tells you to carry it with you. But you have to know what "you" means. At that time, "you" means your intense aspiration. You have become one with your aspiration and inside your aspiration, what looms large is your soul. When you have become one with your soul, you try to go beyond the mind. Now at that time, if the mind says, "Please carry me," you have to ascertain whether the mind is asking devotedly or with a kind of demand, such as this: "I have helped you all this time and now you are going beyond me. You have to take me with you." If it is this demanding mind that wants to be carried with you into the regions of the soul, it is very bad. If it goes there, it will only create problems for you. It will say, "No, no, this place is very unpleasant. Come down, come down. We experienced much more happiness down there. Come down." But if it is the devoted mind that wants to go with you to the Transcendental Beyond, it will not create any problems for you. It will cry for illumination and transformation along with you.

To the demanding mind, you have to say, "No, you have created enough problems for me and now if I go into a room that is all Light, you will extinguish the Light and make me dark again. You will create problems for me no matter where I go. If I go to Heaven, you will create hell for me there."

But the devoted mind will be ready to accept the Light. True, it has created problems for you in the past. Around you is darkness, the mind has created darkness and you are in darkness. But this time the devoted mind says, "I have tortured you for a long time. I am very sorry. Forgive me. Now I want to go to the place where you are going. I want to share the Light with you. I, too, want to grow into the Light. I, too, want to become a conscious instrument of the Light."

134. Are fifteen or twenty minutes enough for meditation, or should I spend an hour?

Sri Chinmoy: It depends on you. If you are able to meditate for more than fifteen minutes, then please do so. But it has to be absolutely sincere and soulful. To sit for an hour just to show that you can meditate for an hour will be a mistake. The soul will not be there. You may meditate for five hours, but the meditation will not give you any joy. It will not be fruitful at all. If a person can meditate for fifteen minutes most soulfully, and after that, if he feels that he has the capacity to continue, then he can continue. But if he doesn't have the capacity and just wants to make himself feel that he can meditate for an hour, it will be a waste of time.

In your case, I know your capacity. You can easily meditate for more than fifteen minutes. Without any difficulty you can meditate for half an hour. After that you can stop. Certainly you can meditate for more than fifteen minutes.

135. Please tell me if I am right. Meditation is the easiest thing in the world when we think of the Supreme with devotion, surrender and pure love.

Sri Chinmoy: You are absolutely right. Meditation is the easiest thing on earth because our inner divinity has not only the capacity or the quality of meditation, but practises it at every moment. Now whatever I do constantly will naturally be the easiest for me to do. Otherwise how can I do it at every moment? So when you are identified with your inner divinity, you will see that meditation is being constantly done for you. It is being done within you and for you, and if you are identified with the inner divine entity which is doing it, then meditation is very, very easy. Otherwise it is most difficult, for the mind will tell you during your meditation, "I am allowing a stranger to enter into me." The vital will say, "I am entering into an alien world." The physical will say, "You are trying to make me think that I am a fool. I still want to enjoy the world. I don't need your Heaven."

All this happens when you are not identified with your inmost divinity. But if you are identified, you can truthfully and spontaneously say that meditation is the easiest thing in the world because in meditation reality grows and the life of creation flows.

136. When I meditate, I enter into the inner world and if certain good vibrations help me, I see things which materialise in the outer world in a few months. Should I try to transcend this?

Sri Chinmoy: You actually enter into the soul's world and see these things which materialise a few months later. No, you don't have to transcend this. There is no necessity. However, you should be aware of whether or not you are crying to know these things. If you are meditating with a view to finding out what is going to happen in the future, then you *do* have to transcend this. If you say during your meditation, "O God, tell me what is going to happen to my husband or my son," then it is a mistake. But if you are not curious and are always trying to go deep within to have a serious, profound meditation, if that is your aim, then I can say that God wants to show you these things for a divine purpose. He wants to show you the future; He wants to give you these experiences. You must not try to transcend these experiences because, in this case, it is God's Will that you are fulfilling and not your own desire.

137. At times during meditation, I feel that the physical heart stops for a few seconds and then it resumes beating.

Sri Chinmoy: When you feel that the physical heart stops, this is a very good experience, but you must not be afraid of it. What does it mean? Only that the physical in you has totally surrendered to the spiritual in you. You won't die at all. In the spiritual life, many Masters, in order to enter into the higher regions during meditation, consciously stop their heartbeat. When I was a boy of fourteen or fifteen, I tried this and then I did it many times. My first experience was at the foot of a mango tree. In front of our dining hall in the ashram there was a garden, and in that garden there was a mango tree. I used to go there and meditate when I was fourteen or fifteen years old. One day, while meditating, I said to myself, "The yogis are able to stop their hearts. Let me see if I can do it. Is it true or not? I may suffer a little or I may die. If I suffer or die, no harm." I stopped my heart and then went on meditating for twenty minutes or half an hour. Nothing happened.

But only yogis and spiritual Masters can do this. Out of His infinite Compassion, God has given you a glimpse of this experience. You should be very happy and proud. Then when you become a yogi, it is up to you whether to stop your heartbeat and then meditate. What it means is that the physical has totally ceased and the spiritual is reigning supreme. At that moment, you do not need the physical. At the present time, the physical being is ruling the spiritual. But when the heart is stopped, it is the spiritual which is ruling the physical and at that time, we become consciously one with God.

138. How many times should one meditate daily?

Sri Chinmoy: As I said in my talk, you have to know what you want. If you want the specific divine qualities that I mentioned, Peace, Power, Joy, etc., then you can meditate at those particular hours. Again, if you want to meditate only once a day and you want Power, for example, but cannot meditate at noon, no harm. You can knock at God's door at any hour of the day or night and He will give you whatever you want: Peace, Light, Love, Bliss or Power. But at those particular hours that I mentioned, it becomes easier. Everything has its own time. Early in the morning you eat your breakfast. At least you call that meal "breakfast". But if you prefer to eat that food in the evening, you can easily do so. It is nourishing food and that is why you can take it in the evening even though you call it breakfast.

So let me come back to your question: how many times a day should you meditate? Please remember what I said in answer to Vijaya's question. How many minutes can you meditate soulfully? That is the most important thing. If you can say that you can meditate devotedly for fifteen minutes and during those fifteen minutes you are sincerely crying for Peace or Light or Bliss, then your meditation will be purposeful. If you are crying for Divine Power, the power that will give you the inner strength to fight against ignorance, God will give it to you. Human power breaks, Divine Power builds. Human power tries to possess and crush; Divine Power tries to enlarge you, expand you and free you from the fetters of ignorance. So you can decide for yourself how many minutes you can meditate devotedly without being interrupted by the doubting mind, by the suspecting mind, by the unlit mind. If after some minutes of pure meditation, the mind starts functioning and disturbing you, you can say, "Let me stop now. It is useless to go on. I shall start again later when everything is pure and fresh." So you will meditate as long as you can do so soulfully, devotedly and divinely. It need not be four or six times a day. People who meditate six times a day are not more spiritual than you people who meditate once a day most soulfully. Some people think, "Oh, God will be very pleased with us if we meditate five or six times a day!" It is not so. Meditate for fifteen minutes or half an hour, twice a day, morning and evening. That is more than enough for you at the present development of your consciousness.

139. Master, what is the difference between meditation and inner concentration?

Sri Chinmoy: Concentration is one-pointed; it is one-pointed awareness. It does not look forward or backward or sideways. Inner concentration tries to penetrate the veil of ignorance, so that ignorance is totally conquered.

In meditation, you have to feel that you are consciously trying to enter into the infinite expanse of consciousness. Everything here is finite. Everything there is Eternal, Immortal. When you are in a high meditation, you do not concentrate on anything. At that time, you only throw yourself into the Infinite Vast of Light, Peace and Bliss. You throw yourself into Infinity, Eternity and Immortality. Concentration is one-pointed. If concentration is aimed at ignorance, it tries to destroy ignorance. If it is aimed at knowledge, it tries to enter into the very breath of knowledge.

140. How do we start meditation?

Sri Chinmoy: In this world, we do everything because we have a love for it. We do things for human beings, for our relatives, our children, because we love them. We acquire skills because we have a keen interest in them. If we feel that we have a real love for meditation, then we can easily meditate. We have to grow within us a love for meditation. Meditation is not an object. It is a subject. We enjoy studying history because we have a love for knowing about the great events of the world and the great figures of history. Similarly, if we have a real love for God, then we will do the thing that is necessary to love Him. We will start meditating.

You asked how we can start meditating. It is by a spontaneous love for God. You don't need any specific meditation now. Only ask yourself the question, "Do I love God?" Don't ask, "Does He love me?" It is your business to feel within yourself whether you love Him or not. Then you should answer with a "Yes" or a "No". If you say "Yes", then ask yourself further, "How can I prove that I love Him? What can I do for Him? The proof is my self-sacrifice. Every day I shall sacrifice my life-breath to Him." And when you feel that you are ready consciously to sacrifice your life-breath to God, devotedly and spontaneously, then I tell you that your meditation has started.

141. Sometimes after meditation I touch things and find that they are not solid; they are fluid. They lose their solid state.

Sri Chinmoy: Actually they do not lose their solid state. After your deep meditation, when you touch a wall or some other solid object, you feel that it is soft and that you can even bend it. But you have to know what has happened to your consciousness at that time. After meditation you are totally relaxed and very peaceful. Your identification with the consciousness of the wall has also become most intense and intimate. Because your own consciousness is soft and yielding, you feel that the wall is also bending. Your own consciousness, in fact, has entered into the solid wall. As it is very light, relaxed and soulful, naturally, anything your consciousness touches will get its very own vibration.

To give you an analogy, when I touch someone from my highest consciousness, that person may not be in *his* highest consciousness. His mind may be roaming here or there. But if I consciously identify myself with that person, immediately he gets my consciousness even though one minute before that, he was like a solid wall spiritually. So I touch him and give him Peace, Light and Bliss. On the strength of my identification with him, that person receives my own divine consciousness.

So when you have come out of a deep meditation and touch something, you will feel your own consciousness in that solid thing. You will see that the solid object is accepting you, embracing you. It has opened its heart's door to become one with you.

142. When meditating, inside I feel very strong and outside I feel very soft. But as I go deeper, I start expanding.

Sri Chinmoy: That is wonderful. You feel strong inside because you bring down divine Peace, Bliss and Light into you. The more you consciously and devotedly bring down from above these divine forces, the stronger you become inwardly. You will feel that these things from above are helping you to expand your consciousness.

Now outwardly you are feeling soft, you say. It is not actually softness. It is the inner peace and inner confidence that grow in your outer being. One who is outwardly strong, like a great boxer or a great sovereign, has inside him infinite confidence and great peace because he fears no one. Inside his confidence, he is totally relaxed. In great power, there is quietude. But if a person is not very strong, he clenches his fists and gets ready to defend himself for he feels that his enemy is right in front of him. He has to show that he can fight with him. But when one has boundless inner strength, one does not have to display it outwardly. He doesn't have to clench his fists. He is relaxed because his inner strength has given him inner confidence. He is like a divine hero. At any moment, he can defeat the enemy or surmount any obstruction outside himself. He is relaxed because he knows that whoever is in front of him is no match for him. The more inner confidence we have, the more we can outwardly relax.

143. Master, you said before, "Let Thy Will be done and not my will." Therefore, is it better for us not to try to help other people by our own small will?

Sri Chinmoy: I am very glad you have asked this question. Normally while we are trying to help someone, we are not helping him at all. We are only creating more problems and more complications for him. Always, the greatest and the best spiritual disciples try to please God in God's own Way. Otherwise there is no benefit in helping others. You are using your own small will. You try to grab this and grab that and while you are trying to possess someone by helping him, you are yourself possessed.

Another thing that people think is, "Oh, if I do this for the Master, people will see how devoted I am. I will feel that I have really done more than others. Many people will say that I am very devoted." But I must tell you people that the Master will not be pleased. He will be pleased only when the disciple pleases him in his own way. I often tell someone to do something and he immediately says, "Oh no, how can I do that? What will people think of me? What will society think of me? What will humanity think of me?" At that time, he is pleasing himself, he is pleasing society, but he is not pleasing the Divine within him, the Supreme within him. If you are going to please God, or the Master who represents God, everything has to go: society, morality, friends, relatives, members of the family. Everything has to go if you want to please your Master who represents God. You think, "I have pleased the Master because I have done this and that for him." But the Master only smiles. Naturally if you give me a blade of grass or a flower, I will give you a smiling face. You have given me something, but it is something I didn't want at that time. At that moment, I didn't want a flower. Perhaps I asked you to cook for me or do something that seemed absolutely meaningless to you. Perhaps I asked you to read the newspaper to see what was happening in the world atmosphere. You thought that by bringing me a flower, you would make me happy. I say, "No, at this particular moment, I want you to read the newspaper and tell me what is happening in Rome or Germany." So if you want to please me by doing what I asked, then naturally, as I am identified with God, I immediately say, "God, he has pleased me." If you please the Highest with all love, all affection, all concern, how can the Highest, the Dearest and the Deepest create problems for you? Even in the ordinary life, when you please someone according to your capacity, that person comes to help you, comes to your aid. But if you please the person the way he wanted to be pleased, naturally he will give you much more, beyond your expectation. And when you please a spiritual Master, who is one with God, then naturally Infinite Joy, Infinite Peace, Infinite Bliss will be yours because he is dealing with Infinity. He is not dealing with society or friends or relatives. He deals with Infinite Peace, Light and Bliss.

If you want to remain in the Source, if you want the Eternal and the Infinite, then try to please the Master in his own way. To please the Master is to please God. Otherwise, to feel that the Master is someone and God is someone else is to make a terrible mistake. The disciples must always see inside the Master the living presence of God. If he fails to see God inside the Master, he is not a disciple. He is simply fooling himself; he is creating a barrier between himself and the Master and between himself and God. He is not fit to be a disciple. What more can I say?

144. When I meditate, I see within and without that everything is alive and has millions of patterns. I see something like a Living Presence in everything.

Sri Chinmoy: This is absolutely true. This is a very high kind of meditation because inside everything is God. And where God is present, life is bound to be present. Life and God can never be separated. Where there is life, there is God and where there is God, there is life. It is a wonderful experience.

Now you see infinite patterns. Inside one thing you are seeing many varieties. Here the One is being expressed in many forms and many patterns. Look at a lotus flower. It is one flower, but it is expressed or manifested by many petals, by the leaves, the stem and the pollen. In one lotus you see the manifestation of reality through various forms. You touch one particular part of the lotus, the leaf, for example, and you say, "This is the lotus." Then you touch another part, the stem, and again you say, "This is the lotus." God is there in all parts of the flower; that is why you feel that each part is the whole. God is present wherever life exists. God is endless in expression. He is endless in manifestation.

145. When I meditate, I start repeating my name a hundred times as you told me to do. But I lose track of the count, so I have to go back and start counting again.

Sri Chinmoy: When you are counting your name, count up to fifty most soulfully. Soon you will be in another world: the world of the soul's divinity. Take some rest. Then you can start counting again. Suppose you make a mistake in your counting. Pay no attention to it. Or suppose you lose track of the number. Do not be worried. You have to understand why I ask you to count. When you count, you separate your consciousness from other things. If you are saying, "Mangal, Mangal," at that time you will not be thinking of someone else or something else. So once you start counting and you begin to feel that you are meditating only on yourself, saying, "Mangal, Mangal," your consciousness will be focussed on your divine qualities. Then if you should enter into another world, whether it is the world of sleep or a world of silence, you don't have to count at all. If you have already entered into a deep meditation while you are counting, then forget about the number of the count completely.

When a runner begins a race, when he is about to run, he is full of conscious awareness. He has to be in the right position when the starter fires the gun. The runner's hands, knees and feet all have to be in the right place. But when he is in motion, running at top speed, he cannot think of his movements. He does everything automatically.

In the beginning, you have to be conscious. When you start a vehicle, you have to mesh the gears and press various levers and pedals. But when the car is under control and going at full speed, you don't think of all the things you have to do. They are simply done spontaneously. Similarly when you are deep inside the consciousness of your soul's name, you don't have to count. The runner is running. He doesn't think whether he is placing his legs properly on the ground. He just runs. He does not look back. He looks forward. Lo, he reaches his goal. Indeed, each seeker is a divinely inspired runner, running consciously and speedily toward the Goal of the Beyond.

146. Why is it that sometimes when a person is apparently making fairly good inner progress in the spiritual life and aspiring very well, we seem to not always see a real reflection of this? Sometimes the outer life does not seem to reflect the progress made. Or is this just an illusion?

Sri Chinmoy: The thing is that there are two worlds, the inner world and the outer world. If someone is making real progress in the inner world, then his progress is bound to be shown in the outer life also. It is a matter of time. Sometimes it happens that you are under the impression that the person in question is making a certain amount of inner spiritual progress, but it might not be so at all. There are many times, we have seen, when people make a show, a parade, of what they think is their inner progress. Without having any sincerity, they will appear to meditate well in a group or work hard with others for a joint cause. First of all, an aspirant has to know whether he is totally sincere or not. If he is, then he is bound to make real inner progress. When he makes real inner progress, he has to manifest it in the outer world. This inner achievement will have to materialise in his outer life also. It is also a matter of time.

147. Guru, are there negative forces, or is it just ignorance that we think of as a negative force, things that make us feel bad and things that seem to put obstacles in our way?

Sri Chinmoy: Undoubtedly there are negative forces in us and around us in the cosmos. But, again, the source of these negative forces is ignorance. Now, we can go to the source, but it is very difficult for us to do so, whether the source is the light or the source is the night. To go to the light is extremely difficult. To go to the night is comparatively easier because we are already in the mire of ignorance. But now the source is ignorance and from the source comes the negative force. The negative force means the destruction of one's inner possibilities. The positive force which energises us is the force of our soul. The force which comes from the unconscious level within us is a negative force which will try to destroy all our inner possibilities. So, when there is a thought inside us looming large which says, "You cannot be God's chosen child. Impossible. You have done many things wrong," immediately we have to tell this negative force, "True, I have done quite a few things wrong, but it is none of your business. I am not taking shelter in you. I don't want to be under your wings. I want to be under the protection of the Omnipotent, the Omniscient." This way I can strike back at the negative force. The negative force will tell me that I cannot become the perfect instrument of God, or cannot grow into the very image of God. These two things the negative forces will tell me. The positive force will tell me that I am indeed the chosen instrument of God. Unfortunately, most of us are not aware of it, and we are suffering because of it. Another thing: we are growing into the very image of God because God Himself is evolving in and through us. Rest assured that the positive force will tell us that we are God's chosen children.

Then every day, early in the morning, at least for five minutes, we have to exercise our positive thought, positive will, positive force. What do we mean by positive force? We mean that the Truth exists within us and is being realised. Then we try to feel that the Truth is already embodied. Finally we try to feel that the Truth has to be revealed and manifested in us and through us. Each aspirant has to feel that. Then there can be no negative force to disturb us or destroy our aspiration. Very often we allow the negative forces to attack us. If we don't give them the chance, then the negative forces have to remain thousands of miles away from us.

Now, there is another process. If we constantly harbour good thoughts, divine thoughts, pure thoughts, then the negative forces cannot stay with us. If we cherish undivine thoughts, then the Divine Force cannot enter into us because it knows that the moment it enters into us it will be suffocated. But, unfortunately, human beings get immense pleasure in cherishing undivine thoughts. After cherishing divine thoughts for five minutes, they find it relaxing to cherish undivine thoughts. Now when we can recognise negative forces, that means we are already awakened. For an unaspiring person there is no such thing as either negative or positive forces. He cannot discriminate. And he has already surrendered to the dark forces which are around him most of the time: his fate. Here is the difference between an aspiring soul and an unaspiring soul. An aspiring soul will never surrender to fate; only to his Inner Pilot, the Supreme. But an unaspiring soul will surrender to his fate. What is fate? It is only the obstruction created by limitation. This limitation has come directly from darkness and this darkness is the child of ignorance. So now let us try, all of us, early in the morning, to welcome divine thoughts, divine Purity, divine Light, divine Truth. Then the negative thoughts, negative ideas, negative forces will not dare to enter into us. Later on, they will not even be willing to appear.

148. In the Bhagavad-Gita, Krishna tells Arjuna that he should go into battle and fight; but I think we are not supposed to go about harming people. I don't understand how Arjuna could kill people.

Sri Chinmoy: You mean to say that Krishna was very immoral. What kind of spiritual Master was he? He asked his devotee to kill.

Krishna asked Arjuna to kill cousins, uncles, etc. You feel that it was a very horrible mistake on the part of a spiritual Master.

Now, first of all, Krishna tried his best to avoid the war. He literally begged the Kauravas to come to some agreement. But they didn't listen to Him. So necessity compelled Krishna to ask Arjuna to fight. What was this supreme necessity? He saw that the evil forces were reigning supreme at that time in the Kaurava family, and they were not opening to the Light. He also knew perfectly well that if the so-called outer destruction took place, a new life would dawn. Then, (I am sure you have read the Gita) in the eleventh chapter Sri Krishna showed His Universal Form to Arjuna. What was He showing? These people were already killed. By whom? Not by Arjuna, but by Krishna Himself. Then He said to Arjuna, "They are already killed. You just become My instrument."

Further, from the spiritual point of view we come to learn that Krishna was not actually destroying them, but was transforming their unlit consciousness so that they could have better lives in their future incarnations. He saw clearly what their future possibilities were. Morality will never allow you to fight against your nearest and dearest ones, but only this much does morality teach you.

Morality cannot see an inch further. If you want to go beyond morality, then you have to obey the express will of the spiritual Master, the divine representative of God. If the spiritual Master asks you to do something, immediately you have to give up all your morality, for he knows what is ultimately best for you and your soul. In order to realise the Highest, if the Highest demands that your moral thoughts and attitudes be changed and transformed, then naturally you have to surrender to the Highest. It is the Highest that can fulfil your life. So you have to know where you stand. Krishna asked Arjuna to be His instrument because He knew well the spiritual capacities of his disciple. He didn't take just anybody as His instrument. So, if I ask you to do something, and if you think that it is touching your morality, please do not misunderstand me. I shall not ask you to go back to your animal life just to please me. But I may ask you to do something which has been commanded by the Supreme. He knows His cosmic *Lila* [Play] better than anybody else. Your life has to be totally dedicated and surrendered to one Person, the Inner Pilot, the Supreme. So I wish to tell you that Krishna did the right thing. He saw the future and did absolutely the right thing. In the inner world we see and feel that He had infinite Compassion. He wanted to expedite the evolution of the unawakened, unlit, unprogressive and undivine human beings.

149. Sometimes in the morning after meditation, I fall into a doze, not a sound sleep. But it doesn't seem to be a conscious meditation. Is this good?

Sri Chinmoy: Unfortunately, it is not a good thing. It is not sleep and at the same time you are not fully awakened. So after you meditate, try to be absolutely dynamic. It means you will not allow sleepiness to enter into you. Before you meditate, try to breathe in a few long breaths and make your whole body energetic. Your dynamic energy will help you enter into meditation. Unfortunately, many disciples don't get enough inspiration to energise them for aspiration. Some days you get inspiration all at once. Other days you don't get any inspiration at all. If the fire is already burning inside, you don't have to do anything. But when there is no fire, what do you do? The best thing is to breathe in, or you can jog a little. Make yourself feel that you are entering into the battlefield where you have to fight against ignorance, doubt, imperfection and death.

It is always better for the aspirants not to meditate while lying down. At least in your case, the time has not come for you to meditate while lying. After you have meditated three or four hours and you want to have a relaxed feeling, you can lie down. But there are some who think that when they lie down, they get abundant inspiration. I wish to tell them that they are only fooling themselves. If you don't want to keep your back erect, no harm, but you have to sit up and be fully alert during your meditation. If it is possible, in the morning before you start meditation, take a small quantity of hot juice or milk, something liquid and hot, before you enter into meditation. Then your whole system will be attuned to the divine energy. That divine energy will take you to the proper plane of meditation in your inner consciousness.

150. Guru, how is it possible to have both our inner and outer life synchronised so that we feel we are one person? I often feel like I am two people.

Sri Chinmoy: Well, here we have to know that two things cannot be given equal importance. One thing alone has to be given prime importance and that is the inner life. It is from the inner life that we can enter into the Source. So, if you are really satisfied with your aspiration, meditation and contemplation in your inner life, if you are paying true, sincere attention to your inner life, then you are going towards the Source. Whether or not you have outer success, whether you are able to cure a particular client, student or yourself – that is immaterial. Your business is to enter into your own deepest Source. From there you will get your inspiration. In the outer life, you must not care for success. If you care for success, you are acting like a beggar. That does not mean that you will not work. You will deal with your clients and work with them, but, when you care for success, you know that the forces around you will mock at you.

Now you want to become one man, inside and outside. For that I wish you to pay infinitely more attention to the inner life than to the outer life. In the outer life, the world may call you a failure, but in the inner life you will achieve tremendous success. If you want to compete with others and be judged by others, no matter what you achieve in your outer life, you will always feel that someone is doing better than you. In the field of competition, you will always see somebody above you or below you. But, in your case, you really want to be one integral person. Inside, you have to become successful and, if you are truly successful in your inner life, you are bound to get outer success. And you will see that the outer life is a mere replica of your inner life.

151. Do our past lives have any effect on our present lives?

Sri Chinmoy: Certainly, on the whole, we are carrying the past inside us. There is a continuous flow from past to present. As you sow, so shall you reap. Whatever you have done in your past incarnations will be given to you by God in this incarnation as a result. The fruit of karma, I must say, in the case of an ordinary, unaspiring person, is unavoidable.

But I always say, "The past is dust." I say it because the past has not made you what you want to be. If you care for the past, and if you go backward (our race is forward and not backward), perhaps you will see that in one of your incarnations you were a thief or someone abominable. Again, if you enter into one of your past incarnations and see that you were president of the United States at one time, what happens? When you enter into the inner world, you will see that the president was filled with miseries and he was not satisfied. None of this knowledge gives you joy. An aspirant wants inner joy. So, if you enter into the thief incarnation you will be miserable, and in the president incarnation you will also be miserable. When a seeker enters truly into the spiritual path, he has to go forward with his own aspiration, concentration and meditation. If he had actually begun his life of aspiration in one of his previous incarnations, he will usually have started aspiring in his present life at a very young age. If somebody was spiritually sincere in his last life, he will not wait until old age to start his spiritual life of Yoga again.

Now it may happen that circumstances in the new life are bad; the environment is not encouraging. So, he will have to go more slowly and steadily, because he does not get enough help from his parents. But, if he was a great aspirant and did not realise God, then in that case he will come into a very high spiritual family and he will enter early into the spiritual life. Most of the great spiritual Masters entered into very high spiritual families. But God's Play is not bound by any plan and it is also possible that He will send a spiritual Master into a very unaspiring family. When an aspirant enters into the true spiritual life, then the law of karma, if it is his bad karma, can be negated and nullified. Otherwise, the law of karma is really merciless. You have to pay the tax; there is no other way. And only God's infinite Grace can nullify the result of bad karma and expedite the result of good karma. So here the aspirant gets the opportunity to go faster with the help of God's boundless Grace. If one really wants the spiritual life, then by sincere practice every day, one can, to some extent, stand above the law of karma, for God is bound to shower His boundless Grace on the devoted head and heart of the aspirant. But if you are an ordinary man, you have to abide by the law of karma. Fortunately, you are a true aspirant.

152. How can one increase one's inner drive, one's aspiration?

Sri Chinmoy: There are various ways to increase one's inner drive, inner urge. If one is absolutely a beginner and is eager to enter into the spiritual life, then the first thing one has to do is pray to God. His prayers should be very simple, very sincere and spontaneous. Prayer is most effective in the early stages of spiritual life, and it is prayer that will increase the inner urge in a would-be true seeker. At the beginning, when one is just curious or a little bit sincere, we cannot call that person a real seeker. If one is a step ahead in the spiritual realm, he will not be satisfied with the rest of the world or even with himself. He wants a better creation in himself, and in the world at large. Then he has to feel the necessity of the fulfilment of God's Will on earth and of taking a conscious part in fulfilling God's Creation. Such being the case, God is bound to give him an additional amount of inner urge. Then, if a time comes when he feels that he can exist without everything, but not without God – when he has such inner strength that he does not need mother, father, brother, sister, wife, children – when the aspirant comes to that state where he needs only God, he becomes the real pride and real instrument of God. At that time, automatically, his aspiration is increased in boundless measure from deep within.

I wish to say, in answer to your question about how one can increase one's inner drive, that in general one can do it just by accepting the life of sincerity and the life of dedication, the life of absolute surrender. If one has a Master, then one has to be absolutely sincere to the Master. Sincerity is the safeguard. If one has dedication, then his dedication has to be total and complete to the Master; and if one has surrender, this surrender has to be implicit and unconditional. Then you will see that automatically, spontaneously, this inner drive will increase. But if one does not have a Master, what should one do? He has to go deep within and try to feel the Inner Pilot. The Inner Pilot will speak through his conscience. He may not see the Inner Pilot – to see Him, the Supreme, is a very rare experience – but the Inner Pilot is always ready to act through one's conscience. And if one listens to the dictates of his conscience, then naturally his aspiration is bound to increase.

153. Would you explain what your chant means?

Sri Chinmoy: I was chanting AUM. AUM is the Mother of all *mantras*. Mantra is a Sanskrit word. Its English equivalent is *Incantation*. Now, AUM has three sounds: A, U, M. *A* represents God, the Creator. *U* represents God, the Preserver. *M* represents God, the Transformer. So we invoke God in His three Aspects all at once when we chant AUM. I have written considerably on this subject. As a matter of fact, for the beginners I wrote a pamphlet entitled *The Significance of AUM*. The question that you have asked me has been asked quite a few times by other seekers, and I have answered them elaborately. I have told them how to chant AUM and how to derive the greatest benefit from chanting AUM. The most important thing is to know that AUM is the Mother of all our Sanskrit mantras. AUM has to be chanted first and foremost when we chant any mantra. It is from AUM that the creation came into existence. Again, the creation will find its ultimate Goal only in AUM.

154. How can an artist dedicate his painting to God?

Sri Chinmoy: Let us take the artist as a creator and his painting as the creation. Now, this artist has to realise that he is not the Supreme Artist and his creation is not the Supreme Creation. The artist has received an iota of inspiration from the Supreme Source, and this inspiration he has manifested in the form of his painting. Now, the artist, if he is a seeker, naturally would like to derive joy from his creation, as we all do. But when an ordinary artist paints something, he feels that since he is the creator, he deserves all appreciation and admiration from others. But he who is going to be a spiritual artist will have a different view. He will see that he gets inspiration only when some Divine Forces work in him, through him and for him. He feels, however, that the divine inspiration is not at his own command. There are many times when he wants to paint something but does not get the necessary inspiration and cannot paint at all. And again, all of a sudden, he is inspired and the result of his inspiration is a wonderful painting. So he knows that he is not the Source. When he enters into the Source, he gets something remarkable, appreciable, etc.

Now when an artist creates something, he gets some limited joy, but he will get infinite joy only when he offers his creation consciously to the Source Supreme. When the Supreme gives us inspiration, we receive it according to our capacity and receptivity. If He gives us beyond our capacity, then we will not be able to hold it, and the vessel will give way. If He gave us less than our receptivity, then He would be doing an injustice to us, which He would never do. So, according to our capacity or receptivity, the Supreme gives us joy. When the artist wants to offer something to God, he has to know why he is offering it. If he does not know that, today he will give something to God on the spur of the moment, but tomorrow he will try to argue and say he made a mistake in offering his creation to God. Once we have established in our mind and heart that we must give our creation to God, we do it, not to get something from Him in return, but just because we feel that this is what we have to do.

Now, your question is, "How can an artist dedicate his painting to God?" He can dedicate his painting to God just by thinking that he is the instrument and not the Creator. It is the

Creator who acts in and through the instrument. But he has to be the conscious instrument. When he knows consciously that he is a mere instrument, then he feels that it is the Supreme Duty of the Supreme to act in and through him. Further, he has to realise that God is offering His Message of divine manifestation through the seeker's painting. He has to feel that the Supreme Artist is God, and that God is manifesting in and through him. Undoubtedly, this artist is a true seeker-artist. His is the life of conscious consecration to God and constant aspiration for God-realisation.

155. My question concerns the soul's reincarnation and higher states of consciousness. Does the soul have a form; is it a separate entity? And if it is part of one universal Soul, then how can it reincarnate?

Sri Chinmoy: Each soul is a spark of the Infinite Consciousness. The soul can take any form. If you want to feel that the soul is a Divine Entity, and you want to have your eternal existence in the soul, then you have to feel that here on earth and there in Heaven, the soul is the very essence and the divine reality of each substance.

Now, let us speak about the form. We cannot see the soul with our human eyes, but with the third eye, when we look at the soul, we see that it can take any form. It can be tinier than the tiniest and larger than the largest. You can see the soul in the form of a little baby, or you can see it again in the form of an adult. It depends upon the development of the individual soul. True, the soul can assume any form, but it can never be bound by any form. At its sweet will it can enter into the form and go beyond the form.

When the Master says that he speaks to your soul, you have to know that he speaks to the supremely beautiful child in you, the divine portion which comes from the Transcendental Consciousness of the unmanifested Self.

In your question you have also asked about the soul's reincarnation. The soul wants to manifest the divine here on earth in infinite forms and boundless measure. In one incarnation we have thousands of desires, but we can only fulfil a few. So we see that even the fulfilment of all earthly desires is impossible in one incarnation; how can we dare to imagine the fulfilment, in one short incarnation, of our heavenly aspiration, God-realisation, which is infinitely more difficult. It is the soul that comes back again and again to give the physical consciousness the highest realisation and also to manifest the Divine fully here on earth. It is the soul that reincarnates again and again. It is the soul that enters into the new bodies. When the soul leaves the body, the body dies; the physical enters into the physical sheath, the vital into the vital sheath, etc. Finally, the soul flies back to its own region. Ordinary souls usually take at least six years to come back. If the souls are more developed, they take a rest of twenty or thirty years. In the case of the spiritual Masters, it usually takes a very, very long time, but if it is the Will of the Supreme, even spiritual Masters of the highest order have to come down within a short span of time. But before it again enters into the world, each soul will have an interview with the Supreme to see how much it has achieved in its previous incarnation and how it is going to manifest on earth in the next incarnation. At that time the Supreme either entirely approves of the soul's coming into the world, or He may accept and sanction the decision of the soul; sometimes the Supreme merely tolerates it. Some souls that are bound to the earth want to come back immediately and enter into the world of their previous emotional turmoil. At that time the Supreme just tolerates this. The souls that have started to aspire and want to realise the Supreme for an inseparable oneness with Him and also to reveal, manifest and fulfil the Supreme, receive a blessingful sanction from the Supreme. The souls who are very highly developed or fully developed in the spiritual life come into the world only to serve God in humanity. At that time, the Supreme with His divine Joy and Pride approves of their divine journey.

156. I understand that preparatory to realisation it is necessary for the ego to die.

Sri Chinmoy: You have to know that nothing dies. If the ego is dead, or let us use the term "extinguished", then we get nothing out of the uniqueness that the Supreme has given us. We have to use the word "transformed". Only if we transform the ego do we get something out of it. In the spiritual life, if you kill the ego it is like taking the life of some living thing. This is not the right thing to do. You must tame the ego, not kill it. The ego says, "I, mine, my husband, my wife, my children, etc." That ego is binding. But if you say, "I am everywhere, I am Universal, I am God's son," this kind of feeling liberates you. When Christ said, "I and my Father are one," He said it on the strength of His total Oneness with the Highest. But we do not have that total Oneness with the Highest. If the ego that you are referring to constantly binds you, then you will always remain bound in the ignorance of the world. But if you say, "No, I am all-pervading," you will be freed from ego. Try to expand yourself, and the more you expand your consciousness, the wider will be your vision. Your limited consciousness is your ego, but when it is expanded it becomes universal. There you are one with the Source totally. Ignorance we have, but if we do not transform it, we remain in ignorance. My advice is this: don't destroy it, but transform it and use it with your inner wisdom. Now you have a knife. With this knife you can come and stab me, but if you use the same knife and cut a fruit and give me a portion, then you are doing the right thing. Similarly, when you can utilise the ego for a divine purpose, immediately it changes its face into a fulfilling reality. Even when your ego is unlit and impure, use it for the service of God and don't use it to destroy the world. While you are serving God, your ego will become purified and in its complete purification, your expansion of consciousness will take place. When your consciousness is expanded you will see that the whole world is yours and that you truly belong to the world of aspiration.

157. When I try to get rid of the ego, I seem to be more bound by it.

Sri Chinmoy: I am sure you always think of your ego. If you really want to get rid of your ego, then think of your soul always. Take the positive side. Try to have an inseparable oneness with the vast. When you concentrate on the limited consciousness, you will, without fail, be more bound here in the limited outer life. But with your eyes wide open, try to feel your own identity with the vast sky. Try to enter into the infinite Sky with eyes wide open. It is on the strength of your identification that you will be bound or freed. Vastness will free you, whereas the puny ego will bind you ruthlessly.

158. Why did God create all this misery and unhappiness if He is the Creator? Why did he not create perfection?

Sri Chinmoy: I have answered this question quite a few times. God has created us and we have also created God according to our own ideas and conceptions. Why did God do this? Why did He not do otherwise? Now, we have to know that God is the Creator. He is also the Player. He is playing His eternal Game. The more we play, the more we become conscious of the fact that we do nothing and we can do nothing. We are all instruments. He, Himself, is having all experiences in and through us. When God created the world, He gave each individual very limited freedom. Unfortunately, we have been misusing this freedom. He gave to each person limited capacity. But this capacity we have been using for the wrong purpose. Early in the morning we know that we have the time to do whatever we want to. What do we do? We get up late. We know that at 5:30 a.m., if we want to, we can pray to God and ask for His Blessing and receive His Joy and Love. Instead of getting up early in the morning, we get up very late. What is worse, we don't meditate at all. So you see how we misuse our limited freedom and capacity. We misuse His precious Concern for us, His Compassion for us. Now, the creation is in the process of evolution. In this creation we see two things, inspiration and aspiration. You are inspiring me and I am inspired. I am aspiring. My aspiration can kindle the flame of aspiration in you.

Now, realising the truth is one thing and manifesting the truth is another. There is a vast gulf between realisation and manifestation. All great spiritual Masters, Krishna, Buddha, Christ and spiritual Masters of the nineteenth and twentieth centuries did realise the highest Truth. Their message was that human beings would no longer remain animals but be transformed into divinity. But, when they wanted to offer their own realisation to the world, the world mocked at them. As far as realisation was concerned, they were perfect; but when the manifestation was going to take place on earth, that very earth-consciousness denied their inner wealth. Most of the spiritual Masters were not accepted. Even when some of the disciples knew who their spiritual Master was, they betrayed Him or did not listen to Him.

Now, you see that earth is the field of manifestation. Here on earth one person realises the Highest and wants to offer it to the world. Why does the earth-consciousness revolt when it is going to get something divine and fulfilling? Precisely because the earth-consciousness wants to remain in bondage and ignorance.

The camel eats the cactus and his mouth bleeds. But a few hours later the same camel eats these thorns and bleeds again. Here also, ordinary human beings do not want real Joy; what they want is pleasure. There is a great difference between pleasure and Joy. Pleasure is something which is immediately going to be followed by frustration. But Joy, which resides here inside our heart, knows only how to increase. An iota of Joy expands itself and becomes vast. As human beings, we want pleasure and not real inner Joy. Now, first we have to know, with our limited capacity and aspiration, what we want. If there is aspiration in our heart, then perfection will eventually dawn. But you look around and, out of thousands, how many people really want God? They don't have five minutes to meditate daily on God. Days will run into weeks and weeks into months, but to your utter amazement, they will not have meditated even for five minutes. Now the world of realisation and manifestation can be established only on the strength of aspiration. The world unfortunately is wanting in aspiration. It is filled with desires ever on the increase. When we aspire, it is not like that. We try to have only the boundless, the infinite, the measureless. Only when each individual wants to sing the song of Infinity, Eternity and Immortality can God offer here on earth the message of perfection. How can perfection dawn? It can dawn on earth only through mutual acceptance. God is perfect. We are imperfect. Only if we accept God as our very own, can He give what He has and what He is. But we don't take God as our own, we only take the nearest, dearest ones as our own. God does not come first in our lives. This is what an individual feels. God comes last. When somebody dies, we cry, "O God, God, God!" Otherwise, how many times have you uttered God's name during the day and how many times have you uttered your own children's names during the day? He is your Divine Child who has the message of Perfection, not the ones whose names you utter thousands of times. So if we know the right Person, then only can we expect the right thing. If you knock at the wrong door and it opens, you will see that the Real Person is not there. But if you knock at the right door, perfection comes to receive you. God wants us to be perfect and to be fulfilled, but if we go deep within we see that we are satisfied with our pleasures, desires, limited consciousness, jealousy, doubt, fear, negative thoughts, etc. When we are satisfied with something undivine, how can we blame God? How can we say that He is not giving us the right thing? Let us not want these negative things. Tomorrow God will come and knock at our door. He will give us Peace, Love, Joy, Concern and Compassion. Even the limited capacity that God has given us, we are not offering to Him. If a child finds a penny while walking along the street and gives it to his mother, the mother becomes so pleased. She sees that the child could have kept the penny for himself. But he did not do that. The mother is highly pleased with him and gives him a quarter in return. The child could easily have thought that the penny was his own possession and he could have been bloated with pride with the money, but his heart spontaneously compelled him to give his greatest treasure to his dearest mother. The same thing happens when we give a little bit of our aspiration to God every day for five minutes. He will be so pleased with us, and He will bring down Peace, Light and Bliss for us in boundless measure. God is for us, and we have to know and feel that He is doing everything for us. At His choice hour He will grant us the Supreme Realisation. When we aspire and enter into the Highest, it is He who takes us to our destined Goal. If we don't want to do that, God says, "Sleep, baby, sleep. The time has not come for you."

III – QUESTIONS AND ANSWERS, AMERICAN INTERNATIONAL SCHOOL, ZURICH, SWITZERLAND

159. The ideas from your talk – are these your own or based on your religion or some other religion?

Sri Chinmoy: My talk was based on my own inner experiences, my own inner realisation. I was born a Hindu, so you can say that my religion is Hinduism. Others will say that. But I wish to say, being a spiritual man, that I welcome all religions as my own. And at the same time, being a lover of God, a seeker of the infinite Truth, my inner Being compels me to say that I transcend all religions. Each religion is right, absolutely right in its own way, but when one cries for the highest Ultimate Truth, at that time God becomes his only Religion.

So in my case, what I have said is on the strength of my own inner experiences and realisations.

160. In connection with your meditation, do you follow any dietary rules, and if so, what are they?

Sri Chinmoy: I do follow some rules of diet in connection with my meditation. I have a few hundred students, disciples, all over the world and I tell them that they have to be vegetarian (it really is very simple – anybody can do it), because if they eat vegetables, the mild qualities of vegetables will not interfere with their meditation. In our spiritual life, when we meditate, very often we feel an inner agitation or excitement. When we eat meat, our inner vibrations become excited and this excitement we have to conquer. We eat meat; the quality, the propensity, the nature of the animal, enters into us. We see the animal right in front of us. We see how animals behave, how they quarrel and fight. The animal consciousness is aggressive, damaging and destructive. So it is advisable for the sincere aspiring seekers to be vegetarian.

Then again, some people are of the opinion that it is helpful to fast quite often in order to purify themselves. Here I say that purity does not come by constant fasting. It is impossible. You see, a snake eats only twice a year. I don't think a snake is purer than anybody here on earth in the realm of consciousness. So we have to eat normally. If we fast once in a blue moon, it will help us to purify our outer aggressions, outer greed. But to fast quite often, or on alternate days, is foolishness.

So to come back to your question about diet, I wish to say that if you are a vegetarian, then you are helping your inner being or the aspirant in you to strengthen your own existence. Inwardly, you are praying and meditating and concentrating. Outwardly, the food that you are taking from Mother Earth can also provide tremendous energy. You will get not only energy, but also aspiration. When we look at nature, when we look at a tree, we get inspiration and aspiration. Similarly, when we see the vegetable kingdom around us, we also get inspiration and aspiration.

Most spiritual seekers have come to the conclusion that a vegetarian is in the best position to make quick progress in the spiritual life. Of course, along with a vegetarian diet, one must practise spirituality, Yoga. Only then can one make considerable progress. Otherwise, there are many people on earth who are vegetarians. In India, for example, the Hindu widows do not eat meat, fish and so forth. All Indian widows are not God-realised souls. Impossible. So, if we just abstain from eating meat and fish, we are not qualified to reach the highest Truth or Light. It is impossible. Along with our aspiration, our inner cry, if we have vegetarian diet, then it adds to our inner aspiration. So, whatever adds to our inner aspiration we must try to adopt in our day-to-day life.

161. You said your talk was based on your inner experiences. How did you get these experiences?

Sri Chinmoy: From meditation. From my concentration, meditation and contemplation. I was in a spiritual institution for twenty years, from the age of twelve up to thirty-two. You study in the school, college and university and get your Master's degree. Similarly, if you spend say, fourteen, sixteen, twenty years in spiritual practices, naturally you will also get inner knowledge in abundant measure. From the age of twelve right up to thirty-two, I went through rigorous spiritual discipline – concentration, meditation and so on. It took me ten hours, twelve hours, fourteen hours daily to achieve what little I have right now. In the inner life when you enter into deep spiritual life, one day you know, you discover your own hidden truth. The truth is within you, within everyone, but unfortunately it is inside a box, a treasure box. The wealth is inside the box. Now, as here your professors are teaching you, they are offering you knowledge and you are gaining knowledge and wisdom; so also when one concentrates, meditates and contemplates, one enters into the world of Inner Wisdom, Inner Light. From there he can bring to the fore at his sweet will the Light, the Bliss and Power that he has achieved.

162. When you meditate, do you hold any special position, like they do in yoga?

Sri Chinmoy: It is an individual matter. Are you asking me what I do or what others do? If you ask me what I do, to be very frank with you, when I meditate, now being an expert in spiritual life, I can meditate while I am walking, while I am running, while I am driving in New York. But this I can do now, not twenty years ago – oh far from it! So, for a beginner, yes, one has to sit in a quiet place and, if possible, one has to sit on the floor, keeping the backbone erect and trying to breathe quietly and slowly. A beginner has to go through all kinds of discipline. I did it. Everybody has to do it in the beginning. One cannot be a good dancer overnight. It takes considerable time, then automatically the steps fall correctly. One cannot be a good runner overnight. It takes time. When one becomes a good runner, everything – his hand movements, his leg movements – is perfectly coordinated. So, in the spiritual life, for the beginner, those who want to launch into the spiritual path should sit at a particular place and try to breathe as slowly and quietly as possible. They should keep the back erect and try to focus their attention either here, on the third eye between the eyebrows, or on the heart centre, here. Here we have a major centre, the third eye. From here we envision the past, present and future. This is the place for meditation. Again, here in the middle of the chest there is another centre. If you want to identify yourself, if you want to be inseparably one with the universe, with the universal consciousness, then meditate on your heart centre. There are six major centres. If you follow the kundalini yoga, you will know all about them. And, I wish to say, for the beginner it is always safe to meditate on the heart. If you concentrate here, on the third eye, you will be meditating on the mind and inside the mind; then doubt may come. Doubt may assail you. You may think, "Oh, I am doing something wrong! It is all futile." If you do not get considerable encouragement or inspiration or result from your daily meditation, then naturally you will be disappointed and you will leave the spiritual life; whereas if you meditate here, if you concentrate on the heart centre, you will get a constant feeling of security, joy. So it is safer to meditate on the heart centre.

163. A question a lot of people have asked me is, "Why must there be a God?" So now I ask you: why must there be a God?

Sri Chinmoy: Why must there be a God? Why must there be yourself? Why must there be a human being like you? If somebody says, "Why must there be a God?" then I immediately say, "Why must there be you on earth?" We know that there is something called the Source. We must know that there are parents on earth. That is why we have come into existence. We must know that there is a seed and the seed germinates into a plant and the plant grows into a huge Banyan tree. So there is always a source. We see that from something, something else comes. So we came into existence similarly from God. Our Source is God the Light, God the Delight and God the Perfection. There *is* a God. For me the question "Why must there be a God?" has no meaning. When you have known God and spoken to God, this question sounds entirely foolish. Only someone who has not seen you personally can ask, "Why must there be a boy like that?" Similarly, before one has felt the presence of God, he can ask this question.

164. When you meditate, are you conscious of what is going on around you?

Sri Chinmoy: It depends on what kind of meditation it is. If it is the highest type of meditation, then one goes deep within and there one sees everything that is happening, but he is not disturbed by anything external. Within and without, one will be aware of what is happening, but at the same time one will not be affected at all. This is what happens when one is in the highest state of meditation. But, if he is a beginner, when he sees something, immediately he will be disturbed. If the beginner is meditating and right in front of him there is a cat moving around, his attention will be diverted. His meditation is gone. Anything, even the slightest noise, will affect his meditation. He will be disturbed. But, if one is advanced, really advanced, then he will not be disturbed, in spite of seeing things happening in front of him, right in front of his nose. He will not be disturbed. He will be aware of it but he will not be disturbed.

165. Do you feel pain while you are meditating? Do you feel any pain? If something should hit you, would you feel pain?

Sri Chinmoy: If somebody strikes you while you are meditating, will you feel pain? Am I correct? Now, if it is the highest type of meditation, you will not feel any pain because at that time you are not in the body, but in the soul. In the body, if somebody pinches you, immediately you will feel pain because your consciousness is in the physical. But, if you are in the soul, you will not be affected. The soul is the divine part in us, the divine light, which is the representative of God. This soul cannot be disturbed, cannot be burned, cannot be destroyed. This is something in us that is immortal. So, when you are doing your best meditation, your highest meditation, you are not in the physical, you are in the soul. You become one with the soul. Here we live in ignorance. That is why somebody can come and strike you. Somebody is in darkness. That is why he is disturbing you. But, if that particular person is in the Light, he will not bother you. He will not disturb you. He will never pinch you. On the contrary, when he sees that you are meditating, he will come and he will also start meditating with you because he feels that you are doing something right, something good, something divine. Naturally, he also wants to do the same thing, so that he can be a divine child.

166. Is there such a thing as destiny? Please tell us something about the law of karma.

Sri Chinmoy: Destiny is there. Fate is there. But again, fate can be surmounted. Fate can be transcended. Yes, God is within us. This is true. And if one meditates, one can realise God. But again, if one takes help from others who have already seen and realised God, then one expedites one's journey.

Now, about the law of karma. We all know "tit-for-tat": a tooth for a tooth, and a nail for a nail, but again we have to know that there is something called God's Great Compassion. Suppose you have done something wrong, that you have hurt someone and that your father is right beside you and has seen you do it. Then, suppose the other fellow comes to strike you because you have done something wrong to him. Since he is strongest, your father, in spite of knowing that you were wrong, may not, if he so wishes, allow you to be beaten by your enemy. Your father has the strength. Similarly, in your inner life, suppose you have done something wrong and you cry to God; He will come to you as Compassion and Forgiveness. God's Compassion and Forgiveness have infinite power. God has the power to nullify your mistake. You and your father are bound with an inner link, you have a close inner connection. So your father came to your rescue. Similarly, your ignorant or wrong action can be forgiven by God's Grace and you can be saved and illumined by God the Eternal Father.

God's Compassion descends into human beings and into earthly laws; these laws too, are His laws. He is the Maker of all Universal Laws. He is dealing with clay. He can give it any form He wants to. Right now, He is making a particular form. You are saying that this is the way things are, but no. He can immediately change His Mind. He is the football player who is kicking with both his legs. Right now, the player is trying to aim at the goal from a particular corner and everyone feels that it is going this way, but no. Immediately he changes his course to another angle.

So, when we are doing something wrong, if we know that there is Someone who has boundless Grace, boundless Compassion, then let us go to Him for rescue. But now we have to understand consciously also that we should not do things that are wrong because the law of karma, the law of action, will call on us. If I go on doing wrong things, how can I expect a better life, a more fulfilling life? No. I have to pay for it. Every moment God has given me the chance either to do the right thing or, if I make friends with ignorance, to do the wrong thing. So it is up to me. If I do the right thing, naturally I will have God's Light, Peace, Bliss, Harmony and Perfection in my life, and if I do wrong, I have to pay the price exacted by the law of karma.

167. What do you mean by highest meditation?

Sri Chinmoy: The highest meditation is when you do not have any thought at all. Now when we are meditating, usually we are victims to many thoughts, undivine thoughts, ugly thoughts, evil thoughts and so forth. Then, we can do a kind of meditation where we get fairly good thoughts, divine thoughts, fulfilling thoughts and illumining thoughts. This is a higher state. But when we are in the highest meditation, there will be no thoughts, either good or bad. There it is only Light. Now, in Light, Vision and Reality are together. Now, you are sitting there and I am standing here. You are the reality. I am the vision. I have to look at you. You are the reality. Then, I have to enter into you in order to know that you are the reality. But, when you do the highest meditation, at that time it is not like that. Reality and Vision are one and the same. Where you are, I have to be. Where I am, you have to be, because we are one. So, in the highest meditation, Reality and Vision go together. That is why we do not need thoughts or ideas or anything. First a thought enters into us. Then we give it form. Then we come to understand what is going on, or what we are talking about. But, when you see the Truth, when you see the Knowledge and the Knower and the Thing that is to be known all together, then it is the highest type of meditation.

168. In your talk you said that man has received from God more than he deserves. Can you explain this?

Sri Chinmoy: Certainly. You see, I can justify it on the strength of my own inner experience. If a man is sincere, if he is really sincere and if he goes deep within even for five minutes, then he will see how many things he has done wrong consciously, not to speak of unconsciously. Unconsciously we have done millions of things wrong. Even during one day, we do hundreds of wrong things unconsciously. But consciously and deliberately, how many things have we done wrong? How many times do we cherish in our minds jealousy and hypocrisy? We belittle others constantly. When others are doing something right, good or divine, immediately jealousy enters into us. We cherish all kinds of undivine thoughts and ideas. We do not want to allow our fellow-brothers to be above us. We try all the time to lord it over others. We want to be the best. We want to be the highest. We always try to keep others under our feet. Now, these are the things we see in our day-to-day experience. Consciously and deliberately we are doing these things.

We sometimes act like animals. We justify it. How? Because we feel that everybody is doing it. "Everybody is doing it. That is why I can also do this and I am in no way inferior." But, if I am really sincere, if I really care for Truth and Light in my life, then I see the difference between what I want to be and what I am now. I want to be a divine child and I am really an animal. Now, at this animal stage, I am doing everything wrong, destructive. But look, even then I am not punished in the way I deserve. In our outer life, if somebody tells a lie, if he is caught he gets a slap; if somebody steals something, immediately he is put into a prison cell. Now, how many times in my mind, in your mind, how many times during the day do we consciously and deliberately commit a crime? Now, what happens? God knows everything within us, whatever is happening. If He wants to punish us for all our misbehaviour, for all the wrong actions that we have committed in the mind, in our inner life, then where do we stand?

What has God done? He has given us a nice mind. He has given us a sound body. He has given us a strong vital. He has given us many things to appreciate. He has given us receptivity. Let us fill our vessel full to the brim with good thoughts, divine thoughts. He has given us the potentiality, the possibility plus the opportunity to develop our good qualities. So then, do we deserve it? If one is really sincere, one will feel that God has given him Blessings beyond his capacity – not only beyond his capacity, but beyond his necessity.

169. If a man is able to control his fate, will he not have the qualities and the capacity of God?

Sri Chinmoy: Certainly, he will. But right now man cannot control his fate, because man is not aspiring. He is now in the world of desire. He is trying to possess and be possessed. But, if that particular man wants to live in the world of aspiration, when he wants only to live here on earth for God, for Light and for Truth, if that particular person wants Infinity in his life or for the world – Infinity, Eternity and Immortality – and nothing mortal, nothing transitory, then that particular man also can achieve all these things in his life.

170. So, at this point then, we have no control over our fate?

Sri Chinmoy: If we aspire, we can control our fate. If we aspire, Light descends, or our own inner light comes to the fore. Just because we are in darkness, we feel that it is impossible. Now, as soon as we go out of this room, if we extinguish the light, there will be no light until you turn it on. So, when you come here tomorrow, you will again turn on the light and you will get light. At that time, you are controlling it. In the spiritual life, automatically light is controlling you. Light is saving you, protecting you, illumining you. Let us see the point from another angle. One thing is to go to desire and be caught there. Then we will always be caught in the meshes of fate. But the other way is to enter into the vast, which is spirituality, the inner life, the yogic power. Then you will find no necessity to control fate, because automatically your nature is being purified, your nature is being transformed and illumined. Rest assured, at that time you have gone beyond the laws of fate.

IV – QUESTIONS AND ANSWERS, UNIVERSITY OF BRISTOL

171. Why is darkness impermanent and light permanent?

Sri Chinmoy: Darkness is impermanent, light is permanent, precisely because our Source is Light. God is all Light. We come from Light. In Light we grow. And through Light we fulfil our inner task. God is the Permanent, the Eternal Source. We are His children. God-realisation, which is the flood of infinite Light, is our birthright. The more we go deep within, the easier it becomes for us to realise that there is something within us which is everlasting. There is darkness around us now. We are enveloped by the night. We have been sleeping, for a few years or for a few incarnations. But a day will come when Light, Infinite Light, will dawn on us and make us feel what we truly are. So, I wish to say, since the Source, our Source, is God who is Light, we eventually have to grow into the Light, because we cannot permanently do anything contrary to our Creator's Nature. It is the Creator who has created us and we have to eventually grow into His very Image.

And what is Light? Light is Delight. The inner Light is Delight. And Delight is immortal Nectar. In one of our *Upanishads*, it is said that we, all human beings, come into the world from Delight. Again, Delight is God, God the Light. We grow in Delight but we do not feel the Delight because we live the surface life. We live in the meshes of ignorance. That is why we do not see the inner Delight. We grow and, at the end of our journey's close, we enter into the effulgence of Delight. We came from Delight. We grow in Delight. And at the end of our journey we go back, we retire into Delight. But this experience we get only when we meditate.

When we meditate, we get inner peace, peace of mind. Delight is visible, palpable, tangible only when we have peace of mind. Unfortunately the modern mind, the intellectual mind, the doubting mind, the sophisticated mind does not care for this kind of Delight which is nothing other than Light. It cries for information, outer information, or it cries to achieve some partial truth. Again, while achieving the Truth, it negates the Truth. It doubts the Truth. The mind sees the Truth for five seconds and, at the time when it is about to achieve the Truth, it doubts the possibility, the potentiality of the Truth. Then who is the loser? The Truth or the mind? Undoubtedly the mind. But if we live in the heart, then the heart gives us the message of identification. Here there is no doubt if we identify ourselves with the Light, immediately we become the Light. Inside the heart is the soul. So, if we can live, even for a minute daily, in our inner existence, then we can see Light in abundant measure. We see it. We feel it. When we feel this Light, we feel the possibility of growing into the effulgence of Light. We feel this possibility. The moment we see Light within us, within our inner Sun, which is infinitely brighter than the star sun, we feel the ignorance-night of millennia is gone. So let us try to go deep within and enter into the inner Sun, the cosmic Sun that we have. There we shall see that the Light, the infinite Light, is waiting for us, crying for us. It only needs our conscious approval, our cooperation.

To come back to your question, anything that is really infinite is permanent. Light is infinite. Hence it is permanent. It is eternal.

172. How does one get benefit from books on meditation in case one does not have access to a personal teacher?

Sri Chinmoy: If one does not have a personal teacher, how does one get benefit from books on meditation? If one does not have a spiritual Master, one has to read spiritual books. It is preferable to read books written by the spiritual Masters in whom one has implicit faith. There are many who have written books on spirituality, but do not practise spirituality. To be very frank with you, I have seen many sincere seekers at the universities who have meditated for many hours and with great sincerity. They are more sincere and they have paid more attention to their inner lives than some of those who have written books on spirituality. But again, there are Masters who have really attained to the highest level of consciousness. There *are* such Masters. There *were* such Masters. So, if you read, kindly read their books and you are bound to get inspiration. Their books will not supply you with inspiration only. There is aspiration within them too, and in aspiration you will get your illumination.

Now, here is the thing. Take a thief and a liar. A thief may tell you, "Don't steal. Don't steal. It is very bad!" A liar will tell you, "Don't tell a lie. Don't tell a lie. It is very bad!" If you listen to them, you will not commit a theft, you will not tell a lie. But, if you hear the same thing from a saintly person, it will be quite different. If he tells you, "Don't tell a lie, don't commit a theft," then immediately you will get tremendous strength, tremendous energy and will-power within you. You will feel that in this life you will never tell a lie or steal anything. When a spiritual Master tells you something, he injects you with tremendous will-power. He may say the same thing as the others. A liar will tell you not to tell a lie. But, when a spiritual Master tells you, "Do not enter into a life of falsehood," immediately you will see that there is tremendous inner power. You also have tremendous inner power. But it is the Master who has the capacity to bring your inner power to the fore.

Your question is very nice. I wish to advise you to read books by spiritual Masters. If you want to read on Indian spirituality, you can read the books that were written by Swami Vivekananda and others. Paul Brunton has written on Ramana Maharshi. Vivekananda has written on Sri Ramakrishna. There are others. Sri Aurobindo has written many books. There are genuine spiritual Masters whose books you can read. But in the bookstores I see hundreds and thousands of books written by people who have not meditated sincerely and devotedly even for one year. Now what will their experience be? What can they do? How can they help you in your aspiration? Since you are a sincere seeker, I wish you to read books written by the spiritual Masters. If not by the spiritual Masters, then by seekers of the higher level. You can read them and you will derive much help, inner and outer, from their books.

Have you been studying some books, spiritual books?
Seeker: Yes, by Prabhavananda.
Sri Chinmoy: Oh yes. Certainly. Please read Prabhavananda. In him there is Sri Ramakrishna's Light. Yes, Prabhavananda was a very great seeker.

173. What do you believe happens when we die?

Sri Chinmoy: When we die, what actually dies is our physical body. This physical body came into the world from the five major elements, called *panchabhuta*. These five elements, earth, air, etc., enter into their own five sheaths after we die. But the soul, the divine within us, the immortal within us, will never die. It cannot be pierced by weapons. It cannot be drenched by water. It cannot be destroyed by fire. It cannot be blown away by the wind. It is indestructible. When the body dies, this soul passes through the physical, the vital, the mental, the psychic realms, and it finally enters into its own region. It rests for a few years there in the soul's region. When the time comes for the soul to descend, the soul goes back to the Highest, to the Supreme, for His Sanction and Approval. Having obtained this Permission, the soul comes back into the world of revelation and manifestation again.

Each time the soul enters into the physical world, it comes with a new promise to the Supreme, to the Highest, that here in the physical, through the physical, it will reveal and manifest Him. The physical is the fort. It is the house. It is the temple. Inside the temple is the shrine. The soul is inside the shrine. What happens is that in one short span we cannot accomplish everything. We have to accomplish, not with the sense of possession, but with a sense of offering our inner wealth. First, we have to be aware of the inner wealth. The soul makes us aware of the inner wealth when we meditate and concentrate. Then the soul gives us the capacity to reveal the inner Light to the world at large. While revealing, we are manifesting the divinity within us. Now, unless and until we have manifested the Highest Divinity, our game is not over, not complete. So, when we die, the physical dies, not the soul. The conscious instrument, the direct representative of God which is the soul, does not die. It comes back. And each time it comes back to earth, it is with a new hope, a new light and a new aspiration. For spiritual seekers of the highest ultimate Truth, there is no death. It is only a short rest. The divine soldier enters into the battlefield of life. He fights against fear, doubt, anxiety, worries, imperfections, limitations and bondage. When he conquers all these imperfections and negative forces in the battlefield of life, the divine victory dawns on him. So, it is the body that dies and not the soul.

Again, this body will one day be a conscious instrument. Now, the body does not listen to the dictates of the soul. That is to say, the physical mind revolts. On very rare occasions, it listens to the dictates of the soul. Our soul tells us what is good and what is bad. But, in spite of hearing the message from our soul, we do not do the right thing. We are weak. The physical is weak. The physical mind is weak. But a day comes when the soul is in a position to exercise its divine qualities. When the physical and the vital consciously want to listen to the soul, want to be instructed and guided by the soul, then here in the physical we will have a divinised consciousness and an immortal life. The physical will take time to be transformed. But it has to be transformed, totally transformed, so that the physical life can be immortal like the soul.

174. Why do we have the body, the physical?

Sri Chinmoy: We need the body, the physical, for the manifestation here. In the soul's region there is no manifestation. For the realisation of the Divine on earth we have to come here. The soul may realise something here on earth; then it goes up for some time and stays in the higher worlds with its realisation. But for the manifestation, it has to be here in the body. The body is the outer structure. Now, here we are talking about the spiritual life. Here is a building, a house of this university. If there is no house, no room, no hall, where are we going to give a lecture? Similarly, the soul is inside the body. As I said, it is the inner deity. It needs a temple. Everything needs protection, outer protection. If we don't have a house, where will we live? In the street? No, we will be blown away. We will be destroyed. Similarly, we need a body in order to house the eternal wealth within us. This body lasts for fifty, sixty or seventy years. Then the body dies because it is not in tune with the eternal Life, whereas the soul is always in tune with the eternal Life. Here on earth God feels that His Absolute Manifestation must take place. For that He needs the outer structure, and this body plays that role.

The soul has realised the Truth, but the soul has to reveal and manifest the Truth. For revelation and manifestation the soul needs an instrument and that instrument happens to be the body. Without the body we cannot reveal and we cannot manifest any Truth. For revelation of the Truth and manifestation of the Truth, the soul must needs have the physical body.

175. Do you think that all religions lead to the same Truth, but maybe by different routes?

Sri Chinmoy: I do, absolutely. I fully agree that all religions lead to one Truth, the Absolute Truth. There is One Truth. There is only one Goal, but there are various paths. Each religion is right in its own way. But, if one religion says that it is the only religion, or by far the best, at that point I find it difficult to see eye to eye with that particular religion. If a religion says, "My religion is true. Your religion is equally true," then I wholeheartedly agree. But, if I say that our Hinduism is by far the best and that your Christianity is nowhere near Hinduism, then I am the worst possible fool on earth. If I say, "If you accept my religion, then I will take you to the Goal sooner," and if I try to convert you to my religion, then again I am committing a Himalayan blunder. No. Each religion is right. A religion is a house. I have to live in my house. You have to live in your house. I cannot stay in the street; you cannot either.

But a day comes when we widen our vision. We feel that beyond the boundary of the rites and rituals of religion lies a higher Goal. Then what can we do? We can try to perfect the imperfection in the religion. Then immediately we will come into conflict with the fanatics. Or we find that we are not in a position to change the rules and canons of the religion. Then we are miserable. But, if we follow the spiritual life, the inner life, we are not in conflict with any religion. So we say that those who want to follow a religion should follow it. But those who want to follow a still higher Goal, that is to say Yoga, the conscious and constant union with God, must follow the path of Yoga. There, on the strength of our Oneness with God, we say that the entire world is ours. Each human being is our brother, our sister. When you launch into the field of Yoga and want to realise the highest Truth, absolutely the highest Truth, at that time I wish to tell you that you can be above your religion. That is to say, if you don't want to follow your religion or any religion, you are free to do it because you are crying for the Highest in a special way. Your religion and my religion, in spite of their respective imperfections, are aiming at the same Goal. But now you may feel that you have a tremendous inner urge to reach the Highest without involving yourself in the so-called limitations of your religion, my religion and other religions. Then naturally you will try to reach your Goal without disturbing us, without disturbing others, and at the same time you yourself will not be disturbed.

To come back to your question, I wish to say that each religion has the message of the highest truth. No man is perfect. Similarly, no religion is perfect perfection. At the same time, no religion is to be condemned; far from it. Nobody is perfect, nothing is perfect here on earth. So, when it is a matter of religion, how can we say, "Religion has to be perfect"? Are we perfect? Is anybody perfect? Nobody is absolutely perfect perfection. Similarly, when I am not absolutely perfect, how can I dare to expect perfect perfection from you or from anybody? But I know, you know, that there is Someone who *is* absolutely perfect and He is God. So, if I have the inner cry, inner urge, I will try to go towards Him. For that we practise Yoga, conscious union with God. At that time, on the strength of our deepest meditation, we can feel that if we want to transcend the barriers of religion – Hinduism, Christianity, Buddhism and all other religions – there is nothing wrong in it. But if we don't have the cry for the highest Absolute, we may only fight and wrangle with other religions. We may say, "No. My religion is best. Yours is no good." Then no path, no religion, not even our own religion will come to our rescue. If I speak ill of Christianity or of any other religion, my Hinduism will not take me or carry me faster towards my Goal. My true Hinduism will condemn me. It will say, "You fool! You are finding fault with your brothers."

What I actually wish to say here is that each religion, knowing perfectly well its shortcomings, must never condemn the followers or votaries of other religions. It is the votaries of a particular religion and not the founders who find fault with other religions. When we practise Yoga, we hear the message of oneness. Religion is also included there. Everything is included there. My enemy is included there. Everyone. But then what happens? We are not totally satisfied. We want to transcend this realisation. With my imperfection, with your imperfection, with others' imperfection, we are living together. There is no satisfaction because perfection has not yet dawned. That is why we try to transcend ourselves consciously. When we try to transcend ourselves consciously, we reach the Goal. When you reach the Goal, when I reach the Goal, when she reaches the Goal, we will see that it is the same Goal. There are many roads that lead to Rome. It is up to you to select the road and then walk along that road, but not to change the road every day. If you change the road every day, then you will never reach the Goal.

Now what happens? Sometimes, even if we are conscious followers of a particular religion, we become very critical of our own religion. Being a Hindu, I will say, "No, no, no! My religion is very bad. There are many things wrong. Let me now follow Christianity. There is some message there that is really unique." In this way I condemn my religion and try to follow the teachings of Christianity. But unfortunately, tomorrow I will find something wrong with Christianity and I will say, "No, no, no! This is not perfect. Let me enter into Buddhism." Then Buddhism also will not satisfy me. This will go on. But, if I am a wise man, I will try to take the quintessence of each religion. Staying in my house, Hinduism, I will try to get the divine qualities, the absolute quintessence of the Divine Message of all religions. Then, when I gather the quintessence of all religions, I see that it is only One Truth. No religion will say that God is not required. God is wanted by all religions. There is no religion on earth that will deny the existence of Truth which is God in Reality. If we can have the essence, the quintessence of all religions, then we see the necessity of God, the highest Truth, constantly looming large. Indeed, this is the message of religion. Let us try to get the real message of each religion which is Truth. If we really want Truth, then every day we have to meditate and offer our conscious living breath to the Inner Pilot.

V – QUESTIONS AND ANSWERS, ST. DAVID'S COLLEGE,
UNIVERSITY OF LAMPETER, WALES

176. Would you tell us why God chooses to manifest Himself in transient beings on a transient earth?

Sri Chinmoy: God and His children play the Cosmic Game together. That is what He wants. We call it the *Lila,* the Divine Drama. Here we know that the earth is finite and here we are all earth-bound. God wants to offer His message of the Infinite to the finite. He wants to offer the message of the Immortal in place of death, the message of the Eternal in a fleeting second. It is our desire that binds us to the finite. We try to possess and be possessed. But, in God's case, God does not possess us. He plays the Game and He feels that He is playing It with His utmost inner Concern, Compassion and Love.

Now, if we go deep within, we see that we are not the doers. We are only taking a conscious part in God's Lila, His Game. He is the Doer. We are His multiple instruments. He is One, but He felt that He wanted to be many. He felt that He wanted to enjoy Himself, to fulfil Himself in a million forms and shapes. This is Divine Enjoyment, not earthly pleasure of course. That was His original Play. You can say, "Why did He want that kind of play?" God Himself only knows. He felt that, being One, He was not fully satisfied. He had to be many. Why should He be satisfied with only being the One Infinite? He could also be the multitudinous finite. God is Omniscient, Omnipotent, and God is infinitely Vast. This is our conception. It is absolutely true. But, if He is Omnipotent, then why should He not become like an ant, an infinitely tiny creature? With His omnipotent Power, we immediately think that He has only to be very great. That is our conception of God. Just because He is Omnipotent, He has to be very big; He has to contain millions of buildings and other things within Himself and so forth. No. That is only one way. In another way, He can show His Omnipotence in a tiny insect.

So now God is playing His Eternal Game in and through you, through me, through human beings who are finite, who are weak, impotent, ignorant. He feels that through His Eternal Game, His Divine Game, He can play in us and through us here in the earthbound Consciousness. Because He is Omniscient and Omnipotent, He feels that He has every right to play the Game. When we go deep within, we see that it is He who is the Player and He who is the Game and we are just the witnesses.

177. Do you have any concept of salvation for the soul?

Sri Chinmoy: In the Western world, we use the term "salvation of the soul", which has its own truth. Now, in our Eastern world, we use the words "illumination", "liberation", "realisation" and so forth. When we use the term "the soul", we mean the *Atman*, the representative of the Supreme in the individual body.

Very often, in the West we use the term "the soul" for a human being: "He is a nice soul." That means his personality and individuality are nice. We observe his personality and individuality and we say that he has a nice soul. That means his outer being is nice, kind and affectionate. But, if we use the term "salvation of the soul", we refer to the real inner soul, and we have to be really wise in our usage. The soul has already achieved its salvation. According to our Eastern understanding, right from the beginning, the soul, which is the representative of the Supreme here on earth, has already achieved salvation. So now what is it doing?

It has the outer body, this body. The soul is the deity and the body is the temple. The soul wants to offer its realisation, as you term it, its "salvation", to our earthbound, limited consciousness.

So the soul, through many incarnations in the process of evolution, is offering this salvation to our outer being, our outer consciousness. But the soul, the real soul, has *already* achieved the highest possible salvation. What it requires now is the revelation of its Divinity – Light, Peace, Bliss and Power – here on earth. And the medium is the human being. Through our earthly human consciousness, the soul is trying to reveal its inner Divinity. First, it reveals. Then, revelation is not enough, the soul feels that manifestation is necessary. You have something. You can reveal it to me, but if you do not manifest it here on earth, then I cannot get it. You have a dollar and you just reveal it to me; but if you put it here, then I can have it. Finally, the soul wants to manifest its Divinity here on earth.

178. Speaking in purely human terms, do you believe that all curiosity is the fear of truth?

Sri Chinmoy: No. All curiosity is not fear of truth, but when the divine truth comes to transform or illumine us, immediately we are afraid, for we are earthbound, we are full of ignorance, we are swimming in the sea of ignorance. At that time, when truth comes, or light comes, we are horror-struck.

Now, Light is good. Everybody knows we need Light. But, as soon as somebody has the Light or wants to offer the Light, what happens? The other person acts like a thief. He feels that he will be caught, he will be exposed. Many people do not go to spiritual persons. Why? They feel that spiritual Masters will immediately see through them and say, "Oh, you did such bad things just yesterday or a few months ago!" People don't want to be exposed to the Light, although they need Light.

Unfortunately, what happens when people run towards the Light out of curiosity is that fear immediately follows, because they feel that they have, by that time, yielded to enough temptation in their life. They fear that the light will expose this life of temptation or pleasure. But it is all a deplorable mistake. They are not wise enough at that moment to feel that this light will not expose them. The spiritual Light will never expose anything. On the contrary, it will illumine and transform them.

We use the ordinary electric light to see. When there is darkness in this room, as soon as you turn on the switch, it is all clear. Immediately, we know what has happened. Here, by this physical light, you may be exposed, but in the spiritual Light, inner Light, the curious person should know that he cannot be harmed or exposed. No. The spiritual Light only wants to illumine and transform him.

179. I should like to ask also whether man may achieve this enlightenment by himself or whether, for most people, it is necessary to communicate with a Master, a Guru.

Sri Chinmoy: Thank you. Now, the first person who realised God on earth – whom did he have as a Master? Nobody. God came to him inwardly as a Guide, as his Inner Pilot. That is why he was able to realise the highest Truth in God.

But now what do we see here on earth? We know that Mother-Earth has been blessed with many, many spiritual Masters down the sweep of centuries. We have to know what kind of teacher the spiritual Master is. Is he a schoolteacher or a college professor? A spiritual Teacher is a private tutor. A professor will examine the student. He will pass him or fail him. He is entitled to do so; he is competent. He sees the papers of the student and then, if the student does well, he will give him good marks. If he does not do well, he will fail him. A private tutor does not do that, as you know. He encourages, inspires and helps the student at home wholeheartedly so that he can pass the examination well. Now, the business of the spiritual Teacher is to inspire and arouse the aspiration in the seeker so that he can realise the Highest at God's choice Hour.

For everything you need a teacher. If you want to learn how to sing, you need a teacher. If you want to swim well, you need a teacher, specially at the beginning. Here, you want to have knowledge. That is why you have come to this university. Now, you know that there have been very few, very, very few, real men of knowledge who did not attend any university. There are exceptions. Every rule admits of exceptions. As I said, the first individual who realised God — whom did he have as a Teacher? Nobody. But again, we see that for most things we need a teacher. To learn the ABC, we need a teacher. To learn higher mathematics, we need a teacher. If you want to acquire scientific knowledge, you need a teacher. For everything we need a teacher. God-Knowledge is also a kind of knowledge. It is called Spiritual Discovery. For that, if you take help from a spiritual Teacher, then it facilitates your journey. It expedites your journey. Now, if you say that you want to swim alone across the sea of ignorance, then it is up to you. But how many years, or how many incarnations, will it take?

A spiritual Master will come to you with a boat. He will say, "Come. If you want to go, I have the boat. You be seated here. I will take you." Now it is up to you. You may say, "No. I don't need anybody's help." If you want to swim across alone, you can. But it may happen that after swimming for some time, you will be totally exhausted and then you may drown; whereas, if you have a boat, you have a fair chance of reaching the other shore, the Golden Shore.

So, as we need teachers for our outer knowledge, to illumine our outer being, so also we need a spiritual Master to help us, to guide us, in our inner life. In that way we expedite our journey.

VI – QUESTIONS AND ANSWERS, THE AMERICAN CENTRE FOR STUDENTS AND ARTISTS, PARIS, FRANCE

180. In your talk, which five things did you mention? Love, concern, sacrifice and there were two other things you said. "Love for the sake of love. Concern for the sake of concern. Sacrifice for the sake of sacrifice," and two other things I don't remember. And also I wish to know your concept of God-realisation.

Sri Chinmoy:

Love for the sake of Love.
Concern for the sake of Concern.
Sacrifice for the sake of Sacrifice.
Realisation for the sake of God-Fulfilment on earth.
Manifestation here for the sake of the Divine Manifestation.

About God-realisation: we want to realise God, not so that we can show the world that we have realised God. No. We shall realise God because He wants us to realise Him. We shall manifest Him because He wants to manifest Himself in and through us. Now we have to know that one way to please God is with our individual effort and aspiration. We all know that if we do this, then God will be pleased. If we say this, God will be pleased. If we act like this, God will be pleased. If we meditate, God will be pleased. This is our human way of understanding how to please God. Another way, which is more important, is to please God in His own Way. Now, this moment you are inspired to meditate. You think that if you meditate right now, God will be very pleased with you. No. If God wants you to secure good marks, high marks in your examination, then He wants you, at this moment, to study. He is inspiring you to study instead of to meditate. So you are fulfilling God in His own Way by studying. But if you meditate at this point, feeling that God will be pleased if you meditate, He will not be pleased. His Ways are different.

So right now, when each human being accepts the spiritual life, he tries to fulfil God and please God in his own way, according to his human understanding. This is good. At least he is trying to please God and not please ignorance. It is infinitely better to please God in your own way than to please ignorance and darkness. But there comes a time when you want to please God in His Way. If you want to do something in your own way to please Him, that is good. But, if you please Him in His Way, naturally He will be more pleased. In our path, in my own path, I always tell my students and disciples, "Try to go deep within and ask the soul what God wants for you, not what you want to do for God. If you want to fulfil God in His own Way, go deep within. Or, if you find it difficult to go deep within, I am ready to dive deep within you on your behalf. I will let you know what God wants you to do, and you do it." My sincere, dedicated, devoted disciples listen to me. They also listen to the dictates of my soul, my inner Being, and they are making very fast progress.

181. I would like to know what is your opinion regarding sexual love?

Sri Chinmoy: Sexual love, love of the lower vital, has to be transcended, but it depends entirely on the seeker. An ordinary person who does not want the spiritual life can remain with sexual love. But, if one wants to have real joy, everlasting joy, then he has to transcend the need of sex. It has to be done slowly, steadily and unerringly. If you tell a seeker who has just entered the spiritual life that he has to give up his sex life, naturally he will be frustrated. He will be broken and he will make no progress.

I tell my disciples who have entered into the spiritual life, those who are still beginners, to deal with sex as you deal with tea. If you take five cups of tea daily, then try to make it four cups. Then, after a few months, try to make it three cups a day. Then after a few months, two. Like that, gradually, you have to diminish your need. Your sex need also has to be transcended in that way. Otherwise, if you want to conquer sex as soon as you enter into the spiritual life, specially when your vital is not ready or pure, then what will happen? It will destroy your aspiration. There will be a tug-of-war between your aspiration and the gross physical need. Your nature will only be purified slowly and steadily on the strength of your inner urge, your aspiration. Then you will see that there is a great difference between pleasure and joy. Unfortunately, unaspiring people are making a Himalayan blunder when they think that pleasure is a form of joy. We always see pleasure is followed by frustration, and frustration is followed by destruction. But joy is followed by more joy and abundant joy. And then what happens? In joy, within joy, we get real fulfilment. So it depends entirely on the sincere seeker. If he wants to be inundated with boundless Peace, Light and Bliss, then he has to purify his nature. He has to transcend his sex need eventually. Otherwise, the transcendental Peace, Light and Bliss will remain a far cry for him. It is like this. We cannot taste sugar and salt together. If you want to have the taste of sugar, you have to take sugar. If you want to have the taste of salt, you have to take salt. In the spiritual life one has to make a decision and then go slowly and steadily. One has to be prepared for the Hour when human emotion is to be transcended. At that Golden Hour, the seeker has to be fully prepared to transcend his physical needs for the realisation of the highest Absolute. But I advise my disciples not to be in a hurry. Go slowly, steadily. Slow and steady wins the race. Otherwise, if you are not prepared and if you want to run very fast, but you do not have the capacity to run fast, you will simply drop in your tracks. Then you will break your legs. Similarly here – you will lose all your aspiration, the limited aspiration that you do have. So the best thing, according to one's outer and inner inspiration and aspiration, is for one to try to gradually overcome the physical need, the need of the lower vital. Then, on the strength of one's sincere inner urge, he has to run towards the Light. It is in Light that there is fulfilment. It is in Light that there is perfection.

182. How can you attain inner serenity and peace when you look around and see what goes on in the world: war, violence, poverty, hunger, drugs, death? How would you reach the inner peace?

Sri Chinmoy: Again I repeat: that is why there should be an inner hunger. If somebody is not satisfied with the outer world, then he wants to enter into, dive into the inner worlds. I have twenty or thirty disciples who once upon a time used to take drugs. They did many things wrong, but later on they found that it was not satisfying them. Then they felt the inner hunger. They were pinched with inner hunger and they came to me. They entered into the life of aspiration. When the outer world, the so-called outer world, fails us or disappoints us, at that time some of us become awakened. We say, "Let us see the other shore. Since this shore has disappointed us, now let us see what the other shore has to offer."

Similarly, those students of mine wanted to enter into the inner world, to see if there was any Truth, any Light, any Fulfilment there. When they entered into the inner life, they found the answer. One has to see whether the outer life has satisfied him or not. If the outer life has not satisfied him, then naturally he will try to enter into the inner worlds. Then, what is inside has to come to the fore. If I cry for Light and dive deep within, then I see the Light. I grow into the Light. Then I try to offer it to mankind. Mankind receives the Light according to its own receptivity.

183. If you have a job and you work, can you meditate at the same time?

Sri Chinmoy: Certainly. When you become an expert in meditation, you can do many other things at the same time. In the beginning, it is different. Say you are a dancer. When you are just learning how to dance, you will always be conscious of your steps, seeing whether they are coming correctly or not. Then, when you become an expert, it becomes spontaneous. While you are dancing you are observing the room, looking at all the people and doing all sorts of things. In the beginning, when you learn how to drive, you cannot do two things at once. You are always afraid that you will have an accident. Then, when you become an expert, what do you do? You look to this side, that side. You talk to your friends and you do many things. You can do this when you are an expert driver. Similarly, when you become expert in the spiritual life, you can do many things. When my students were beginners, absolute beginners, they had the same problem. They used to say that while they were in the office for instance, while they were typing something, only typing would exist for them. They could not meditate on spirituality or even think of the spiritual life. Now the stenographers and secretaries are doing very high meditations while they are typing and taking down notes from their bosses in their spiritual way. The bosses are surprised when they look at their secretaries. They feel, "How is it that her face is shining with divine light?" It is because these particular girls are all meditating while doing their work. Again, it is a matter of time. In the beginning they could not do it. But they meditated systematically, say for a few months, six or eight months, and naturally they have developed this capacity. It is only practice. By practising every day one becomes an expert.

VII – QUESTIONS AND ANSWERS, CONWAY HALL, LONDON, ENGLAND

184. How can one overcome fear?

Sri Chinmoy: Fear. You have fear in the physical. You have fear in the vital. You have fear in the mental. Again, you have fear, unfortunately, in the heart also. First of all, you have to know where the fear looms large and important. If there is fear in the gross physical of a particular person, then I wish to say that that person should concentrate on a particular centre. That centre is the navel. We have several spiritual centres. We call them *Chakras*. There are six major spiritual centres. Now there are many ways to overcome fear, but if one can concentrate on the navel centre and be one with the life force, the life energy, in the physical, one can conquer fear there.

Now, if one wants to conquer fear in the vital, then one should concentrate on one's own inner being. This is one way, concentration on the inner being, but it is difficult for beginners. So I tell them if they want to conquer fear in the vital, they should try to expand the real vital in themselves. We have two types of vital consciousness. One type, the undivine one, is aggressive; the other vital is divinely dynamic. We use the aggressive vital, its fighting quality, daily. The dynamic vital, though, wants to create something sooner than at once in a divine way, in an illumined way. So, if we can concentrate on that vital, or focus our attention on it, the dynamic vital, then we expand our consciousness there in the vital also. Then there can be no fear there.

Now, fear in the mind. Try, if you can, to empty your mind daily. The mind is full of doubt, obscurity, ignorance, suspicion and so forth. Early in the morning you can try, say for ten minutes, to conquer thought – not to allow any thought to enter, good, bad, divine or undivine. No thought. Feel that your mind is like a vessel. First you empty it. Now you are waiting – for what? For Peace, Light and Bliss. But if you do not empty the vessel, when Peace, Bliss and Light descend, they will be contaminated. How can you make your mind totally empty? Just do not allow any thought to enter your mind. No thought. If thought comes, try to kill it. Then, after some time, after a few days, allow only the divine thoughts which are your friends. In the beginning you do not know who your friends are and who your enemies are. You have to be very careful. Later on, you allow only your friends, that is to say, divine thoughts, progressive thoughts, illumined thoughts. These thoughts will undoubtedly conquer fear in the mind on your behalf.

Why is there fear in the physical, in the vital, in the mind? Precisely because something in you does not want to expand your consciousness. I am separate from you. You are separate from me. That is why I am afraid of you and you are afraid of me. This is what happens. But, if we realise the Highest, then immediately we feel the length and breadth of the world, the whole universe, as our very own. Only in expansion can we expel fear. If you expand your consciousness, then you become part and parcel of others. You belong to others; others belong to you. How can you be afraid of anybody else when you represent Divinity in humanity, and they represent the same Divinity in humanity? There can be no fear.

Now, fear in the heart. The aspiring heart has no fear, but the unaspiring heart has fear. The aspiring heart has a flame, a burning, mounting flame. Where there is light, there cannot be fear. The aspiring heart has a burning flame that mounts towards the Highest. Fear is bound to play its role in the unaspiring heart.

Now how can we conquer fear in the unaspiring heart? Here we have to take help directly from the soul. Where is the soul?

How many of us have seen the soul or felt it? When you meditate here, directly on the Heart centre, first you have to know if you are really and truly meditating on the Heart centre proper. Then, try to feel at every moment, or, let us say, every time you breathe in, you are digging into your heart. This is not violent digging. No. It is only a divinely intensified feeling you have inside your heart that you are going deep, deep, deep within. Each time you breathe in, feel that you are going deep within. And then, a few days or a few months later, you are bound to feel a twinge or you will hear a very tiny sound. When you hear the sound, try to see if the sound is caused by anything or not. That is to say, when we want to hear a sound, we need two hands to clap. But try to see or hear if the sound you are hearing is the result of something struck, or if it is spontaneous. Here the sound is automatic; two things are not struck together. It is spontaneous. So, when you feel that sound inside, like a celestial gong, then you are bound to conquer fear in your unaspiring heart.

But, to come back to your question, fear in every sphere of our being can be conquered through our inner cry, and this inner cry we call aspiration.

185. Can you tell us the place of the will?

Sri Chinmoy: Yes. Will-power is of paramount importance. But we have to know which will-power we are discussing. The soul's will-power is here, deep within. We also think of will in an aggressive sense, in an aggressive way; we use our undivine vital power to destroy. We make a mistake if we take the undivine vital power and the soul's will-power as one. That vital power does not come from the real will-power. Real will-power we get directly from the soul, here within, and this soul's will-power we all truly need. If we do not have the power from within, the soul's power, we will not succeed in achieving anything in the spiritual life. In the outer life also it is of great importance if we can bring to the fore the soul's will-power, soul-power. Now, how can we do it? How can we develop it? How can we cultivate this will-power?

One takes exercise every day if one wants to be an athlete. If one day he takes exercise and then for ten days he doesn't take any exercise, then he cannot be a good athlete. In the spiritual life also, we are all divine soldiers. At every moment we are fighting against our inner enemies. Our inner enemies are our doubt, fear, suspicions, worries, anxieties and so forth. At every moment, we have to hunt these inner animals, and here, what is our weapon? Aspiration. With our aspiration, we can hunt, we can kill all these animals, the animal qualities, animal propensities in us. Along with aspiration, we have to have will-power also. It has to be cultivated and developed. One cannot have abundant will-power or adamantine will-power overnight. If one is wanting in will-power, then you can be sure that that particular person will not be able to realise the Highest. He can make progress in the inner life, but this progress is of no great value. Will-power means immediate progress, immediate success and immediate achievement and fulfilment. This we can and we will get directly from the soul. The soul's Light, when manifested in a dynamic way, is called will-power.

186. I wonder, could you tell me, this ignorance that we have, how did it come about in the first place?

Sri Chinmoy: We started our Journey with Knowledge, with Wisdom, with Light. At the birth of our Journey there was no ignorance. But, what happened? God gave us freedom, even in our outer existence; limited freedom. We misused it. We allowed the dark and undivine forces to enter into our consciousness. From there, they entered into the whole world. He has given something to us. Suppose he has given us a knife. With this knife, what are we doing? We are stabbing each other. We are not cutting fruit and sharing it with each other.

When we go deep within, we see that even in our outer existence, God gave us some limited freedom. It is like a cow tied to a tree with a rope – it has limited freedom. Now, our Goal is right in front of us, but what happens? Whenever we do something wrong, we feel that life is gone. This life cannot link us to the Goal any more. But this very idea, again, is ignorant. Now, today, we have not reached the Highest, but that doesn't mean that tomorrow we will not reach our Goal.

To come back to your question as to why ignorance started. There was no ignorance in the beginning. It is we who have created our ignorance, mostly through our mind. We do not live in the heart. We live in the mind. Now, a mind that is earthbound, physical – we call it the physical mind – needs abundant Light either from within or from above. But we do not seek that. We are using our mind constantly in the wrong manner. We think we are far superior to animals. When we look at animals, we think, "They are constantly fighting. They are killing each other. They are living in ignorance." But, when we go deep within, we see that we are also doing the same things in our mind: fighting, thinking ill of others, disturbing our soul, our inner voice.

187. I would like to ask you: in your analogy of the cow, why would the cow be ignorant, just remaining on its own patch?

Sri Chinmoy: If the cow sees something within its own boundary, it simply destroys it. I have seen it many times. If you leave some toy or something nice near it, the cow just destroys it. I was just giving an analogy to show the sort of things we do with our limited freedom. So, here the cow is destructive. I am not saying that we are cows, but I am saying that we are acting like cows. God has given us freedom to go high, very high, but we are not using our freedom in a divine way. As I was saying about the knife, He has given us freedom to do whatever we want to do with the knife. But we are stabbing each other instead of doing something good with the knife. The knife is the instrument that is freedom. That He has given. But how are we using it?

Again, if we do the right thing, immediately the Divine within us, the Liberator within us, liberates us. It is like filling a jar. Drop by drop we can fill it. We say, "Oh, it will not do it. It is only a tiny insignificant drop." But, drop by drop, we can fill the whole jar. Similarly, we started our journey many, many hundreds of years ago and from the very beginning, unfortunately, we started walking in a wrong direction. That is why it has become so difficult. But if we, again, slowly and steadily run towards the Goal, then the Goal cannot deny us. We have to reach our Goal which is Light, through Light itself.

188. How can I sublimate or conquer my desires?

Sri Chinmoy: If you want to sublimate them, if you want to conquer your desires, there is only one thing to do. You have to pay more attention to the Light, in a positive way, but not by hook or by crook. If you try to subdue your physical or vital power in any kind of repressive way, then you will never be able to conquer this physical need. But, if you open yourself towards the Light, if you reach or feel the Light within you, then you will think more of the Light than of the darkness. You may feel that by thinking constantly of your desires, your vital, sex life, you will be able to conquer them, but it is impossible. Even if you want to think of them with a view to conquering them, you are making a mistake. Think of the other things, Light and Joy, which you need and which you actually want. Through concentration and meditation, you can have inner Joy and inner Light. You will try to bring them into your gross physical, and your physical being will also feel divine Joy and divine Light. At that time the life of destructive pleasure will leave you and the life of fulfilling joy will embrace you.

189. What should one's attitude be towards things that one did before, when one's higher mind, knowing it was wrong, was not in control? What should be one's attitude towards guilt resulting from these former actions?

Sri Chinmoy: One's attitude at that time should be that the past is buried in oblivion. You have done something wrong. If you cherish the idea of guilt, "I have done something wrong," you are being sincere, but thinking of your mistake, having this sincerity, does not help. Yes, you have done something wrong. But by having a guilty consciousness, you do not get Light or Wisdom. You have done something that is not right. Then, try to do the right thing, the divine thing. This second, this minute you have used. You could have used it either for a right purpose or a wrong purpose. All right, you have used it for a wrong purpose. Then use the following minute for a divine purpose, and if you use it for a divine purpose without thinking of the previous minute when you did something wrong, then what happens? Your positive strength, this will-power you have used to do the right thing will then have the power in entirety, in fullness. But, if you think of the past minute with a sense of guilt, that you have done something wrong, and then you think that the following minute you are determined to do the right thing, half of your power is again lost in darkness and only half can be utilised for the following minute of right action So, I tell my disciples to try to bring to the fore their full power in the following minute and nullify the previous mistake.

If one cherishes or broods over misdeeds, then one is again strengthening one's own guilt unconsciously. I may think, "I am repenting." But why should I repent? I have done something wrong. I am a hero; I am ready to face the consequences. If I have done something wrong, then I have the capacity to do the thing right. Again, by focusing all the attention on the right thing, we are adding to our positive strength. The sense of guilt, the constant feeling of self-reproach is, unfortunately, all-pervading in the Western world. If my Source is God, the Absolute infinite Light, if I know that it is from there that I came, then some day I must go back to my Source. During my stay on earth I got, unfortunately, some unhealthy, unaspiring and destructive experiences. Now, I have to get rid of these unfortunate experiences. I have to get fulfilling experiences in my life. So for that I have to concentrate only on the right thing, the divine thing which will fulfil me, and not on the things that have stood in my way.

190. When one is looking for the Inner Light and opens oneself to the Inner Light, does this necessitate a withdrawal from the material life?

Sri Chinmoy: When we look for the Inner Light, we don't have to give up the material life at all. We have to live on earth. If one gives up the members of his family, his children, his parents and his dear ones, then tomorrow he will give up the inner life also. Then what is he going to get? Where is God? God is inside everyone. Now, what is he going to give up? He is going to give up ignorance. He is going to give up bondage. He is going to give up temptation, his own temptation. The undivine things he is going to give up. But if you say that you have to give up your earthly existence in order to realise God, then it is a mistake. It is not required at all. God is here on earth as He is in Heaven. Now, if you look all the time up in the sky – as Bernard Shaw said, "Beware of the man whose God is in the skies" – then you are consciously negating God who is also the Creation. We don't have to be satisfied only with God the Creator. God the Creation we also have to accept. Otherwise, God is not complete. He is both Creator and Creation. We have to realise and fulfil Him here in the Creation itself.

191. Many times in one's life, one comes to a crossroad – not just in metaphysical things – when one doesn't know which way to go and one is looking for some kind of direction. Is there any way one can know what to do? Any sign?

Sri Chinmoy: There are two ways that can be taken when one is in that kind of difficulty, when one can't make a decision about what to do and what not to do. One way is to go to a spiritual person who can easily enter into the soul of the person who has the problem. The other way is to go deep within to get the Inner Light. The soul knows what is best for the individual. Now, we do not know, when we are doing something, whether we are doing the right thing or the wrong thing. Why are we uncertain about our own action? It is we who, after all, do something in our life, for our life. We are uncertain just because it is not coming directly from our soul or because, unfortunately, the physical mind is not able to grasp the message of the soul. Now, if you don't want to follow the spiritual path, if you find that impossible, and you just want to know what is best for you, then you have to go to some spiritual Master who will immediately enter into your soul and tell you what is best for you to do.

Needless to say, it is always good to aspire. If you aspire, God will shower His choicest Blessings on you. Eventually, you yourself will come to know what to do and what not to do. You will see not only the Way, but also the Goal.

VIII – QUESTIONS AND ANSWERS, UNIVERSITY OF GLASGOW

192. Does one have to have a spiritual Teacher in order to follow the spiritual life?

Sri Chinmoy: The necessity of a spiritual Teacher in the spiritual life is of paramount importance. As you know, a teacher is necessary in our outer life, no matter what we want to learn. If you want to learn how to swim, how to dance, or how to play a musical instrument, you need a teacher for some time. This is university. Here, all the students are studying under professors. The professors also, once upon a time, had to study. They themselves were students. Now they are in a position to teach and the students are learning from them. Soon, the present students will also start teaching. So it is not that one has to study all his life with a teacher. One studies for fifteen or twenty years. Then one gets his Master's degree and he starts teaching. In the spiritual life, one has to learn how to meditate, how to concentrate. This subject also one has to learn from someone, from an adept, from a spiritual Master. In the spiritual life, if one learns how to meditate and gets inner knowledge, inner illumination, then he will be in a position to communicate with God constantly. Something more, a spiritual Teacher does not act like a teacher or a professor. That is to say, a teacher or a professor will pass you or fail you according to the papers that you have submitted. If you have done well, he will give you a high mark. If you have done badly, he will fail you. But a spiritual Teacher acts like private tutor. He helps you wholeheartedly and unreservedly to pass the examination. And what is the examination? It is to cross the sea of ignorance, which is right in front of human beings. The spiritual Master himself has crossed the sea of ignorance. Then he teaches the aspiring seekers, disciples and followers how they too, can get across the sea of ignorance. This is what he does. He is like a private tutor.

To come back to your question: everybody needs a Teacher. Then when one gets his own illumination, he does not need a teacher any longer. But, you can ask, who was the teacher for the first God-realised soul? He didn't have a Teacher. He who realised God for the first time didn't have a human Teacher, it is true. But, we have to see how many God-realised souls Mother-Earth has been blessed with: many, many, many. Most of them, if not all, had a Teacher for three years, ten years, twenty years or forty years. Especially in the beginning, one must have a Teacher. Otherwise, one will be terribly confused. One may get high, elevating experiences, but he will not be able to give adequate significance to his own experiences. He will have high experiences and he will tell his friends, his intimate ones. They will say, "It is all your mental hallucination. Forget about the spiritual life." Then if you have faith in your friends, you will do away with your spiritual life. But if you go to a spiritual Master at that time, he will encourage you. He will inspire you and give you proper significant explanations of your experiences. Again, if you are on the wrong path, doing something wrong in your meditation or concentration, he will be in a position to correct you. So, the role of a spiritual Master is that of a private tutor.

193. If one doesn't have a spiritual Master, will one be able to achieve God-realisation?

Sri Chinmoy: Yes. But if one does not have a spiritual Teacher, then his path becomes extremely difficult. Then, you know, he will be in a difficult position. Sometimes he may get high experiences. Then, doubt will eclipse his mind and he will say, "How can I have this kind of experience? It is something so high; yet, I am an ordinary person. I cannot have this kind of experience. Perhaps I am just deluding myself." But if there is someone who knows what the Reality is, then he will say, "Don't act like a fool. The experiences which you have had are absolutely true." He encourages the seeker and inspires him. If he sees the seeker is doing something wrong, he shows him the right path. I do not say that if one doesn't have a spiritual teacher, then one will not achieve realisation, far from it. A spiritual Teacher is he who is an aid, a considerable help to the seeker. You know, in this world when there is someone to push or pull us – pull us from above or push us from below – then we go faster. The Teacher is a source of inspiration to the seeker. He will offer inspiration. You know, when you are inspired, you write, you compose wonderful music, you write wonderful stories. But when you are not inspired, you cannot. You cannot achieve something remarkable without inspiration. In that way also, a spiritual Master is of help to us.

194. How can man, a limited human being in the finite, realise Infinity in his life?

Sri Chinmoy: When we say "man", we have to know what we are referring to. Is it a man who is five feet, eight inches tall, or six feet, two inches tall? If his human height, earthly height, is the "man", then I wish to say that that is not "man", "man" the consciousness, "man" the everlasting consciousness. We all have consciousness within us. We have two types of consciousness: finite and Infinite. Now, we are expressing our finite consciousness in our day-to-day activities. But, deep within us, we have also an Infinite Consciousness. So, when we ask how a man can achieve infinity in his life, we must know that it is not in his physical body, or in his arms, or in his feet, or inside his eyes that he will achieve infinity. It is in his inner consciousness. Even after a spiritual Master has realised the Highest, he eats, he sleeps, he mixes with his friends. Everything is normal. If a spiritual Master has achieved realisation, it doesn't mean that as a man he will have two big horns, or a long tail, or something else. No. He is normal. Spirituality is normal. Spirituality is absolutely normal. But unfortunately, we have made it seem abnormal because we feel that spiritual people are all in the moonlight; they are not facing the earth or the earth's problems; they do not face reality. This is a deplorable mistake. Real spirituality is the acceptance of life. We have to accept life as such, as it is now. Then we have to try to change the face of the world with our aspiration and with our realisation.

To come back to your question: man, in his outer life or his outer achievements, is very limited. But the same man, when he enters into the inmost recesses of his heart, feels that there is something constantly trying to expand itself. This is consciousness. This consciousness links him with the Highest Absolute. He has the potentiality and capacity deep within him to be one with the Absolute. So, when one realises the Highest through a spiritual Master, it is in his consciousness that he has received the infinite Light, infinite Peace and infinite Bliss which the Master offers to his disciples, his spiritual children, when they meditate on him. The Master is standing or sitting right in front of his disciples, and they feel from him, in him, Peace, Light and Bliss in boundless measure. Where do they get these qualities from? From his consciousness. Not from his arms or from his nose or from his limbs. They come directly from the very depth of his consciousness. Consciousness always welcomes us. It is in the consciousness that we invoke, receive and offer boundless Peace, Light and Bliss.

195. If a man rejects the existence of a Deity, what will be his fate?

Sri Chinmoy: Well, if someone consciously and deliberately rejects the existence of a Deity, if he wants to remain in ignorance, then for him ignorance is bliss. Let him be happy in his belief or disbelief. However, if he feels that he is not getting any energising Light, Joy, Bliss or Power from his feeling, then he must leave the realm of ignorance.

Now, about the Deity. According to our traditional Hindu philosophy, there is a Supreme Deity and also many cosmic gods and goddesses. If one has faith in the highest Deity, whom we call Brahman, that is more than enough. One has not to go through all the hundreds of Indian gods and goddesses, demigods and so forth. If one has faith in the Supreme Reality, the Supreme Deity, that is more than enough. But, if somebody says that he does not have faith in the Deity, assuming that he means God, then what happens? He is not going to be condemned. God has given all of us, each individual, some limited freedom. It is up to us to utilise this freedom, to exercise this freedom divinely or undivinely. Again, there is something called God's Hour. From the spiritual point of view, you know that each human being has an hour. God has chosen an hour. God does not want anybody to remain unrealised on earth. Why? God's only Message is fulfilment. He wants Himself to be fulfilled, and He wants us to be fulfilled. This is freedom. So, if someone consciously or deliberately ignores his divine potentiality, if he has no faith in God or in the Deity, if he is still in the world of sleep, then God says, "Sleep, baby, sleep."

But a time comes when the mother, for example, sees that the son is not getting up. It is very late. It is high time for him to go to school. Then, the mother comes and knocks at his door. Here, the mother knows the actual hour when the son has to go to school. If the son is good, obedient, intelligent and has a sense of responsibility, he will not wait for his mother to knock at the door. He himself will be up in time to go to school. So, in the spiritual life also, those who are sincere, earnest in their spiritual pursuits, have the conscious inner longing for the fruit, for the Light, Peace and Bliss. When we say God-realisation, what do we actually mean? We mean our conscious, inseparable Oneness with God. We are all in God, but few, very few of us are consciously aware of God's Existence. A spiritual man has free access to God's Consciousness. He feels and knows that he has established his conscious Union with God. This is the difference between an ordinary man and a spiritual man. A spiritual man wants to establish a conscious Union with God, and an unspiritual man does not even want to achieve this state of consciousness.

To come back to your question: again I wish to say that if somebody denies the existence of the Deity, the Supreme Reality, let him deny it. Let him continue to deny it for one year, four years or twenty years; indefinitely. But a time will dawn for the poor fellow because God Himself will never allow anybody to remain unrealised. God does not want to live unfulfilled. Neither will He allow this particular man to remain unfulfilled. So, at God's Hour, God consciously arouses him, awakens his consciousness, so that he can launch into the life of spirituality. But he who, on his own, already has a deep inner urge, feels the necessity to run towards the Light, towards the Destined Goal. Naturally he is expediting his journey with God's Grace and with his personal efforts. When God's Infinite Grace and man's sincere efforts go together, then the Goal cannot remain a far cry.

196. Many young people are interested in expanding their consciousness with drugs. What do you think of consciousness under drugs, like LSD?

Sri Chinmoy: First of all, I am not an expert, an authority on LSD, so I can only speak from the experience of some of my students. I have not taken any drugs and will never take them in my life, so it is only from the experience offered by my disciples that I can speak. I am not able to help drug addicts, hippies and people with alcoholic problems, serious perverted emotional problems and similar conditions. Now, of course, there are spiritual Masters who have them in their families, among their students, but I am not competent to have them in my family. Just to give you an experience – I have a Centre in San Juan, Puerto Rico. One day, about twenty drug addicts came in during the meeting. They started arguing with me and saying that they had wonderful experiences, high, elevating experiences with drugs. I said, "Wonderful. You stay with your experiences. Then what do you want from me?" They said, "We want to have spiritual experiences from you." I said, "If you want to have spiritual experiences from me, then you have to give up your drugs. I am not going to your place to have the experiences you have had through drugs, but you want to have the experiences that I can offer. If you want my experiences, spiritual experiences, then you have to give up your drugs here and now. Otherwise, tomorrow I will not allow any of you to come to my Centre. This is my place. I am not giving a talk in a public hall where I have no authority. Here I have a right to exercise my authority. This is my Centre, and I will not allow any of you to come to my Centre unless you come tomorrow with the idea that you are going to give up drugs." The following day, nineteen out of twenty came up, and they stood in front of me and said, "We want to have the experiences that you want to offer, so we are giving up drugs." I said, "Then you meditate here for a month or so. But, during this month you have to be sincere to me and sincere to yourselves. If you do not get any experiences during the month you can leave me and you can go back to your old life." From that time, they started coming regularly to the Centre. They were having true spiritual experiences. They told me the difference between the experiences they had with drugs and the experiences they were getting from inner aspiration, from the spiritual life. One of them said to me, "Drugs gave us the message of self-deception. Spirituality has given us the message of self-perfection." Now they have become true jewels of my Puerto Rican Centre.

197. Have you considered establishing a Centre in Scotland, and if so, where?

Sri Chinmoy: To be very frank with you, I have not the slightest idea of running a Centre here. But, if some of you are interested, after the meeting is over, then I will speak to you. Yesterday, after the meeting was over in Ireland, a few sincere seekers came up to me. We have a Centre in London. There, a young boy named Patrick, who has become my disciple, said that he had three or four friends in Ireland. From London he informed his friends who are studying at Dublin University that I was going to give a talk in Ireland. After the meeting was over, they came up to me and said, "Here we would like to have a Centre under your guidance." They are really sincere and with them we have formed a Centre at Dublin, Ireland. Here also, if you want me to open up a Centre, then kindly see me after the meeting is over.

IX – QUESTIONS AND ANSWERS, UNIVERSITY OF LEEDS

198. How do you suggest that a genuine Western student should go about learning to discover these concentration and contemplation exercises and the techniques of meditation in order to follow the spiritual path, and run faster than the average?

Sri Chinmoy: If a student wants to learn, what does he do? He goes to a school, college or university. Why? He goes because he feels that there he will find a professor who will be able to illumine him. Similarly, in the spiritual life, if a seeker, who is the student, has the inner cry to learn how to concentrate, meditate and contemplate, he goes to a spiritual Master. As a student has faith in his teacher, and therefore goes to school and learns from him, so also the sincere seeker goes to a spiritual Master in whom he has implicit faith, and learns from him. But in a school, when there is a class, a teacher sometimes finds it difficult to give individual attention to the students. He tells them something, and they listen to him collectively, and learn as much as they can. In the spiritual life, if the Teacher sees that an individual is making great progress, but is in a group with other students who cannot keep up with him, then the spiritual Teacher will always give the good student special lessons so that he can run fast, faster, fastest towards his Goal. He will not make the good student wait for the others.

One should always go to a spiritual Master in order to learn concentration, meditation and contemplation, because a spiritual Master knows how these things can be taught. Just as an ordinary teacher will know all about geography, science, philosophy, history or some other subject, so the spiritual Master will know about concentration, meditation and contemplation.

199. Here in the West there is an acute shortage of spiritual Masters. How does one find one?

Sri Chinmoy: In the spiritual life, there is a ladder, and this spiritual ladder has quite a few rungs. The first rung is inspiration, and the next rung is aspiration. In aspiration are contained the seeds of concentration, meditation and contemplation. After aspiration, the next rung is realisation. After realisation comes revelation, and after revelation comes manifestation.

Let us start with inspiration. You know that there are millions of books. You have already read hundreds of books. If you read spiritual books, preferably written by spiritual Masters, you are bound to get inspiration. When you read a history book, you become inspired to learn all about history. When you read spiritual books, you enter into a new field, a new domain, a new consciousness. You get inspiration when you read in these books that somebody attained Peace, Light or Joy. Immediately you want to have these things yourself. As you say, there is a shortage of spiritual Masters. But if you read books written by spiritual Masters, you are bound to get some inspiration.

Then a day will come when you will realise that this inspiration is not enough. Your inspiration will give birth to aspiration, the inner cry. A child cries. The mother immediately comes running. Why does she come? Because her child is crying. The mother cannot stay in some other place at that time. She has to come and care for her child. In the spiritual life also, when you have aspiration, this inner cry for God, no matter where He is, He has to come to you. And how does He come? He comes in the form of some spiritual persons who have seen Him or felt Him, or who have received some inner message from Him. When you go to school, you are expected to pay a fee for the opportunity of studying. In the spiritual life also, there is a fee. This fee is called aspiration. If you have this aspiration, the fee, then how can you be denied your inner education? God is bound to help you at that time. You may not get a real Guru, the highest Master, but you are bound to get someone. For some time you may have to wait for the teacher who will be able to give you a Master's degree, but there are many people in the West who can help you at the very beginning. In the spiritual life, this elementary help is as important as the kindergarten or primary school.

Then, if you are not satisfied, if you want to go higher and deeper and farther, if you want to make faster progress, I tell you, your inner cry will never be denied. You will find somebody else who will help you on your journey, and finally, you will get someone who will be able to take you to your Destined Goal.

So, your first spiritual Teacher is spiritual books. You will learn many things from books. These things may seem theoretical at the beginning, but if you learn something theoretically, then you will have some inner confidence in it. For practical knowledge, you must get a Teacher. No sincere cry has ever been denied. It is only a matter of time. If somebody really wants to do something, to achieve something, he may not be able to do it immediately. But if he has a real, sincere, genuine aspiration to do it, then it is only a matter of time. In one year or two years, in one incarnation or two incarnations, he is bound to get what he wants. The very nature of God is fulfilment. God wants fulfilment for His own children. If our Father eats a mango, He will not deprive us of the mango. He will also give us a mango so that we can eat with Him. So, since God wants fulfilment for us, His aspiring children, we can certainly expect fulfilment from Him.

200. Having been born and brought up in India, many of us have been surrounded by much of the spiritual philosophy and mysticism of the country, not necessarily because we are great believers, but because it is part of the environment. Over here, I am constantly being asked by my friends what spirituality is, and what are we trying to do with it in relation to the starvation and poverty in India. They ask me how is it that our spirituality does not cure everything miraculously? I can't answer this question. Can you help me? Can you tell me what actually spirituality has to offer to mankind?

Sri Chinmoy: From real spirituality, we have to know what we can expect and what we cannot expect. Unfortunately, what not only the Western world, but the entire present-day world expects from spirituality is miracles. At every moment, the Western world and the Eastern world are crying for miracles. Spirituality, they feel, has to cure everything and solve all problems in one instantaneous stroke. Why do people expect this from spirituality? Real mysticism, real spirituality, is not miracle-mongering. The message of spirituality is to live a higher life, a transformed life, a divinised life.

A sincere seeker sees inside himself many animals: fear, anger, doubt, anxiety, temptation, greed and jealousy. These animals have to be conquered in order to attain the highest Goal of spirituality – conscious oneness with the Supreme. So if the seeker has doubt, if he has fear, if he has jealousy, he has to conquer them. He has to conquer all the animals inside himself.

The message of spirituality is the transcendence of our present consciousness, which is half animal. We want to be divinised, we want to go high, higher, highest, so that we can become totally one with the rest of the world. This we can do through real spirituality. But most people expect something quite different from spirituality. They want to have their diseases cured, or their fortunes told. No. Spirituality will give what spirituality has to offer. Spirituality will give inner Peace, inner Light, inner Joy to those who practise it. A divinised life is what spirituality wants to offer, and this is what we can expect from spirituality.

201. Can you please define for us concentration, meditation and contemplation, and tell us how they differ from each other?

Sri Chinmoy: Concentration. When we concentrate, we focus all our attention on a particular subject or object. When we try to concentrate, we have to feel that right in front of us there is nothing but that object. [Holding the petal of a flower.] This is the petal. I have not to see anything else. I do not have to see my finger, or the rest of the flower. No, only this one petal. Feel that only you and the petal exist, nothing else; not the rest of the world. From this kind of concentration, you will get the essence, the quintessence of the petal.

Meditation. Let us not meditate on this petal. Let us try to meditate on something vast. When we meditate, let us see right in front of us the sea, or the sky, or the Himalayas. Concentration paved the way. While I was concentrating, I was not thinking of my students, my disciples or my friends. I was only concentrating my whole attention on the petal. While one meditates, one has to try to expand one's consciousness to encompass the vast sea, or the vast blue sky. One has to expand oneself like a bird spreading its wings. We have to expand our finite consciousness, since just because we are bound, we are unhappy. If we can free ourselves from the meshes of ignorance, then we become all-pervading. We enter into the Universal Consciousness where there is no fear, no jealousy, no doubt, no fault. There is all Joy, Peace and Divine Power. In meditation there is no thought – no limiting thought, no destructive or undivine thought – no thought at all. That is why we can meditate on the Vast.

Contemplation. When we contemplate, we have to feel our entire existence – body, vital, mind, heart and soul – as inseparably one. Again, we have to feel that we are not the body, and that we don't have to be bound by the limitations of the body. I spoke just half an hour ago of Infinity, Eternity and Immortality. These are all vague terms right now. But when we contemplate, our whole existence enters into the consciousness of Infinity, Eternity and Immortality. By concentration we become one-pointed, and from meditation we expand our consciousness into the vast. In contemplation we grow into the vastness itself. We have seen the Truth. We have felt the Truth. But the most important thing is to grow into the Truth. What we have seen and felt in meditation, we grow into and unite with totally in contemplation. At that time, when we look at our own existence, we don't see a human being; we see something like a dynamo of Light, Peace and Bliss. This is what contemplation does for us.

202. You talk about spiritual practices, either elaborate or very simple. When we, as ordinary people, listen to a piece of music or see a very great piece of art, we feel a certain kind of joy. Is the joy you achieve after many years of spiritual practices the same as the joy we achieve momentarily, or is it greater?

Sri Chinmoy: It is something different. When you hear a piece of music, you are temporarily transported to a realm of ecstasy. Then, after five or ten minutes, the music goes away, and the joy disappears. When you make something, you experience the joy of creation. You are in ecstasy for fifteen minutes or half an hour, or for a day or two. Then your joy vanishes. Why? Because the joy that you get from your creation or from somebody else's creation is limited by the quality of the creation. Your creation may have the capacity to give joy for five or ten minutes. Then it stops. This is because you have not created something infinite or eternal. But when you have meditated for fifteen or twenty years, eight or ten hours a day, at that time, after your meditation, you will still have a free access to something boundless and infinite.

When we meditate, we enter into the vast – the vast sea, or the vast sky, or infinite Light. When we enter into the Vast, we become, by God's Grace, a channel which flows endlessly, like the Ganges flowing down from the Himalayas. So, when we meditate, we get a continuous flow of inner joy. The joy which we get from some earthly creation lasts for a short time, because both the creator and the creation are bound. But by meditating, we enter into boundlessness. Then when we get Joy, it is really spontaneous and permanent. When a spiritual Master says that he has inner Peace, inner Joy, inner Bliss, he has these permanently. They flow constantly from within because he has grown into the Source. This Joy is infinitely greater and more fulfilling than the fleeting joy which an ordinary human being may experience.

203. I wonder, Sir, if you could tell us a little bit more explicitly what you mean by the term "God", and whether you could perhaps compare this with what the word "God" means in Judaism, Christianity and Islam?

Sri Chinmoy: First of all, I would like to say that when we try to define God, we bind and belittle Him. God transcends all definitions. But each individual has the right to define God in his own way, in spite of the fact that God is beyond definition. He is infinite. He is eternal. He is immortal. You, as a seeker of the Infinite Truth, may say that God is Infinite Consciousness. The gentleman sitting beside you may say that God is Infinite Power. A third person may say that God is Infinite Energy. And a fourth may say that God is a divinised human being. Everybody is right in his own way. God is what each individual sees Him as. He can be a Man; He can be a Woman; He can be Power; He can be Light; He can be Peace.

If you want me to tell you what I feel, I wish to say that God is man, and man is God. We are all God's children, but we have not yet realised our highest height. Man is God yet to be realised in totality, in the highest plane of consciousness. God is man yet to be manifested fully here on earth. This is my definition. You have every right to define God in your own way. Nobody's definition has to be accepted as the only one with real authority. In defining God, everybody is perfectly right in his own way.

204. Can you tell how spiritual Masters differ from ordinary beings – how they are, as you say, "sons of God"? Can you explain how they are superior to other human beings?

Sri Chinmoy: In the West we know that Christ, the Son of God, said, "I and my Father are one." In India, our Vedic seers said, "Aham Brahmasmi" – "I am the Brahman." On the strength of their highest realisation, they became the Truth itself. When Christ or the spiritual Masters say that they are God, they say it on the strength of their inseparable oneness with Him. This is the essential difference between a real spiritual Master and an ordinary person. A real spiritual Master has become consciously one with God.

A real spiritual Master will never think that he is superior to anybody. He will feel that it is his bounden duty to be of service to the divinity, to the Supreme in humanity. A real father does not feel that he is superior to his children. He feels that it is his duty to bring up his children, because God has given him the opportunity and the responsibility. The matter of superiority does not come into the picture. Real spiritual Masters likewise do not have a feeling of superiority. They only feel that they are fortunate that God has chosen them to be of service to suffering mankind or searching mankind. They feel that in their self-dedicated service, they are trying to fulfil the Divine. Spiritual Masters do not think that those who are unillumined and unenlightened are inferior to them. No. The father never thinks his child is inferior to him. The older brother does not think his younger brothers are inferior. They have simply not had as much experience or wisdom as he has had. If one brother has seen where the Father is, he tells his other brothers where to find Him. He says, "Come with me. I know where our Father is." Then he leads them to their Father, but he does not feel that in doing so, he is superior.

205. You stated that one should live a simple life. How do you define a simple life, and how does one recognise it? How does one live it?

Sri Chinmoy: There are many things we do here on earth that are unnecessary. There are many things we own that are superfluous. You live in a house, and you have a room. In your room, if you want to, you can have a radio, a stereo, a television and many other things which you don't really need. I am speaking from the spiritual point of view. If you want to lead a spiritual life, if you want to live the life of aspiration, if you want to realise God, then to make the fastest progress, it will be better for you to think more of God than of music and television, and all kinds of other things. You have to know what you want. If you want to be a spiritual person, then naturally you have to spend most of your time in spiritual pursuits. All the paraphernalia of the world will only distract you and waste your time.

If you want God, you have to lead a simple life. There are only twenty-four hours in the day, and when they are gone, they do not come back again. If you waste an hour, then it is lost to you forever. You will not be able to retrieve it. You have to decide what you will use each fleeting moment for: for worldly pleasure, or for God. If you feel that your first and foremost necessity is God, then if you simplify your life, you will not be distracted or tempted. If you keep all the objects of temptation around you, then you are consciously and deliberately delaying your spiritual progress.

X – QUESTIONS AND ANSWERS, UNIVERSITY OF ESSEX, COLCHESTER, ENGLAND

206. In your opinion, can one realise the Highest through the use of certain drugs?

Sri Chinmoy: To be very frank with you, everybody has his own way. If somebody feels that by taking drugs he will get inner experiences, highest experiences, then it is up to him. I am not a judge or authority, since I have not taken drugs, but I am offering my opinion based on my inner spiritual understanding. I have meditated and, as far as my understanding is concerned, I have realised the Highest. So, in my case, if somebody asked me what I did, I will say that I meditated for twenty years, from the age of twelve right up to thirty-two. I went through twenty years of sincere and serious meditation, eight hours, ten hours, twelve hours a day, in order to realise God. I can only say that, in my opinion, I feel that God-realisation, the Highest Realisation, cannot be achieved through drugs. That is my personal opinion, and I say it on the strength of my realisation. But, if somebody says that he can get it through other ways, through drugs, then he is perfectly entitled to do so in his own way.

As far as my realisation is concerned, on the strength of my own highest realisation, I wish to say that I worked very, very hard on the spiritual path. This path is really long and arduous. Here, you need a disciplined life. Everything depends on self-discipline. From self-discipline and self-perfection, we get God-realisation. Since you are asking me my opinion, on the strength of my own realisation I wish to say that the use of drugs is not proper. Realisation must come through proper meditation. I have a few hundred disciples in the States and in other places. Thirty or forty students of mine who are now my close disciples used to take drugs. They came to me with the idea of seeing the difference between the experiences that they had had with drugs and the experiences they were expecting from meditation with me. So they stayed for a few days. Then they got real spiritual experiences from their meditation. To my deepest joy and pride, all of them gave up drugs. It is they who are in a position to judge, because they had many, many experiences from drugs. Then they came to me and they got experiences from the meditation. They came to learn from me how to follow the path of spirituality. I taught them and they felt the enormous difference between the two types of experiences.

207. What is your theory about life after death?

Sri Chinmoy: The other day I gave a talk at the University of Kent, Canterbury. The subject of my talk was, "Is Death the End?" My philosophy, or my personal experience, is that death is not the end. Death is just like an ordinary road; life is the eternal traveller. When life is tired and exhausted, life takes a short rest. Then, after the rest, life resumes its journey. Death is not the culmination. Death is just like a room where you take your rest. Some people take their rest for a longer time in a particular room. Some people take a short rest, then again they start working.

It is like a living room and a bedroom. In the living room we have to work. We have to show our friends that we are alive. But, in the bedroom, in the sleeping room, we take rest. There we don't have to show our friends that we are alive. There we take rest for four hours or six hours or eight hours. Similarly, each individual soul comes into the world and plays its role within the physical sheath. This sheath is composed of five elements. Now, when we leave the body, let us say, when the bird flies away from the cage, this physical sheath enters again into the physical world, composed of the five elements. The vital enters into the vital world. The mind enters into the mental world. And the soul goes back to its own region. Then, after taking a short rest or a long rest, whatever rest is required for the individual soul, the soul comes back into the world. It comes with the permission or approval of the Supreme, once again to fulfil the Mission of the Supreme in the world. So death is not the end. It is only a short rest.

From the spiritual point of view, on the strength of my own realisation, I wish to say that death is not the end. It can never be the end. It is only a temporary rest that we need at the present stage of evolution. There will come a time when we won't have to take that kind of rest, when man will have abundant Peace, Light and Bliss, when man will be surcharged with divine qualities. At that time, this temporary rest will not be necessary for the fully developed souls.

208. Do our actions on earth affect our life after we die?

Sri Chinmoy: After we die there is a law of karma. Now, if we do something wrong here, we have to know that either today or tomorrow, either in the physical world or in the inner world, we will receive the result of it. "As you sow, so shall you reap." It is unavoidable. If I constantly steal, one day I shall be caught and put into jail. Today after stealing, I may not get caught; but if I continue to steal, I shall be caught one day. Then, if I do something good, if I pray, if I meditate, if I do good things, divine things, regularly, there too I will get the result of them. It is absolutely true, "As you sow, so shall you reap." The law of karma cannot easily be nullified. It can be nullified only when the Divine Grace descends. I am ignorant, and I have done a few things wrong, or many things wrong, so what happens? If I cry to God for Forgiveness, for His Compassion, then naturally His Compassion will dawn on me. If I sincerely cry, then God has the Power to nullify the law of karma, the law of Action and Reaction. It is by God's Grace that we can nullify it. But if God's Grace does not descend on the individual who has committed a great mistake, a Himalayan blunder, naturally he has to pay the penalty for his misdeeds. There is no escape. There is no such thing as escape. I cannot go on doing something undivine and feel that God, the Cosmic Law, will forgive me. No. But, if I have done something wrong, and I really have repentance, if I really don't do it again, if I shed bitter tears and if God sees a soulful cry within my heart, naturally He will forgive me. He will also give me the necessary strength not to commit the same mistake again.

So, for one who does not aspire, who does not want God's Forgiveness or God's Compassion to overcome the teeming ignorance that he unconsciously cherishes, I wish to say the law of karma is always binding; it will coil around him like a snake. But, if he is really sincere, genuine and aspiring, and he wants to be free from the meshes of ignorance, then naturally he will not do wrong things to start with. He will only do things that are divine, things that are motivated by a divine Will from within. At that time he will know that the law of karma cannot bind him because he is doing everything according to the dictates of his soul, his inner Being. The soul will not ask him to do anything wrong. It is the physical, it is the vital, it is the mind in us that unfortunately compel us or instigate us to say and do the wrong things. The soul will never ask us to do anything wrong. On the contrary, the soul will inspire us to say the right thing, to do the right thing and to grow into the right thing. The law of karma will bind us at the point when we are wallowing constantly in the mire of ignorance. This is not our first, and this cannot be our last incarnation. When we come back in our next incarnation, naturally we have to start our journey according to the result that is destined. If I have done many things wrong, I cannot expect to realise the Highest Truth in my next incarnation. But, if God's Grace is there, we can easily nullify the results of all our wrong actions.

209. How can we enter into the life of self-discipline?

Sri Chinmoy: Now we have to know that self-discipline is not just a word that we come across in the dictionary. If I have to choose which quality is most important and fulfilling at the beginning of the spiritual life, then I must say that it is self-discipline. Now, what we need is a disciplined life. If we don't have a disciplined life, we are in no way better than an animal. We are no better than a monkey who is always pinching and biting.

Now, the mind. Our mind is a victim to doubt, worries, anxieties and so forth. A disciplined life will not have the same fate. It will have joy and peace. A disciplined life comes from constant practice. Nobody can be a world champion overnight. What does practice mean? Practice means patience, Patience-Light. Patience is not something weak. It is something dynamic; it is something illumining. We want it in order to have a disciplined life. Today, if we want to discipline our life altogether, it may be impossible. But tomorrow it will be possible. Slowly, steadily, we have to discipline our life. If we are in a hurry, we can never discipline our life. Suppose we do a few things wrong. Suppose somebody drinks a lot, yet he feels that in the spiritual life he is not supposed to drink at all. What will he do? He has to discipline his life. If he drinks, say six or seven times a day, let him come to realise the fact that it is something harmful, it is damaging to his God-realisation. Then, let him try to drink less. If he drinks six times, let him reduce it to five times a day. Then, after a few days, let him drink four times. Then, after a month or two, or four or six months, let him drink three times a day. Gradually, slowly, let him diminish it.

In our ordinary human life, we know that we are doing many things wrong. If we want to conquer them all at once, we shall simply break. We shall be torn into pieces. No, we have to have a real inner will, will-power, soul's will, to conquer them slowly and steadily so that we will not break. Otherwise, the body will revolt and the body will break.

Now, this disciplined life that you are speaking of can come from only one thing, and that is aspiration, our inner cry. When you cry for outer things, sometimes you get them, sometimes you don't. But if your inner cry is sincere, you will see that the fulfilment dawns. A child cries for milk. He is crying in his cradle in the living room. The mother may be in the kitchen. Wherever she is, when she hears his cry, the mother comes running to feed the child with milk. Now why? The mother feels the cry of the child is genuine and sincere. Similarly, in the spiritual life we have an inner cry. If you have that inner cry, then it does not matter when you cry. It may be at one o'clock or at three o'clock or at noon, in the morning or in the evening. At any hour, that inner cry reaches God, and God is bound to fulfil that inner cry. If one wants to discipline himself, if one is dissatisfied with his loose life, and if he feels that from a disciplined life he can have realisation, he can have real fulfilment, perfection and satisfaction, then God is bound to help that particular sincere seeker. If there is an inner cry, then nothing on earth can be denied. No fulfilment can be denied to an individual who has an inner cry. We cry as human beings for name and fame, for many things. But we do not cry for the one thing which is of paramount importance, and that is God's Inner Wealth. What is that Inner Wealth? His inner Wealth is Divine Fulfilment, Divine Perfection. We are all imperfect. No human being is perfect. No. But again, our aim is to be perfectly perfect. This perfect perfection can only come from self-discipline. God is all ready. He is more than eager to offer His perfect Perfection. But for that perfect Perfection, we have to grow into a mounting cry which we call aspiration, constant aspiration. When this flame of aspiration rises towards the Highest, it illumines everything around it which is dark. Then, the higher it goes, the greater and more fulfilling is our manifestation. You want me to tell you how you can, or how we can, have a disciplined life, a really disciplined life. I wish to say that the answer lies only in our inner cry, our aspiration. With our inner cry we can have a self-disciplined life. With self-discipline we can get the inner wealth of self-discovery. Self-discipline is the precursor of self-discovery. Self-discovery is the harbinger of God-Manifestation.

210. When you say "God-realisation", what does it actually mean? How are we supposed to grow into it?

Sri Chinmoy: One has to realise one's own Highest. Now, as human beings we feel that the infinite Peace, infinite Light, infinite Bliss and the infinite Divine Power are all sheer imagination. We are in the finite, quarrelling and fighting. We are victims to doubt, fear and negative forces which we feel are quite normal and natural. Peace of mind is a far cry. We do not see peace of mind here. We do not see a peaceful atmosphere around us. There is no such thing as Peace, Light or Bliss around us. But, when we talk of God-realisation it means that our inner existence is flooded with peace, poise, equanimity, light and so forth. Now, according to unaspiring people, this is something vague, a fantasy of our imagination, a chimerical mist. But those who practise meditation go deep within and see that there *is* real Peace, Light and Bliss. It is not merely imagination. It is absolutely real. They get enormous, boundless inner strength, and they see that doubt can be challenged and conquered. Now we are victims to doubt. Each moment we are killing ourselves with this slow poison. Moreover, we cannot love anything. We cannot love anyone. We cannot love ourselves. But once we have achieved God-realisation, there can be no shadow of doubt. It is all certitude. It is all love. It is all illumination. It is all Bliss.

XI – QUESTIONS AND ANSWERS, UNIVERSITY OF NOTTINGHAM

211. You said that because we desire, the light within us is eclipsed. Now, we have got basic necessities, for which we require food and shelter, speaking of two on which our lives are based. Is it possible to eradicate desires?

Sri Chinmoy: If you follow the spiritual life, it is quite possible to eradicate desires because God's Will, first of all, helps the seeker to minimise his desires. Now, you say as a human being you have to take care of your family, friends and so forth. This is one way. But there is another way. This we call the divine duty. When God inspires you, you will still spend time on the members of your family, providing for them food, clothing, a good education and other necessary things. There is abundant light in that. But, as human beings, what we feel is that, if we have one car, we want to have two cars. If we have one house, we want to have two houses. We try constantly to increase our material possessions instead of existing with the minimal things we need to live here on earth. God gives us enough capacity. If one wants to aspire, He gives him enough time. There is nobody here on earth who can say that he wants to pray to God but has no time. No. Here we have to see that, if we are really sincere, God will immediately give us the time. He also gives us the capacity. When God asks us to do something, we have to realise immediately that He has given us the capacity which is already within us.

So, as a human being, if somebody says that he has to work for these basic necessities, certainly he has to. But he has to know how many things, unnecessary things, he is crying for. And he is not crying for Light; he is only crying for material possessions. For basic things, yes, we have to work; we have to eat, we have to feed ourselves. But for that God has given us the necessary wisdom also. You have to know that if we constantly desire more material possessions, naturally we are eclipsing the inner Sun, which is the Light within us. Then we will not aspire.

God wants us to live on earth. God does not want us to live in the Himalayan caves and negate the world. Far from it. Those days are gone. Let us accept the world as such, and then, on the strength of our intense inner cry, God will tell us, "Try, my children, to change the face of the world." When we think of desires, there is no end. They are like teeming clouds. But, when we think of aspiration, it is only one thing: God, God the Truth, God the Light. So, if we think of only God the Truth and the Light, we will see that automatically the world of desire will fade away. It is like two poles: the North Pole and South Pole. If I am running towards the North Pole, towards my Goal, and it is aspiration that is carrying me there, then naturally I will not be able to see the South Pole. So, overcoming desire is like that. If we aspire, God will give us the necessary strength to be freed from teeming desires. Each human being has the potentiality.

Now, if the human being wants to be a seeker, he has to give primary importance to aspiration. If he cries for God, God knows that his body here on earth is of great importance. The body is the fort. The body is the temple. If there is no temple, how can there be a shrine? So, God will protect him. God will give him the necessary capacity to protect the temple as well. Otherwise, if the temple is broken, the shrine inside the temple cannot remain. God will give us what we need to sustain the body. We have to accept the world, and for that God has given us a body. If we utilise the body properly and divinely, then here on earth we can work for God.

212. So, if God gives us succour, helps us, and we aspire for God, will those necessities and our desire to satisfy them remain as long as we are alive?

Sri Chinmoy: No. No. No. We have to know that there are two things here on earth. One thing is pleasure, another thing is joy. We know that there is a great difference between pleasure and joy. What is actually happening is that the human world, the outer consciousness, is crying for pleasure; and each time pleasure is fulfilled, we see that frustration looms large in our pleasure. But, if we feel that joy is coming into our lives, then joy grows from joy into more joy, abundant joy, boundless joy. So, when there is real joy within us – when we meditate for five minutes or ten minutes – we get inner joy that fulfils us. But, when we think of pleasure, of buying something unnecessary like a Cadillac or something of that sort, we are fulfilling our pleasure there. Soon after, we are frustrated because the one we have got is not big enough; we want something more comfortable. We are running after comfort here. If we run after comfort with the help of our desire, then naturally we will not be satisfied. But, if we cry for joy, inner joy, then each time we run towards fulfilment because inner joy wants us only to fulfil God; and only by fulfilling God can we be really fulfilled.

213. You quoted some words of Jesus Christ, whom you called the Son of God. When some of his followers asked him the way to God, he said, "I am the Way. No one comes to the Father but by me." How important do you think Jesus was?

Sri Chinmoy: How important to whom? To me, or to everybody? I cannot speak on behalf of humanity. I can speak only on the strength of my inner realisation. He is highly important, most important. When he says that he is the Way, he is speaking on behalf of his Father, on the strength of his inseparable Oneness. Here he is not speaking as an individual human being who says, "If you want to see the Truth, I am the only person who can show it to you. You have to come through me." No. He is not speaking in that sense. Nor is he speaking as an ordinary human being who is jealous of others, or who feels that he is the only person who is realised, so that others who are not realised must go through him. No. Here it is his inseparable, his highest Oneness with the Way and the Goal. He feels that it is through him, the Christ, that everybody has to go; not through the human personality, Jesus, but through the divinised, absolutely Realised Being. So, when he says that everybody has to go through him, that he is the Way, we have to know that it is he, the Saviour, who actually had the highest, most all-pervading Realisation, and not the human being who stayed on earth for thirty-three years.

214. I would like you to clarify your concept of God. You jump from the Upanishads to the Bhagavad-Gita and over to the New Testament with this unifying element of God. But it seems to me that the Judeo-Christian concept of a God that is both personal and infinite is a little different from the idea of God as the Absolute, the One, the Supreme Being who is obviously Infinite but, it seems to me, Impersonal. Could you please clarify your concept?

Sri Chinmoy: Everybody has to define God in his own way. God is Personal. God is Impersonal. God is everything. Now, if somebody says that God is this and He cannot be something else, then you and I will naturally contradict him. What right has he to say that God is only this? He may say that God is Personal. No. I have experienced that God is Impersonal. Now, somebody will say that God is infinite Light. A third person will say that God is infinite Power or Energy. God, being the Infinite, has given us the opportunity to realise Him in infinite ways. Each one is right in his own way, on the strength of his realisation. So some of the spiritual Masters, including the Christ, say that God is a Personal Being, the Father. All right. Now, let us take Him as the Father, Divine Father, All-pervading Father. There, immediately you may think of Him as Personal.

Sri Ramakrishna used to call Him Mahakali, Mother Kali. In this case, He was seen as a personal Deity, or Transcendental Mother. Again, there are some spiritual Masters who did not meditate on God's personal Aspect in this way. They meditated on God in His Impersonal Aspect, as the Infinite expanse of water or Light. They are also right. You, as a seeker, have to feel which aspect of God is best suited to you. Perhaps you don't want to be satisfied with only one aspect of God. You want to realise God in various aspects. You want God the Personal, God the Impersonal, God the infinite Light, God the infinite Peace, Bliss and all that. So God, being All-Compassionate, is bound to fulfil your aspiration in that way too.

So, in our spiritual life, each seeker has to feel the necessity of realising God in his own way. In that way he will be most convinced and he will be most fulfilled. God defies all definition, but again each individual, when he meditates or prays to God, feels that there is a way for him to realise God. When he sees God in one aspect, he feels, "Oh, it is more than enough for me!" The Ganges runs all the way from the Himalayas, yet, at any one particular point, if you taste just a tiny drop of the Ganges, you can feel that you are drinking the water of the Ganges. So, in the spiritual life also, when you think of infinite Light or Peace or Bliss flowing down, you also feel that just an iota of this peace, light and Bliss is fulfilling you; at that time, God's Impersonal Aspect may not or need not bother your aspiring soul. Right now, many people are afraid, if I may say, of the Impersonal Aspect of God. They want God the Personal.

They want to see God, talk to God face to face, as a human divine Being. But again, there are some who want only God as an infinite expanse of Light, Peace and Bliss. They are perfectly right in their aspiration and when they realise God in that aspect, their realisation will be equally important and fulfilling.

215. If we have an experience which we feel may be coming from God, in objective truth, how do we know we are experiencing God, the Devil or anything but our own imagination?

Sri Chinmoy: God the Devil will destroy you, but the real God, the compassionate God, will fulfil you. Here, when you meditate, if you get inner peace, or inner joy, then immediately you feel that there is some truth, there is some light that is compelling you to go faster, to move forward, or to go upward, or to dive inward. But if you feel that it is the opposite of that, then naturally some wrong forces, hostile forces, are entering into you. Where there is Light, you have to feel there is joy; and where there is joy, real joy, divine joy, there fulfilment is bound to take place. You must know that the spiritual life is not a life of imagination. It is something real, absolutely real.

216. How does death affect a human being's quest to aspire and to come face to face with God?

Sri Chinmoy: Yesterday I gave a talk on this matter at Kent University. The subject was, "Is Death the End?" I spoke elaborately on this yesterday, but now I wish to say regarding death that nothing is ended. If someone has aspired here, say for ten, fifteen or twenty years and has not yet realised the highest Truth, he will come back again. He has to realise the Highest here on earth; God-realisation has to take place here, here on earth.

Death is like a stopping place on the road of Eternity and life is the traveller, the eternal traveller. The soul is the guide. When the traveller becomes tired and exhausted, the guide says, "Take a rest, for a long or a short time, and then afterwards start your journey again."

In our spiritual life, when we meditate, we see that we have gone far beyond the domain of death. The eternal Life, the boundless Life, is here in our consciousness. We come into existence and here we stay and play our roles of transitory life for fifty, sixty or seventy years. Then we pass through a transitory period of death, which is rest.

The body dies. The soul goes back to its own region. The soul knows how much it has achieved or how much it has offered to the world at large here. Now, before it enters into the world again, it will have an interview with the Highest Supreme and will make a solemn promise to Him concerning what it will do in its next incarnation here on earth. Then, with the Blessings of God, it will come down again.

So now, the progress that the soul has made through its aspiration here, towards its own self-revelation, is not lost at all at death because the soul has carried with it all the light that it has acquired.

If we live the life of aspiration, nothing is lost. Nothing. Temporary rest we take, like a soldier who is tired and takes rest for some time and then returns to the battlefield. Here, the soldier has to fight against doubt, fear, worry, anxiety, imperfections, limitations and ignorance. These are the enemies he has to conquer.

But, to come back to your question: nothing is lost. The soul will come back again to this earth arena which it has left. It will return with a higher promise, a higher light, a deeper message from God.

217. If meditation is the only way of seeing God face to face, how would you advise the man who has a family to look after, to lead the spiritual life and see God face to face?

Sri Chinmoy: The family man, early in the morning when he gets up, what does he do? What does he think of? He thinks of the members of his family, the education of his children and so forth. But if, before he enters into his earthly activities, he can meditate, if he can think of God, say for five minutes, this five minutes nobody can steal from him. Yes, he shoulders responsibility, he has to think of his whole, large earthly family. But again, who shoulders the responsibility of the entire universe? Not he, not the members of his family, but God, God Himself. God Himself shoulders this problem of the entire world.

Now, if for five minutes the family man, the head of the family, meditates on God, on Light – for God means Light – then the Light descends. It starts to decrease his worries and anxieties. When you concentrate for any purpose, perhaps to learn something, whatever you want to do becomes easier. A student, when he does not concentrate on his studies, may read a poem ten times to commit it to memory. He finds it difficult, he cannot do it. But, when he concentrates for five minutes and then reads the poem, he learns it. He just reads it once or twice and it is all memorised.

So, similarly, if an individual who has big family problems meditates for five or ten minutes before he thinks of his family, it will immediately help him in minimising the difficulties he faces and also the Light that he will receive will operate in him. He has not to meditate ten or twelve hours like others. He knows that his progress will not necessarily be very fast. Slow and steady wins the race. But, he has to know why he is thinking of his children and members of his family. Not because they are dear to him. No. But because God is inside him and inside his dearest ones. If every day you try to feel God, the living God, inside your children, then immediately you are seeing and feeling the Light within them. It is also a form of real meditation. But we don't do that. We look at our children as our possessions and feel that we have every right to mould them and guide them according to our sweet will. We feel that we know best. But, if we see, if we feel that we love our children, the members of our family, precisely because God is inside them, and if we think of that and we meditate on it, we will see that we are doing the highest form of meditation. The son should be dearest to the father, not because he is the son, but because the father feels the son embodies the highest Light, which is God. If he loves his son for that purpose, knowing that God is inside him, then he is doing his meditation.

XII – QUESTIONS AND ANSWERS, AMERICAN COLLEGE, PARIS

218. Are you the basis of some religious group? What is the name of the religion that you stand for? What do you do?

Sri Chinmoy: I happen to be a spiritual Teacher. I have a few hundred disciples in the United States and in various places all over the world. I teach them concentration, meditation and contemplation, the things that are required in order to realise one's inmost Truth. I act like a private tutor. I help them in their search for God-realisation. My disciples come to me for inner guidance. I have Centres in quite a few places. I visit these places from time to time. My headquarters are in New York. I have been in the States for the last six years. I have come to this part of the world and here, if somebody wants inspiration, it is my hope that I may be of some service to him. From inspiration one enters into aspiration. Those who are already aspiring can go deeper and higher, in order to realise the highest Truth. So, I move around and if I can help any sincere seeker who needs my service, I feel I have played my role, I have played my part. This is what I have been doing so far.

219. What is your approach to the Truth?

Sri Chinmoy: My philosophy is Love, Devotion and Surrender. There are various approaches to the Truth. There are many roads that lead to Rome. My philosophy is the philosophy of divine Love, divine Devotion and divine Surrender. Human love we all know. It is nothing uncommon to us. Human love means possession. It culminates in frustration. But divine Love is expansion. Here there is no bondage. Here one does not bind anything. One tries to free oneself and one tries to free mankind on the strength of one's conscious oneness with God.

220. Is this true what you talk about? The Realisation of God?

Sri Chinmoy: This is my realisation and I am trying to offer it to those who are sincerely seeking the Truth, to those who are interested in my path. This is my own realisation based on love, devotion and surrender. This is my approach. There are many paths, but my path happens to be this.

221. Have you heard of the International Society of Krishna Consciousness? Do you share the belief that the animals, plants and all objects are just another physical embodiment of the Spirit's soul?

Sri Chinmoy: Yes, I have heard of them. I wish to say that God is everywhere. God is in this table. God is in the chair. God is in the wall. He is everywhere. So I believe in God the Omnipresent. As I believe in God the Omniscient, Omnipotent, so I believe in God the Omnipresent.

222. Don't you believe in hell?

Sri Chinmoy: We don't believe in hell according to the way the Christian belief goes. We believe that hell is right inside us and Heaven is also right inside us. It is all in the mind. This moment, I am thinking of something good, something divine. I pray, I meditate and I try to offer the inner light that I have gained from my meditation and prayers. This is when I am living in Heaven. But this moment, if I think evil of you, criticise you and cherish wrong thoughts about you, then I am in perfect hell. Hell we create. Heaven we create. With our divine thoughts we are creating Heaven. Again, with our wrong thoughts, silly thoughts, undivine thoughts, we are creating hell within us.

223. Sir, I have read of astral power, that through meditation one can bring out one's inner part and travel. Have you ever done that?

Sri Chinmoy: Well, I have done it hundreds of times, thousands of times. We call it the astral body. It is inside the physical body. It is the astral body with which we take astral journeys. The astral world is in the vital world. If you practise spirituality you will also acquire this kind of ability. We have six major centres. There is a special yoga called kundalini yoga. If you follow kundalini yoga, you can open up these centres. These centres are not in the physical body proper; otherwise the doctors would have discovered them long ago. They are in our subtle body. If you can open up all the centres in the subtle body, there you can have all the powers which we call occult powers. You can easily travel all over the world with your astral body.

224. How does someone go about meditating if he has never done it before? How is he going to start meditating? What sort of steps should he take and what should he expect? What can help him at the start?

Sri Chinmoy: In the beginning if one wants to start he has first of all to read some spiritual books, religious books, preferably written by the spiritual Masters and not by the professors and scholars. He will soon realise that a writer who has realised the Truth and God can give him infinitely more inspiration than any book written by an unrealised man. Further, inspiration is not enough. The book may have given him knowledge about realisation, but it may not be helping him as a practical guide. So what he needs at that time is a Teacher.

You have to go to a spiritual Teacher who can show you how to meditate. Just because you are inspired, you have every right to go to a spiritual Teacher and ask him for a favour. Your fee at that time is your inspiration and your aspiration. You want to aspire. Since you are offering him your fee, he is bound to accept you. You are studying here at the university. You are paying the fee and you are a student of this university.

Every individual will realise God, but every individual needs help. For your outer knowledge you have come to the university, and there is somebody here to teach you. Similarly, for your inner knowledge also, one who has got inner knowledge will be able to help you in studying the inner subject, which is meditation.

225. Is it possible, without dying, for the soul to leave the body? That is, could you still function without your soul?

Sri Chinmoy: Only for a short time you can. When you are asleep, sometimes the soul moves around. It leaves for a few minutes or for an hour or for a few hours. The soul can leave the body at other times as well for a short period.

226. But what happens to you when you have no soul?

Sri Chinmoy: During my deep meditation many times, like a bird, I go from here to there. I live in New York but I go to Jamaica, West Indies; I go to Puerto Rico and so many other places. My disciples see me there then as clearly as you see me here now. It is a matter of a few minutes. The soul's minutes are different from our minutes. In one second the soul can do hundreds of things, whereas in one second I can only move my finger. I can just move a yard or so. But if the soul really leaves the body, then naturally the body cannot stay without it. If the bird flies away from the cage, then the cage is useless. It is only when the bird stays in the cage that we go and see the cage.

227. I have some friends who do Christian meditation. They read the Bible and they have been inspired by that. They have been able to really meditate on the Bible, but whenever they felt that they had come close to God there was always a presence of evil around. Why is this? Can it be avoided?

Sri Chinmoy: No, that is not true. I mean I am saying this from the viewpoint of our path. I have no right to speak about the Christian belief or your friend. In our path we say that there are two poles: North Pole and South Pole. Let us say the South Pole is darkness and the North Pole is light. Now, if my aim is to reach the North Pole which is all light, then as soon as I enter into my destination it will be all light. There can be no darkness. Yes, for a short while we enter into the corridors of darkness, but we know that our aim is to reach the North Pole where it is all light. Now in this room here, if you turn off the light, then there will be no light. Suppose that for ten days or twenty days nobody enters into this hall. There will be all darkness, true. But the moment somebody comes and turns on the light there will be light. So in the being also, if somebody remains in ignorance, in darkness for ten years, fifteen years, twenty years or forty years, it doesn't mean that he will never be illumined. Yes, for forty years he was in deep darkness. But the moment somebody enters into the room and has the capacity to illumine it, the darkness disappears. Here we need an electrician to bring in light if there is no light. Similarly, in the spiritual life we need an electrician, whom we call a spiritual Master. He helps in bringing us the light. In a spiritual person it is a slightly different matter because the light is already there, in the aspirant. The spiritual Master is not giving his own light. You have the light, only you do not know where your light is. So the spiritual Master helps you in seeing the light within you.

If once you see the light, how can there be darkness? Where is darkness here now? You tell me.

228. This friend of mine had no religion. She didn't care about religion. She was very wild when she was at college. But then she was inspired to open the Bible for some reason. She felt very pulled to it and she started to study it more and more. Then she joined some Christian meditation group. But at one point she said she kept getting things, like somebody was bothering her. She said it was from the Devil. But finally her belief got stronger, so it stopped. What was it that actually happened to her? Was this trouble she had something good for her?

Sri Chinmoy: Yes. It was an experience. As her faith in God was stronger than the evil forces that she was encountering, naturally she could succeed. She did succeed. It is our faith in God that can enable us to overcome all negative forces. But although she was stronger, while she was fighting against evil forces, if she had felt that there was no Light, no Light from within or from the Beyond, naturally she would have become a victim to the evil forces. Then she would have been destroyed. Since her faith in God was genuine and strong, finally she saw the Light. The darkness did not conquer her, could not conquer her.

229. Some people who have reached Enlightenment have felt compelled through compassion to serve other people in the sense of spreading their Enlightenment, like you for instance. Whereas other people have retired with their Enlightenment to live almost solitary lives. Which is the best? What makes them make this kind of choice?

Sri Chinmoy: Now, it is like this. There are many students every year from each university, hundreds of students, who get their Master's degrees. You see though that only a few go on to enter into the teaching line. Some people get their Master's degree and then they enter into some office or industry or some consulate. Again, some enter into the universities and they start teaching. But they all have got their degree. In the spiritual life also, some people have realised God, but they feel that it is not necessary for them to spread light or to help mankind. It might seem as if they have gotten their realisation just for their own sake. But they really have enlightenment, and you cannot deny it. You cannot say that that person has not got his degree, I mean the inner degree of illumination. Again, some others feel, "No, let us help."

Some people get their Master's degree and then teach, while on the other hand, others do not teach after getting their Master's degrees. They do not try to teach at the universities or anywhere. They enter into various fields, various walks of life. In the spiritual life also, some realised souls will feel that they crossed the barriers of ignorance and they are now really tired. It is not an easy thing to realise God, to get illumination. Now they feel that they have acted like real divine heroes in the battlefield of life. They fought against fear, doubt, anxieties, worries, imperfections, limitations, bondage and so forth. They feel they have every right to withdraw if they ask God and if God allows them. If God says, "All right, now you no longer have to take part. Don't take any conscious part in the Cosmic Game. You just observe", then, if they have got permission from God, naturally they can remain silent. But again, those people who are not taking part in helping mankind, say they are meditating, are also doing something very great because their will has become one with God's Will. That is to say, they do not enter into any kind of conflict with God's Will. Ordinary human beings will desire many things, will do many things against God's Will consciously or unconsciously. These realised people, realised souls, may not take active part, they may not go from one place to another or they may not open up spiritual Centres and so forth, but they will offer their conscious good will to mankind. How many people are offering their good will to mankind? We quarrel, we fight, we do many things, we act like animals. But the spiritual people who have got their own illumination will try to offer that illumination inwardly, that is to say through their conscious good will to mankind. They take God's permission and withdraw. God says, "All right, My son, do not take active part, but you be the observer. You be the witness. Let your other brothers who want to work here for us do it. Let them do it." Then they obey Him. So here we cannot say that one is greater because he is crying for mankind, because he is trying to help. Only he is great who listens to God's Will. God has told that particular Teacher, spiritual Master who has got illumination, "You don't have to offer your light. You just inwardly give. Outwardly you do not have to move around and all that. Inwardly give your good will to mankind." Similarly, to me or to others, He will say, "No. I want you to move around and give the light, the inner light that you have. If people want to have it, be of service to them. If they don't want it, it is up to them." So, what is most important is to listen to God's Will at that time. If God tells me to take an active part I will take it. Also if God says, "No, I don't need you to take an active part; you just offer your good will to mankind in silence. That is all," I will listen to His Will.

230. Would God send you a dream? Do you believe in spiritual dreams? What do they actually mean? Can dreams come true?

Sri Chinmoy: Certainly, we do believe in dreams. But we have to know there are many places from which dreams come. Sometimes from the subconscious world we get many dreams which have no value. Sometimes we get dreams from the higher worlds.

When we get dreams from the higher worlds these dreams are bound to materialise. Today's dream is tomorrow's reality. Why? Because the dream is coming from a world which is living, palpable. Only with our limited consciousness we do not know this. When we meditate we enter into many worlds consciously and the reality of these worlds enters into us in our dream. If the dream is from a higher world, it is fulfilled today or tomorrow. It has to be fulfilled. But, if it is just from the subconscious world, where we are quarrelling, fighting and doing so many undivine things, then it need not materialise.

231. How can you tell the difference [between dreams from higher worlds and those from the subconscious world] ?

Sri Chinmoy: When you study you know many things, many, many things, and you know the difference between this and that. So also when you meditate you will come to recognise the difference. When you meditate, immediately you will be able to enter into these worlds, but this takes time. How many years have you been studying in order to get your Master's degree? Similarly, in the spiritual world I spent twenty years studying, practising the spiritual life. For twenty years I was at a particular spiritual institution. Twenty years right from my childhood I spent practising and that is why I am in this position. If you study something for twenty years I am sure you will also be an authority on that particular subject.

232. Six or seven times my uncle has had very vivid dreams which have actually happened on the physical plane after he has awakened. He believes that it is the soul that is giving him the message. Is he right about that? Can we all learn to interpret our dreams?

Sri Chinmoy: It is absolutely true. If you get the messages from up above, they are bound to take place. The thing is that if we meditate, if we concentrate, we consciously enter into the dream worlds. Now the dream world to us is something vague, uncertain, obscure to some extent. But if we study we come to know many things. Because you are studying here you have gathered, amassed knowledge. If you study inner life, naturally you will be inundated with the inner knowledge. It is a matter of studying. Self-knowledge is self-cultivation, inner discovery. When you study you discover many things. Similarly, if you study inwardly, then you will discover the inner life. There everything is recorded; we have only to unfold it.

XIII – QUESTIONS AND ANSWERS, UNIVERSITY OF LONDON

233. Do you suggest any special kind of mantra or meditation?

Sri Chinmoy: In my case, I teach my disciples how to meditate. I have a few hundred disciples. I teach them meditation. I have given mantras to a few, but I prefer meditation. I teach them collective meditation. Again, I teach them individually when I see that they need an individual meditation. They come to our Centres. We have a few Centres and the students come there and I teach them how to meditate. Mantras are important, extremely important, but I feel that meditation includes everything. If you can meditate well for, say, ten or fifteen minutes, then it will serve the same purpose that the mantras serve. When we repeat a mantra, it offers us a particular result. While using a mantra, we may pray to a particular god or invoke some particular god to give us Peace, Light, Bliss or something else that we want or need. But, when we meditate, we enter into a vast expanse of Peace, Light and Bliss. So, in my case I ask my disciples to meditate. Of course there is no hard and fast rule. I *have* given mantras to a few selected disciples. But in most cases I have advised my disciples to meditate.

234. When you say "meditate", do you mean to meditate on something, on some particular god or something? How does one who has had no experience go about meditating?

Sri Chinmoy: First of all, I have to say here at this point that my students and disciples each have a picture of me which was taken when I was in my highest Transcendental Consciousness. All those who claim to be my disciples meditate on that picture every day. I tell them to concentrate and meditate on that picture. When they meditate they either feel that they are entering into me, into my inner Consciousness, or they feel that I am entering into them. I have simplified the matter. There are some among them who have received specific meditations from me. Again, there are many who have recently joined me. I tell them, "I shall meditate on your behalf if you give me the chance." The picture that I ask them to meditate on was taken when I was in my own highest Consciousness. There, I am absolutely one with my Inner Pilot. I tell my disciples, when they meditate on the picture, "Either you enter into me, or allow me to enter into you. Then I shall meditate on your behalf." So this is how my disciples meditate.

About others who are not my disciples, when they ask me individually, say here at the lecture hall, I tell them to try to control their thoughts, not to allow any thoughts to come in. The mind has to be vacant, calm, quiet. At the beginning it is impossible for an aspirant to be free from thoughts, ideas, the memories of the past and so forth. I tell them, "Feel that it is you who have to conquer your nature." Right now, a monkey is beside you, constantly pinching and biting you. You need not be afraid of the monkey. You just exercise your inner strength, inner power, and threaten the monkey. When he is threatened, the monkey stops biting you. Similarly, the undivine thoughts that are pinching, biting and disturbing your mind can easily be conquered by you.

Now, say you are standing at the door of your house. It is up to you to open the door to admit anyone. You are inside. If you see that your enemies are outside wanting to come in, naturally you won't allow them in; but if you see that your friends are waiting, immediately you will allow them in. In the beginning you have to be very careful and cautious not to allow just anybody to come into your house. When you do open the door, your mental door, you will admit only those thoughts, divine thoughts, that will encourage you, inspire you, uplift your consciousness. They are your friends. Doubt, fear, anxieties and worries are your enemies. If they want to enter, immediately lock the door. Don't allow them in. A seeker who has no spiritual Master, who has no guide, has to practise meditation in this way. First he has to make his mind absolutely calm and quiet. No thought, no iota of thought, must enter into his mind. He has to feel that he is standing behind the door. The door is locked. Nobody is to enter. Then, later, he has to allow only the divine thoughts, the divine ideas to enter. He must let them grow gradually, gradually. Also he will sow the seed of divine Truth inside his mind. Then, after a few years, he will gather a bumper crop of realisation. This is what the seekers should do, if they do not have a personal Master or Guru.

But, when you have a Master, a Pilot, a Boatman, once you are in his boat, it is his responsibility to take you to the Golden Shore. While you are seated in the boat, you can sing, you can sleep, you can do anything you want to. Once you enter into the tube, the subway, you can do anything. But, in order to enter, you have to get a ticket. After you purchase the ticket, you have to board the train which takes you to your destination. Now, the ticket for the spiritual life is aspiration. The real fee is aspiration. If you have aspiration, and if you have found your Master, then meditation becomes infinitely easier.

235. At your Centre, if you set one up here, will it be somewhere that people can come at intervals and discuss spiritual matters and meditate? What sort of meetings do you have at the Centres existing now?

Sri Chinmoy: Let us speak about our New York Centre, which is our main Centre. We have a few Centres: New York, Puerto Rico, Connecticut, Miami and the West Indies; but I stay most of the time at the New York Centre.

On Thursdays my disciples come to my place. There I hold a very high meditation. That is to say, during that meeting I don't speak. The disciples come in and for about two hours, sometimes more, they meditate in front of me. Very often, I ask them to come to the front of the room in groups of ten or twelve at a time. They sit in front of me, and I enter into my highest Consciousness. Then I enter into them. I enter into each individual soul, and I see what each soul wants me to offer. Whatever they want I offer them in utmost silence. If they want Peace, they get Peace. If they want Light, they get Light.... There is no talking at all. The disciples receive according to their inner receptivity. Some may be extremely receptive while others are not so receptive. According to their receptivity they receive whatever I bring down from above on Thursdays.

On Sundays I give a short talk on the spiritual life, on meditation, Yoga and so forth. Then the disciples ask me questions. Often I go to the universities to give talks, and my students also attend these. On Sundays, in order to convince the minds of the disciples of the reality of what they are doing on Thursdays, I give talks. I answer their questions. We may meditate and get inner joy. But then when we re-enter the physical mind we are frustrated, we doubt ourselves. We ask, "Was it proper meditation or was it all mental hallucination?" After meditation we start doubting ourselves. But, if the seekers of the truth listen to the spiritual Master, then their doubts disappear. Their mind is also convinced that their meditation on Thursday was something real, genuine, and not hallucination. That is why I hold meetings on Sundays where these things can be discussed.

236. What does the United Nations Meditation Group do? Who belongs to this group? What kind of meetings do you hold?

Sri Chinmoy: The United Nations Meditation Group meets every Tuesday, when I go to the United Nations to hold meditation from twelve noon to one p.m. The representatives from various parts of the world and the staff members of the Secretariat come there to meditate. For about half an hour I meditate with them. I look at each individual seeker for a couple of seconds and try to lift, to elevate, their consciousness. I must say, the seekers who come there are extremely sincere. We hold our meditation in the Peace Room. They come, they meditate and they are inundated with inner peace. After that, usually I give a short talk for ten minutes or so. Then I invite questions, one serious question and sometimes two. We hold our meditation there every Tuesday. I am extremely glad and fortunate to be able to tell you that very recently I received a letter from the Secretary-General U Thant, appreciating our achievements. We have received two letters from him appreciating our spiritual activities in the Peace Room.

237. When you first came to the platform this evening, before you began to speak, you, I presume, meditated a bit. What exactly were you doing? Were you receiving any feeling from the people here this evening?

Sri Chinmoy: Yes. I did quite a few things. First, when I stood up here I personally entered into a very high plane of consciousness. To be very frank with you, it was not my highest plane of consciousness. My highest plane is infinitely higher. But I did go very high. Then I tried to enter into the aspiring souls. Here, most of you are aspiring. I tried to raise you to your divine heights. When I saw that some of you, not all, had responded to my inner call, I felt that the time had come for me to speak. At that time your souls became in tune with my soul. Then, even if I had not spoken a word, if I had not said anything at all and just meditated with all of you here for about half an hour or forty minutes, my purpose in coming here would have been served, perhaps even in a more convincing way. There the communication would have been more meaningful and successful. But unfortunately I have come here to give a talk. In silence, spiritual Masters do infinitely more meaningful and significant things than they do through speech. On the one hand we try to elevate the consciousness of the seekers; on the other hand, it is we who bring down the consciousness in inviting questions. *We* bring it down, but this is unfortunately unavoidable. People come to listen and we try to offer our light. Again, as I said before, it is to convince the physical mind that we do this; we talk and answer spiritual questions. I entered into a high plane of consciousness, and from there I tried to elevate the aspiring consciousness of the seekers here. When I saw that they were in tune with me, I started talking.

238. When you go into your highest consciousness, do you leave your body?

Sri Chinmoy: No, I do not leave my body when I enter into my highest consciousness. Nobody has to leave his body in order to enter into his highest consciousness.

When I enter into my highest consciousness, I do not allow my physical mind to operate, I do not allow the earthly physical consciousness to operate at all. When I give extemporaneous talks, I stay most of the time in a state of consciousness far beyond the mind. But when I answer questions, my knowing and illumining mind operates. Sometimes during my talks I look to this side and that side in order to get sublime ideas. And at that time I get divine thoughts either from within or from without. When I answer questions, it is altogether a different matter.

239. Do you believe that everyone can meditate as you would like people to meditate? For instance, I have been to meditation classes, and I find it extremely difficult to meditate. When I meditate, to a certain degree I feel relaxed. But frankly, I feel no more than that.

Sri Chinmoy: Do you have a Teacher, a spiritual Master?
Seeker: Not really. There is someone I went to who is not a real Teacher, not a Guru.
Sri Chinmoy: Unfortunately there is the difficulty. You need a spiritual Teacher. You need a personal interview with your Teacher in order to discuss the problems in your spiritual life with him. In our New York Centre one has to wait for six months for a personal interview with me. But whenever I go out of New York, if I see some seekers who are really sincere, then I give them a short interview for ten or twelve minutes. At that time the seeker need not be my disciple, far from it. Just because he is a sincere seeker, I try to help him in whatever way I can. But it is necessary to have a spiritual Master of your own. Again, you have to know that a spiritual Teacher is not like an ordinary teacher or professor. He is like a private tutor. A professor will simply pass or fail you in a course according to your own standard. A tutor is not like that. A tutor helps you wholeheartedly and unconditionally so that you can pass your examination well. Your task is to swim across the sea of ignorance with the help of an able Master. You need a spiritual Master. You have to get a Master of your own.

240. Is there a Master that you know of in London that you would recommend?

Sri Chinmoy: I came to London just the other day. I do not know anybody here. I can only suggest to all of you here that, if some of you are really interested in the spiritual life, meditation and so forth, then you must form a small group, like a family, where three or four persons can meditate together. This will help you to some extent in your spiritual life.

Unfortunately I do not know any spiritual Master here, otherwise I would immediately have mentioned someone you could try.

241. On what criteria does a seeker take a prospective Master? How can you tell a good one from a bad one?

Sri Chinmoy: Again, it is a matter of inner feeling. Now you see that you have quite a few universities in England. What do you do? Your inner being or something from within tells you, "Go to London University." In England there are many universities, but you feel from within that London University is better for you than Cambridge or Oxford or some other place. That is why you are studying here. As regards your inner life also, you can make your own selection.

In the spiritual life there is a way of knowing one's own Master. Here, the student, the seeker himself, has to play the role of a teacher. How? He has to give marks to the Master. You know that there are quite a few spiritual Masters all over the world. You will write down their names. Write down the names of ten spiritual Masters. Then, you repeat the name of the first Master on the list seven times. You write him on your heart. Then try to see what kind of feeling you get. If you feel an inner thrill, then you give him sixty per cent or seventy per cent. Then you repeat the next Master's name. If you get no feeling from him, you give him zero. Then again, you meditate on somebody else, the next on the list. Repeat his name seven times. If you find you get a greater thrill than you got with the first one, then you give him seventy-five per cent or eighty per cent. You do this with all the spiritual Masters on your list. Then, the one who gets the highest mark from you is bound to be your Master.

This inner thrill that you feel is not false pleasure or anything of that sort; it is real inner ecstasy that you are getting. The moment one hears the very name of the Master, or one sees the Master, one immediately enters into the highest realm of bliss according to one's own capacity. This has been the experience of many of my students and disciples, just after hearing my name. They have not seen me, but just by seeing my picture in the newspaper, or by hearing someone mention my name to them on the telephone, they have felt an inner thrill from within; now they have become my disciples. Again, there are many who come to me who are not meant for me, who have heard me talking at the universities or some other places, but who didn't feel anything in me. They are perfectly right in going to some other Master who is destined to be their Master.

So, in your case, if you are looking for a Master, you kindly be the judge. You give them marks and see who deserves the highest mark from you. He who gets the highest mark is bound to be your Master. This mark you will give according to your inner ecstasy.

242. *Just following up that question, I feel that I don't require the guidance or tuition of any particular Master. There have been many Masters: the Christ, Buddha, Krishna. Now, I feel that I can get the same from any one of them as I can get from a living Master. Isn't that true?*

Sri Chinmoy: No. Unfortunately that is not so. It is true that Krishna, Buddha and the Christ were Masters of the highest calibre, but what happens is that if you get a living Master then it becomes much easier. Every day, in your daily activities, it will be easier for you if you have a living Master.

Today, if your son falls sick, then you can immediately approach your spiritual Master who is on earth. You don't have to go deep within to contact him. If you are in difficulty today, if you are depressed or some calamity takes place in the family, then immediately you can approach him here. Your living Master comes to your immediate rescue. Further, when it is a matter of aspiration also, he can sit right in front of you and teach you how to meditate. Otherwise, you may meditate for hours, yet you may feel that you are walking through a stony desert, a stormy night. Without a living Master, walking along the path is an extremely long and difficult process. If a living Master is right in front of you, and sees you face to face, then you can give to him all your earthly frustration as a human being – just as in the case of Krishna and Arjuna, who stayed side by side. Arjuna offering his doubts, his fears, his everything, to Krishna. Finally, Arjuna was illumined by Krishna. So similarly, in your spiritual life today, if you get a living Master it becomes infinitely easier.

Yes, if you meditate on Krishna or the Christ, certainly you will realise God. But if you want to go faster, you need a living Master. It will be easier and faster for you if you see somebody who can illumine your consciousness and whom you can approach at your sweet will. It is difficult to approach the spiritual

Masters who have left the body. You have to go deep within, cry deep within, to get their Blessings. If you have a Master right beside you, you can offer to him all your sufferings, all your anxieties, worries and doubts. In this way it is much easier. It is not that the other Masters of the hoary past are not necessary. They are of paramount importance. But, if you want to make the life of aspiration simple, easy, and if you want to run faster and safer, then you have to get the help of a living spiritual Master.

XIV – QUESTIONS AND ANSWERS, KEBLE COLLEGE, OXFORD UNIVERSITY

243. Could you say something about breathing in meditation? Are there any practical ways in which breathing can be regulated which will be beneficial to meditation?

Sri Chinmoy: Breathing is of paramount importance during meditation. Now, I wish to advise a beginner that when he wants to breathe correctly, he should sit erect. His spinal cord must remain erect. When he breathes in, he has to breathe slowly and quietly. Then, after a few months of practising slow and quiet breathing, he can start alternate breathing. That is to say, when you breathe in, you breathe through just one nostril, holding the other closed. Do this a few times and then reverse the nostril.

There is another traditional system you can apply. When you breathe in, you can repeat the name of God, or, if your spiritual Master has given you any mantra, you can repeat that. When you breathe in, try to repeat the name or mantra once. When you hold your breath, repeat it four times. And, when you release the breath, at that time repeat it twice. One, four, two. While you are inhaling, count one. While you are holding the breath, count four. While you are exhaling the breath, count two.

This system of breathing is called *Pranayama*. If you want to know more about breathing, you should go to a spiritual Master who has personal experience in breathing. He will teach you how to breathe properly, step-by-step. I always advise a beginner to breathe as slowly and quietly as possible, then later to do this alternate breathing. Then, after that, he can hold just a tiny thread right in front of his nose as he breathes and see if the thread is moving to-and-fro. If it is moving to-and-fro, that means the breathing is not quiet. There is a restless movement in the breathing. If it does not move, if the thread is not disturbed by the breath, then it is Yogic breathing. This you can try for some time. One has to go to one's own spiritual Master, and he will teach this step-by-step. He will observe the disciple's breathing and correct it if it is improper.

While breathing one has to be very careful. That is to say, one has to think of purity first. If, when one breathes in, one feels consciously or unconsciously that the breath that he is using is coming directly from God, from Purity itself, his breath will be purified. Several things can be done to further develop this sense of purity in the breath. First, for a few minutes, try to imagine a flower right in front of your nose. The flower will automatically give you the sense of purity. Either a flower or a candle flame or incense, something that represents purity, that convinces the physical mind, should be imagined in the beginning.

244. Do you think that marriage is necessarily an obstacle on the spiritual path?

Sri Chinmoy: It depends on the individual marriage. If one has the capacity to think of God while carrying on a married life, if his inspiration is tremendous, his inner cry constant, then there is no objection.

But very often what happens is that when one gets married, one is pulled down because a tremendous responsibility commences for him. He wants to run fast but, consciously or unconsciously, he puts a burden on his shoulders. Now, naturally, if a runner wants to run the fastest, and at the same time puts a heavy load on his shoulders, how can he run the fastest?

But again, if somebody wants to accept life, if he feels, "Here on earth I have to establish perfection," then what will he do?

Man will see God in woman and woman will see God in man. Here God is both masculine and feminine. If a man feels that he should take his other half also, so that his realisation will be integral and complete, then he is again in a position to run the fastest towards the Goal. You know there are quite a few spiritual Masters, even Masters of the highest order, who got married. There were some ancient Rishis who were married. Their realisation was in no way inferior to that of others who didn't get married.

Again, we have to know what God wants from the individual. If God wants you not to get married, it is up to God. God feels that in that way you will reach Him. If God wants your friend to get married, if He feels that your friend needs the experience of married life, then this also is the Divine Will. If your friend follows God's dictates, he too, will reach the Goal. So, there is no hard and fast rule. One cannot say that married life is necessarily a hindrance to spiritual realisation. Again, one cannot say that if one does not get married, his life can never be fulfilled. On the other hand, an unmarried man does not necessarily lead a better or purer life. No. He may not be a married person, but his mind may remain in the ordinary vital, lower world. So he will not make any progress.

We have to know what God wants. When we meditate, when we aspire, we come to learn God's Will. If it is God's Will, naturally there will be no difficulty in realising the Truth after entering into married life. But, if it is not God's Will, then we have to be very careful. We are then, consciously or unconsciously, putting a heavy burden on our shoulders. Each individual has to decide if married life is necessary for him personally.

245. I have read in some places that the use of sexual energy means that you use up some spiritual energy at the same time. Is this true? In that case, what can be done if one wants to lead a spiritual life?

Sri Chinmoy: What you have read is absolutely true. The animal human life and divine God-life do not and cannot go together. But one cannot realise God overnight. It is impossible. You don't get your Master's degree in the twinkling of an eye, or in a day, or even in a year. It may require twenty years of study to achieve. God-realisation is also a study, the most difficult subject. It takes quite a few years. Fifteen, twenty, thirty years, even many lifetimes, many incarnations, are required to realise God.

But if you tell a beginner that he will have to give up all his lower vital life and everything of that sort all at once, he will say, "Impossible! How can I do that?" If he has to give up all his lower vital propensities the moment he enters into the spiritual life, he will never enter into the spiritual life at all. So instead, he has to make headway towards his Goal slowly and steadily. He should not try to give up everything all at once. It is just like smoking or drinking. If someone feels that drinking excessively is a serious obstacle to his spiritual life, let him try to minimise it slowly. If he is drinking five times a day, let him try to drink four times a day instead. Then, after a few months, let him try to make it three times a day. Then, after considerable time, he can make it twice. Gradually, slowly, if he tries to diminish his hankering after drinking, he will be successful. This way, it will not tell upon his health. Otherwise, it will only be a great struggle. The body will resist and it will break down.

So, in the spiritual life also, the lower vital nature which you may call sex, has to be gradually conquered. If one enters into the spiritual life and says, "Today I shall conquer all my lower propensities", he is just fooling himself. Tomorrow his mind will be in doubt. His physical mind will torture him. His impure and cruel vital will try to punish him in every way. He will feel miserable. He will be frustrated and inside his frustration will loom his own destruction.

So I advise my students to go slowly. But you have to know that one day you will have to conquer everything, all lower vital movements. But that day is not going to dawn just now for the beginner. We don't get our Master's degree while we are in kindergarten. We come up to the M.A. degree after we have already passed through all the previous grades. So, in the same way, we gradually acquire the knowledge we need for the Highest Truth. Slowly and steadily. But, to attain to the ultimate Truth, the ultimate Goal, the realisation of the highest order, the seeker needs total purification and total transformation of the lower vital.

246. Would you say something about death? What is it? What happens when we die? Can we conquer the fear of death through meditation?

Sri Chinmoy: Very recently I spoke on death. I think it was my first talk here in England – at the University of Kent, Canterbury. "Is Death the End?" was the title.

Now, from the spiritual point of view, death is not the end. Being a spiritual man, I can say on the strength of my own inner realisation that our soul does not die. The body dies. The body is composed of the five elements called *panchabhuta*. At the time of death, the body enters into the physical sheath. The vital enters into the vital sheath. The mind enters into the mental sheath proper, and so forth. The soul flies back to the soul's own region.

Death is nothing but a short or a long rest for the soul. The soul came into the world, and this world is like a battlefield. The soldier does not remain all the time on the battlefield. He fights. Then, either he loses the battle or he dies, or he goes back victorious, triumphant. In the same way, in the spiritual life, we constantly fight. We do not fight against an enemy outside ourselves, but we fight against our own inner enemies: fear, doubt, anxiety and worry. And our worst enemy is death. We are constantly fighting against ignorance, and death is, unfortunately, the fond child of ignorance.

So, a spiritual person sees and knows that death is not the end. It is just like being on a road. He walks along the road and, when anything happens on the road, he takes a short or a long rest. After the rest he walks along the road again. And what is the road? The road is life. We came from Infinite Life, the Life Divine. That Infinite Life stayed here on earth for a short span of time, say fifty or sixty years, during which time it consciously became earthbound. Then this life again passed through the corridor of death, remaining, say, for five years or ten years, or fifteen or twenty years. The time depends upon the individual soul. Then again it comes down into this world and starts functioning here on earth. Its very purpose of coming into this world is to manifest the ultimate Truth. Until the manifestation is complete, its aspiration, realisation remain unfulfilled. So, from the spiritual point of view, a spiritual seeker will always say that death is not the end. It is only a rest.

Very often I have said that you can take death as your bedroom, sleeping room, and life as your living room. When we are in the sleeping room, we don't have to show our life. There we sleep. We do not have to show our life to our friends. No. When we are in the living room, we have to work, we have to show that we are alive, we have to prove that we exist. In the other room, where we take rest, we do not have to show anything. Death is like a room where we take rest for a short time or a long time. Then again we come back to life, the living room, to fulfil our day-to-day tasks.

So, to come back to your question, I wish to say that through meditation we *can* conquer the fear of death. When we meditate, we enter into the endless Life. However, just by entering into the endless Life, we do not possess that Life. For that, we have to meditate and meditate, and then we have to grow into that endless Life.

247. Can you tell us how to choose a Master? How can we know if we have made the right choice?

Sri Chinmoy: I have been asked this question quite a few times. Now, you want to choose a Master. I wish to tell you that God has given you a unique opportunity to choose your own Master. And God has given you the opportunity to be with your Teacher. Now you are looking for a Master. You are a student. God, at this point, gives you the opportunity and capacity to choose your own Master by doing something very simple.

You will write down the names of all the Masters that you have come across or that you have heard of, or that you have found out about in the books you have read. There may be a few: seven, eight or ten names.

Then, take the name of the first spiritual Master on the list and, as you repeat his name, place your right hand on your heart. Try to feel the sound, the palpitation of your heart as you repeat the name seven times. Follow the list. Repeat the name of each Master and, as you do, immediately try to feel the heartbeat. Then, if you feel any joy, delight or ecstasy, instantly write down a mark for it. Mark it say, sixty out of a hundred, or seventy out of a hundred. You have to determine what kind of joy you are getting and then rate it on a scale accordingly.

For each name on the list, as you repeat it seven times with your hand over your heart, try to feel the heartbeat. Then, give each name marks as you listen. Each time, mark whether you feel joy or not. Suppose you get no response, no joy, no inspiration when you repeat the name of a particular Master, then you are in a perfect position to give him zero out of a hundred.

When you get tremendous response from a Master on the list, say you are thrilled all over. His very name sends an enormous thrill from the soles of your feet to the crown of your head, you are bound to give him ninety, ninety-five or even a hundred. Undoubtedly he is your Master. He is meant for you and you are meant for him. Suppose he is not here. He is in India. Then you have to go there. Or, if he is meant for you, circumstances will bring your Master here. If you are meant for him, if you are a chosen disciple of that particular Master, God will without fail either take you to him or bring him to you.

248. Could you explain the difference between Samadhi and self-realisation? I know they are not the same theoretically, but I don't see why they are not.

Sri Chinmoy: They are not the same. Samadhi and self-realisation are not the same because Samadhi is a state in which you can stay only for a few hours, for a few days. You cannot stay in this state for more than twenty-one days. Usually after three weeks the body does not function. The Infinite Grace of the Absolute Supreme has to dawn and take you into another channel of Divine dynamic Consciousness, if it wants you to work for God on earth. As regards realisation, you have to know that once you have achieved realisation, it lasts forever.

Samadhi is an exalted and glowing state of Consciousness, whereas realisation is a conscious, natural and manifesting state of Consciousness.

There are three stages of Samadhi: *Savikalpa Samadhi, Nirvikalpa Samadhi* and *Sahaja Samadhi.* Usually we speak of Savikalpa and Nirvikalpa.

In Savikalpa Samadhi there are thoughts, ideas, but they do not affect the most advanced seeker or the Yogi. The Yogi remains unperturbed. He functions in a dynamic and confident manner.

In Nirvikalpa Samadhi, nature's dance stops. There is no movement. Everything is tranquil. The Knower and the Known have become totally One. The Lover and the Beloved have become One. The Yogi enjoys a supremely divine, all-pervading, self-amorous ecstasy.

Sahaja Samadhi is by far the highest type of Samadhi. Very few spiritual Masters have achieved that state. In Sahaja Samadhi they walk like ordinary human beings. They eat. They do almost all normal things, the usual things that an ordinary human being does. But, in the inmost reaches of their hearts they are surcharged with divine Illumination. After achieving the highest type of realisation, on very rare occasions one is blessed with Sahaja Samadhi. He who has achieved and remains in the Sahaja Samadhi consciously and perfectly manifests God at every second, and thus he is the greatest Pride of the Transcendental Supreme.

The Samadhis that you know, that you are familiar with, are Savikalpa Samadhi and Nirvikalpa Samadhi. Nirvikalpa Samadhi is the highest Samadhi that most spiritual Masters attain and it lasts for a few hours or a few days. Then, one has to come down. You have to know that one cannot operate from that high state of consciousness. One can never operate from Nirvikalpa Samadhi. It is simply impossible. One has to come down. Then, when one comes down, what happens? Very often one forgets one's own name. One cannot speak properly. One forgets one's own age. Many things happen then. Again, through continued practice of this Nirvikalpa Samadhi, gradually, when one comes down, one can immediately act like a human being on earth.

But realisation is something else. When once realisation dawns, the seeker enjoys freedom from the human personality and the human individuality. It is like a tiny drop of water which enters into the ocean. Once it enters, it becomes the ocean. At that time, we don't see the personality of the one tiny drop or the individuality of the drop. It becomes the entire ocean. So realisation is totally different. When one realises the highest Truth, at that time the finite enters into the Infinite and realises and achieves the Infinite as its very own. Then, when somebody else sees such a seeker, he will see that he has become the Ocean itself in his inner life.

249. Is faith something that is given to an individual or something which the individual can acquire through his own actions?

Sri Chinmoy: Everybody has been blessed with faith. Some have much faith; some have little faith. There is nobody on earth who has no faith, either in himself or in God. But what happens? Ignorance or darkness has eclipsed our faith. Again, faith can come out of the meshes of ignorance.

If we pray or meditate we can increase our faith. It is like a muscle. If we take exercise, we develop the muscle. Inner faith also can be expanded. There are many who enter into the spiritual life out of curiosity. They have very little faith. But they go on; they continue, continue. Then later on they feel within themselves deeper faith, greater faith, more fulfilling faith. So, when one sticks to the spiritual path, one is bound to have more faith.

Faith in oneself and faith in God are both of paramount importance. If somebody says he has faith only in God and not in himself, well, he cannot go very far. If he says he has faith only in himself and not in God; if he acts like Julius Caesar and starts saying, "I came, I saw, I conquered – Veni, vidi, vici," he will eventually be lost totally in the evolving process of time. There is no God. It is all mind. No, we have to feel faith both in ourselves and in God. To have faith in God is not so difficult. It is comparatively easy. Why? We know, we feel that God is infinitely better than we are. He is infinitely more Powerful than we are. He is infinitely more Compassionate than we are. We feel that He is Boundless in every way. So it is easy for us to have faith in God who surpasses us in everything. But, we have to know that we must have faith in ourselves too. Yes, God may be superior to us in every way, but how are we going to have His qualities unless and until we have abundant faith in ourselves, in our receptivity, in the power of divinely surrendered acceptance?

If I say that somebody is superior to me in science or in spirituality, then, just by having a little faith in his achievements, I cannot achieve his qualities. I have to also have faith in myself. I have to believe that one day I can also be like him, a great scientist or a spiritual Master. So, it is only when I have total faith in myself that the divine possibilities I have within me can easily be transformed into divine Reality. We are singing the song of possibility with our limited faith. Here something may happen, or something may not happen. But, when we are endowed with boundless faith, constant faith, it is not mere possibility, but it is nothing short of inevitability. At that time we feel that God-realisation is our birthright.

XV – QUESTIONS AND ANSWERS, KINGS COLLEGE, CAMBRIDGE UNIVERSITY

250. If someone is having great difficulty in meditating because he lacks discipline and cannot concentrate, can you suggest a possible remedy? How can one develop self-discipline and improve his meditation?

Sri Chinmoy: In that case, that particular person should start with concentration. Meditation will be too difficult for him.

Self-discipline comes through proper concentration under the express guidance of an able Master. One has to lead a disciplined life while practising concentration. Otherwise, if his life is not disciplined to some extent, and if he wants to practise meditation, it will be too hard for him. It is like a kindergarten student who wants to study at the high school level. Every seeker should start with concentration in the spiritual life.

Concentration is a vast field. Each individual has to know, or has to learn from someone, how to concentrate. Concentration has to pave the way for meditation. When we concentrate, we try to control our thoughts, our emotions. When we meditate, we must have already disciplined our emotional and restless life to some extent. Through proper meditation we either enter into vastness or vastness enters into us.

To lead a disciplined life, what we need is daily practice, constant practice. Twice or three times a day we feed the body. We do not feed the child divine within us, the soul, even once in a blue moon. When we feed the body, we become strong. We can live on earth. When we feed the soul, we grow. Our inner being grows into the divine Light.

Please try to meditate early in the morning, that is to say at the Hour of God, between three and four a.m., then meditation will be easy for you. If you meditate at seven thirty or eight or nine a.m., it will be more difficult. Mother-Earth commences her dance or her work, the hustle and bustle, by six or by seven a.m. If you can meditate between three and four a.m., no matter of what standard you are, even if you are a complete beginner, you will have very little resistance in your meditation. It is in the early morning that one can meditate best. At that time, one is bound to run very fast in the spiritual life.

To come back to your question, meditation is the only answer which offers us a disciplined life. But, as I said previously, if before meditation one practises concentration, then one can expedite one's inner journey. When one concentrates, one becomes the divine hero. When one concentrates, one enters into the battlefield of life in Light where there can be no doubt, no fear. Fear and doubt will be conquered by concentration. Then, when one enters into deeper meditation, there one gets confidence, inner assurance. Then when one contemplates, one eventually enters into the Goal and grows into the Goal itself. This is God-realisation – where the finite merges into the Infinite, where the Lover and the Beloved become One, inseparable.

251. Does one achieve divine experiences through rigorous practice and coercion?

Sri Chinmoy: Through meditation we are bound to get divine experiences. Meditation is the means. If one meditates, certainly one will get divine experiences. If one doesn't meditate, then one will have only ordinary, human experiences. Meditation is the only answer. Meditation has the key to enter into the divine world. Certainly it requires practice. But coercion exists only until our self-enforced discipline becomes something natural and joyful. If we have to coerce ourselves, it is because some part of us is recalcitrant. Self-discipline will gradually become spontaneous and natural; then concentration and meditation will never seem coercive.

252. Does a divine experience come only through controlling one's emotions and one's senses by force?

Sri Chinmoy: We do not get divine experiences by force or through coercion. It is the divine purity within us that purifies us slowly and steadily and makes us fit for inner and divine experiences. We cannot do it by coercion or by hook or by crook. We have to follow a systematic method, and for that aspiration is necessary. When we aspire, the flame of aspiration climbs up. While it is climbing up, it will illumine our outer nature. Then automatically we will have a self-disciplined life. But, we can never have a disciplined life by force. First it will break our vital being, and then it will tell upon our physical body.

If you believe that you can reach or realise the highest Truth overnight, then you are making a terrible mistake. The truth is, after all, an inner knowledge. We take twenty-five years or even more to complete our earthly education, to get our Ph.D. degree, which is the zenith of our earthly knowledge. In the spiritual life also, we have to devote quite a few years to study and practice. If somebody feels that he can control his emotions in the twinkling of an eye, or that he may realise God in a couple of hours, he is only fooling himself. At the present state of your consciousness, please try to have divine thoughts all the time in your mind. In that way you will make very good progress.

253. You said I must keep divine thoughts in my mind, not undivine thoughts. How do I know which are divine thoughts?

Sri Chinmoy: When we have divine thoughts, we immediately expand and enlarge our consciousness. When we have evil or undivine thoughts, we bind ourselves. We bind everything, we try to possess everything. "I, my, mine, my family, my friends, my country" – there it is all human. But when it is all divine, immediately we say, "we". Then, for the first time we will use the term "we". We may ask where this feeling of Oneness with humanity is coming from. It is coming from the source which is Light.

So, each moment when you get a thought, try to see whether that particular thought is expanding your consciousness or binding you. Please try to observe any idea that enters your mind and see if it is expanding your consciousness or if it is binding you. When a thought comes, immediately please try to enter into the thought and see if it is instigating you to possess something or someone. Then if this is so, you will see that it is human thought. When you try to possess someone, you have to know that you are already possessed. But, if it is a divine thought, there you are not going to possess anybody. You are not going to be possessed by anybody. You are going to liberate and illumine the entire world.

254. Is it necessary to study under a Teacher to achieve self-realisation? What does a spiritual Teacher do? Are there any advantages to be gained by studying with a spiritual Teacher? Do you ever outgrow your need for a Teacher? Can anything be achieved alone?

Sri Chinmoy: Now, to be very frank with you: who was the spiritual Teacher of the very first person who realised God on earth? He who realised God for the first time on earth didn't have a spiritual Master as we have. But he did realise God.

Here we see that every rule admits of exceptions. He did realise God. In that particular case, God helped him, God Himself became his Teacher. Anyway, he realised God. The first realised person on earth didn't have a human being to help him realise God. God became his inner Teacher and outer Teacher.

By this time, there are many spiritual Masters who have really realised God. Again, there are many unrealised persons who claim to be spiritual Masters. There are false teachers. There are genuine teachers. Mother-Earth is cursed with false Masters and blessed with true Masters.

To come back to your question, we have to know the role of a spiritual Master quite well. He is not a school teacher. A school teacher will examine you and mark you according to your merit. If you have done well, your teacher will pass you. If you have not done well in your examination, he will fail you. This is his business. You are always examined by the teacher here. But a private tutor is not like that. A private tutor helps you wholeheartedly, individually, privately, to pass the examination. He will constantly help you so that in school, in college, you can get high marks. This is his role. He will only try to help you, to expedite your progress in acquiring knowledge. So, a spiritual Master, a real spiritual Master, is a private tutor. And what does he do? He helps, he inspires and he kindles the flame of aspiration *in* the seeker *for* the seeker so that the seeker can stand right in front of the sea of ignorance and face it and conquer it. This is what a spiritual Master does.

Now in this world, we need a teacher for everything. So there is nothing wrong in having a teacher for one's spiritual and inner education. But, you may say, for how many years will the teacher be necessary? For five years or ten years or twenty years? To get your Master's degree you have to start at the beginning as a child, in kindergarten. Then after you get your own highest degree, you do not continue to go to the University as a student. Then you yourself start teaching. You have every right to teach then, because you have acquired your knowledge. Now you are in a position to teach others, to help others. In the spiritual life also, if one is wise, one knows that the role of a spiritual Teacher is like a private tutor. You take help from the Teacher for a few years, for as long as you need to get your own inner illumination:

five years, ten years, twenty years or fifty years. Or it may take a few incarnations because, after all, it is a difficult subject.

One may say, "No. God is part of me, He is in all of us. For that, why should I go to others to get God-Knowledge?" I would like to say that it is true. God is within you. God is also inside all knowledge. Why do you then go to a teacher to learn? You go to him precisely because you need his instruction, you need his guidance.

God is within you. But unfortunately, you do not know where He is. God is inside you, but He is seated at a particular place. He is seated on a Throne. You do not know how to reach that Throne. Here the role of the Teacher begins. He comes, he carries you. He shows you God's Throne. Then his role is over. Just take a little help from him. You need it. He is not God, but he has seen God a few seconds before you or a few years before you. Your schoolteacher also learned from someone else what he teaches you now. It is the individual who has to be wise. If he feels that he wants to run faster towards his Goal, then naturally he has to take help from the one who has already seen the Goal, and stays in the Goal.

255. In our daily life are we to work to suppress our emotion? What is the nature of emotion as you see it? Is there any way we can control it?

Sri Chinmoy: No, in our daily life we should not work to suppress emotion. We have not to suppress anything. Suppression is very bad. If we suppress something today, tomorrow we will be subjected to its revolt. Suppression is not the answer. We must not suppress our emotion. What we have to do is to illumine it. While we are illumining it, we shall feel real joy. Now, by suppressing, what do we actually accomplish? Nothing. We are only forcing ourselves beyond our capacity and sincere willingness. As we have a desire to enjoy a life of pleasure, so also have we a desire to suppress life. A life of gross pleasure and a life of suppression are equally bad. They are followed by frustration. Frustration ends in destruction.

Suppression is not the right method of getting joy from life. Let us try to find out the right method. If our aim is joy, we must know that joy is in light. Let us think more of Light than of night. Automatically our inner light will come to the fore.

We have to know that there are two types of emotion: human emotion and divine emotion. Emotion as such is not bad. But human emotion is, unfortunately, bad. With our human emotion, we possess and we are possessed. Divine emotion is something else. It is like this: "I am God's child. How can I do something that is wrong? My Father is All-Light. He is All-Perfection. He is All-Love. He is for humanity. He is for the universe. It is beneath my dignity to surrender myself to ignorance." This emotion comes directly from the heart, from the inmost recesses of our heart. Here, this divine emotion grows and flows. But the other emotion which we observe and to which we are subject, is our vital, human emotion, our lower vital emotion. That emotion we have to transform, illumine. As night has to be transformed into Light, so also human emotion has to be transformed into divine emotion.

If we meditate more on the positive side, that is to say on Light, then Light is going to descend on us. But, if we think of night and are afraid of night, then we are unconsciously entering into the domain of night. Whenever we think of night, of darkness within us, we enter into night's domain. But, if we always think of Light, which is after all our true Joy and Saviour, then we are running towards our destined Goal.

So I wish to suggest to you that when human emotion appears, do not try to suppress it, but try to think of divine emotion. When you are enlarged, when you are in Infinity, you will get boundless joy. You will not then care for tempting and tempted pleasure. We know that when we meditate, we enter into the world of Joy and Delight. We know the difference between pleasure and Delight. Human pleasure frustrates us and destroys us. Divine Delight feeds us and immortalises us.

256. In your talk you said that human love is an express train, destination: frustration; and that divine Love is a local train, destination: illumination. How is it that human love has not been given a divine consciousness or dimension?

Sri Chinmoy: Unfortunately it has not been done. Why? The answer only God can give. In human love we are binding, we are limiting ourselves. But the divine Love does not limit us, does not bind us.

North is north. South is south. When we stand facing the south, we cannot say, "Why is it not north?" It is not north. It is south. We know that this is north; this is south. Similarly, we know what human love is. We experience it in our daily life. We also experience divine Love in our spiritual life. Those who meditate, those who aspire, experience divine Love.

We cannot ask why darkness is not light. They are two different things. However, we see that the Divine can enter into the undivine and change the undivine into the Divine. Light can enter into darkness. Similarly, Infinity can enter into the finite, Eternity into the fleeting second, Immortality into mortality, to transform them.

In the human, divinity is there. In the human body the divine soul exists. Let us use the soul, which is divine. This soul is within us. When we try to offer our identity, let us try to offer our identity as the soul. If I can say, "I am the soul and I am not the body," then I can get a glimpse of inner and outer freedom. I said in my talk, "I am the Knowledge. I am the Knower. I am the Known." If I can say, "The soul is within me. I am the soul. I am not the body," then I can go very fast towards the Goal. But, if I say that by experiencing human love and human pleasure I will get divine fulfilment, then I am fooling myself.

Whenever we want to do something divine, we have to use the divine method. If I want to learn English, I will go to an English professor. I won't go to a history professor. I know that he will not be in a position to teach me English. So, in the spiritual life also, if you really want to have the divine Truth, you need the divine aspiration within your heart. It is through aspiration that the human love can be transformed into the divine Love.

Human love, undoubtedly, will one day be transformed. But if human love claims that by following the human method it will be able to compel the divine Truth, divine Light to reveal Itself, then it is impossible.

Let us take aspiration as a dynamic push from within. This inner push will be met by a pull from above. This pull is God's Compassion. Man's aspiration and God's Compassion together transform man into perfect Perfection.

NOTES TO BOOK 2

108–109. *(p. 85)* Akuti (Miss Dorothy Eisamann), 26 June 1967.
110. *(p. 86)* Ahana (Mrs Blanca Bueso), 26 July 1967.
111. *(p. 87)* Ratna (Mrs Haydee Casellas), 31 July 1967.
112. *(p. 89)* Nydia Caro, 31 July 1967.
113. *(p. 90)* Dr. Carrasquillo, 1 June 1969.
114. *(p. 91)* A visitor, Puerto Rico, 2 June 1968.
115. *(p. 95)* Mrityunjayi (Mrs Margarita Rodriguez), 13 July 1969.
116. *(p. 97)* A visitor, 20 July 1967.
117–120. *(p. 100)* Bodhananda (Mr Saturnino Rodriguez), 20 July 1967.
121. *(p. 104)* Mrityunjayi (Mrs Margarita Rodriquez), 20 July 1967.
122–158. *(p. 106)* A talk to the disciples of the Sri Chinmoy Centre in San Juan, Puerto Rico, on 24 January 1971, in which the Master answers his own questions on meditation and then invites questions from the disciples.
123. *(p. 108)* Sevananda.
124. *(p. 108)* Ashpriha.
125. *(p. 109)* Drona.
126. *(p. 109)* Kalyan.
127. *(p. 110)* Devadas.
128. *(p. 110)* David.
129. *(p. 112)* Mita.
130. *(p. 113)* Pratyay.
131. *(p. 113)* Mangal.
132. *(p. 114)* Sudha.
133. *(p. 116)* Agni.
134. *(p. 117)* Vijaya.
135. *(p. 117)* Sanjivan.
136. *(p. 118)* Gauri.

EARTH'S CRY MEETS HEAVEN'S SMILE, BOOK 2

137. *(p. 119)* Shankara.
138. *(p. 120)* Indu.
139. *(p. 121)* A visitor.
140. *(p. 121)* A second visitor.
141. *(p. 122)* Ashpriha.
142. *(p. 123)* Mangal.
143. *(p. 124)* Ananta.
144. *(p. 126)* Sevananda.
145. *(p. 126)* Mangal.
146. *(p. 128)* Sarama (Mrs Linda Smiler).
148. *(p. 130)* Dhruva (Mr Steven Hein).
149. *(p. 132)* Robin.
150. *(p. 133)* Aditya (Mr Alan Smiler).
151. *(p. 134)* Samrat (Mr Dan Weiss).
152. *(p. 136)* A visitor.
153. *(p. 137)* Mrs Pamela Lenz.
154. *(p. 137)* Miss Kathy Splain.
155. *(p. 139)* Sebastian.
156. *(p. 141)* Mr Frank Finnerty.
157. *(p. 142)* Mr Frank Finnerty.
158. *(p. 142)* Charugita Shukla.
159–170. *(p. 146)* Questions answered at the American International School (High School), Zurich, Switzerland, on 27 November 1970.
171–175. *(p. 157)* Questions answered at the University of Bristol, 20 November 1970.
176–179. *(p. 167)* Questions answered at St. David's College, University of Lampeter, Wales, on 20 November 1970.
180–183. *(p. 172)* Questions answered at The American Centre for Students and Artists, Paris, France, on 14 November 1970.
184–191. *(p. 178)* Questions answered at Conway Hall, London, England, on 3 December 1970.

192–197. *(p. 188)* Questions answered at the University of Glasgow, Glasgow, Scotland, on 2 December 1970.

198–205. *(p. 196)* Questions answered at the University of Leeds on 18 November 1970.

206–210. *(p. 206)* Questions answered at the University of Essex, Colchester, England, on 17 November 1970.

211–217. *(p. 214)* Questions answered at the University of Nottingham on 10 November 1970.

218–232. *(p. 223)* Questions answered at the American College in Paris on 13 November 1970.

233–242. *(p. 233)* Questions answered at the University of London, London, England, on 11 November 1970.

243–249. *(p. 244)* Questions answered at Keble College, Oxford University, Oxford, England, on 19 November 1972.

250–256. *(p. 255)* Questions answered at Kings College, Cambridge University, England, on 23 November 1972.

EARTH'S CRY MEETS HEAVEN'S SMILE

BOOK 3

I

257. I would like to know how you felt the call of God in your life?

Sri Chinmoy: First of all, I would like to tell you that I came into the world with a special mission. I have to tell the truth. It is far from boasting or bragging. When a person comes with a high mission to fulfil God here on earth, he automatically brings with him the love for God, the call of God, the spontaneous feeling for God. Ordinary persons do not have that.

An ordinary person grows slowly and when the years advance on him, he sees around him others who are thinking of God, praising God and people who feel that without God there can be no joy. These ideas enter into him and then, of course, he may also develop a little aspiration for God. Gradually, with the help of others and with his own sincere cry for God, he feels that he has also got the call of God. In my case, though, I came with a very high mission.

Then I had the opportunity to come into a very spiritual family. My parents were spiritual, my sisters and brothers are all living in a spiritual community; they have been there for the last thirty years or so.

When I was a child of a year and two months, my parents took me to a spiritual Centre which in India we call an ashram. From that time on, even my physical being was inspired with the message of my soul's inner call. Then when I was twelve and a half years old, I came to that place to stay permanently and I remained there for twenty years. At the age of thirteen, or when I had completed thirteen years, I became fully aware of what I was in my past incarnations. That is to say, my past spiritual achievements and so forth became revealed to me. Gradually, in the course of a year or two, I became fully aware of my self-realisation in my past incarnation and also my role as a spiritual teacher in my past incarnation.

So if I have to tell you, if you want me to tell you when actually I became fully aware of my spiritual realisation, then I must say that it was when I was between thirteen and fourteen years of age. But the call, if you ask when I got the call, I must say that the call I got or I had when my soul entered into this physical body, this physical frame. And that call I got hundreds of years ago to realise God and to fulfil God here on earth. But in this incarnation, I must say that I became totally and fully conscious of my inner call at the age of twelve and a half.

1966

I – QUESTIONS AND ANSWERS ON 20 JULY 1966

258. How long have you been here in Puerto Rico?

Sri Chinmoy: I came here last Friday.

259. What do you think is the soul development, the vibration here in Puerto Rico?

Sri Chinmoy: Oh, it is wonderful. The spiritual soil is very fertile. People are aspiring, dedicated and they have genuine aspiration. What they lack is confidence in themselves.

260. Do you think that our commodities here in Puerto Rico are a hindrance to the development of the soul?

Sri Chinmoy: Not at all. Commodities are not a hindrance to the soul's development. We have to have a different attitude towards them, towards material prosperity. All hindrance, even if you consider them as hindrances, can be taken as opportunities in your life. If you take them as hurdles, these hurdles will give you an opportunity to surmount them and reach your Goal. What we think of as a hindrance is not a hindrance in God's view.

261. I was thinking for instance, that we have very good TV programmes here and we also have a spiritual meeting. But we feel more inclined to stay at home watching the TV programme than going to the meeting. So I consider that a hindrance.

Sri Chinmoy: That is not at all a hindrance; it is a lack of wisdom. If I have money, that does not mean that I am doomed to squander it all the time. I should know when to use it for a right purpose, for a divine purpose. Similarly, there are many things that might distract me or prevent me from following the spiritual path or the inner life. It is I who am the master of my possession. I shall have to deal with them according to the dictates of my soul. If I have a TV in my room, it is I who use the TV. It is not the TV that uses me. I am the Master of my possession. So long as I am the master, it is I who have to control my mind and say, "No, I have to go and listen to a spiritual talk which is more important than the TV show."

262. But don't you think that if you did not have the TV set, you would be more inclined to go to the meeting?

Sri Chinmoy: Unfortunately, no. That is not the case. At that time, laziness may enter into me and I might say, "Who cares? The spiritual life is not meant for me; it is something unreal. I want to talk to my neighbour." In that case, what you are saying is that the poorest people who cannot afford to buy television sets would all be more inclined to follow the spiritual life than the others. But it is not like that. There are beggars in India who do not care for the spiritual life. Here also. Poverty does not mean that we are one inch nearer to God. It is our mistaken idea to feel this.

The possession is not responsible for what we do; it is the possessor who is responsible. The TV is not responsible; it is the owner. I am sure you have heard the name of King Janaka. He had a vast kingdom and in spite of having this vast kingdom, his whole mind was always devoted to God and God-realisation. Similarly the material prosperity of the West is in no way an obstacle to God-realisation. If you can feel that you are the possessor and that you must not be possessed by what you have, then you will be the master of the situation. Those who don't have money will always harbour the feeling that they are poor and unfortunate. But for them, the same difficulty will arise and it will not be due to their poverty, but to their inner weakness.

You have a TV and you cannot go to attend a spiritual class but the person who does not have a TV will also be thinking of something else. His mind will also be thinking of something else. His mind will also be turned in another direction. Is it clear? Always we have to understand what is the possession and what is the possessor. We have to separate the possessor from the possession.

263. Do you believe there is a great strength in stillness?

Sri Chinmoy: Yes. Stillness is where we get the strength. The abode of stillness is in our higher mind or quiet mind. So if you can stay in that room, the quiet mind, then you can grow in stillness. It is stillness that creates. Creativity actually starts from stillness.

264. Even if one moves he may be still. I think stillness is like the eye of a storm, which is still, but around it, everything moves. I think also that artistic stillness, even if it has a lot of movement in it, has to be quiet at the centre.

Sri Chinmoy: Actually in Sanskrit, they say, "That moves and That moves not." Actually stillness is moving all the time, yet it is not moving. "That moves and That moves not."

265. Let us say that I am at the piano and I am moving my fingers, playing, but if I am a witness of what I am doing, the fingers are moving, but I am not.

Sri Chinmoy: True. You will see both action and inaction together. You will see that you are creating action with your fingers; at the same time you see the stillness that we are speaking of. It is just like the sea; on the surface you see the waves, but when you enter into the depths, you see all calmness. The deeper plane is that which moves not; the outer plane is that which moves. At the same time, you cannot separate the surface from the depth. In that way, your action and inaction go together. Action is on the outer plane; inaction is on the inner. That is why we say, "That moves and That moves not," at the same time.

II – WEEK OF 20 JULY 1966

[On the Master's first visit to Puerto Rico on 20 July 1966, he answered, at great length and in considerable detail, a number of questions on karma, reincarnation, occultism, the Guru-disciple relationship, illness, death, etc. About fifty pages of this material, in manuscript form, were removed and used in a group of booklets published around 1974, including Death and Reincarnation, The Inner Worlds, *etc. In compiling this book, we found that in several cases, we were left with the original question itself, plus a few disconnected, disjointed and unmarked paragraphs of unused material. As we have been unsuccessful in tracing the published material, i.e. the specific answers which originally belonged to these questions, we have had to use whatever material we have, as it is. The asterisks indicate large portions of the answers cut out.*

On a higher level, though, everything that is said by the Master has a universal Truth and Beauty, quite apart from the context in which it is placed. So in whatever publication his teachings appear, and whether his answers appear as originally spoken, or not, his Light and Power as such, fulfil an eternal need in the searching life of the eternally aspiring seeker.]

266. *Had you heard something about Puerto Rico in India?*

Sri Chinmoy: Yes, well geography tells us something, history tells us something, and literature also tells us something. I will tell the children at the YMCA in a few hours my impression of Puerto Rico, strictly from the spiritual point of view, whatever it is; from the spiritual point of view plus a little geography and general knowledge. But it is all based on the spiritual feeling of the island, now that I have seen the place, and since I have been taken around.

But more than that, the moment that I entered and touched the feet of Puerto Rican soil, it has given me the knowledge of what it is. As soon as I landed there at the airport, my first thing was to touch the feet, to touch the soil and be blessed by the Puerto Rican presiding deity. And then she gave me the wisdom-knowledge of what she is and what she represents.

[....]

267. How long will you be staying here: a week?

Sri Chinmoy: Yes, I will be staying one week; then I shall have to go back to New York.

I am not flattering you. All of you are sincere and at the same time, dedicated. My humble request is to please have confidence in yourselves. If you have got a Guru, well and good. If you don't have one, or you don't need one, do not be at all disturbed. The first thing is to have confidence in yourselves, that you are God's child. Say, "I am God's child. I have to realise God. There is no alternative." If you have a Guru, well and good. If you don't, what can you do? If you don't need one, that is also all right. But confidence you must have, saying, "How can I stay, how can I live without God-realisation, without seeing Him?"

[....]

268

[....]

God is our Eternal Father and we are His eternal children. It is only a child that can make progress, not the one who is learned. He will be in his own mental world. But the child knows and feels that he has much to learn and he wants to live in God's consciousness, which is limitless. There is no limit to our knowing and learning. We are all a drop, a tiny drop in the vast ocean of God's infinite consciousness.

[....]

269

[....]

If it touches our mind that we should live a spiritual life, then only will we, one day, begin to do it. Otherwise, if we don't think of the very idea that we should try to live a better life, a spiritual life, then we will never start the spiritual life. If we want to bathe in the sea, we may not jump into the sea right now, but we have to go, at least, to the seashore and stand there and observe the waves. If we don't leave our room and stand before the sea, then we shall never enter into the sea. So at least let us start our journey and then one day we shall reach our Goal.

[....]

270

[....]

If I have a father and a mother and if I am in prison, I must break through the door and go to see my parents. Similarly you know that our father and mother is God. And we have to break asunder all ties of ignorance and go and rush towards God. If we go one step forward, we will see that He has already come hundreds of steps towards us. So my request, my sole request is to please, all of you, have confidence in yourselves. You are God's children and you have to bring Him to the fore. He is already within and you have to reveal Him.

[....]

271. How can imperfection be removed quickly?

Sri Chinmoy: Imperfection? On which plane? If it is in the mind you have to apply one type of treatment, but if it is in the body, you have to apply a different type. But the general rule is that if you feel some imperfection in yourself, please do not think of it as something that is part and parcel of your life. You have to think, on the other hand, that you are perfection itself.

For some time, you have to think, "No, I am not this imperfection. I can never be. I am God's child. How can I ever be imperfect? It is something quite wrong." Go on thinking in this vein for a few days. Then your thinking will be transmuted into feeling. First you will be thinking with the mind, "No, I cannot be that." Then you will feel, "No, I cannot be imperfect. I cannot bind God's child." Then you create, within yourself, a kind of oneness with perfection: "I am all perfect." First you are thinking, then you are feeling that oneness. You will become one with perfection. When you have become one with perfection, will you dare to say that you are imperfect?

Those of you who ask me questions, if my answers are not satisfactory or do not serve you satisfactorily, do tell me. I can try to throw more light on it if you feel that it is not convincing you. I will try my best to convince you, but I may not be able to succeed.

[....]

272. What about sickness?

Sri Chinmoy: There are various reasons for sickness. The main reason is a very material one. A certain internal imperfection or dislocation develops in our organs or our cells. It is natural and it occurs with all living things. Very often, due to that, we fall sick.

The second reason is that certain chronic diseases or fatal diseases may come to us owing to our previous wrong actions.

Then again there is another reason which is deeper still. That is that God wants to give you that experience. You may not have done anything wrong in your life; you may not be responsible in any way, but in this life, you are getting the experience. Why? Because God wants you to have the experiences of poor, suffering humanity.

[....]

III – 20 JULY 1966

273. I would like to know the name of Swamiji.

Sri Chinmoy: It is very kind of you. My name is Chinmoy Kumar Ghose. I was born in Bengal and I was brought up in South India. So this is my name, my Bengali name.

Today we are discussing religion. Until we know what religion is, we will not understand spirituality. And until we understand spirituality, we cannot understand yoga. Until we have understood yoga, we cannot think of God. Tomorrow I shall be speaking on spirituality and then I shall give a few more talks on "The aim of life" and "What is God's Plan?" and the principal Yogas: *Karma Yoga,* the path of Action, *Bhakti Yoga,* the path of Love and Devotion, and *Jnana Yoga,* the path of Knowledge and Wisdom. These are the things I would like to deal with during my stay in Puerto Rico.

[....]

274. With what movement is Swamiji connected in New York?

Sri Chinmoy: I am not connected with any movement.
Seeker: You came by yourself?
Sri Chinmoy: No, I was brought up in a spiritual Centre. I stayed for twenty years in a spiritual Centre in India, the Sri Aurobindo Ashram. For twenty years I stayed there. I went there at the age of one but they were not accepting children. But I stayed there from the age of twelve until I was thirty-two. Twenty years I stayed doing intense meditation and all that. My brothers and sisters were all there. I am the youngest of the lot and my sisters and brothers are still all there. Some of them have been there for thirty years, forty years, in that Centre.

I got the Command from within. The Supreme within me demanded it. In the beginning I was afraid, but I was compelled. My American sponsors also insisted. I said, "Well, if it is the Supreme's Will, I have to accept." And I came here. We do not decide anything. We wait for the Command. Where is India? Where is New York? I had to come.

275. Did you go to Europe first?

Sri Chinmoy: No, I did not go to Europe. Only on the way we stopped there for two and a half hours. Otherwise I did not go to Europe. I have been here in the U.S., in New York. I have gone to quite a few states to give talks. I went to Canada. Most probably at the end of my visit here, I will go to California. Again, these are all speculations. We do not know actually what will happen. Here I have come. Who knows if I may come here again. I may not come here at all.
Disciple: You have to come back again.
Sri Chinmoy: We don't decree such things.
Disciple: But you must try to arrange it.
Sri Chinmoy: We say that the Guru is always at the command of his disciples. If the disciples want him, the Guru is bound to come. There is no alternative.

If a child cries, the father will not feed himself, but he will remain unfed and he will come to the child, to try and feed the child. It is like that.
Disciples: We need to be fed.
Sri Chinmoy: You have here so many spiritual figures for guidance. I am so glad that at least Puerto Rico has been blessed with spiritual figures. There are places, unlit places, where spiritual figures have never come and it is quite unfortunate.

276. What is the name of your magazine?

Sri Chinmoy: The name is AUM. You know *A* represents Brahma, the Creator, *U* represents Vishnu, the Preserver, *M* represent Lord Siva, the Destroyer. So what happens is that when we say AUM, we are invoking the Creator, Preserver and Destroyer. I beg to be excused, but in my philosophy, I feel that there is no destruction. It is all transformation. As a matter of fact, we can't destroy anything. First we create something, then we preserve it. Then what do we do? Transform the thing. So: Creation, Preservation and Transformation. Brahma is the Creator, Vishnu is the Preserver and Shiva is the Transformer. If it is destruction, who is destroying whom? God only transforms us. In our creation, we enter into ignorance and we do many things wrong. For that He has to transform us and again take us back into His bosom of infinite Light.

IV – AT SRI CHINMOY'S HOME

277. : Gurudev, the word "Yoga" means "union with God"?

Sri Chinmoy: Yes.
Kalipada: The union of the individual soul with the God-Soul.
Sri Chinmoy: Yes.

278. But in ordinary experience, all of us know what this is. I can stretch out my hand to Mr Friedman. I can talk to him; I can communicate with him. Now when we want the Goal, the abode of spiritual union, what is this? What is the experience? What is it like?

Sri Chinmoy: The thing is this: you can touch Mr Friedman and communicate with him. You may even feel that you have become one with him. You get a kind of vibration or feeling that you have united with him in the spiritual sense. But actually, you have not really become one with him in the inner planes; you have not achieved a union with his inner being or with his soul. You have the feeling that Mr Friedman's thoughts and ideas have entered into you. This comes from your intellectual closeness to him and your heart's ties. You do have a deep affinity with Mr Friedman and a fine understanding of him. But the feeling that you have fully entered into him or that he has entered into you is partly your imagination and partly your mental projection. It is also due to your sense of affinity and the closeness that you feel towards him. But it is neither *your* inner being nor *his* inner being that has united you two. Needless to say, your souls do not enter into the picture here at all.

Kalipada, it is very difficult to achieve a union with another person's soul without first having achieved union with the Supreme Soul, God. You have correctly stated that Yoga is union with God. When you have achieved union with God, you get the

Consciousness of God. When you achieve union with someone's soul, however, you get a glimpse of God's Consciousness. You see an aspect or a facet of the Divine Consciousness. The more developed the soul is, of course, the more powerfully and beautifully will God's Consciousness be manifested in that person. But in union with God Himself, you feel that you have become inseparably one with Him. Not only do you feel it and see it, but actually you have become one with what He eternally is. In Yoga, through your aspiration and meditation, you consciously enter into the Ocean, which is God, the Supreme. Like a drop, you enter into the Ocean and you lose your individual, separate existence.

Now if you touch Mr Friedman, you will get a partial glimpse of his existence, his feelings, thoughts and vibrations. But you will not really become one with him. It is only a momentary oneness. But in Yoga, when we identify ourselves with God, we become like a drop in the Ocean and we lose our very existence. At the same time, we become the Infinite Ocean itself. The union with God is different from the union that we try to achieve by identifying ourselves with someone, especially when it is a limited identification such as we get by touching or talking to someone.

In the true spiritual union, what actually happens is this: the union with the Highest may last for a few days or a few months and then you lose it until you have created a free access to the Highest, until you can go there at your command or bring it down at your command. When you can do that, it becomes something permanent. Otherwise it may last for a few hours, a few days or a few months. Then it vanishes. But in our inner consciousness, it is all being recorded – how many times you have gone up to your highest consciousness and how many times you have come down. You have the experience a number of times and then you make it a living reality. Eventually it becomes a permanent realisation.

279. One further question on this. If anyone here in this room or anywhere else, for that matter, attained union with God in some previous life, but in this present life they have not yet attained it, how does that previous attainment affect him?

Sri Chinmoy: If he had already attained realisation and in this present life is not conscious of it, how can he become aware of it and how can that previous realisation affect his everyday life?
Kalipada: Yes.
Sri Chinmoy: It is through the same process. It is through Yoga, by practising Yoga. All the great spiritual figures, you know Krishna, Buddha, Christ, Sri Ramakrishna.... they all attained to the greater part of their spiritual perfection in their previous lives. But even then, they had to practise Yoga for quite a number of years to get back to their original Home. Then, of course, once they get back to their original Home, they bring down all of their spiritual wealth.

Here also, I must say, most of you.... no, all of you, all ten of you here in this room today accepted Yoga in your previous lives. Some of you are conscious of this and some of you are not. Those of you who *are* conscious of it, how have you become conscious? You did not become conscious overnight. Only by practising Yoga for a number of months, and in most cases, a number of years, did you become aware that you did something previously in your spiritual life. Something reveals itself inside you.

Revelation comes in the course of time. Then you go spontaneously, openly, freely back to your original Home, the Home of your true existence. Then you bring it down to affect your present incarnation.

All spiritual figures, the Avatars too, in the beginning, were unconscious of their total realisation. They acted like ordinary human beings, but inwardly they had a great inner urge and surge, and in the course of time, what happened? They entered deep within themselves and they got back their Realisation, their old Realisation.

280. Gurudev, when I come into contact with Mr Friedman or anyone else in this everyday experience, I get a certain joy and sometimes a certain pain in that association. Now what do you experience when you are in union with God?

Sri Chinmoy: When we are in union with God, we experience Absolute Bliss. There is no suffering at all. At the same time, if you see, within God's Consciousness, the cosmic suffering, that suffering itself will be experienced as a kind of joy.

You have perhaps noticed that many times in a spiritual seeker's life, when he has a terrible headache or a stomach-ache, in the beginning he has unbearable suffering. Then what happens? He brings down Peace from above and that Peace touches the suffering itself. And when it touches the suffering, the suffering transforms itself into joy. The seeker gets enormous joy.

I remember once in India I was undergoing a small operation; I was having a boil opened. The doctor was an intimate friend of mine. He said, "Please be calm and quiet for a few minutes." And I did what he asked. While the doctor was performing the operation, I was actually smiling at him. It was not that I wanted to show that I was confident. No, I was actually deriving joy. The pain was unbearable, but while he was operating, I was getting joy and I was smiling. The doctor said, "What is the matter with you? Are you cutting jokes with me?" I said, "No, I am getting joy from the suffering."

In your case also, you will see that if you enter into God's Consciousness, the first experience will be Absolute Bliss. Then when you see that the universe and nature are within God Himself, you will see, from the human point of view, that the world is truly full of suffering. But the suffering world is also contained within God's Consciousness. Then you will see, in the period of a few seconds, that inside the suffering there is great joy. The suffering transforms itself into joy and there is no suffering as such.

281. Now once I have entered into this Ocean of Bliss and I come back down to my normal self, would I be normal in the sense that I was the same as before I went into this Ocean, or would I be radically different?

Sri Chinmoy: Certainly you will be different. There will be a radical difference from your old consciousness. You will be a totally different man. And your intimate ones, your wife and daughter, will see a great change in your movements, your conduct, your attitudes.

I attained my highest experience at the age of thirteen. I became conscious of what I was. Then again I had to toil. At the age of thirteen, I knew what I was and what realisation I had achieved and all that. But again for years I had to struggle to make it permanent. To know something and to make it permanent in one's life are two different things. It takes time.

282. Sri Chinmoy asked each disciple present to place his hand on his heart. The Guru then concentrated intently on each person. He then offered the following message.

Today at about a quarter to three [half an hour previously] the Supreme came to me and gave me a Special Blessing and Power. I was commanded to share it with all of you. The most effective way, I find, is when you place your hand on your heart. It becomes very easy to part with the inner Wealth, the Wealth that I received. So it is in order to give you something most valuable, invaluable, most precious, that I requested you to do this. That invaluable thing, the Blessing, the Power that the Supreme gives, I offered to all of you here now. And now it is working. All of you will make great progress by the very touch of the Supreme within your heart. You may not feel it right now, but within an hour, in the early evening or at night, you will feel that something most special has entered into you.

And now I wish all of you to place your hand on your heart individually when I look at you. That is to say, I wish to concentrate on that particular person most intensely, spiritually and divinely. And that concentration and meditation will be meant only for him or for her. After that we will have a general meditation. In that meditation, all of us will aspire and invoke the Supreme and all of us will be benefited.

Just one thing more I wish to say to Kalipada. It takes many, many years for a spiritual seeker to identify himself spiritually with what he was before, to get back his old realisation in his present incarnation. I know people in India who were once realised souls. They *had* achieved Realisation. Now, although they have become aware of it, they have not been able to bring down their Realisation into their mental and physical consciousness. In their deep meditation, they feel a kind of revelation, but they have not been able to bring their Realisation, their highest

Realisation, back into their outer existence. In some cases, it takes forty or fifty years. In some cases, at the end of their lives or on their deathbed, they get back their Realisation.

In my case also, it took years.

283. Suppose one achieves Realisation, say, at the age of twenty. Does this Realisation wipe out all karmic debts for that individual?

Sri Chinmoy: Yes. After you have achieved your Realisation, you are no longer bound by karmic laws, cosmic laws or universal laws. What you do is that you surrender; you become one with God's Will and Decision. At that time, suppose you still have some suffering or pain, it is not because of your previous karma, the reaction to your previous actions. No. Once you have consciously realised God, karma cannot bind you any more. But if God wants to give you a particular experience, then you have to accept it.

It is like Sri Ramakrishna's cancer, you know. He took it from his disciples; it was not that he did something wrong. Certainly it was not his karma. No. Mother Kali wanted to give him that experience. He took it gladly. This experience is different from the experience of a normal man. A normal man has to undergo this suffering because of his previous karma. But a spiritual figure, a yogi, does it for a different reason. He accepts the burden from his disciples because he feels that he and the disciples are one. He has to accept it because the Divine within him wants to give him that particular experience. After all, the experience and the Divine are eternally one.

1967

284. Is it correct to think of love, forgiveness and wisdom while one pronounces the name of the Supreme?

Sri Chinmoy: No. Do not think of anything at all. When you invoke the Supreme, do not keep anything in your mind. Try only to feel that your whole existence is inside your soul. If, from the soul, love comes, wisdom comes or forgiveness comes while you are chanting, well and good. But mentally do not formulate any thought or concept regarding the Supreme. The divine aspects of love, forgiveness and wisdom are wonderfully inspiring. But while you are chanting or invoking the Supreme, please do not try to formulate with your mind any of these divine attributes.

Let the Supreme work through your soul and bring to the fore the divine qualities that He wants to reveal or manifest in your outer life. This will be the best attitude. Let Him work in and through your soul.

285. Is it possible to realise the Supreme in one life?

Sri Chinmoy: I am repeating Lakshmi's question. Is it possible to realise the Supreme in one incarnation? I wish to add: has one to come back into the world and have many incarnations in order to realise God? The answer is: it depends on the individual soul, how advanced the soul is. In one human incarnation alone, nobody can realise God. Impossible. No human being on earth realised God in his first human incarnation. In his first human incarnation, he is a semi-animal. Even after many incarnations, we have many animal qualities in our nature. In the first incarnation, it is simply impossible for a human being to realise God. He has to come through many, many hundreds of incarnations. Then when his aspiration develops through each incarnation and he enters into higher worlds, deeper worlds, he grows nearer and nearer to God.

Finally if he becomes fully consecrated and devoted, if he has the deepest aspiration for God-realisation in one particular incarnation, and if he gets the help of a spiritual teacher in that particular incarnation, then it is possible for that person to realise God in that life-time. If, however, he has to do it by his own personal efforts, it will take him another several incarnations; perhaps eight or ten or twelve more in spite of having the deepest aspiration. This is because the process is very arduous, very difficult.

But as I have said, if he is of a high calibre and extremely sincere, if he has abundant receptivity, if he has the highest aspiration and if he wants to dedicate his life only to God and no one else, and if he gets a spiritual Master who is a realised soul, who has the capacity to help him in his realisation, then in that one incarnation it is possible. That is what the greatest spiritual Masters do for their most advanced disciples but not for all disciples.

286. Is there a difference or distinction between surrender, devotion and selfless love?

Sri Chinmoy: Now, let us take them. Wonderful! Selfless love, devotion and surrender. Now, let us put them in order. Let us put devotion first; you used the word "selfless"
.... selfless love, second, and surrender, third. One, two, three. Devotion, selfless love and surrender.

Devotion is wonderful in the inner life or in the outer life. Devotion: what does it mean? It means to devote oneself to and to serve with total absorption something usually apart from oneself. If you devote yourself to something or someone, then sooner or later, you will achieve success in whatever you aspire for. Then also, devotion is something very intense, especially if it is used in a spiritual way. Devotion need not, or at times it may not be pure, because of thousands of desires which the individual has or by the impure motives of his devotion. Somebody is devoted to me, but at the same time, he may be assailed by thousands of desires and then each desire is like a drop of poison in his system. But he is coming to me with devotion. It is wonderful. But he is unaware that he is bringing this poison also. But if his devotion is freed from desire, at that stage, we have come to selfless love.

Here we go one step ahead. We love but we don't care for any return. In devotion, there may be a kind of give and take. "I devote my entire life to you. You have to give me inner Realisation or Illumination or something else." In selfless love, when you come to this stage, there you are loving selflessly and you are becoming one with the object of your adoration. Then, in that love, there is a subtle understanding that He will give you the best reward because you do not bother Him with your silly emotional problems or desires. You no longer say, "Give me this or give me that." That stage I have gone through. In selfless love, you know that He will give you something worth possessing.

Now let us take surrender. It is the best stage. There the disciple will say, "I do not care for Heaven. I do not care for Hell. Only I care for my spiritual Master." (This is what you have said in your unique poem, Madhuri. Whatever he wants to give me or do with my life, with my existence, I am ready. I fully surrender my very breath, my existence. Then, even if he does not want my help or assistance, or my life, I am still happy. In one of your poems, you have said this. I expressed the thought conveyed at the end of your poem.) This is the truest surrender. There we want only the Will of God, the Supreme.

Let Thy Will be done. That is the highest Surrender. It is very easy to say, "Let Thy Will be done." But that is when we identify ourselves with God's Will. When you really surrender, then you become one with God's Will. And there can be, in the spiritual life, no greater achievement or more powerful weapon with which to enter into the spiritual life than surrender, which is most difficult, especially in the West. In the East, it is much easier, the practice of surrender. So .... devotion, selfless love and surrender.

287. Does resurrection come when perfection in body and mind is attained?

Sri Chinmoy: Man's perfection in the body and mind? Man can be perfect in the soul, in the heart, in the mind, in the vital and eventually even in the body. Perfection must dawn on all levels. If man achieves perfection in the physical body, then the body will be automatically transformed, but it will take a few centuries.

There are two processes. What you call resurrection, I wish to call transformation. Resurrection would mean (as it does in the Christian tradition) that we would leave the physical body, ascend to a higher world, then come down again and animate the inert body with a higher consciousness than it had before. This process would not be necessary. For millions and millions of years, the body has been in darkness, this physical body, but not the heart, not the soul, not the mind. So this physical body, in the march of evolution may take a few hundred or even a thousand years to be perfected. When perfection has dawned in the mind, in the heart, and in the soul and when the soul within the body is fully realised by the outer being, at that time there would be two ways of living on earth. One way is this transformation which is the complete perfection of the body.

The other way will be what you can call the divinisation of the body. Right now, if you want to speak in the strict sense of the term, the body is undivine; it is not divinised. However, with aspiration and inner realisation, everything will be divinised. So one process is the transformation and physical perfection of the human body here on earth, which is similar to what you call resurrection; the other is divinisation in which all the functions of the physical body lose their mechanical, automatic nature and are controlled directly by the inner will. Everything in the body will be luminous, malleable and totally at the direct, supple service of the inner divinity, the soul.

An ordinary seeker in the future will have the capacity to transform his physical body by using his spiritual Light and his inner spiritual powers. His bodily perfection will be divinely "normal" at that time. In the case of a realised person, however, his physical body will be not only transformed and made perfect, but it will also be divinised. He will not have to go back and take another incarnation in order to have a divine or perfect body.

Then there is a third method. That method is that the beginning of human existence would not take place here on earth. The soul will take its physical form, its human shape in the psychic world. In the psychic world, the soul will be able to unite with a physical sheath or form, a divine body already created. Then at that time there will be no necessity for the spiritually realised soul to enter into a human mother, the human body. At that time, procreation will be stopped for those spiritually realised persons. They will no longer enter the earth through human birth. But in ordinary human beings, procreation will go on.

Just as we came out of the animal kingdom and we still see around us monkeys, elephants, dogs and all, so these divinised beings will be surrounded by ordinary human beings. But after thousands and thousands of years, millions of years probably, there will be a golden creation. It will be the creation of divinised, transformed beings. It will be a new Golden Age.

288. Is all that happens to a human being caused by karma or by trials or by a third force? Can we call that third force "will"?

Sri Chinmoy: Actually, let us not use the word "trial". You may call it a trial, but the actual truth of it is experience. The law of karma and experience – either one the soul wants to give you or the Divine wants to give you or else, it is the law of karma which is giving you the experience. Although the law of karma can be separated from experience, at the same time, karma itself is an experience. So the law of karma may be an experience that God wants to give you or the soul wants to give you.

The third thing that causes things to happen in the human being is will-power. In its purest term, in its highest term, will-power is inner determination. But in ordinary terms it is desire. At its highest, it is the inner urge; at its superficial level, it is an outer, shallow tinkering or wanting. So you can call the third force, will-power or desire.

Lastly there is God's Vision in Reality and Reality in Vision. God has All-Vision and that Vision is surcharged with Reality. So now these are the four things that affect us: the law of karma, experience, will-power or desire, and God's Vision in Reality. So there are the four major reasons for things that we see happening in the world.

289. How can we succeed in breaking loose from the bonds of karma?

Sri Chinmoy: Man can free himself from the bonds of karma by divine Grace and by his own aspiration. Who is the cause of karma? Man! But if you go deep within, you see that it is not the man but some other force, an inner force or law which initiates the karma. Now if you carry this inner force to the original source where karma and its results stay together, there karma cannot be separated from its results. I shall explain. We have done something today; the next moment we will get the result; or it may be years later or perhaps a few months later. But if one can stay where karma and its result are conceived or formulated, then that is one way of freeing oneself from the law of karma. Needless to say, this method is not widely applicable.

The easiest and most effective way of freeing yourself from the bonds of karma is to feel that you are not the doer. You are just an instrument. An instrument is not responsible, but the Doer, who is God, is responsible. If one can feel all the time that there is Somebody else who is the Doer and he is merely the instrument, then who will be responsible? The doer. If He does something wrong, He is responsible; if He does something good, He will be appreciated. Unfortunately in ordinary life, it is impossible for the average human being to think or feel that he is not the doer. If he does something wrong, immediately he curses himself and says, "I made a mistake." If, on the other hand, he does something right, he is bloated with pride and feels that he alone did it. Our human action compels us to feel that we deserve the fruit. But if we feel that we are not the Doer, that the Doer is God, immediately the fruit, the result, goes to the One who has actually acted. And who is that person? It is God, the Supreme.

So any human being, any man on earth, can free himself from the bonds of karma just by changing his attitude towards karma.

"He is the Doer, I am the instrument." This may be very difficult, but at the same time, it is the only way for an aspirant to free himself from the bonds of karma. And if the aspirant is sincere and aspiring, sooner or later, he will be granted liberation, self-realisation and all that. When one has realised God, one has liberated himself from the fetters of ignorance. Then one is not bound by the law of karma. He does another kind of karma which in Sanskrit is called *Agami karma*. Agami karma is done by the liberated soul, the realised person. When he works, he is not bound by the results of his work, either good or bad, because he knows perfectly well that he is the instrument and he is not the doer. Another kind of karma is *Sanchita karma*, accumulated karma which brings together the results and the consequences of a great deal of past karma all, more or less, at the same time. There is also *Prarabdha karma*, the actions that you have done in the distant past and for which you are now reaping the results.

So after realisation, after being liberated, one feels that he can never be bound by any karma. At the same time, he will have to work here in the world to manifest the divine, the Supreme here on earth. Liberation does mean abstention from work. Liberation means the acceptance of the work and the manifestation of Divinity within us. This manifestation can be achieved here on earth when the seeker feels that he is only the channel, the instrument and that God is the Doer.

290. Please explain the relationship between karma and fate.

Sri Chinmoy: Let us start with karma. In the West, very often this term is used erroneously. The word *karma* comes from Sanskrit and often it is translated into the English word "action". Action does not convey the same meaning as the word karma. It is not just any kind of action being done. It is not like that. Karma is something significant and it conveys an esoteric meaning. When we use the expression "the law of karma", it is used in a spiritual way. It refers to a cosmic law in which actions and reactions, causes and effects are part of a chain of experiences given to us by a higher Power.

Karma can be done physically, vitally, mentally, psychically. We can work with the heart, we can work with the soul. And again, in silence we can work. Silence is a kind of karma, if there is the power of conscious determination behind it. And that karma is most difficult: to remain silent, not inert, but dynamically silent.

Now to come back to your question. You are asking if whatever is happening is destined. Today's suffering or tomorrow's joys, is it all destined? Today I run into an accident. Is this destined? Or could I have avoided this accident to some extent, or could I have totally freed myself from that accident? Here we have to know whether there is something called Divine Grace. That Divine Grace can protect us totally or partially or it may not interfere at all in our day-to-day activities. It enters, it permeates our being only when we are in the field of aspiration.

Now another method you can adopt to obliterate the law of karma is the exercise of will, adamantine will. That will is not desire proper. It is adamantine will-power which we get through aspiration, through meditation.

You speak of karma, but there are many people who call it fate and do not differentiate between the two. A spiritual person says, "Fate shall be changed by an unchanging will." Right now, most of us do not have that unchanging will. We have only a bundle of desires. Desire is not the same as will-power. We are always saying, "Give me, give me" like a beggar. We have to be conscious of what we are praying for and that is our oneness with the Will of the Supreme. When we can identify ourselves totally with the Supreme's Will, we develop and we possess that will-power. That will-power is our soul's power.

Let us come back to Grace, Divine Grace. In our ordinary life, we often see people attacked. Immediately the person who is wronged tries to take revenge. But there is or can be a third power. This is the intervention of Divine Grace which is infinitely mightier than my action and your reaction. If I do something wrong, immediately you will take revenge, you will punish me. But my wrong action can also be obliterated by Divine Grace and at the same time, your power, your revenge cannot take place in my life.

Here is an analogy of a child who goes and strikes his friend. He expects his friend to strike him back and he is afraid. He runs to his father. The father has compassion for his child. He knows that the child has done something wrong, but at the same time, he does not allow the second child to strike his child back even though his child deserves it. In this way, when we do something that we ought not to do and we run to God, God nullifies our karma. He prevents it from coming back to us out of His Infinite Compassion and Love for us. So if we have complete faith in God and we surrender to Him and we immediately run to Him with our wrong doing, our error or our defects, He will bless us and protect us from the karma which would have normally come back to us.

291. I believe that if we live our lives according to the laws of nature, most harmoniously with the laws of nature, we won't have as much suffering as we now have, because everyday we are actually violating the laws of nature.

Sri Chinmoy: Yes, that is true, we are violating the laws of nature. That is why we are suffering. But again, just by following nature we will not reach our Goal.

292. I think that one should not try to imitate the laws of nature, inasmuch as each one has his own nature which is more important to him. We cannot imitate a tree. The tree does not have to know that it is a tree to be a tree. A man has to know that he is a man to be a man. We have to be conscious, but the tree is not required to be conscious.

Sri Chinmoy: But the thing here is that God wants all human beings – all His creations – to have an individuality of their own. Creation is such that in God's manifestation, no two human beings are alike. Not even my two fingers: one is shorter, one is longer. So in His creation, God wants to enjoy Himself in infinite ways. No two beings are the same. So we should not be a carbon copy of anything else. A man is a man and a tree is a tree. Each has its unique divine essence. I have my human individuality. This individuality is not the individuality of ego or pride. This individuality is the expression of God's infinite Self-Expression. And each divine individuality has its own degree of conscious awareness. The tree is fulfilling God by being a tree, whether or not it is aware of being a tree. But you are absolutely right in feeling that since we are more conscious than the tree, we should not try to regress to the tree-consciousness. The tree is playing its part; we must play our part. A tree is a tree. It need not be conscious (although many large and old trees are deeply conscious of their existence). But a man is a man, and to fulfil his divine destiny, he has to be conscious of his inner reality and his soul's oneness with the Supreme.

293. We try to live the spiritual life and then we feel that the forces of the world seem to act apart from us and try to drag us down. When we give in to those forces, something happens and then we lose our contact with the Divine. We get mixed up with the things of the world. We have desires, passions, and we ask God for material things. Then when we try to go back to the spiritual life, we find that we do not deserve it.

Sri Chinmoy: The thing is, first of all, that we are making a great mistake, a serious mistake, when we say that we don't deserve God. If you don't deserve God, who does deserve Him? God-realisation is your birthright. From whom did you come? From God and nobody else. And where are you? In God. When you go back, where will you go? You will go back to God. God-realisation is your birthright. So the first thing is to annul the idea that you don't deserve Him. You do deserve Him. We came from God and certainly we should be an exact prototype of the Father, the very image of God. And we deserve Him because He is deep inside us and we have come here to express Him, to reveal Him. So we fully deserve God-realisation.

The thing is that sometimes we sleep. What you say, that you have entered into the ordinary world, you have forgotten God and that you harbour these ugly forces like passion, anger, fear and all that — let us take that as sleep or rest, conscious rest. Now sometimes, instead of sleeping for eight hours, we sleep for twelve hours. Why do we sleep? Sometimes the body needs rest but sometimes out of laziness or mere whim, we are inclined to sleep more than our due. Similarly our outer being wants to take rest, or sleep, for a few years. It has meditated for so many years and it could not keep up the continuous prayer and meditation, the mounting cry which I always speak of. The flame of aspiration, consciously or unconsciously I can extinguish. The flame is extinguished and then for some time, I sleep. Then after four or five years, ten years, again I light the flame. Then my aspiration mounts.

Now the truth is that we don't lose anything. God is in this room. You have been trying to come here from the other room. There is a passage and you are about to knock at the door. Instead of knocking at the door, you stand in front of it for a few hours or a few days. You changed your process of entering into God's room.

You felt either that you were frustrated in the world, frustrated with the world, that there was no God, or that in the material world God was there, but in desire, in fear, in passion. In whatever you were doing, you discovered that God was there. Here, however, you are making a mistake with your human mind. Certainly in everything there is God, but we have to find out where precisely God can really illumine us. God is in dirty water as well as in pure, distilled water. But what do we want? We want pure water which will give us new life and not dirty water which will make us sick. Similarly we should not try to find God in the most ordinary, obscure and impure activities and foolish desires.

But what is the opposite of desire? It is aspiration. It is like the obverse and reverse of a coin. When we are on one side, it is desire; when we are on the other side, it is aspiration. What do we want to do with that aspiration? We are trying to bring down Peace, Joy, Light and Bliss, all these things. So we can go on living in this world. It is like two brothers: one brother is desire, the other brother is aspiration. If we enter into aspiration's side, we see in everything the living face of aspiration. The chair is aspiring because in that chair there is a soul. The world is aspiring because in the world there is soul. We have to see with the eye of aspiration and then everything is changed.

So to come back to your point, Agni, you have not lost anything. You have not lost anything. In the Gita, it is mentioned that, if, owing to circumstances, a man could not stay on the spiritual path and adopted a path of enjoyment, he would not necessarily come back in his next incarnation as the most ordinary man, but that he would again enter into an aspirant's family. Suppose a man for twenty years has meditated and practised the spiritual life. Then for ten or fifteen years, he enters into the world of enjoyment. Then, what will happen? Does it mean that he will never regain the spiritual life? No, he will get it either in this life, in the evening of his life or in his next incarnation. Again he will be given the opportunity to enter into the spiritual life. God will give him another opportunity to enter into the family of a spiritual seeker. So he will lose nothing.

The only thing is that the sooner you can come back to your inner life, by emulating the aspiration of others, the better it is for you. By observing the aspiration of others, you get inspiration again to start treading the path. They will inspire your own aspiration. That is what a spiritual person does. He does not speak. When a disciple has lost aspiration for a month or two, if he is sincere enough, he will just come and look at his Master and then just by looking at his face, he will get back his long-forgotten aspiration. In your case, I am elaborating on your personal question, so that if there is any further question on this, you please tell me.

Agni: It is very clear. Thank you.

Sri Chinmoy: So nothing shall we lose, nothing shall we lose. The only thing is that if we are wise, we can get back our own wealth sooner by seeing true aspirants. And there is also another process which is the process of devotion, which is difficult in the West. In the West, devotion should grow a little more. First of all, in the West they do not know the meaning of devotion. They think that showing me devotion means that if I am the Himalayas, then you are just a hill. No, devotion actually means that you are showing loving care and service to your own Highest. When you look at me, if you show devotion, it is not to me that you are showing this loving concern, but it is to the Highest within me and that Highest abides within you as well. The moment devotion comes, you have to feel that you are showing devotion to your own Highest which you consciously want to become.

Now you know that you have a highest and a lowest consciousness. We are living, most of the time, in the lowest consciousness. The highest consciousness we don't see, but at the same time, we want to become it. How can we become our highest? Only when we see someone who is constantly trying to bring forward that highest and that is the Guru or the Master or the illumined Teacher. And that Teacher is not, even for a second, separated from you, because his Highest and your Highest are the same. Only he is conscious of the fact that he has free access to that Highest and you are not. Otherwise his Highest and your Highest are the same. So in the West, if the westerners cultivate more the soil of devotion, they will grow faster. In the East, in the Orient, there is devotion, but at the same time, the East is lethargic. In the West, there is dynamism, but this dynamism is used as restlessness. So again, when you are acting like a restless fellow, you are misusing your dynamic faculties. When we are not aware of devotion, we cannot identify ourselves with the Highest. Devotion immediately becomes one with the object of its love. Like this it comes and it touches and it becomes what I am, what I stand for. "I" means your own Highest.

When you lose faith in yourself or faith in God or faith in your own achievement and fulfilment, the best thing is to bring forward your own devotion which is here in the heart and let it come out and grow. As the inner devotion starts growing, your outer life will also start blossoming. This is the first, fundamental preliminary step, without which one can never, never realise God.

294. How do you find a Guru? This is all new for me in this life. Idle urge is already there, but how does one know?

Sri Chinmoy: It is not a matter of knowing. It is a matter of feeling. Please go deep within and shed bitter tears and pray to God: "I have wasted my life, all my life; now You must tell me whether I am meant to have a Guru." Then God will say, "Yes, you are meant." You will ask God, "Who is my Guru? I implore You to tell me." If you are totally sincere, then God will immediately answer your prayer. A child, when he cries bitterly in front of his mother, how long can she, if she is a real mother, deny him what he wants? You are also a child of the Supreme. If you sincerely cry, it is a matter of hours or days. The Supreme will quickly make you feel whether I am, or someone else is, meant for you.

The thing is – whom do you actually want? Do you want a Swami or a Master or a Guru? Mahatma Gandhi, whom you were speaking about before was not a realised soul; he was a saint who expressed his love in a patriotic way. A saintly patriot need not be a great spiritual Master. Mahatma Gandhi was not an authority on the inner life or the spiritual life. He was a supreme authority on the moral and religious life; he was an authority on what was decent, proper and necessary in Indian social life and Indian politics. He was a very great man and a very great soul. His illumining vision was much higher and wider than that of his fellow men. He showed his heart's deepest compassion and oneness for the simple Indian villagers who were downtrodden and neglected. He offered his whole life to help raise the condition of the Indian masses. But as far as self-realisation is concerned, all spiritual Masters know – I am not the only one – that Mahatma Gandhi did not have this. He was not a man who had realised God. He was not a second Sri Ramakrishna or even a Vivekananda. He was nowhere near them. He was not a spiritual figure according to our definition of the term.

It is true to say that spiritual figures are not as easily available as before, but it is simply a wrong idea to say that there are no spiritual figures any more. It is as I told you before that in order to recognise a yogi, one has to be a yogi. But there are spiritual Masters available, and if you are sincere, even though you may not be able to recognise one yourself, the Supreme will lead you to a genuine yogi.

Coming back to Mahatma Gandhi, he was a saintly person, a wonderful character and full of heart, sacrifice and inner strength. But when the question of realisation arises or of his being a great spiritual Master, he was unfortunately not in that category. I have a great admiration for his complete identification with the Indian people in our India's independence movement.

295. In the Bible, it says that there will always be a Joshua to follow a Moses. Joshua was Moses' disciple. I see also in Indian books that there is always a disciple who starts a line of followers. Is this spiritual chain a necessary part of the manifestation?

Sri Chinmoy: It is not quite like that, actually. If the spiritual Guru is really great and has real power, it is quite possible that his power will be given to a spiritual descendant. Sri Ramakrishna had a spiritual descendant, Vivekananda. But at the same time he had a few more disciples who were spiritually great. Undoubtedly, Rakhal (Brahmananda) was one of them. You can say that a Master might have one major disciple, but you cannot say that all his spiritual Power, all his Light he gives to this one person, while the others get next to nothing. It is not like that. When the Master realises God, he represents the Divine to his particular disciples. Indeed, because he represents the Divine, his spiritual Power, Knowledge, Peace, Light and Delight are unlimited. Each disciple can get boundless Light, Delight, Peace and Power. "When Infinity is taken away from Infinity, Infinity still remains the same." This is what the Upanishads teach us.

One disciple can play the part of a leader and he can be described as the Master's spiritual descendant, but the Master's spiritual powers and achievements are given to each disciple according to his capacity and receptivity. The Master may make one disciple a leader, as Sri Ramakrishna did with Vivekananda. Everybody cannot be a leader. But even the leader will receive from the Master according to his own spiritual capacity and receptivity. There are many sincere disciples who do not have the capacity of leadership, but at the same time, they most sincerely aspire. If they are sincere they, too, can get everything.

Actually, each disciple can think that he is the dearest. How can he know? The moment the disciple feels that he has offered everything, his outer life as well as his inner life, to the Guru, he can feel that he is the dearest and closest. He lives just because the Guru wants him to live. He lives for the sake of the Guru, for the sake of the Divine. If any disciple can do that, undoubtedly he will feel that he is dearest to his Master. This feeling of his is absolutely true. Nobody will have to reassure him on this point. No one will even have to tell him. If any disciple can make a constant, cheerful and unconditional surrender to God, then I must say he is or she is the dearest disciple to the Master. Just to fulfil the Will of the Supreme in the Master, he or she is on earth. This absolute surrender to the Will of the Absolute has no equal in the spiritual life.

296. This state or condition of complete surrender is not easily obtained. On the other hand, you cannot obtain liberation until first you reach the condition of complete surrender. However we find out that we cannot reach that Goal unless we bypass the limitations and self-consciousness of the limited mind, be it in the sphere of the personality or elsewhere. To by-pass that self-consciousness, we find that we cannot do so by the development of the intellect or by the development of the reasoning power because this condition transcends the sphere of both, of the intellect and the reasoning power. And there is a difficulty here because to attain this condition you cannot be consciously immersed in life's problems. I mean to say, we cannot be attached or chained by those problems. Yet life is a challenge that we must meet because life is the process by which the Atman will develop the power and the wisdom to merge with the immanent and transcending power of the Divine. Now the question is: on the one hand we cannot run away from life, but I have found now that this is true only until a certain stage. The stage comes when you have to pull out from this daily turmoil so that you can concentrate and develop or not, but at least get in contact with the inner powers of the Self. For that we need to retire in solitude and meditation so that we will not be disturbed. And my question is: is this retirement indispensable? Is it also indispensable at this ultimate stage that you have the guidance and help of the Guru to attain that condition of complete surrender? Is it indispensable? Once you have attained that condition, then can you come back into life and serve in whatever position that the Supreme wants to put you into?

Sri Chinmoy: Well, thank you. Many, many questions in one question and if I forget any question, you will afterwards tell me.

To start with, you are absolutely right when you say that it is extremely difficult to make a surrender. Even a partial surrender, not to speak of a total surrender, on the one hand is difficult. On the other hand, it is said that without a complete surrender, you cannot realise God. Both are equally true. Now, how can we solve the first problem or make it easier? We say that it is extremely difficult to surrender to God or to the Guru. But everyone consciously or unconsciously has to surrender; God Himself is helpless in this respect. If one does not surrender to God or to the Guru, he is bound to be unfulfilled, since the entire purpose of our existence is to fulfil the Will of God. So here I wish to tell you how one can surrender.

If one has sincerely accepted a spiritual Master — I am using the word "sincerely" because it is not a matter of just saying that one has accepted a Master in order to show off: "I have the greatest spiritual Master on earth. My Master has miraculous powers, my Master has written hundreds of books, my Master knows all the inner worlds and outer worlds," — no; I have accepted the Master just because I felt in him my real existence, not because of what he has achieved or what promise he is going to make or what he is going to manifest. Some Masters are absolutely illiterate. They can't read or write. Other Masters are thoroughly conversant with both Eastern and Western philosophies and scriptures. So whether your Master is a scholar or a fool does not matter. No. You have accepted the Master because in him, in the Master, you feel your highest existence, your highest reality. Only for that reason have you accepted him, not for what he has achieved or what He is going to give you.

If the disciple comes to the Master with the expectation that the Master will give him liberation, realisation, that is a wonderful idea. The Master will give them, He will bring them from God. But a real disciple is he who comes to the Master saying, "Master, take my life. Do anything. If you want me to be your eternal slave, I shall be one. If you want me to realise God, all right, take me. I am at your feet. My realisation is at your feet. My total surrender, my life is for you. Either use me as an eternal slave or use me as a king; for me it is the same." But if you have the expectation, "Oh, the Master will make me a realised soul," it is a wonderful expectation, but what happens? When the expectation is not fulfilled today or tomorrow, frustration comes, anxiety comes, worries come, fear comes and doubt comes. "I have been on the spiritual path for forty years; what is wrong with me? Still I am not getting the sense of realisation, not even a glimpse of it!" But where is your surrender? When you accept the Master, if you say, "Now I have totally given myself to you. Use me the way you want, not the way I want," that is the correct way. But if you say, "I want to be a realised soul, I want to help humanity. I say 'I' referring to my highest Self and I do not care for myself, but only for humanity," that, too, is wonderful. But again, how do you know what is best for you, to help humanity or to realise God first? God knows best. God knows the hour, God knows what He wants, in and through your life.

So you must feel that all your expectations must also be offered to God, to your Master – your expectation to be the highest person or the greatest person on earth or to be a great spiritual Master yourself. If all these expectations you can consciously surrender to the Master – good expectations, highest expectations – then it becomes very easy to make a surrender.

After you have got rid of desire, you have come into the field of aspiration. A time comes when you have to give up your aspiration also. To give up aspiration does not mean that you won't pray or meditate. No, you will. Giving up aspiration means that the result of aspiration, which is expectation, that also you have to give up. Ramakrishna used to say, "When you have run a thorn into your foot, it is that desire has entered. Now, what do you do? You take another thorn and pick out the first one. Then you throw away both thorns. You do not keep them." So first you have ignorance. Then you take knowledge to remove your ignorance. Then you throw them both away and you go beyond both ignorance and knowledge. In the Upanishads, it is said, "Through ignorance, we conquer death and then through knowledge, we get Immortality." Yet a time comes when we have to go beyond both ignorance and knowledge. When you can transcend them both, at that time your absolute surrender comes.

So what I wish to tell you in this matter is that you must give what you have and what you are, if you want to fulfil the Divine in your life. Are you a beggar that you expect this and that? If God is your real father, if you have a spiritual Master, he has to do everything for you. Yesterday I told the disciples that whenever I accept a disciple, I consciously make a promise both to the disciple and to the Supreme that I will take responsibility for this person for Eternity or until he has realised God. Until then, I am responsible for him. So when I make that commitment to the Supreme, the Highest, I have to be sincere and honour it. Some people come and accept a spiritual Master; then after a few months or a few years, they leave him. Their own promise, however, is never ever over, because they have made the highest commitment to the Supreme. They haven't only made a commitment to their own individual soul. But it seems that often, an ordinary person, when he makes a promise to the Master, just takes that promise as nothing, as drinking water. Tomorrow he leaves the Master and enters into the ordinary life.

The role of the Master is the role of a private tutor. The disciple has to offer his aspiration, his conscious desire, his outer existence, his inner existence to the Master, to the Supreme in the Master. He should say, "I do not expect anything from you, good or bad. From my Master I know I will get only good things, but my only prayer to you is that you utilise my life, you will mould my life, you will shape my life."

You must go beyond expectation. When you go beyond expectation, at that time you will get everything in plenitude, in infinitude. There, at that point, you make your surrender very easily. Surrender becomes extremely easy when you have the feeling that the Master thinks of your life more than you do yourself, because the Master had made a commitment, not only to you, but to the Supreme to liberate you. If you are sincere in your belief that the Master's commitment to the Supreme is absolutely binding, then your expectation, although you have long ago transcended it, is bound to be fulfilled in infinite measure. In this way, surrender becomes absolutely easy.

Now to come back to your question as to whether surrender is only one thing but the first thing is God Realisation. If, after accepting a spiritual Master, one wants to go this way or that, or one wants to turn back to one's own personality and individuality, then that is no surrender at all. You have to surrender to your Master or to the Inner Pilot or to God. These are all the same. The Master is representing God. The Inner Pilot in human form is the Master and in the Divine form, is the Supreme. So one has to surrender to one of the three in order to realise God. If one has no Master and he thinks of God, all right, he has to surrender his existence to God. But if one has a Master, he has to surrender to him, or, if he cares for the Inner Pilot in the human form, who is the Master, and in the spiritual form, the Divine and the Supreme Himself, he has to surrender to them. This is the first fundamental preliminary step, without which one can never, never realise God.

Now you said something about bypassing the mind?
Anugata: By "bypassing", I meant transcending.
Sri Chinmoy: That is very good. That is true. Otherwise "bypass" is not the right word. We cannot really bypass, but we can transcend. Now the thing is that here we have to ask how, while staying on earth, we can remain above the earth? While you are

mixing with people or talking to people, while you are amidst human life, how can you think of the divine life? Here I wish to tell you that the divine life has to be manifested here on earth. How? How are you going to be unaffected when you are mixing with ordinary people who are not aspiring around you? You have to remember that a boat is inside water under water but is not affected by water. We don't say that the boat is composed of water, but while it is carrying passengers from here to there, it is on top of the water. Similarly you are amongst unaspiring, insincere people. But on the strength of your own sincere, spiritual life, you are carrying them to their destination. That is what the boat is doing, sailing in the water, but not being affected by the water. You can be in the ordinary life, amidst your friends and neighbours, but you need not be affected. Why? Because you have your inner urge to realise the Highest, to fulfil the Highest on earth. If your aspiration is sincere, your aspiration is like an arrow which pierces into the heart of others to stab their own ignorance. But if your own aspiration is very meagre, not sincere, rather hesitant, then where do you go? You cannot inspire anybody, you cannot kindle the flame of aspiration in anyone. There you are lost. First of all, you cannot enter into them, then you can do nothing for them. So you have to know what wealth you already have. If you have the purest, which you have, the purest aspiration, then you can rest assured that you can mix with anybody because aspiration itself is the strength, the purest strength of God in human beings, in the aspirant. So if you have true aspiration, you can mix with anybody. Anybody, men, women, anybody, they will not be able to take away your aspiration. But if there is no aspiration, you are lost to the world, you are lost to yourself. Aspiration has a burning quality, but this fire does not burn people; it illumines people. Ordinary fire will simply turn everything to ashes. But the fire of aspiration, only illumines, illumines our lives. So when you are taking that kind of fire to the darkness, it is only illumining the darkness. The darkness is being illumined by our aspiration which is the constant inner fire. Easily you can stay amidst the world. What am I doing? It is my aspiration that gave me realisation. Now I am doubly secure, with my aspiration and realisation. Now you have the aspiration; what you need is realisation. Right now your own realisation is that you have to surrender your own existence to a spiritual Master who is totally one with the Supreme. So if your surrender to me is complete, then immediately we are one. When you are one with me, you are one with God. Then you need not be afraid of anybody. We are not afraid of ignorance.

297. I cannot see anything created by God as imperfect. How can He create a soul that is not perfect and then say, "Alright, you go ahead in your own free way; develop the best you can?"

Sri Chinmoy: But God does not just throw the soul into the manifestation and leave it there helplessly. He Himself is going there. He is in the soul and with the soul, guiding it constantly.
Arati: Good! G-o-o-d!
Sri Chinmoy: God is....
Arati: Perfect.
Sri Chinmoy: Yes, God is perfect – the Absolute God who is above all. The Highest is perfect, who is the Supreme, the Self. The God who is One Soul without a second, He is really perfect. But the God who has entered into the multiplicity, the One who has donned these clothes, Chinmoy, He is imperfect because He is now taking this human consciousness which is full of limitations and full of imperfections.

God Himself is in the process of making. I should say that He is going from imperfection to perfection. God wants to make me perfect. The potter, when he makes a pot, changes it constantly, moulding and changing the shape until it comes to perfection. So God is also perfecting Himself through humanity because He is the Spirit. He has descended into matter. This is His game. You can say it is a cruel game, but it is His game.

I say, we say, that we are all God, we have come from God. But where is our Realisation? Where is our perfection? We are in the process of Realisation: we are in the process of perfection.

When each individual represents God, what is actually happening? Even though that individual has not fully realised God, still we can't separate God from that person's existence. So much imperfection we are seeing in this world. Do you think that God is not there in that imperfection? God is everywhere. God is in a thief just as He is in the honest man. He is there; He is getting experience. God can be everything: He can be the Highest and He can be the Lowest. Of course I don't want to be the God who is in the lowest. I want to be the God who is in the Highest. God is in dirty, filthy water as well as in pure, distilled water. If I want to survive, I shall drink the pure water and not the filthy water; otherwise I would die. Similarly, if I want to be good, perfect and serve the Divine, I have to become Divine.

In our ordinary existence, during one day, how many times does each human being become the victim of ugly thoughts, undivine thoughts and all that? At the same time, you will see that he gets divine, fulfilling and sublime thoughts, too. So when God is in the uncomely thoughts as well as in the divine thoughts, how can He separate His existence from ours from one hour to another? No, He is in our imperfection and in our aspiration.

So God, the Spirit, has entered into matter, yet matter is ignorant, sleeping. There He is, awakening and pushing matter forward. Open your eyes, open your eyes; you have to grow into the Infinite. God is everywhere. God is in darkness and in Light.

But with our knowledge, with our wisdom, with our aspiration, we have to grow towards the Best, towards the Highest, towards the most fulfilling.

Our conception of God is that He is up there and cannot come down, that my Father and I may be one, but that my Father is in Heaven and I am doomed to rot on earth. No, if I am in hell, my Father is also here in hell because my Father cannot remain in Heaven if I am in hell. When I say that I and my Father are one, if I am in the most abysmal hell, He will be there also. He cannot be up there. He is where I am, if He is really my Father. My Father will not be able to suffer the separation. If I am in prison, my Father will come to prison with me. He cannot separate Himself from me; He cannot remain aloof from me if He is my true Father.

298. I would like to know why I have many times seen that when a person comes into profound practice of the spiritual or inner life, so many difficulties arise, many times discouraging the aspirant to go on in his practice?

Sri Chinmoy: You want to practise the spiritual life, you want to see God, realise God, become God. You want to achieve the highest, the greatest, the most fulfilling thing on earth. To do that, you also have to pay the price. Now the first thing is this: if we are sincere to ourselves, we will know that it is not God who is testing us. God never tests the sincere seekers. He never does. He knows how much capacity His daughter has and has no need to test her. But what actually happens is this: there are many hurdles right in front, between the seeker and his goal. When the seeker sincerely prays to God to see and to realise Him, very often it happens that by God's own Grace he is able to encounter most of the difficulties that otherwise he would have met and gone through all his life, or even in some future incarnations. Suppose you have hundreds of difficulties when you accept the spiritual life. These difficulties you had before. Under ordinary circumstances they would come to you – one, two, three, four, like this up to the last moment of your life. But if you accept the spiritual life, the inner life, God is most gracious in bringing all these difficulties right in front of you at the same time. At the same time He showers His special Grace on you so that all the difficulties may be overcome sooner. It is His Grace. And what actually happens to our limitations, imperfections, and ignorance? These are lions and tigers within us that we have been feeding. These tigers and lions are our desires, our wants that we have been feeding all the time. With God's Grace, they disappear.

299. In relation to Sudha's question, are not other personalities sometimes involved in keeping the soul in its present condition? For example if you are attached to someone?

Sri Chinmoy: It is absolutely true. Very often it happens like that, that if you are connected with someone, you are trying your best to go up, up, up; but the other person keeps pulling you down.

And in connection with Sudha's question, I am glad to say one thing: if we go deep within, we shall see one thing, that the difficulties that we are now facing after we accepted the spiritual life, we had almost ninety-nine per cent before we accepted the spiritual life. At that time we were not conscious; we were unconscious of them. Each difficulty we had. Just because you are unconscious while you are eating, whether you are eating rice or bread or fruit, you are still eating. But when you eat consciously, you know whether it is rice or bread or fruit. Similarly in the spiritual life, if we are conscious of the fact, then we will see that these difficulties almost ninety-nine per cent of them we had before we accepted the spiritual life. At that time we were blind. We were ignorant. We were foolish. We did not know what actually was happening in our life. But now that we have become conscious, we are aware of the difficulties that rise to fight against us. We are glad not only that we have become conscious but that there is Somebody, there is some higher factor, God and His miraculous Grace, who are more than eager to help us. As we have become conscious, we reach Him, realise Him. So we are most fortunate to be conscious of the difficulties that we have and we must never try to avoid difficulties. Accept them....and we know that with us, for us, and in us is the omnipotent Grace of God.

300. I would like to know if there is a point after pain? We live in pain, but then do you believe that there is a point beyond pain?

Sri Chinmoy: As long as we are in the physical, if our consciousness is all the time in the physical, certainly there is pain. But if we can withdraw our consciousness from the physical, then there can be no pain. Many spiritual figures have done it. They are undergoing a major operation, even without anaesthetic. Then what do they do? They put their conscious force on that particular place and then they smile. They smile while the operation is going on. I remember one such incident. A girl cousin of mine went with one of her friends to the doctor. My cousin was undergoing an operation, a tremendous one. When the doctor started operating, she looked at the doctor and started smiling, but her friend, who was supposed to help her if she was crying, fell down on the floor and fainted. The actual person who was undergoing the operation started smiling! And I have seen quite a few times that the doctors in India do not use chloroform or ether.

Once I had three big boils here and the pain was unbearable when I went to the doctor. I raised my hand; the nurse was holding my wrist and I was looking at the doctor, smiling. Before the actual operation took place, for ten minutes I was concentrating. When the doctor was operating, I was looking at him, smiling.

There is another way to overcome pain. If you can consciously enter into the pain itself and stay in the pain for a few minutes, then the pain does not torture you as pain. For when we become the possessors of the pain, we can transform this very pain into joy. When you enter into the pain, you become the possessor of the pain. Right now, the pain possesses you; you are a victim of the pain and it keeps torturing you. But if you can possess the pain, you can actually inject into that area anything that you want. With your conscious power, you can inject delight, joy, whatever you want. It is quite possible and practicable. Many people have done it and the doctors have admired it. If you want to inject joy into the pain, you can feel it in that very spot.

Then, of course, if we can separate ourselves from the body-consciousness, it becomes easy. Ramana Maharshi suffered from a cancerous tumour. He used to laugh and say, "That gentleman has now come." "That gentleman" referred to the pain and he mocked it. Pain can easily be transformed into joy if we consciously enter into the pain or if we separate our body-consciousness from the pain itself. In two possible ways it can be done. Either you can enter into it and possess it and when it is possessed, you can give it your own joy. Or you can separate your body-consciousness from the pain itself. These are two possible ways.

301. But do you think that a person can go on like this and not have to come back and stay in the physical plane? I mean, can he stay in a state of joy?

Sri Chinmoy: Yes, a person can easily stay in a state of joy and, at the same time, remain on earth. There are many levels of consciousness. In one particular level, if you can retain that constant joy, you can stay there, while at the same time your other parts are remaining on another level. Realised souls, when they get news of suffering, say the death of their parents, for a time, suffer as intensely as ordinary people. At the same time, there is another part which is detached, completely detached. There it is all joy, all delight. On one plane, they are suffering like ordinary human beings and on the other plane, they are completely detached. So a human being can retain the consciousness of joy and at the same time, can operate on the physical level. It is quite possible. One can function on two different levels at the same time. That is what spiritual figures do.

Is it clear to you, Akuti? It is quite possible. Even in your meditation, if you go and enter into the place of Peace and Bliss, you retain a higher level of consciousness while you are doing your daily work. Even though you are involved in thousands of activities, you can consciously retain that beautiful state of Bliss. Although you are talking with your friends and are involved in physical activities, you are retaining the consciousness of Peace and Bliss.

In our *Mahabharata,* India's greatest epic, the mother of the Pandavas used to pray to the Lord, Sri Krishna, to give her pain and suffering so that she would think of God all the time and pray to Him. "O Lord, give me pain, give me suffering, so that I can always think of you." But in this evolved world and in our society, this should never be our attitude. We should pray to God to go towards the Light. "Give me Light so that I can think of You all the time in Light, in Joy, in Delight." But she prayed for pain. "If I am in joy, I will forget You", she said. That should not be our attitude.

On another human level, there are many people who cherish suffering. They feel that if there is no suffering, the day is not complete. There are many couples who feel that the day has ended properly when they have some calamity in the family among the relatives or friends; the day has played its part. But that should never be our attitude. Our attitude should be to invoke Light and to grow in the Light because God Himself is All-Light and All-Joy. Very often we invite suffering and pain just to justify and prove that we belong to this world. God does not want that kind of suffering and pain.

302. Will you speak about the Divine Mother?

Sri Chinmoy: The Mother Divine is the Divine in its feminine aspect. As in the physical world, so also in the spiritual world: just as it is usually easier to please the mother than the father in the physical world, so also in the spiritual world, it is easier to please the Mother Divine. This is because She, the executive Force of the Supreme, the Divine Shakti, has Herself created the earth and therefore she identifies Herself with the earth-consciousness. All our imperfections and struggles rest upon Her infinite Heart of Compassion. Yet the Mother Divine does everything in consultation with the Lord, with the Supreme. And He consults the Divine Mother in all His Supreme Movements.

There are four major aspects of this Mother Divine, the transcendental Mother. The first aspect is that of immensity, power, vastness and majesty. That aspect we call Maheshwari, the Great Mother. In another aspect, we call her Mahakali, the Great Mother who is all the time fighting against the undivine forces, yet who is full of compassion. Of course, all the Mother-aspects of the Divine are full of compassion, but this Mother, it seems, has more compassion than the others. Now this Mother, Mahakali, does everything very, very quickly towards the final achievement. She cares only for those who sincerely aspire. She does not care so much for perfecting the seeker, but she cares for the highest height. If she is satisfied with the aspiration and sincerity of her disciples, of her devotees, then what she does is to give them, in a day, the progress which otherwise would have taken those particular aspirants fifty or sixty years. She works so fast; this is the Mother Mahakali, Great Kali. She is my favourite, my most favourite of all the goddesses; but we cannot separate one goddess from another, since these are only aspects of the one Divine Mother. I cannot separate my right arm from my left arm. In the same way, all the different aspects of the Divine Mother function in their own unique way, but they work together.

And I must say that the Maheshwari aspect of infinite wideness has another emanation, another personality, whom we call Durga. Durga is one of Maheshwari's aspects. Durga and Vijaya are the same goddess. Vijaya is also an emanation of the Goddess Maheshwari. She fights for the Divine. She fights for the victory of Truth and Light. One of our great Avatars – an Avatar is a direct descendant of God – whose name was Ramachandra, the first Avatar, while he was fighting against the demons, prayed to this particular Goddess, Durga. Durga was pleased with his prayer and Ramachandra was able to conquer the hostile forces and win the victory. He brought back his wife, Sita, who had been captured by the demon chief.

The third goddess is Lakshmi, Mahalakshmi. She is the Mother of beauty, charm, sweetness and fragrance. She is the Mother who creates in every aspect of life, a divine harmony. Most Indian women are inwardly connected and influenced by Mahalakshmi. She has infinite patience, whereas Mother Kali does not want to wait; she does not have patience. In our human sense, we can say that Kali won't wait. Immediately she will know whether I am sincere or not. If I am insincere, she will simply throw me away. But Mahalakshmi will wait and wait, no matter how insincere I am, no matter what my imperfections are. She is for each and every soul on earth. She wants a peaceful harmony in this earthly life; beauty, softness, sweetness, splendour, all of these heart qualities. So those who pray to her will naturally get all these divine qualities, but they do not go as fast as the devotees of Kali do. These want only liberation, the disciples of Kali; they go right to the Goal. Then after reaching the Highest, if the Supreme wants perfection in their nature, then they have to perfect themselves; and become perfect perfection. I want to say one more thing about Kali: she is the Mother of aspiration also. She kindles the flame of aspiration in the sincere seekers. She does this immediately on seeing real sincerity.

Now there is a fourth goddess. Her name is Saraswati, Mahasaraswati. She is the Mother of Divine Learning, Knowledge and Wisdom. In India, when a child begins to learn to read, he is taught to invoke the Goddess Saraswati and at the same time, to learn a particular mantra [an incantation] and *shloka* [a verse] which he will repeat so that the Goddess Saraswati will be pleased with him and bless his endeavour. Even when an adult person sits down to read in India, he will often invoke the name of Mahasaraswati to bless him with divine understanding and ultimate knowledge. I still remember the shloka which I had to learn at the age of four and a half or five. We had to say it repeatedly, so we learned it. It was in Sanskrit. "I bow to Thee, O Saraswati, who gives knowledge and wisdom, and whose eyes are very wide and who plays the vina." This goddess plays the vina, the Indian stringed instrument. She wants perfect perfection in her disciples. As I said, she is the Goddess of Learning and Wisdom, Knowledge and divine Understanding. She wants perfection in every minute detail. She is the Mother of Perfection. In everything, she wants divine perfection. Mahasaraswati is most gracious, most beautiful in this unillumined, ignorant world. She is the youngest and most recent of the four aspects of the Divine Mother.

So these are the four divine emanations of the Mother Divine on the transcendental plane. Through these four aspects, She manifests Herself here on earth. And at the same time, one disciple, one aspirant, can be the follower of all these four aspects, because ultimately one is praying to the one Mother Divine, only One. But in Her manifestation, she has taken four forms. Suppose, in my case, although Mahakali is my dearest, I have satisfied, pleased, all the aspects of the Mother. I do a little bit of writing. This writing, music, poetry and all this, I get from this Mother, Saraswati. Secondly, I am ugly now, but I think I have retained just a little beauty. In my childhood, I was not as ugly as I am now, I must tell you. I lived in South India, where it is very hot, so my skin is dark like this. But Mahalakshmi did bless me as a child. Then Mahakali – she has given me everything, so-called liberation and all that. The other Divine Mother who is immensity, vastness and who is unfathomable in Her highest aspect, Maheshwari – she has also blessed me. So I must say that any aspirant can be blessed and helped by these four aspects of the Divine Mother.

303. Do you have pictures of the different aspects of the Mother?

Sri Chinmoy: Yes, we have. Here in Puerto Rico we have a picture of Mahakali. In our reception room here, we have Saraswati. In our Centre in New York, we have pictures of all the goddesses.

304. In that picture, Mother Kali is represented doing different things with her four arms. What is she actually doing?

Sri Chinmoy: These paintings are done by contemporary Indian artists. They are usually calendar illustrations. The ones of Kali show her in her vital aspect, not as she appears in the highest transcendental worlds. There she is all golden and extremely beautiful. But in these paintings, we see Kali as the divine warrior, sometimes looking very grotesque and even hideous. She wears a garland of skulls and has her tongue stuck out. The objects in her four arms differ according to the particular artist, but often with one arm she is blessing. With the second arm, she is holding the beheaded Ravana, the embodiment of evil. With a third arm, she is fighting the hostile forces with the bloody scimitar, and in her fourth arm, she is holding Lord Shiva's trident. I shall explain this later. Now in the picture, Kali is placing her foot on the chest of her husband, Shiva. How can a wife place her foot on her husband's chest? In India especially, this is unbelievable. Some people say that she brought out her tongue in surprise when she realised that she was stepping on her husband's chest. But it actually means that when this particular Mother was fighting with the hostile forces and their blood was running profusely, she was drinking the blood of these hostile forces. That is why her tongue is stuck out. When Kali was killing the great hostile force, Ravana, she saw that from one drop of his blood, millions and billions of hostile forces were taking birth. So after killing him and cutting off his head, she is drinking his blood so that no more hostile forces would be born. In some pictures of Kali, instead of one hand blessing the divine forces, this hand holds a bowl, into which is dripping the blood from Ravana's beheaded head.

And now, why is she seen to be standing on her husband? When she was fighting, it was all water and flowing blood. She needed space. When the divine starts fighting, both the dynamic and the static states are brought into play. Dynamism can take place only where there is a static base. Somebody must remain solidly anchored and still; Kali's own husband offered. She was moving while fighting, so she needed some place where she could get a footing. Lord Shiva played the part of her static base by lying down and allowing her to stand upon his chest.

Each goddess has a secret and special name. While this Goddess is normally known as Kali or Mahakali [Great Kali], her secret name is *Kring*. Many years ago, when I started worshipping her, I had to say her name most powerfully: AUM, Krinng, Krinnng, Krinnng.... All fear, all the world's fear has to leave when you repeat her name, her secret name. I used to repeat her secret name thousands and millions of times when I was thirteen or fourteen years old.

With other goddesses, for example, if we invoke Saraswati, it is a softer and more gentle vibration. Saraswati's secret name is *Oihing*. You invoke Oihing, Oihing, Oihing. Sarawasti will bless you with inner illumination, musical capacity and perfectionism. But for this Goddess Kali, you have to break your palate when you invoke her mantra, Kring. Here I am not doing it powerfully. When I used to chant it repeatedly in full voice, it was infinitely more powerful and sonorous than now.

305. What is true humility and how does true love for mankind manifest in us?

Sri Chinmoy: Humility, what we call humility is truly the divine dignity. It is God's true divine pride. "Therefore know by that humility that thou art God."

We cannot be abused. We do not allow anybody to stand on our head. We do not allow anybody to treat us mercilessly. God.... let us look at God. He lives in the grass. Early in the morning we walk on the grass and how it is crushed and spoiled, but there He is. Without humility we do not, cannot, possess the divine dignity. And what is this divine dignity? Divine dignity is the knowledge that we exist in everything. I am God, so I exist everywhere, in everything. So now, if one wants to realise God, the first and foremost thing that will be necessary is humility.

Now to go deeper; when one is humble it does not mean that he is weak, he is a beggar. No. Humility and humiliation are two totally different things. Very often here in the West we take humility as humiliation. Why should we allow anybody to trample us, to degrade us? No, that is called humiliation. But humility is something that spontaneously grows in our day-to-day life because it is the sweetest, softest, mildest and at the same time most fertile ground in us. Look at this Mother Earth. Can there be anybody or anything as humble as Mother Earth? Mother Earth is holding us, receiving all impacts from us, guiding us. She is all love, all compassion and at the same time, all powerful. But when we look at Mother Earth, the first thing that comes to our mind is humility. How humble! We see this when we appreciate nature and natural beauty all around us. How humble they are! The more humble one is, the greater is his strength. God is omnipresent. That means He is everywhere. Just because He is everywhere, He is also omnipotent; He is all powerful. So when we are humble, when we know the true meaning of humility, we immediately become one with the Person who is around us, in front of us, and one with the Object that is around us. The moment we become totally one with God or Light or Duty or Power or with Consciousness, we become the All-powerful, the Almighty in our inner life, as well as outer life.

So humility is the secret to show us the oneness with the outer world and also with the inner world. When we have true humility, we unite both worlds, the inner and the outer. When we unite the worlds, then we see what else is required: possessing the world. When we possess the world, what else is required? We become the real rulers of the world. This ruler does not dominate. No, he will be the conscious guiding light of the world.

To come back again to your question, true humility is man's true dignity: God's divine pride. We say "humility" and God says "God's divine pride" which is expressed not like the human pride of arrogance. No, God's divine pride is in everyone, in everything, and that divine pride you get only from humility.

306. Does the spiritual life preclude other kinds of normal activities in life? I mean .... does the spiritual life mean that you have to give up what you happen to be doing at the time, say, being an interior decorator?

Sri Chinmoy: Not in the least. The spiritual life, if it is the true spiritual life, will never negate anything. It will always accept. First it will accept, then it will embrace; then it will become one with the activity itself. What for? For its transformation. It identifies itself with the activity in order to transform it. The spiritual life will never reject anything. If it is the true and integral spiritual life, it will accept each and every activity as an opportunity to go to God and manifest God.

You asked about work. Now there are two kinds of work: in the ordinary kind of work, you do something and then immediately you ask for the result. Then when you get the result, you say, "No, perhaps I could have got a better result." There is no end to it. If you want real joy, you will not get it by fulfilling a desire for a particular result. You won't get real joy. But in the second kind of work, in true spiritual work, you do the work but you do not care for the fruit or the result. Only by having the right attitude, will you become a happy person. If you do the work with a divine attitude, then it will not be the result which gives you joy, but the very act.

So within the spiritual life, we can easily house the outer life. But the true spiritual life will never ask the outer life to remain separate. No. What it does is that it enters into the physical life or the outer life and it tries to expedite the movement and progress of the outer life in a divine way.

What do we mean by the spiritual life? We mean that it is a life of inspiration, aspiration and inner communion. When you are able to meditate for a few minutes, the mind does not become a victim to doubts, impure thoughts, and unhealthy ideas. When there is no doubt, you can do some work in a very few minutes. If there is a little shadow of doubt, though, it may take an hour or even a day. So even in your day-to-day activities, the spiritual life is a great help in achieving success. And if you really and truly accept the spiritual life, you will see that in the twinkling of an eye, most of your difficulties not only decrease but disappear. This happens because in your spiritual life there is abundant strength which you don't have in your outer life. This abundant strength, when it comes to the fore, makes the outer life surrender automatically to the inner life. And when it surrenders, it is not from compulsion, but from a spontaneous, inner feeling. It surrenders with joy because it feels that in surrender itself, it gets the full power and total bliss of the inner life.

So to come back to your question, the spiritual life is the greatest help to the outer life. You can say that it is the elder brother of the younger brother. The elder brother will always beckon the younger one. In every way the spiritual life helps the outer life. Unfortunately, people harbour a wrong conception of the spiritual life when they think it means giving up the world. If you give up the world, where are you going to establish God's Truth, God's Kingdom? It is right here on earth that Self-realisation or God-realisation can take place. Not in Heaven. Heaven is a state of consciousness. And here, earth is also a state, but it is a physical place where one has to manifest God. And it is through the spiritual life that the synthesis of the spiritual life and the outer life can be made. Again it is only through the spiritual life that God-manifestation can take place on earth.

307. If there is no perfection in the body and no perfection in the mind, then my question is: would the soul's light lead the body and the mind towards perfection?

Sri Chinmoy: Yes, if the body and the mind become the conscious instruments of the soul and say, "We shall work along with the soul," then the soul's perfection will automatically lead them towards their own perfection. If the mind, the body and the vital are not fully surrendered to the soul, then the soul's full manifestation can not take place. And if the soul's manifestation does not take place, it means that the soul is not fulfilled. It has to be fulfilled. Since it wants fulfilment, we will see that one day, the body, the vital and the mind will consciously obey the divine in us, our soul.

308. Do the body, mind and heart function differently when they function with the light of the soul?

Sri Chinmoy: Certainly, they do act differently; that is to say, they act divinely when they function with the light of the soul. With different eyes they see the truth, with different hearts they feel the truth. Always they function differently in the sense that they are tinged with God's Light. Their act of seeing and feeling is done through the play of energy. This energy is totally different from the usual physical energy. That is why we call it spiritual energy or cosmic energy. Cosmic energy is totally different from physical energy. When we draw in cosmic energy even for four or five minutes, we can overcome the need for rest or sleep most effectively. It is also the cosmic energy that quenches our inner thirst for Truth and Light most adequately.

309. Can we draw upon the cosmic energy by going deep within ourselves?

Sri Chinmoy: Yes, we can draw upon the cosmic energy by entering into our deeper consciousness, the all-pervading consciousness, which is here, there, everywhere. There are various types of "consciousness" in the spiritual worlds. It is the inner consciousness, the inmost consciousness, that touches the springs of the cosmic energy. If we can have a free access to our inmost consciousness, the cosmic energy is bound to come to the fore if you go deep within, it comes like a spring, a never-failing spring. And when it comes, it permeates the whole body.

Unfortunately we look at the spiritual life with our outer eyes. It is here that we make our mistake. But if we look at the inner life with our heart's feeling and our soul's light, then we see that the inner life has already housed the outer life, energised the outer life and perfected the outer life. The deeper we go within, the greater will be our fulfilling and fruitful achievement without.

310. What did you mean when you said that now we have a choice with regard to the discovery of the inner life, but that some day we wouldn't have that choice?

Sri Chinmoy: The thing is this.... we all know that in the world, opportunity is something that never knocks at our door twice. In the spiritual life, this is also true. But in the spiritual life, when one has entered into the inner life and is living the spiritual life, he feels that it is impossible to believe that this spiritual life might not be permanently meant for him. He feels that this possibility is only something imaginary. It is very good for him to feel this because God's Hour, which is now – and I shall explain it to you – will never come back. It does not come twice.

Those who have an inner Guide, a spiritual Guide or a Guru are extremely blessed. This is what I mean by "God's Hour". But out of their obscure folly, very often, disciples try to judge their teacher according to their own light. And they leave the Path. According to the Divine Law, you may leave the person, but you may not leave the Path. But very often, when people go to their spiritual teacher and are not satisfied, they become dissatisfied with the Path as well; that is to say, with spirituality itself. Here they make a great mistake. If they leave the spiritual Path, once having seriously entered upon it, they forfeit the Grace of God's Hour. And it does not return for thousands of years.

Now the Hour has come. Evolution, both the inner and the outer, has come to the stage where people have developed the conscious mind. Formerly the conscious and developed mind was lacking. In our human evolution, it was the animal mind that was working. Now the animal mind has been transformed into the conscious, developed, human mind. Consciously man knows what is right and what is wrong in his own life. In spite of that, man often does the wrong thing. But now man's conscious, developed and searching mind has become illumined to some extent by an inner light and by his heart's constant cry.

Evolution, not only of the mind, but of the whole being in general, is a spiral. It is not a straight or a direct movement, like climbing up a ladder. It is rhythmic, like this.... like the waves of a spiral movement. It goes round and round in a circular motion, going higher and higher at each round. It comes back to where it had started in the spiral, but on a higher level. As the line of development comes full circle, there is almost a meeting of the new level with the old level. In the process of evolution, man's mind has become illumined and although he still appears to act in his old unlit way, he is actually higher than he was when there was no light at all in his mind.

Now here, in the world, the Divine, the Supreme, is trying consciously to awaken each individual soul because He feels that the time has come for the human to be transformed into the divine. Formerly, even in the spiritual life, there was only a one-sided aspiration, that is to say, aspiration from the soul or from the heart or from the mind – but only from one part. Now people have discovered the truth that the body and the vital also have to aspire. Formerly in the East, and in the West, too, they neglected the body. They thought that if the heart aspired or the soul aspired, then that was enough. But now it is not like that. Now at each moment we can serve the Divine with the physical consciousness – in the workshop or in the office or in the street. Our physical consciousness has been developed to such an extent that it can consciously aspire to enter into the Beyond. This is the time called "The Hour of God". It is a very special period. If we deliberately pay no attention to it, then what will happen is that we will lose the Grace, the Infinite

Grace. Then we shall have to work with our own strength which is very, very limited. It will take us lives to accomplish what we can do in a matter of months with the Divine Grace.

After this special period of Grace has ended, after forty or fifty years or even a century, or at most two centuries, there will be a compulsion from above, a force that will propel people forward. This will not be an opportunity but a coercion. Right now, there are some souls who have consciously accepted the inner life, the spiritual life. They are marching forward and accelerating their progress. They are moving consciously towards God. They have to be followed by those who are still sleeping. At that time, the push will come from God. Those who are now awakened are marching forward towards the Goal, but those who are not awakened will be forcefully compelled to arise and follow the awakened ones.

The human mind has achieved extraordinary marvels; the scientific mind is the proof. The scientific mind in the beginning was confused, but now it seems to be going in the right direction, and if it really and truly enters into the spiritual mind, then the success of mankind will be beyond measure. Now the Hour of God has come. Some of the scientists in the West do believe in God or believe in something that they call "even higher than God". Wonderful, as long as they feel that there is some conscious Force or Power in the universe! So when science sees, in the material world, the possibility of some inner truth, then it can easily enter into that Truth and ultimately understand that Truth. Here also the Hour of God has dawned. The animal in man has played its part, whether successfully or unsuccessfully, God alone knows. But the very animal in man is no longer satisfied. At the same time, it is unable to go beyond the animal kingdom. This is the opportunity, here and now, to go beyond. By our conscious aspiration and by God's constant Grace, we can bask in the sunshine of this Hour of God, once and for all time transcending ourselves, and becoming true divine beings – our real destiny!

311. Why would God take the trouble to compel slackers like myself to accept the inner life?

Sri Chinmoy: We know that in the process of evolution, we came from the mineral life to the plant life, then to the animal kingdom and finally to the human consciousness. Now God wants a different being to descend on earth or to take incarnation. This being we can call Divine Man or Superman. So now God is trying to bring this being into the manifestation. With those who are consciously abiding by God's Will, God is happy and content. But the hour will come when God sees that some people have the potentiality and yet are neglecting this potentiality, which has been given by God Himself. He says, "Let the instrument himself consciously aspire." Then a day comes when God says, "I have given him the potentiality, the capacity, everything. Even then, there is no conscious striving, no aspiration, no prayer. Then let Me use force." When God uses force, it is a kind of blow which forces the person to come out of his usual unaspiring consciousness.

People are coming here to this Centre. People are going to churches, temples and synagogues. They are praying or meditating at home. They are doing all this consciously. Inside they are feeling an inner urge to move forward, to grow. They feel that they have some inner awareness, some inner capacity. God sees and observes and God is pleased with them. But when God sees that this same potentiality which He has implanted in all is not being utilised by some, He says to them, "No, I won't allow you to lag behind. You must follow those who are consciously awakened." And for that, He compels them.

The inner, divine qualities or the spiritual quintessence that you have and that somebody else has do not lead to the same results. In your case, you are awakened and you are happy and God is happy. You are marching. The other fellow who has the capacity and potentiality is sleeping. He is not aware; he does not care. He is engrossed in the material world. God says, "Now is the time. I have given him what he needs. If he doesn't grow, I have to compel him."

It is like two sons of a mother, standing in front of a pond in an Indian village. One child feels that his mother will be happy if he jumps into the pond and takes his bath. He knows that he has the capacity and that he himself will be happy. His mother also knows that he has the capacity and that he will happily jump into the pond which he does. The other son also has the inner capacity, but he is lazy. He says, "It is cold and anyway I don't want to take a bath." Then what does the mother do? She waits for a few minutes, observing whether or not he will do it. Then she finally pushes him in. So the second son eventually has to take his bath. In the beginning the mother gives the same opportunity and capacity to both of them. One jumps in willingly and the other, after some time, is compelled. Similarly in the spiritual life, everybody has the inner urge. One uses it, the other does not. Then, just as with the two sons, when one refuses to use the urge consciously, the pressure comes at that time, to which he has to surrender. This is how God compels slackers.

312. There is still something I don't understand. You said that there is the opportunity at the Hour of God and yet you said that He could take away the Grace. Then if so, how is He divine?

Sri Chinmoy: He takes away the Grace for some time. The person who does not use the Hour of God forfeits God's Grace. I have just explained that later on, God will compel the slacker. But at that particular time, it is an act of withdrawal on God's part. Of course, one day everyone will realise God, but when God withdraws, it is a matter of centuries and not just years.

313. But if His Grace is Infinite, how can He take it away for a while?

Sri Chinmoy: Yes, God's Grace is Infinite, but God is working through the finite. When the finite is unable to receive the Grace, due to its limited receptivity, the Grace is forced to withdraw. God can stay in you only according to your receptivity and capacity. He is Infinite, but I am finite. If the vessel in me is very limited and He is limitless, how long can He stay? Only according to my receptivity can He pour down His Grace. And if my vessel is very tiny, poor God!

314. I ask this question mainly because I wonder why the greater part of the holy men or yogis that I know are unmarried or do not have a family life. I just wondered if marriage would be a deterrent.

Sri Chinmoy: No. It depends on each individual soul. You were saying that most of the Indian yogis are not married, but at the same time, there were many great spiritual Masters who were married. For example, Sri Ramakrishna, one of India's greatest spiritual figures. He was married. And many of the ancient Rishis, the greatest sages of the Vedic era, were married.

In fact, only ten or twelve – some say six – of the Vedic rishis were unmarried.

Then in India, there is something called a spiritual partner, a collaborator. The Sanskrit term is *shakti*. They are not legally, or in the human sense, married, but on the highest spiritual level, they are divinely one. For God's Creation, man and woman must go together in some cases, and some spiritual Masters have a feminine counterpart.

But there are some spiritual figures who agree with our silly scriptures that woman is the door to hell. Our scriptures say, *Nari narakesya dwara,* "Woman is the door to hell." Women, on their part, can say and feel the same thing: "Man is the door to hell." But that is not the thing. The reason that men say this, is that they feel that women, in general, being bound to Mother-earth, have tempted them, pulled them down and bound them. But who is at fault here? Men. Why? By nature, women think of earth more than they think of Heaven. That is, they are always thinking of their children and family and they do not get the time to enter in the deeper world. But men have never given women the opportunity to cultivate their inner life, their spiritual life. And, of course, when the question of temptation arises, who tempts whom?

Apart from all this, many Indian seers and yogins think that it is an extra burden to get married and have children. They say, "We are going to our Father. Why should we have a heavy burden on our shoulders?" If one is married, he may say, "Let me save myself first and let her come in her own time. When she is ready, she too can see God." This is how they reject women. The ones who said, "Woman is the door to hell," when they finally achieve their own realisation, understand that it was not their women or wives who were the problem; the defect was in their own consciousness. With the others, it is a question of how much they can carry, how much responsibility they can bear.

If they feel that they can get married and have children and still lead a higher life, the life of true fulfilment, then God tells them to carry on. They are absolutely doing the right thing according to their inner understanding and their inner necessity. God's door is open to all. But I must say that this is an extremely difficult process.

315. Referring to your talk on Illumination, I want to ask: in our daily life, when frustration and adversity attack us, how can we orient ourselves so that we know what to do about it?

Sri Chinmoy: Let us not bother ourselves with frustration, suffering and all that. Yes, they are all here, but let us try to bring down God's Grace. If He Himself wants to carry our frustration, we will be making ourselves happy, happier. If God does not take our pain, however, we can still let the flow of His Grace and Compassion descend into us; then immediately it will illumine everything, illumine all our suffering, frustration and adversity. Then let us use another process. This process is to see God's existence in everything. God does not give us pain, first of all. He does not give us suffering either. It is we who make mistakes in our day-to-day life or in our attitudes and ideas. But if we have frustration and suffering, let us enter into that frustration and suffering and see there the existence of God. So when the adverse forces attack us, they will not be able to do so fully because behind it, we are seeing the existence of someone who is all Love, all Affection, all Concern for us. And we can easily enter into that person to be saved.

It reminds me of an incident many, many years ago. In India at the time of the British occupation, an English soldier with a bayonet was about to kill an ordinary innocent man. That man immediately cried aloud without fear but with a soulful emotion, "You, too, are divine." When he said, "You, too, are divine," he actually saw in the bayonet the existence of God. The soldier did not kill him because at that moment he did not see in the innocent man anything aggressive or destructive, anything to feed his own aggression. Through the intercession of the Divine Grace, the soldier also saw something luminous in the man and was struck by it. Here also when suffering comes, if you say to the suffering, "You, too, are divine; in you, I am seeing the existence of God," then immediately the wrong forces of suffering which are disturbing you will also leave you.

What you are now doing is that you are separating God from the suffering. Suffering we do not invite; far from it. But if it comes, we have to see in it the existence of God. If you do not separate God from the suffering, then your own life-breath and God's Compassion will meet together. Otherwise you are not allowing God's Compassion to touch your life-breath, you are not seeing God's existence in everything. We say that God is everywhere. If God is everywhere, is He also not in suffering? Is God not in frustration? Or is God so weak that He has to be only in Heaven and not in our painful earthbound existence? When we suffer, God is there. We have to see His Face and not the face of the suffering that tortures us. So if we can do that, if we can see God's Face in pain and in everything, then we will see that suffering and frustration cannot exist. They have to be transformed into joy, constant joy, because our sweet Father, our affectionate, compassionate Father is there in everything to protect us and save us.

316. When you tell us to learn by heart twenty meditations, are you not establishing a kind of competition among the disciples?

Sri Chinmoy: The world is full of competition. In the ordinary life, we are constantly competing. I am competing with you; you are competing with me. All the time, we are competing. But this competition must not take place in the spiritual life. In the inner life, the spiritual world, there is no competition. It is only you and God. We are not in competition, but if you say that there is competition, let it be between you and your ignorance.

How fast can you leave aside your ignorance and go towards your own Goal? Competition, if it is at all necessary, should be to see how far behind us we have left ignorance and imperfection and how fast we are running towards our Goal. Let there be two sides: one, perfection's side; the other, imperfection's side. How fast are we running from imperfection and ignorance towards the positive side of Perfection, Truth, Light and Bliss? That and not rivalry with others, should be your competition.

II – TV PROGRAMME, WKAQ, CHANNEL 2

317. Introduction

Sudha: Good afternoon, ladies and gentlemen. Thanks to the courtesy of *Foro de la Comunidad* [Community Forum], I have the privilege and the pleasure to introduce to you the figure of Sri Chinmoy Kumar Ghose. To many here in Puerto Rico he is well known. Many know, "Una Pausa en el Día" ["A Pause in the Day"], the column in *El Mundo,* the daily newspaper where Sri Chinmoy expresses his teachings. Sri Chinmoy is a spiritual figure, a great Master, philosopher and Hindu yogi. He is the spiritual director of the AUM Centre in San Juan and the AUM Centre in New York. Sri Chinmoy is with you.

Sri Chinmoy: Thank you. I am extremely happy to be here at this TV station and at the same time I am most grateful to the authorities of this TV station WKAQ for granting us the opportunity to be here. We do hope that we will be able to serve, to some extent, those who will be seeing us and listening to us. Again I wish to offer my deepest sense of gratitude to this TV station, WKAQ.

318. Master Chinmoy, I believe that there are two wars, the inner and the outer. When and how will these two wars stop?

Sri Chinmoy: You are right, there are two wars, the inner and the outer. The inner war is the war that our inner being or the soul fights against limitations, ignorance, doubt and death. The outer war is the war that man fights with man, nation fights with nation, country fights with country. Now the question is: when and how can these wars come to an end? These wars can come to an end only when the inner war first stops. That is to say, when in the inner world, the inner being or the soul conquers ignorance, fear, doubt and death. Then in the outer world there will be no necessity to wage war. *We fight because deep inside us there is disharmony, there is fear, there is anxiety and there is aggression.* When deep within us there is peace, joy, plenitude and fulfilment we shall not invite war. So the outer war will come to an end when the inner war is resolved, when the inner war stops. Both wars will come to an end and are bound to end in the process of human evolution.

319. Master Chinmoy, I have read in some Eastern books that man is greater than the gods. I wish to hear from you if this statement is correct?

Sri Chinmoy: Thank you. I am glad that you have read Eastern books. There often it is mentioned that man is superior to the gods. What we actually mean by that is that there are many, many gods in the vital world. According to our Indian scriptures, as many human beings, so many are the gods. So, these gods, what do they actually do? They help us at the time of our need. When we suffer from headache or stomach-ache or some minor diseases they come and help us and we pray to them. But there is something else that is called liberation. Liberation or Self-realisation can be had only by a human being. When a soul enters into the human being and starts making progress, in the process of evolution, his soul becomes fully liberated and fully realised; when this particular human being has fully realised himself, he has realised God also. But the gods do not have that opportunity. They do not take the human form. They live in the vital world and from there they operate. So, unless and until they enter into a human body and human form and go through the process of reincarnation, they cannot have the Self-realisation or liberation that we human beings have. When we have Self-realisation, we know that there is nothing greater than that Self-realisation. That means we have crossed the barriers of ignorance and travelled across the sea of ignorance and death. That is why we say that man is greater than the gods, superior to gods, because man gets Self-realisation whereas the so-called gods who are in the vital plane do not care for it and do not get it.

320. Can you explain further what liberation is?

Sri Chinmoy: Liberation means the actual freedom from fear, freedom from doubt, freedom from ignorance and freedom from death. Now, as soon as you come into this world you become a prey to ignorance, fear, limitation and doubt. But through our spiritual practice and by living the inner life, we enter into the consciousness of the Divine and there we start growing and a day comes when we are well established, fully established, in the spiritual consciousness of inner life. We become totally free from ignorance. Now we are caught by ignorance, we are wallowing in the pleasures of ignorance; but a day dawns when we will be free from ignorance, and the moment that we are free from ignorance, we are liberated for good.

321. Is there a special means that would accelerate this process of liberation?

Sri Chinmoy: Yes, there is a special way and is called "conscious aspiration", and this conscious aspiration should come from the body: from the physical, the vital, the mental, the psychic and the soul. Of course, the soul has been all the time aspiring. The physical, the vital, the mind and psychic have to be aware of this aspiring consciousness, and when we consciously aspire in all different parts of our being we will be able to accelerate the achievement of liberation.

322. Master Chinmoy, from the spiritual point of view does the New Year have any special significance? Please let me know.

Sri Chinmoy: From the spiritual point of view the New Year has a special significance. On the eve of the New Year, a new consciousness dawns on earth. God once again inspires each human being, each creature with new Hope, new Light, Peace and Bliss. God always wants us to move farther, farthest; He does not want us to look back. We know when a runner runs fast, while running fast if he looks back, he drops to the ground. Similarly, if we constantly look behind at the year that we are leaving aside, thinking of our sorrow, miseries, frustrations and all that, we lose everything that we gained. But if we look forward, ahead, we see hope dawning deep within us, we see a new light illumining our consciousness.

Each New Year is like a rung on the ladder of consciousness; we have to climb up the ladder of consciousness and each New Year serves the purpose of a rung in the ladder. When the New Year dawns, we have to make ourselves conscious of the fact that we are going to transcend ourselves. We have to go beyond the present capacity, beyond our present achievement. And when we have that kind of firm determination, God showers His choicest blessings upon our devoted heads and He says, "New Year dawns, a new consciousness dawns deep within you. Run towards the destined goal." And we listen to God, we listen to the dictates of our inner soul, we run towards the Ultimate Reality. The New Year energises us, encourages us, inspires us to run towards that Ultimate Truth.

323. When God thinks of me what does He really do?

Sri Chinmoy: God actually thinks of you *all the time.* It is I or somebody else that has to think of you *at a particular time.* But in God's case, God being All-Awareness, He always thinks of you. But He does not use his mind to think of you. We use the mind to think of a human being. In God's case, the mind is not required. So whether we think of God or not, God is constantly thinking of us. So in your case God has been thinking and will think of you, because deep within God it is you who are always there and at the same time, in you is God's Own Reality. So God does not need to think of you. He is All-Awareness and we are deep in His Heart all the time.

324. Master Chinmoy, will you explain briefly to us what is Yoga?

Sri Chinmoy: Yoga means union. Union with whom? It is the union with God. By practising Yoga, that is, spiritual discipline, we unite ourselves with God.

1968

325. I believe that Adam and Eve were Vitudha and Atman and then they underwent that transformation. Is this true?

Sri Chinmoy: Both Adam and Eve were individual souls. It is not that one was the divine soul and the other, the human soul. No, both of them were human souls. In the field of manifestation, Paramatman or the Supreme took both Adam and Eve for His experience and for His manifestation. Now through silence, He embodies Peace and that embodiment takes place in man. Then through Power, God reveals His manifestation and that manifestation takes place in woman, that is to say, in Prakriti. So in order to embody Peace Infinite, God needed Adam. In order to manifest Power Infinite, God needed Eve. One for the embodiment of Peace, the other for the manifestation of Power. But both of them, Adam and Eve, were individual souls created in order to manifest and embody the Truth. God needed both of them. Not Adam, the cosmic soul and Eve, the individual soul. No. Both of them were individual souls, but God expressed Himself through them in two different ways in order to achieve the fullest Truth here on earth. Neither one was superior to the other: both of them were equal.

326. When we reach the Pralaya, *how can the souls who have not attained the highest and are not pure blend into the Divine Purity if they themselves are not pure?*

Sri Chinmoy: *Pralaya* is the dissolution or the final destruction of the universe. Now where is the destruction? You feel, Gauri, that when the Pralaya takes place, there will be souls who will remain unrealised, who will not realise God, that everything will be destroyed. But where will the Pralaya be? It will take place in the earth's atmosphere, not in God's Consciousness. There is no destruction in the Infinite Consciousness of the Supreme. In destruction we only see that a few trees are blown out or a hurricane has taken place, an earthquake has occurred and thousands of people have died. But this destruction is not the destruction of Consciousness. Although we say that the world is destroyed, it is not destroyed in God's Consciousness. It is only destroyed, part of the world, in the physical, geographical sense, but not in the sense of God's infinite and immortal Existence.

When a country is destroyed, you think that all human beings are likewise destroyed. No. Only the earth, the external manifestation is annihilated. But the beings go back to their Eternal Abode. That Eternal Abode is the Supreme's Consciousness. There they have their own shelter. Then they can, at God's own hour, be given the chance to come back to earth to fulfil God's mission or their own self-realisation.

Gauri: When they come back, do they come all pure?

Sri Chinmoy: No, they do not come at all pure because purification has to take place here. However, they will not be destroyed because the soul is immortal. Purification and realisation – everything – has to take place here. Here is the field of experience; here they have to be purified; here they have to realise themselves. When we are speaking of the dissolution of the manifested cosmos, Pralaya, we have to be aware that destruction does not take place in Consciousness. It takes place only here in the manifested material world. A few million miles may be destroyed, but consciousness can never be destroyed. Human consciousness can never be destroyed unless it is the Supreme's Will.

327. Many good people, spiritual people, are depressed by the things that are going on. How do you get these people to have hope without saying "Pollyana" to them?

Sri Chinmoy: You are speaking about "spiritual people", but I wish to tell you that a spiritual person will never be depressed, because he knows what is going to happen in the future. You say that they are depressed and you want to carry the message of hope to them. I wish to tell you that if a person really wants to be happy or wants even to be hopeful, then he must not expect anything from the world. If he expects something, even from another person, he will be miserable. He has to expect only from God. Even from Him, today you will expect something and tomorrow you will try to get it from Him; if you don't get it, you will feel frustrated. The person may think he is extremely sincere. It may be true; he may be sincere, but the time has not come for his expectations to be fulfilled by God. It is only when one is totally in tune with God that one can legitimately harbour any expectation. You can expect everything from God only when you are totally surrendered to Him. As for expecting anything from human beings, if you do, you will be frustrated and miserable. There will be no end to your disgust and frustration.

Now again, your expectation from the Supreme also has to be surrendered to patience. We expect something from Him and then we put a limit on our expectation in that we fix a time: tomorrow or the day after, God has to fulfil my desire. Here I am making a mistake. I do have a right to expect everything from God, but as to when my expectation will be fulfilled, it is not my business. My need will definitely be met by God, but the choice hour has to be fixed by God Himself. The hour and the moment must be surrendered to Him.

Now you asked about hope. Hope is one way of getting true wisdom in our life. There is another method. That method is to enter the consciousness that constantly wants to free us or transform our day-to-day life. We have a very limited physical consciousness, that is, the consciousness that is aware of the ordinary things and events in our outer material life. The moment, however, that we come out of the physical consciousness, we see that there is another consciousness which is the universal consciousness. If we can enter into that universal consciousness, we will see the entire world, the universe and the reason for the happenings of the world. We will see the creation of the world with its meaningful purpose. And if we enter into the region of the cosmic soul, the universal soul, we shall see the clear future in today's reality. When we see that future, we also see that everything is perfectly all right. So, what these distressed people need is the Light of Patience, because ultimately, everything will be all right.

II – TALK AT THE RETAILERS' CENTRE IN HATO REY

328

Dear President and dear Vice-President: I am extremely glad to be present at your Centre. I offer to all of you present here my deep sense of gratitude. We were under the impression that there would be a large gathering here, but owing to circumstances, the actual situation is different. But let us try to observe the situation from the spiritual point of view. It reminds me of an incident that took place in India. A spiritual speaker came to our place to give a talk on spirituality. Unfortunately there were only two persons present to attend the meeting. So the spiritual teacher said, "Well, had there been no listeners at all, I would still, with my deepest joy, have said what I intend to say to the walls. The walls would have responded to my heart's soulful words. The walls would have been my listeners."

Let us not feel disappointed and let us carry on with today's significant talk, on the topic "I know what to do". When I say that I know what to do, most of you will misunderstand me and this misunderstanding of yours will be quite natural. But at the very outset, I wish to defend myself. I wish to state my faith most humbly. I have just said that I know what to do. Now I wish to tell you the inmost secret of my statement. I know what to do precisely because God does it for me. You may, in no time, ask me why God works for me and not for you. No, God is not at all partial. I know that I do nothing, I know that I can do nothing. God is the Doer, God is the Action, God is the Fruit thereof. Unfortunately, there is a slight difference between you and me, between your approach to God and my approach to God. I am sure that all of you are well aware of the statement made by the Son of God. He said, "I and my Father are one." I try to live this paramount truth. In the same vein, our Vedic seers of the hoary past said, "I am the Brahman. The Brahman is me. I am the One without a second." I have also learned from Sri Krishna, one of the greatest spiritual Masters of India, nay of the entire world, in the Bhagavad-Gita, the Song Transcendental, that a man is made by his faith. Whatever his faith is, so is he.

Now you are apt to cherish a surprising ideal. With your kind permission, I wish to cite your part-time ideals. You get pleasure, joy, in telling the world there is no God. You try to parade your views. You say, "Had there been a God, how could this world of ours be so full of suffering, pain and untold misery?" Even now if you feel that there is someone called God, that there is a God, you say that this God is for others and not for you. God is for others. Now your sincere belief makes bold to say that God does not care for you. God thinks of the rest of the world, but He has no time to think of you or care for you. To be sure, this is the acme of stupidity. Something more. You feel that God is terribly angry with you because twenty years ago, you told a lie or you deceived someone in your business or in your profession. And that is why God is terribly angry with you. Now He wants to punish you ruthlessly all the time. Poor God, as if He had nothing else to do! Believe it or not, God the Almighty, God the All-Compassionate, God the Transcendental Reality has many things to do with you, your life. Not one thing, but countless things He wants to do with your life and for your life.

God sings the song of Immortality within you, He sees in you the embodiment of Existence, Consciousness and Bliss. You are God's unparalleled pride, you are God's only dream, you are God's only Reality. For you, God exists throughout Eternity. He shapes you, He moulds you, He guides you, He transforms you into His very image, into the everlasting Life of the Beyond.

Friends, sisters, brothers, you are now in the same Boat as I am. Together, united, let us sing, "I know what to do because

God does it for me. In addition to that, I know what to say, what to pray for, what to aspire for." With the blessing and benedictions of the Upanishadic seers, I wish to chant and sing the soul's message, a message of the Indian seers that has been ringing in the firmament of India for many centuries.

> Lead me from the unreal to the Real.
> Lead me from darkness unto Light.
> Lead me from death to Immortality.

III – QUESTIONS AND ANSWERS FOLLOWING SRI CHINMOY'S
TALK AT THE RETAILERS' CENTRE

329. Is there a co-ordinated effort in all countries to study yoga, philosophy and transcendental truth, searching for a spiritual approach to God?

Sri Chinmoy: To some extent, there is. Most countries are aspiring and praying to God according to their own capacity. What I spoke on today was based on Indian philosophy, spirituality and yoga. Here, at the same time, I must say that when I use the term "Indian", it is not that I come here to preach Indian thought and Indian ideas. Far from it. God-realisation, spirituality and yoga are for each individual and for all countries. But there are specific methods we apply to realise God. As far as aspiration is concerned, the entire earth is aspiring. At one particular place we can notice that the aspiration is intense, whereas in some other places, the aspiration may not be so intense. Mother Earth is aspiring, whether we believe it or not. Whether we are conscious of it or not, Mother Earth is constantly aspiring to embody the highest Truth, to manifest the highest Truth here on earth. So aspiration is all-encompassing and all-pervading, and, at the same time, its mounting radiance is an ever-burning flame.

330. Is Yoga philosophy something similar to Unity, where one mission or one congregation or a series of ministers or self-abnegated servants of Christ are spreading the seed to teach people how to come nearer to, and enter into, pure Christianity?

Sri Chinmoy: If you ask whether Yoga is similar to Unity, the group that is so famous and well established, it is not actually so. Yoga, according to the strict concept, is something special.

We have various kinds of yoga, mainly the yoga of Action, the yoga of Love and Devotion and the yoga of Knowledge and Wisdom. All these paths lead to the same goal. Yoga ultimately leads us to God-realisation and to Self-realisation. In India, the practitioner, the aspirant who wants to realise God takes the guidance of a spiritual Master. A teacher is required in order to help the aspirant in his self-discipline in his inner life and spiritual life.

However, according to my own understanding, Unity is something quite different. I have been to a few Unity groups. Last year I went to Kingston, Jamaica, West Indies. There are large gatherings of at least five hundred people at the Unity of Jamaica. I spoke there. Unfortunately, the minister had not actually achieved the consciousness of a spiritual teacher, not to speak of a realised person. He teaches, he give sermons and the members of Unity try to utilise the truth of the sermon according to their capacity and receptivity. Farther than that, that particular minister could not go. He did not have the capacity to enter into the individual aspirant or seeker in order to help him in his self-discovery. Whereas when one practises Yoga, in India or somewhere else, one is supposed to have a teacher who knows the spiritual life thoroughly. We need a teacher in every walk of life. In order to learn singing, we need a teacher. In order to play the piano, we need a teacher. Similarly, in order to learn the inner discipline and make progress in our inner life, we likewise require a qualified teacher. And Yoga means "union with God". This union can be effected through the constant guidance and help of a spiritual teacher.

In Unity, however, whether they care for union with God or not, they lack that kind of spiritual Master who has a small (or large) group of his own, where he can pay attention to each individual and see where each one actually stands in his progress towards God-realisation.

So here is the vital difference between Unity and Yoga. If you take Unity as a spiritual discipline, inner discipline, I must say that you are right, it is true, for we are all moving towards the same goal; but Yoga is something absolutely deeper. It deals with all kinds of spiritual problems, inner and outer, and Yoga tells us that man is nothing short of the veiled God.

I wanted to avoid this question because I enter into a controversy when I say that Unity and Yoga are not one. Unity, as far as the teachings and the movement is concerned, is very high and true. But when we use the term "unity" in the deeper sense of the term, Yoga is that union or unity with God.

IV – TV PROGRAMME "TEMAS DEL MOMENTO"

331. [Introduction by Sri Chinmoy]

God is seated in the hearts of all human beings, so when one practises Yoga, one is entering into God's presence. Yoga is not a religion; it is something infinitely deeper than religion. The so-called religions are satisfied with moral canons, ethics, creeds, and so forth. But Yoga helps a human being to transcend these finite, human standards. That does not mean that one has to act like an animal or violate civilized morality. It means that one has to be constantly in touch or in contact with one's Inner Being and listen to the dictates of his Inner Being. One has to go beyond the snares, the boundaries of morality. So we can say that religion is a human endeavour, while Yoga is a soul endeavour. The difference between Yoga and religion is the difference between the body and the soul. At the same time, there is no ultimate difference, because the body needs the soul and the soul needs the body. So religion needs Yoga and Yoga needs religion.

332. Interviewer: Sri Ghose, what is the advantage to the human body in being influenced by learning Yoga philosophy?

Sri Chinmoy: There is abundant advantage in accepting Yoga in our day-to-day life. First of all, everybody wants to simplify one's outer life. One wants to free oneself from fear, doubt, bondage, limitation, imperfection and ignorance. Now, if one practises Yoga, one enters into the deeper reality of human existence. And when one has free access to the Inner Being, one is in a position to have a better life and have a more satisfactory human existence. Right now we see frustration all around us. Each human being has become consciously or unconsciously a victim of frustration, worry and anxieties. But Yoga assures us that we can easily free ourselves from this frustration if we follow the path of inner self-discipline.

333. Interviewer: Is it necessary for a person to abandon his religion, let us say Catholicism, in order to adopt the Yoga teachings?

Sri Chinmoy: One does not have to abandon one's own religion or one's own faith. If one abandons one's own religion, then he will be committing a Himalayan error. One must live in one's own religion, in one's own faith. Religion is like a house. In your own home, you have complete security, you have a place to live and rest, you have a place to do your work, to be with your own family, you have a place of your own where you can be comfortable and at ease. Similarly religion has to be accepted. One should live in one's own religion, though, at the same time, aspire to realise God. Nobody is required to relinquish or abandon his religion in order to practise Yoga. If one does so, he is making a mistake. But at the end of his journey's Goal, when a person is liberated from suffering and feels that he is one with God's consciousness, then he knows that he can transcend all this. But at the beginning, one need not leave one's religion aside to attain liberation or to practise Yoga. No.

334. Interviewer: What made you come to Puerto Rico?

Sri Chinmoy: First of all, I would like to tell you that I came to the West in 1964. I came here on the invitation of some of my friends, admirers and disciples from the West. They invited me to come in 1964.

335. Interviewer: And this is your seventh visit to Puerto Rico?

Sri Chinmoy: Yes, this is my seventh visit.

336. Interviewer: What other Centres do you have?

Sri Chinmoy: We have four Centres: one in Puerto Rico, one in New York, the third is in Jamaica, West Indies and the fourth is in Miami, Florida. There we do our spiritual and yogic activities. Puerto Rico happens to be the first Centre and the name of our Centre is AUM Centre.

337. Interviewer: Does that have a meaning?

Sri Chinmoy: Yes, AUM is a Sanskrit word and it means God in three aspects: God as the Creator, God as the Preserver, and God as the Destroyer or Transformer.

338. Interviewer: Is the membership of the Centre here almost one hundred per cent Puerto Rican?

Sri Chinmoy: A little less than one hundred per cent. We have one German disciple and three Americans who have lived in Puerto Rico for many years. The others are all native Puerto Ricans. All are most dedicated and most sincere in their spiritual approach.

339. Interviewer: Do they follow your teachings with enthusiasm?

Sri Chinmoy: Mostly; and they have an earnest seeking for the Truth. They pursue their spiritual discipline most devotedly and satisfactorily during my absence.

340. Interviewer: How many days do you spend in Puerto Rico when you come and engage in these teachings?

Sri Chinmoy: Each time I come here, I try to spend about a month or so, but this time, I shall be here for about six weeks.

341. Interviewer: Then from here, where will you go?

Sri Chinmoy: I will go back to New York and there is every possibility of my going to Germany, Italy and a few other places in Europe.

342. Interviewer: You don't have established headquarters in New York or in Puerto Rico aside from all these centres?

Sri Chinmoy: Yes, we do. I have my permanent headquarters in New York, but these are all permanent Centres with a resident president in each place. They function here all the time without me, although I offer them spiritual guidance inwardly and by mail and telephone. I spend eight or nine months a year in New York and the rest of the time I spend in Puerto Rico, Miami, Jamaica, West Indies and other places. Then I go out on occasion when people invite me to speak on Yoga, philosophy, etc. I give a great many public talks in churches, synagogues, schools, hatha yoga groups, etc.

343. Interviewer: I want to inform the television audience of the location and telephone number of your Centre.

Sri Chinmoy: Our Centre in San Juan is located in the San Marcos building in Santurce, at 659 Miramar Avenue. The telephone number is 724-7286. Every week we hold special meditations and classes. On Sunday morning at 11:00 a.m. we have a special meditation and a discourse. On Wednesday evening, we start meditation at 8:00 p.m. and end at 9:30 p.m.
Interviewer: Thank you, Master Chinmoy Kumar Ghose, Master of Yoga philosophy for the privilege of having you here on *Temas del momento*. Goodnight.

344. Is the earth planet like a final stage for perfection? Do we have to go through the other planets first and then come here?

Sri Chinmoy: The earth is the only place to realise God. To other places, humans go as visitors, as you would visit your friends' or relatives' houses. According to what your own inner affinities are, you might like the place and stay, or else complete this incarnation and go back there. But there you do not make any progress. You do not meditate there or do anything to further your spiritual evolution.

This is the world where you have aspiration and where you practise meditation. No soul, no human being is able to realise God on other planes; only here on earth. That is why an Indian poet said, "Man above all." No one is superior to man because man is tomorrow's God and God is today's man, concealed but not revealed. Man is tomorrow's God revealed, whereas God is today's man concealed.

When the soul aspires in other worlds, it gets experience. Aspiration is itself an experience. But manifesting the divine fruits of aspiration can only take place here on earth. Here alone is the field for manifestation and here alone realisation can be had. Realisation is the culmination of the soul's evolution and it can only be had here on earth. The planet earth represents and embodies spiritual evolution. The soul incarnates in a human body in order to give liberation or realisation to human beings and at the same time the soul manifests the Infinite and the Highest.

V — RADIO PROGRAMME "THE BARBER'S VOICE"

345. [Introduction and talk were not transcribed]

[Introduction by the President of the Barbers' College.]

Sri Chinmoy: Thank you very much, Mr President of the Barbers' College.

[Questions following Sri Chinmoy's talk.]

346. What do you mean by scepticism? Do you mean by the term the same thing that religions mean when they say that somebody is a sceptic?

Sri Chinmoy: Scepticism means absence of belief. It means the denial of the existence, of the reality, of Truth. A sceptic can exist in any walk of life. We can see people doubting religion, doubting ethics, doubting the capacity of others. So one can be a sceptic in any walk of life. By doubting somebody else, do we get any true benefit? Do we derive any benefit? No. When we doubt someone, we actually weaken ourselves. Truth always exists and Truth ultimately prevails. One who doubts the Truth will always starve. The one who believes in the Truth will be fed by the Truth. Truth is the all-nourishing food. The more we doubt the existence of Truth, the weaker we become. By doubting Truth, we never reach the Goal, whereas by believing in Truth, by staying in Truth, by feeling Truth, we finally become the Truth itself.

347. Can a man be something else than what he thinks himself to be?

Sri Chinmoy: There is a saying that, "A man thinks, therefore he exists." Also there are people who hold the opinion that man exists, therefore he thinks. Both theories, both views are correct. I exist, therefore I think. If I am dead, if I am not alive, how am I going to think? At the same time, I think, therefore I exist.

Now to come back again to the question. Can a man be something else than what he thinks himself to be? A man may think anything he likes, but in the field of expression he may not be embodying what he thinks himself to be. A man may think wonderful thoughts, have wonderful ideas, but in his outer life, he may be extremely cruel and act like a beast. So he thinks that he is a wonderful person, but in his action he is worse than any ordinary human being. His thinking and action are totally different.

Let us go a bit deeper. There are people, renowned people on earth who thought that they were useless, nothing. But friends inspired them, teachers or great personages told them that they had tremendous possibilities or inner capacity to do something great, unique. Then they followed some technique or teaching or they entered enthusiastically into their respective creative fields and they became well known all over the world.

Now, let us go a bit deeper. There are people who feel, who think, that they can never realise God. In their thinking, they feel that God is somewhere else, in Heaven, that they are not God's children, they are useless and will never realise God; they are weak, they are ignorant, etc. But this kind of thinking is again absolutely wrong, for God is seated inside each human heart. Every one, sooner or later will realise God, no matter how many times one thinks that God-realisation can never take place in his life. So in his thinking, he may be afraid of God-realisation, the Infinite Truth, Eternal Life, but a day will dawn when to his widest surprise, he will not only see the Ultimate Truth, but he will become the Ultimate Truth. So I wish to say that if one negates the Truth in his thinking, then he is mistaken. One will ultimately have to recognise the Truth. This is the only way of entering into the Truth. That is to say, think of Truth and Truth alone. The more we think of Truth in its purest term, the sooner we grow into the Truth. At that time we can say, "As we think so we are."

But if we think wrong thoughts, we must not say that we can never have true thoughts, we can never become the possessors of real Truth. Thank you.

348. What attitude should we take towards religions other than our own?

[This is Agni's summary of Sri Chinmoy's answer as no tape recorder was available on that day.]

Just as God has given us a free choice to follow any path, so we must give freedom to others to follow their own way. There are dozens of roads that lead to God. Each one has a right to choose the road that suits his temperament, his degree of evolution and his present needs. Tolerance and acceptance are fine, but we must go even further and feel that others' religions are as important and necessary as our own.

When you are in a family, true, it is very difficult to manage when everyone is going along a different path. And there is a great temptation to say, "You are a fool. You are wasting your time going along that particular path." But you must allow the other person the same freedom of choice that you yourself want. At the same time, you have the right to inspire others with your enthusiasm and your devotion. However, if they argue with you and constantly criticise you, it is better to act on them silently. At night, when everyone is sleeping and you are in your most peaceful consciousness, put all your sweetest and purest aspiration into the sleeping consciousness of the one whom you want to influence. Feel that your path will help him and that you are inwardly meditating on him. By acting silently, you help him most.

One should follow one's own path steadfastly and not worry about shaking hands with another religion until you and the other person have come to the end of your Goal. If you go to this Temple today, that Synagogue tomorrow and this Church the day after, you will never make any progress. You must take one path and follow it to the very end. Then you can shake hands with the followers of the other paths. If you shake hands in the middle of the path, you will only break each other's arms.

349. How should a disciple of yours meditate?

[The following is a summary of Sri Chinmoy's answer, as offered by Agni.]

There are two ways for Guru's disciples to meditate. They can either try to open themselves to Guru and allow him to enter into them, or they can try to enter into Guru. Both are effective, but Guru feels that the latter method is somewhat better. When the disciple tries to allow Guru to enter into him, fear may develop and prevent the disciple from receiving Guru. He may think that, "I told a lie this morning or did some undivine thing", and so he may feel that Guru will be like an inspector coming into a dirty or impure room. But when the disciple enters into Guru, He is all compassion. Guru keeps his room clean and pure, so the disciple can always enter and be cleansed, purified and elevated.

On the other hand, when the disciple sees Guru standing in front of him, he may be frightened or awed by His vastness. However, he needn't worry about being impure, since when he stands in front of an ocean, even if he is covered with sand and dirt, he can just dive in and he will be cleansed. So the disciple should feel that Guru is a Sea of compassion and he has but to dive in and become part of the Sea. The drop will not lose its individual self-awareness inside the vast Sea, but the drop will expand its individuality until the wideness of the Sea and the drop are one and the same. The drop becomes a conscious portion of the whole ocean without actually losing consciousness of itself. Rather, the drop receives the consciousness of the whole ocean: Peace, Power, Wideness, Depth and Unfathomable Divinity.

VI – INTERVIEW WITH BOHEMIA

350. Mr Roberto García: What was the main purpose of your visit to Puerto Rico?

Sri Chinmoy: I have come to Puerto Rico to inspire the seekers of Truth. There are persons who have an inner aspiration to realise God and I have come to help the Divine within them. This is our Centre and here I teach the correct way to practise meditation. I give talks and they ask me questions about the inner life and about some problems of day-to-day living. I try to bring down Light so that the person can face his particular problems and solve them.

351. Mr Roberto García: Do your teachings constitute a religion?

Sri Chinmoy: No, I do not preach any religion. I teach Yoga and philosophy. Each religion is confined to a group: Hinduism, Buddhism, Christianity and others. Yet any person belonging to one of these religions can accept our path without detriment to his own religious background.

352. Mr Roberto García: Why do you say that?

Sri Chinmoy: I think that any person who wants to realise God will not have any difficulty in accepting our path. Our path is the path of concentration, meditation and contemplation. A person can follow this path and remain in his own religion.

353. Mr Roberto García: These, concentration, meditation and contemplation, are they a means towards obtaining something?

Sri Chinmoy: It is my way of entering into Infinite Peace, Infinite Bliss, Infinite Harmony and Infinite Light and Power.

354. Mr Roberto García: Can a human being know the Infinite?

Sri Chinmoy: Certainly. If you can enter into my consciousness you can realise the Infinite.

355. Mr Roberto García: But you are not Infinite.

Sri Chinmoy: You are seeing me now as a man, but if you can enter into my consciousness, you will see there the infinite Consciousness. If you meditate with me, I can penetrate into you and see the infinite Consciousness that is within you. But you do not have that power. You are not only a human being with hands and feet. You come from God and have within you all the possibilities to realise God. But you have not cultivated them. If a person does not learn to read he remains ignorant. If he does not learn a certain type of work he will remain ignorant of what that work signifies. By the same token, if he does not meditate, how can he enter into that inner world? This outer world that we perceive with our physical senses is not the only world. There exist seven different worlds. An ordinary person knows nothing about those worlds. He only perceives this physical world with its buildings, roads and all that and he thinks that this is the only world.

But if you enter into meditation you will see another world that is much bigger. You will see lights and see other beings and many other things. A spiritual person practises concentration and meditation because to him this world is not enough. If one is satisfied with this present world, he is not invited to practise meditation; but if he is not satisfied, we invite him to come and meditate with us, so that he can see that other worlds exist.

356. Mr Roberto García: Do concentration and meditation have something to do with the power of the mind?

Sri Chinmoy: They have nothing to do with the mind. This is something that anybody can practise. The thing is to go beyond the mind. What you call the mind is an ordinary human mind. With this mind we cannot meditate or contemplate. We have to go beyond that mind. The mind thinks something now and the next moment thinks something totally different. It is always full of ideas and thoughts like a monkey standing in front of you pinching and biting you continuously. You have to enter into meditation and make the mind stay quiet and calm, like a lake without waves, perfectly tranquil. One has to go beyond the mind to be able to perceive Peace, Light and Bliss.

357. Mr Roberto García: By means of this meditation you try to obtain peace, only peace?

Sri Chinmoy: Not only peace. In peace there is Light, there is Joy, there is Power.

358. Mr Roberto García: One can obtain peace for a moment but then when he goes out from here, he will go back to the same hustle of human life.

Sri Chinmoy: This happens to ordinary people. You have to know that there is a big difference between a really spiritual person and one who only goes to church to pray for half an hour, obtains a little peace and then goes to the coffee shop and gives his peace to the coffee shop. But if he meditates for long hours and establishes this practice firmly, then he will get durable results. If you start to run, you will not do it very well for the first few days. The same thing with dancing or any other activity. Only continuous practice will give you satisfactory results. The same thing happens in the spiritual life. When you are advanced you can retain the benefits for a long period of time, but not at the beginning. What you say is absolutely right, you obtain peace for a moment and when you go again to the world, restlessness comes back to you. But if you can enter into the deepest world and stay there for some time during your meditation, a day will come when, in the midst of the outside world, in front of people, speaking with people, mixing with people, you will possess your own deepest Peace. This Peace remains imperturbable, unmoveable.

359. Mr Roberto García: What is the meaning of the word AUM?

Sri Chinmoy: It means God in His Three aspects: God as the Creator, God as the Preserver and God as the Transformer. He who transforms our ignorance into light. He who transforms our limitations into plenitude. It is a Sanskrit word that is used in all our spiritual disciplines and in our spiritual philosophy.

360. Mr Roberto García: If you are preaching something about God, that is religion, not philosophy. Philosophy knows no God.

Sri Chinmoy: This is an erroneous concept of Western philosophy. All Indian philosophy, the Vedic Scriptures begin with God, Brahman, the Infinite, the Supreme without a second. Indian philosophy starts with the Vedas, the Upanishads, the Bhagavad-Gita and others. Modern Indian philosophy, too, begins and ends with God.

361. Mr Roberto García: Do you think that Westerners can understand Eastern philosophy?

Sri Chinmoy: Some understand it perfectly. Those who have no interest in understanding it must suffer for their lack of understanding. The Western mind finds it difficult to understand Eastern philosophy because in the East, philosophy is not separated from the true spiritual life and yoga. In the West, this is not the case. Here they say, "This is religion, that is philosophy, this is life. All are something different." In India, spirituality has a perfect right to call itself philosophy and philosophy to call itself spirituality. Both of them are interlaced.

362. Mr Roberto García: What is the rational and logic base for your philosophy?

Sri Chinmoy: Every man has the right to an inner life, a life of plenitude and joy and every man can feel and realise God. That is the base of my philosophy. Now man is immersed in suffering, in slavery, imperfection, ignorance; but if he has true aspiration he can very easily be freed from fear, anxiety, doubt, worry and all that. For that, one has to meditate. It is not precisely that he has to come to me; he can go to another spiritual teacher. He can meditate in some other place, but he has to meditate, he has to contemplate.

363. Mr Roberto García: How many times have you come to Puerto Rico?

Sri Chinmoy: I have come seven times.

364. Mr Roberto García: Did you come to preach your philosophy?

Sri Chinmoy: No, I came because I was invited by my most dedicated disciples. I come here because I have disciples. This is our Centre where I give lectures. My disciples ask spiritual questions and I teach them how to meditate and tread the path of spirituality.

365. Mr Roberto García: About the truth, is there more than one Truth?

Sri Chinmoy: There is only one Truth. In Sanskrit there is a saying that Truth is only One but it is expressed in various ways. I own a truth, you have a truth, another one has still another truth. In the field of expression, Truth expresses itself in different ways. But truth is only One and my truth can never be different from your truth nor can your truth be different from mine.

366. Mr Roberto García: Does any religion possess the Truth in itself?

Sri Chinmoy: All religions claim one essential Truth and that Truth is their union with God. But in the field of manifestation one says: "If you do this, you will realise God." But in the last analysis we are teaching one and the same thing. All roads lead to Rome but you follow one road and I will follow another road. Yet when we reach the goal, this will be Rome. There exists only one goal that is Truth, but this goal is expressed and at the same time is sought in different forms.

367. Mr Roberto García: How many disciples do you have in Puerto Rico?

Sri Chinmoy: Here I have forty-eight or fifty disciples.

368. Mr Roberto García: During how many years have you obtained these disciples?

Sri Chinmoy: In three years, more or less. But the important fact is that I don't care to have a great number of disciples. I care for the sincerity and aspiration of the student. There are some teachers who want a great number of disciples. I, on the contrary, am very strict with my disciples. I do not accept hippies, alcoholics, or drug addicts, or those with problems due to a perverted nature. There are spiritual teachers who accept all comers. In my case I say differently. A person must at least be ready to follow this path. This does not mean that those persons cannot go to other teachers to learn about Truth. There are different methods.

369. Mr Roberto García: What do you feel about hippies?

Sri Chinmoy: I do not say a single word about them, only I said that they cannot follow my particular method of teaching.

370. Mr Roberto García: Maybe they are seeking for peace?

Sri Chinmoy: Maybe. I am not qualified to judge them. I do not hate them, I love them. But what I say is that I do not have the capacity to teach them. Other teachers can guide them but I cannot advance them by my method. They are looking for happiness, but it is a different kind of happiness from the one I can give them.

371. Mr Roberto García: Maybe you could help them?

Sri Chinmoy: If I were a doctor and you asked me a question about medicine I could answer you easily but not one about politics. I cannot help the hippies because the kind of happiness that they want I don't have. Other teachers say that they do have that kind of happiness and the hippies are satisfied with those teachers.

372. Mr Roberto García: And what do you think is the reason that so many hippies and so many people are opposing society?

Sri Chinmoy: When they fight society, the simple reason is that they are not satisfied with society's norms. Why do people fight? Dissatisfaction, disharmony. They want society to give them something different from what it can offer them now.

373. Mr Roberto García: Do you think it is society's fault?

Sri Chinmoy: I do not know because I do not represent society. I cannot say a single word in favour of society or against society because I do not represent society. I only represent my inner truth. If society is guilty or not, only society knows. I can only speak for what I represent. If you ask me something about our Centre here or about my disciples then I can tell you.

374. Mr Roberto García: Are you trying to give some message to society?

Sri Chinmoy: No. I am not in a position to tell society that it is making a mistake because society is not paying special attention to me; it is not following my path. If it followed my teachings I would be in a position to tell society, "This is the Truth." For those who do not believe me, why should I interfere in their way of approaching Truth? Society has a particular method of approaching Truth. Hippies have the belief that they know a better truth. I have my own way of approaching Truth. I think that in this world instead of trying to correct somebody, the best thing that we can do is to try to correct ourselves.

375. Mr Roberto García: Did you found this philosophy? Did you discover it?

Sri Chinmoy: No, I did not discover this philosophy. It was discovered by our Vedic seers four thousand years ago. Our most important books are the Vedas. Nobody can claim that he founded this philosophy. And philosophy in its Sanskrit concept means the direct vision of God, the vision of Truth, of unity in all. Each individual has his own personality, his own illumination. With this illumination the person tries to supply the proper method to be followed by his disciples. So I have my own way of working with my disciples, spiritually, inwardly and with my writings about spirituality.

376. Mr Roberto García: When did you come to the United States?

Sri Chinmoy: In the year 1964.

377. Mr Roberto García: Are you the only priest preaching these teachings in the U.S.?

Sri Chinmoy: There are many, but I do not consider myself to be a priest. I am a spiritual person, a spiritual teacher. I teach the way by which a person can realise God and become conscious of the Truth.

378. Mr Roberto García: How did you come to Puerto Rico the first time?

Sri Chinmoy: The president of this Centre invited me to come to Puerto Rico. I gave a few lectures and many persons became interested in my teachings and formed a study group. I have study Centres in Puerto Rico, in New York, in Miami and in Kingston, Jamaica, West Indies.

379. Mr Roberto García: What is the meaning of that painting?

Sri Chinmoy: It represents the Divine Mother. We conceive her with four aspects. This one represents power. According to Indian philosophy she offers Infinite Power to her devotees. At the same time she has great compassion for all our sufferings. Her name is Kali.

380. Mr Roberto García: Do you have Christians among your followers?

Sri Chinmoy: Yes, most of them are Christians in the West. I also have some Jews. There are Catholics, Protestants, Jews and a few others from other religions. All religions can come to my teachings because this is something interior. In the way we practise meditation, it does not interfere with religion. If it is a true religion it cannot say anything against meditation because any true religion advocates God-realisation and Truth. You can realise God in your own room or in the street but you have to realise Him.

381. Mr Roberto García: Do you charge a fee to sustain your Centres?

Sri Chinmoy: This depends on the regular members. Those who come to hear my lectures are not obliged to give anything. My disciples and followers sustain the Centres contributing according to their capacity or wish. Visitors can give a love-offering but they are not obliged to do it. My disciples feel that their Centre is their own house and they sustain it because of the feeling of oneness they have with me. It is not that somebody compels them but that they inwardly feel the desire to help pay the costs of rent, electricity, printing, postage, flowers, incense and so forth.

382. Mr Roberto García: How many followers do you have in the United States?

Sri Chinmoy: Of disciples who strictly follow the discipline that I impose on them I have about fifty. There are admirers and persons interested in the teachings who come to my lectures and form a much bigger group. These have no obligation but they cannot have me as their teacher. If, for example, something disagreeable in their family comes to happen, I am not obliged to give them help.

383. Mr Roberto García: I think this is enough for today.

Sri Chinmoy: I feel very happy that you have asked all these questions and it is with real joy that I have answered them. At the same time I wish to say that this house is open for all, but only those who have a genuine interest in these teachings can derive benefit from them. If you want to buy a pair of shoes you go to a shoe store. If you want to buy a suit you go to a clothing store. In the same way we here offer something that is of interest only to those who want to acquire Truth. Thank you.

VII – TALK TO AND QUESTIONS FROM THE FINANCE DEPARTMENT STAFF, PUERTO RICO

384. Talk to members of the finance department of the government of Puerto Rico

Friends, sisters and brothers, I am extremely happy to be here. This morning I wish to say just a few words. I am looking at the picture of Christ, the Son of God, the true Son of God. The Son of God has taught us that all human beings come from the same source, the Eternal Father. Now what are we? We are also the children of God. We are His chosen children.

Each human being has three teachers: the mind, the heart and the soul. The mind tells us that God is a sempiternal mystery; the mind cannot fathom God's mystery. The mind tells us that God is an eternal mystery. The heart tells us that God is an eternal experience. Now the soul. The soul which is a portion of God tells us that God is an eternal achievement. At each moment we are achieving something from God, either consciously or unconsciously.

What does the mind need? The mind needs clarity. The heart needs sincerity. The soul needs spontaneity. Clarity is the mind's joy. God walks inside the head of our clarity. God sees through the eye of our heart's sincerity. God fulfils Himself in the nectar flow of our souls, His Divinity in us. When we think of God, we see Him standing behind us. When we pray to God, we see Him standing right in front of us. When we meditate on God, we see God deeply seated within us. When we devote ourselves to God, to God alone, we see God within, God without and God in His manifestation all around. Finally, when we surrender ourselves to God, to God alone, we become God's veritable child.

Man dies. When he dies for God, he lives eternally in the heart of God. And when man lives for God, in order to dedicate himself entirely to serve humanity, to help humanity, to illumine humanity, then he becomes the very breath of God.

This is the Department of Finance. Here I wish to say one thing. What is our necessity? What is our true necessity? We have only one necessity and that is God's Blessing. How can we have it, this Blessing of God? We can have it just by borrowing from God's bank. We can have this blessing only from God's bank. If we want to pay our debt, what are we going to do? Again we have to borrow from God's bank. There is no other choice. Once we have borrowed His blessings, now we want to pay Him off. But how can we do it? We can do it only by borrowing once again from the bank. But this time we have to borrow only one thing and that is His Wisdom: the Eternal Infinite Wisdom. We do not commit any mistake. We grow in Light, we grow in Peace, we grow in Joy, in sublime Bliss. So if we can grow in God's wisdom, we embody everything. Let us try to grow in God's adamantine protection and at the same in His Infinite Wisdom.

385. Is Yoga a religion, an art or a science?

Sri Chinmoy: Yoga is neither art, science nor religion. Art itself, from the strict spiritual point of view, is not yoga. Religion which is man-made and which is fighting against other religions, is also not yoga. Yoga is conscious aspiration for God. Yoga feels that to realise God is necessary. At the same time it is in religion, in science, and in art, but it is not like them. It is like a boat which is inside the water, but is not of the water. The boat is detached; it is not affected by water although it is in the water. Similarly when we paint something, draw something, and do it with our aspiration and our yogic concentration, that is wonderful. If we want to discover something scientific, if we can pay attention or concentrate for the purpose of scientific discovery, then that too is yoga. If instead of fighting each other, all religions meet together and say there is only one God, then that is yoga. So yoga is inside each study and at the same time, yoga transcends everything because yoga says, "The main thing is to realise God." When we realise God, when we become one with God's consciousness, then we see God's presence in everything. Right now, theoretically we are saying that God is here. But can we feel it? No. But if you practise yoga, you will see in everybody, even in each material thing like this desk, the presence of God. So in that way, yoga exists in everything. Otherwise yoga transcends everything; it transcends art, science, religion and all.

386. Please tell me about the basic principle which I understand you yogis follow very consistently about the respect for life. You see life in insects and in every animal and you respect such life. Is that a principle in yoga?

Sri Chinmoy: We should have respect for life in everything, in grass, in insects, in animals. This is the supreme knowledge: God is inside everything. But what is God? God is eternal Light, all-pervading Life. So we must have respect for all life. But in the field of manifestation we have to accept the fact that there are certain things we utilise for our own existence. Suppose when we are walking on grass, we know that the grass is being hurt. But can we fly above the ground? In the field of manifestation we have to adjust ourselves. Some animals eat grass; it is their only food. Some persons eat meat; it is their only food. The Eskimo, if they do not eat meat, they die; they cannot exist. And if the animals do not eat grass, they die. Now, what is the secret?

We know there is life; even then we are killing and destroying it at every moment. The secret is that the life that is being killed is not killed. We see the insect, just press it and it dies. But inside that life there is eternal life. We believe in reincarnation. This insect is not dead. It is dead in our physical eyes, but the eternal life that the insect possesses will immediately spread all over the cosmos. Then after some time, the insect's soul will enter into some other animal and progress gradually until it comes into human life. No life is destroyed because there is an Eternal Life. And this Eternal Life existed before the creation; it is in birth, it is between birth and death, then it goes beyond death. Eternal life started before existence. It is in birth, it is in death, it is between birth and death. This Eternal Life animates the things that we are using in our day-to-day life for our own existence and maintenance, but we have to see that there is no other way. But that does not mean that we have to go and fight and kill someone. That is not so. When it is unavoidable for our own existence, we have to use what we need. I need food; I personally do not eat meat or fish. But there are some persons who eat meat and fish. What are they going to do? They have to eat. An animal has to be caught. An animal itself has to eat grass. But we have to go beyond the ordinary life to the Eternal Life and then there is all peace. Who is destroying whom? Life the Eternal can never be destroyed.

VIII – TV PROGRAMME ON CHANNEL 2, TELEMUNDO

387. Presentation

Agni [Mr José Luis Casanova]: Greetings, televiewing friends. By the courtesy of Telemundo and the programme *Community Forum* we are going to present a programme of the AUM Centre. This Centre is dedicated to the study of Yoga and spirituality. It opens its doors to all persons interested in spirituality and inner development. It is located at 659 Miramar Avenue, Santurce, Puerto Rico. The telephone number is 724-7268. Meetings are held at 8 p.m. on Mondays and Wednesdays and at 11 a.m. on Sundays.

Poet, philosopher, thinker and spiritual guide, Sri Chinmoy Kumar Chose is now here with us. He was born in Bengal, India. This is his seventh visit to Puerto Rico. He is the spiritual director of the AUM Centre in Puerto Rico and the AUM Centres in New York City, Miami, Florida, and Kingston, Jamaica, West Indies.

According to the philosophy of Sri Chinmoy, life must be accepted fully, life must be transformed devotedly and unreservedly, life must be lived in an integral and divine way. The Master teaches his followers, students and disciples that spirituality can never be an escape from the world of reality; on the contrary he says that spirituality is the only assurance we have in life, of solving the world's problems. It is spirituality that can and will change the face of the earth. It is spirituality that brings forth the inner life and manifests the Infinite here on earth.

With us also here today are Mr Ramón Torres Peña, Mrs Rose Albin, Miss Petrita Hernández and Miss Lotti Wolff.

388. What is detachment and what do we actually derive from detachment?

Sri Chinmoy: Detachment is true wisdom. Detachment is our divine Divinity. Nobody can be as happy as a man who has detachment. We are under the impression that a man can be happy only when he is attached to something or to someone, but this is a great mistake. When we are attached to something or someone, we actually become a prey to them. We actually become a victim of that person or that thing. So in this world, if we want to have true joy, true peace and true divine qualities, then we must be totally detached. This detachment does not mean that we shall not work for the world; no, we shall have to work for the world, in the world, but should not allow ourselves to be caught by anything.

389. Could you tell me what is freedom, where is it and how can earthbound man have it?

Sri Chinmoy: True freedom is infinite joy, boundless joy inside us, around us, everywhere. This boundless joy we get when we see true freedom in us. Where do we get this true Freedom? We get it when we live in the soul, when we are able to utilise our soul's will-power, when we are one with God's consciousness consciously. That is to say, when we are aware of our oneness with God, consciously we become the possessors of true freedom.

Now earthbound men can easily have this freedom. A day will dawn when each man on earth will be blessed with this freedom. Now each human being, most of the time, lives in the body, that is to say in the physical being. The body is limited, the physical is limited. It is like a prison cell; but inside the body there is something called the soul; this soul is a portion of the infinite. If a person lives in the soul then he becomes aware of the Infinite within him.

When we say it exists in us, we will have to make ourselves feel that our very existence depends on the soul's will, the soul's achievement and fulfilment. If we live in the soul, we are bound to have true freedom, and this freedom is infinite Joy, Peace, Power. To have this infinite Joy, we have to live in the soul and not in the body.

390. Most of the ordinary human beings take life seriously; should spiritual persons take life seriously?

Sri Chinmoy: Like ordinary human beings, spiritual people too take life seriously. I must say, most seriously. There is only a slight difference. An ordinary human being could be excited, worried, depressed and so forth the moment something goes wrong in the family or in his life. If somebody drops suppose a book from this table to the floor, immediately the man will be excited, disturbed. No matter what happens in his day to day life, he says, "This is life, I should take it seriously." But a spiritual person takes life in a different vein, a different form. To him each second is most significant because he feels that when he misuses a second, he is not able to go closer or nearer to God. Each second, each moment he takes as an opportunity to realise God. He wants to possess the infinite expanse of Consciousness. He feels that life is most significant, and when one is endowed with life, one has the opportunity to realise God here on earth. And in this short span of life if he misuses it, then he has to come back to this earth again, he has to come back into the world to fulfil his mission. So he is always conscious of the value of time, he wants to enter into the Timeless by utilising each moment divinely, spiritually, because he feels that he has to go far, very far, to the farthest end. If he loses time, he will never reach his Goal. The goal will remain a far cry to him. This is the difference between the seriousness that a spiritual man feels in his life and what an ordinary man feels in his day-to-day ordinary life.

391. Please tell me what is wrong with the world: it seems to act like a madman and it seems to be running towards its own destruction; what is wrong with the world?

Sri Chinmoy: To start with, I wish to tell you that there is nothing wrong with the world but everything is wrong with you and me and the rest of the human beings. Poor world has not committed anything wrong; it is we who are misusing the world. Now let us focus our attention on the poor world. God has created this world; we are utilising the world. We can use it in our own way. We can either destroy it or we can manifest the Divine, the Infinite Peace here on earth. This world is the field of manifestation where we can manifest our inner divine qualities. At the same time, instead of manifesting the divine qualities deep within us, if we want to destroy the world, which is what we are actually doing, it is up to us. Let us take the world as an instrument. If we play the wrong note, then who is responsible? The player, not the instrument. If we use the world in a divine way, then we shall see that there is no problem with the world. It is we who have the capacity and we can utilise the world in a divine way to fulfil the Divine here on earth.

Agni: Thank you, respected listeners who have lent us your attention today. In the name of Sri Chinmoy and the AUM Centre of Puerto Rico we give you our heartfelt thanks. We also thank Telemundo and the *Community Forum* for their courtesy to us this afternoon.

VIX — TV CHANNEL 6, WIPR INTERVIEW

392. Hector Campos Parsi: Good evening, Master Chinmoy. It is marvellous to have you here with us again in Puerto Rico. I have been informing our audience that this is the seventh time, I believe, that you have come to Puerto Rico, and you are with the AUM Centre group here, orienting them in their spiritual progress. I would like to ask you a few questions if I may.

You have been here several times. Is there any particular reason, special reason that you come or do you come to visit Puerto Rico and be with your followers? Is there any special reason?

Sri Chinmoy: There is a special reason why I come to Puerto Rico. This is my seventh visit to Puerto Rico. First of all, I come here because I love this place very much. The aspiration of this place has conquered my heart. Here the spiritual soil of Puerto Rico is extremely fertile and I happen to be a spiritual farmer; so being a spiritual farmer, I come to this most beautiful and most fertile land to cultivate the soil, and here I get the bumper crop. The aspiration of this place, this island, has touched the very depth of my heart.

This is one reason; then there is also another important, most important reason. I have here a well established Centre called the AUM Centre. Here I have quite a few sincere, dedicated and devoted disciples who are absolutely dedicated to their inner call and God-realisation. I come here to inspire them and help them in their inner life and their discovery. Then, there is another particular reason. I come from India and I see many things in common between India and Puerto Rico. There are many things which unite India and Puerto Rico. The qualities of this land immediately remind me of my India. The qualities of the heart, the qualities of the soul, the peace-loving qualities. Peace-loving countries have much to do in common. So for all these reasons I come to Puerto Rico, and I am pretty sure that I shall be here many, many, many times during my lifetime.

X — INTERVIEW AT RADIO STATION WKYN, SAN JUAN

393. Your name is Sri Chinmoy Ghose?

Sri Chinmoy: Yes.
Interviewer: "Sri" means Mister? In what language?
Sri Chinmoy: In both Sanskrit and in Bengali. Sanskrit is the mother of all Indian languages, as Latin and Greek are for the western languages.

394. Would you be classified as a Swami?

Sri Chinmoy: I should be classified as a spiritual Teacher.
Interviewer: I thought that was primarily what Swami meant?
Sri Chinmoy: A spiritual Teacher can be of various types and of different calibres. He can be called a Swami or Guru or can be addressed by a number of other titles like Acharya, Sant, Yogiraj, Nath, Rishi, etc. But I prefer to be called a Spiritual Teacher.
Interviewer: So there is not really any difference between a Guru and a Swami or other titles?
Sri Chinmoy: Yes, there is a difference in grade. A Guru is supposed to be one who has inner identification or conscious oneness with God, whereas the Swami need not be spiritually fully awakened or spiritually realised.
Interviewer: This is, of course, in Yoga?
Sri Chinmoy: Yes, in Yoga.

395. And is there a particular branch of Yoga in your philosophy?

Sri Chinmoy: Yes, my philosophy or my approach to Yoga is the acceptance of life. There are many approaches in Indian philosophy and yoga which do not accept life. In my case, my Yoga accepts life as it is and then transforms it.

396. You have a Centre in San Juan. What is its name?

Sri Chinmoy: AUM Centre, spelled A-U-M.
Inteviewer: Does this name have a particular meaning?
Sri Chinmoy: Yes, AUM is supposed to be, and actually is, the mother of all our spiritual mantras. A mantra is a syllable or a particular word which we chant or use in order to realise God. By repeating this AUM or a few other mantras, we feel that we can realise God.

397. I read that people who embark on one of the varied spiritual programmes are usually given a particular sound for them. Is this based on a particular thing, or just a feeling at the time, or is there a way of determining what this sound is for the individual?

Sri Chinmoy: Each mantra or sound carries a special significance. It depends on the individual soul, that is to say, the individual aspirant. So when you give a particular sound, a particular mantra, one has to know whether the mantra is actually going to help the person. Any mantra cannot be given to any aspirant. Only the teacher is in a position to see the spiritual faculties, qualities, tendencies and aspiration of the aspirant and the teacher gives a suitable sound, a mantra, to that individual seeker.

398. But you have to know the individual fairly well?

Sri Chinmoy: Certainly, one has to know the individual seeker first and then one has to enter into the soul of the seeker and then give a special sound, the mantra.

399. At your AUM Centre, you are preaching life? Is this the idea that I get from you?

Sri Chinmoy: In my AUM Centre, I teach them, first of all, how to meditate and how to concentrate, so that they can enter into the deeper layer of their existence. Then I give talks on the Inner Life, on Spirituality and Yoga, so that they can have mental illumination. I also hold special meditation classes almost every evening.

400. Where is the AUM Centre located?

Sri Chinmoy: It is located at 659 Miramar Avenue, Santurce.
Interviewer: So that is not too far from here?
Sri Chinmoy: Not far.
Interviewer: And you have these meetings every evening?
Sri Chinmoy: Every evening and on Sundays in the morning at eleven o'clock.
Interviewer: You are not here yourself constantly, are you?
Sri Chinmoy: I am the spiritual Director of the Centre but I live in New York. I have four Centres: one here in Puerto Rico, one in Miami, Florida, one in Jamaica, West Indies and the main one in New York City.
Interviewer: So you travel between the four of them? How long have you had your Centre in San Juan?
Sri Chinmoy: It completed its second year on the twentieth of July.

401. Do you find that the Western mind has difficulties in grasping the implications of the Eastern philosophers?

Sri Chinmoy: To some extent, it is difficult for the western mind to approach, or should I say, appreciate Eastern philosophy. But when the question of inner illumination and self-realisation come in, then I find that Westerners have no difficulty in approaching the inner life, that is to say, their self-discovery.

402. If you had to wrap up your philosophy in one sentence, could you do it?

Sri Chinmoy: Yes, I can.
Interviewer: Would you?
Sri Chinmoy: Yes, I accept life, I face life, I discover the significance of life and I try to transform life into the everlasting Consciousness of the Supreme. This is my philosophy.

403. If people want more information about this, can they come down to your Centre?

Sri Chinmoy: Certainly. I would be most happy.
Interviewer: Where is it, when they come down?
Sri Chinmoy: 659 Miramar Avenue in Santurce. If they want further information they can speak to the President of the Centre, Miss Carmen Suro at phone number 724–7286.
Interviewer: When are the meetings that you have?
Sri Chinmoy: Every evening at 8:00 and on Sundays at 11:00 a.m.
Interviewer: I thank you very much for stopping in and talking to us, Sri Chinmoy Ghose.

XI – QUESTIONS AND ANSWERS ON 17 AUGUST 1968

404. I realise many times that people want to be involved and do things for the betterment of humanity, but for some reason, their inadequacy or their inefficiency does not allow them to do this. Or they cannot come forward and do what they would like to do. They think often about it but they cannot come forward and do it. What can they do?

Sri Chinmoy: Some people feel, from deep within, an inner urge to serve humanity, and at the same time, they feel their inadequacy. How can they help or serve humanity? Now there are two ways. According to strict Indian spirituality, philosophy and yoga, one has to realise God first and then one can try to illumine others. If it is a question of illumination, first one has to be illumined and then he can illumine others later. If one wants to serve humanity, first one has to serve divinity within himself. Then divinity will tell us how we can effectively serve humanity. Otherwise it would be placing the cart before the horse.

But there is another process. When a spiritual Master takes full responsibility of a particular disciple, he may say, "Now, you help people, serve humanity. I am within you, with you. I am taking full responsibility. The more you help humanity in my name (that is, in the name of the spiritual Master) the swifter will you make your own inner progress and fly to your own self-realisation." Like a flower, you yourself will unfold by the Grace of the Supreme and the Master. At the same time your very unfoldment will inspire people in their self-search, in their spiritual life, their inner discipline.

So either one has to be fully awakened and realised, or one has to be commissioned and authorised by a realised spiritual Master. When the spiritual Master says that he takes full responsibility, at that time you are not making any mistake in the beginning, because he is taking the entire responsibility. He is the Doer. He is in you, with you, through you and for you.

But if, out of self-imposed sympathy, kindness and concern for humanity, one tries to serve humanity, then actually instead of serving, one will be only feeding one's ego consciously. So I wish to tell you that the involvement that you are speaking about should be with the Guru, the Master, for the Supreme. To be totally one with the spiritual Master physically, vitally, mentally, psychically, with His infinite consciousness which represents the Supreme, is one alternative. Or, as I explained first, one must wait until one has totally realised God. This is the traditional, time-honoured and time-proven Indian spiritual method. Either of these two can be followed.

In the ordinary world, if one does not want to go farther, if one wants to remain satisfied with what one has (very little capacity), one will quite naturally try to help others according to one's own capacity. But that kind of help does not help much in the long run. It is just like a blind man leading another blind man. Very soon his wisdom or his light will be totally exhausted. But if there is full realisation or inner oneness with the Supreme or with the Spiritual Master and, at His divine command, the spiritual Master asks a particular disciple to help others, inspire others, at that time, the disciple can, with the deepest joy enter into the field of service. This service will all be dedicated to the Divine, the Supreme, and its dedication will all be offered to the divinity in humanity.

405. I have always wondered if the AMEN of our Christian religion was originally meant to have the same significance as the AUM of the Hindu religion?

Sri Chinmoy: They are totally different. AMEN is said at the end of a prayer and means "So let it be." We have, in Sanskrit, a similar phrase, uttered at the end of invocations to the deities and prayers to God: it is TATHASTU and it means "May that be so." But the syllable AUM is a mantric sound. It is used in a completely different way from AMEN or TATHASTU. AUM is the actual sound of the creation; it is the Originator, the Mother, the Breath of Creation. From the sound AUM, Creation came into being. AUM is also the expression in sound of God in His three aspects: Brahma, Vishnu and Shiva. Before AUM, nothing in the manifested cosmos existed. The Supreme began the Creation with the supreme sound of AUM.

When we say AMEN or TATHASTU we are praying to have something we want fulfilled. The AMEN is always preceded by something else, whereas AUM is not like that. AUM always precedes everything. When we begin any religious or spiritual activity, when we start any mantra, we start it with AUM. We can also end any mantra with AUM if we want to, but we have to start it with AUM. In the Western religions of course, we do not start anything with AMEN. It always comes at the end, after a prayer. Moreover, the significance of AUM is infinitely more soulful and more intimate in the realm of reality and God's vision than is AMEN. When we say AMEN, immediately our physical consciousness enters into the fulfilment of some desire or prayer. But in the case of AUM, this does not happen. AUM will inspire the very existence of the seeker and then, after the inspiration is over, it will energise the seeker to enter into aspiration. When aspiration starts functioning, then AUM takes the aspiration of the seeker into the highest and the deepest in that individual's soul.

I am very glad that you have asked this question. The function and significance of AUM and of AMEN is not at all the same.

406. In the Gita, it says that we must have discrimination. What is meant by this discrimination and how can we obtain it?

Sri Chinmoy: The Sanskrit word for discrimination is *viveka* and it refers to the power of discrimination which actually comes from the soul. Viveka comes not from the mind but from the inner being. Our mind can discriminate in its own way: this is right, this is wrong, he is the best person, he is the worst person. But having made an assessment, the very next moment, the mind contradicts itself. First the mind gets a kind of satisfaction in achieving a decision and then the following moment it sees that its judgement was absolutely useless. Because the mind is not at all poised, it is not in a position to address itself to its own truth which it has already decided upon. The mind can never be in a position to discriminate. It is our soul's wisdom, our soul's knowledge that can discriminate. We can make the discrimination between the false and the true, between light and darkness and between two pairs of opposites on the strength of our soul's light.

You were reading the Gita. Yes, from the second chapter onwards, discrimination is enjoined upon Arjuna by Krishna. Let us start with duty. Each human being on earth knows what duty means. But the real duty, very few of us know. What is the real duty of our inner being? In the process of discrimination, we come to understand that our real duty, our entire duty, is our self-discovery or God-realisation. *Neti, Neti,* "Not this, not this." Then what do we want? I don't want this. I don't want that. What do I want? I want only the Real, only the True, only the Ultimate which is God Himself.

By discriminating, by separating the true and eternal from the false and transient, I come to a point where I can see my Goal. Then I step upon the path leading to my Goal. In our day-to-day life, if we want to emphasise our duty, then there is no end to our ordinary duties. I have to eat, I have to meet my friends, I have to see my family, I have to go to college. All kinds of duties I have. But we have to know that beyond these duties there is a real duty. These mundane duties we are fulfilling daily, but they do not bring us in any way nearer our Goal. Are we fulfilling any ideal in life? No, to fulfil an ideal, we have to select or adopt a Goal. There is only one Goal for each human being and that Goal is God-realisation. This does not mean that in order to realise God, we have to discard humanity. Far from it. We do not have to throw away members of the family: wife, sisters, brothers, parents, children. No. We have to see in them the existence of God. This is one of the major duties of each human being, to see the existence of God in children, in friends, in everybody on earth.

Then one also has to know that his true duty lies not in what he does, but in how he does it. If an ordinary human being knows what he has to do and why he is doing it and also how he is doing it, then in his very action, he is approaching God. You are a student, Chaitanya. You want to study in order to have more knowledge and wisdom in the field of psychology. The reason you are studying is that you want to widen your knowledge and by this means, you want to help humanity. Now, how are you doing it? Are you studying devotedly, soulfully, or we may ask, are you studying for the Grace of God? That is to say, does God want you to take up this particular subject? Why are you studying psychology? If you know that God wants you to do it, then here you get your real duty. How are you doing it? You are doing it with the conscious approval of God. Is your soul making you feel that it is the subject that you want to study in order to manifest your soul here on earth?

So I want to tell all of you here, when you do something, when you perform any action, first you have to know whether that action is really important in your life and will take you nearer to your Goal. Then if you feel, "Yes, it is required," do the action, but after the action, you may look for a result, either success or failure. Now here is the most difficult situation. If you have failed, you will feel that you are totally lost, frustrated, that you can never get the satisfaction that success would have given you. But after separating success from failure, if you can throw both success and failure into the hands of God, then you will see immediately that you are going beyond both, beyond the capacities of both success and failure. Here you are going beyond even discrimination.

First we have to start with discrimination – discrimination between darkness and light, falsehood and truth. First we have to start with morality and immorality; then we have to go beyond morality and immorality, beyond light and darkness. One has to remain only in the consciousness of the Supreme. So when we speak of discrimination, we have to know that we are dealing with our day-to-day life's duty, duty that takes the form of thought, feeling and so on. For example, discrimination can tell us which thought is a divine thought, which feeling is a soulful feeling. At each moment, let us try to see our soul's mission in each activity which presents itself to us as duty and let us discriminate one from the other. Then, at the end of the path, we shall have to go beyond both, beyond even discrimination, beyond viveka.

407. When Arjuna refused to kill, was he discriminating?

Sri Chinmoy: Arjuna wanted to abstain from the fighting that was his duty. He did not want to fight. He thought, "If I don't kill anybody, they will think highly of me, appreciate me and be my friends." Sri Krishna said, "No, your warrior's duty is to fight this righteous battle, because it is the Divine Will. You are not to behave like a Brahmin who has to spurn earthly activity and dedicate himself to the interpretation of the scriptures. What God demands from you is to protect your subjects. You have to protect the world. Your duty is to fight."

At most you can say that Arjuna was ignoring his own *dharma* or inner law and indulging his own feelings of weakness and fear. This is not *viveka*, the soul's discrimination.

408. Does not this battle of Kurukshetra mean that one is fighting against his own wrong ideas and ignorance, fighting an inner battle and not actually fighting to kill somebody?

Sri Chinmoy: No. The battle described in the Bhagavad-Gita was a real war, a literal battle. It is not a symbolic description of an inner battle. Arjuna did indeed have to fight against his own ignorance, fear and cowardice but when he fought, it was as a real warrior. He thought that he was the doer and he had to kill people who were his relatives. Sri Krishna said, "No, you are not the doer, they are already killed. You just have to be the instrument." Outwardly Arjuna had slain hundreds of persons in other fights, but here he was assailed by powerful doubts and fears. What would people say? "They will say nothing," claimed Sri Krishna, "because you are fighting for the right cause, the divine cause."

His enemies, the Kauravas, were forces of evil incarnate and it was God who had made the decision to have them destroyed.

In the name of morality and self-righteousness, Arjuna was absorbed in self-pity but Sri Krishna wanted to show him that he had to fight against evil, against ignorance, against darkness. Arjuna thought that he was fighting against human beings. Sri Krishna said, "No, inside human beings there is darkness, there is imperfection, so I want you to do God's Will and kill them."

409. When one reaches the highest levels, does he have to come back to the world?

Sri Chinmoy: If one wants to work for the world, in the world, then no matter how high he goes, he will be granted the opportunity to come back; not only the opportunity but the assurance of the Divine that he can come back because God wants him to work for the world and manifest the Divine here on earth.

410. Once I met a person who said that he did not believe in God because he could not see Him or hear Him. He said he believed in his wife because he could see her and hear her, and his child. What can we do and what can we say to persons who think that way, because we try a lot of arguments but to no avail.

Sri Chinmoy: So your friend does not believe in God, but he believes in his wife because he sees his wife and hears her voice. We can approach this question from various angles. First of all, although he sees his wife's face and hears her voice, is he satisfied with his wife? Does he feel that his wife is in a position to give him everything that he inwardly wants? No, there are many things his wife cannot do because she does not have enough power. Now the question is: if he does not want to believe in God and wants to believe in his wife, a spiritual person will say, "Fine, let him believe in his wife." Even though he is actually having faith in someone physical, his faith in itself will immediately take him beyond the boundary of the physical. He will enter into the spiritual realm, the realm of vision. Unconsciously he is having faith in some other world, but he does not know what that other world is. He sees his wife only in the physical world and that is the reason why his wife is all to him, physically, spiritually, inwardly and outwardly.

But we know that the Infinite Truth lies inside us and that Infinite Truth or Reality can only come to the fore when we consciously try to bring it to the fore. Now, in your friend's case, he does not want to know the Truth or see the Truth, feel the Truth or become the Truth. No harm, as long as he has faith in his wife, but his wife need not be a spiritual person. She *may* be a spiritual person. Let him give all credit to his wife because for him his wife knows everything and his wife satisfies him. We suppose all this because he does not want to progress beyond the achievements or capacity of his wife. But his wife, I do hope, will feel that the satisfaction that she is giving to her husband is actually coming from some higher or deeper source. And that deeper source is God or God's Light.

Now if that person deliberately wants to negate the existence of God, it is not advisable on our part to insist to him, or compel him to have faith in God. It is a waste of time. So long as he has faith in something, that is enough. In India, there are people who have great spirituality but who do not actually believe in God. They do believe in something. He says that he does not believe in God, but he does have faith. There is not anybody on earth who does not have a belief in something, even in negation. This man is negating, negating, negating the Truth. That very negation is an affirmation of Truth expressed in a negative way. So let us allow him to continue to negate the Truth, but at the end of the journey he will see that the negation itself is being transformed into something positive.

So I wish to tell you – please do not try to impose your ideas, your immediate feeling about God on this person. It will be a waste of time. Only try to observe what his actual feelings are. If his actual awareness of Truth lies in his wife, then let us not disturb him because God is deeply seated in his wife and it is God who is working through his wife in order to change and transform his mind and heart.

411. I am deeply disturbed. I want to have peace. My greatest ambition is to study languages, but I cannot concentrate on the simplest things of life. This makes me feel sad, deeply sad and I cry a lot. I feel dispersed, I am so deeply disturbed. I want to regain my happiness, my tranquillity of spirit and mind. I would like you to help me, to lead me. I will follow you.

Sri Chinmoy: You are using the term "regain". Now if you say that you want to regain your peace of mind and tranquillity, that means that once upon a time you had peace of mind and tranquillity.... if I understand you correctly.... Now when we lose something, it means that we have done something wrong. If we have something in ourselves and we are constantly doing the right thing, we are not going to lose the precious jewel inside us. Why do we lose it? We lose it because we run after worldly things, empty things, temporary joy or temporary pleasure. Or what we do is to enter into others' business which is not our business. So there are various reasons for losing our peace of mind, the peace of mind that we once had. Now your question is: how can we get back that peace of mind which is our true treasure?

Each person present here knows what the Truth is. But just by knowing the Truth, one cannot be satisfied. One has to try to live the Truth. When one wants to live the Truth, the real problem arises. We know the Truth, all of us, but in our day-to-day life, when we want to follow or live this Truth, even an inch of the Truth, an iota of Truth, problems arise. If we could practise the Truth, most of the problems would be solved. Now, how to know what Truth is and what falsehood is. It is very difficult. In this world, very often Truth and falsehood are intermingled. We have to separate them. For that, we need God's Grace and our utmost sincere effort. When God's Grace and our own sincere effort go together, we shall not only see the Truth and feel the Truth, but we shall become the Truth. When we become the Truth, infinite Peace will be at our disposal.

Now we are running after Peace, but Peace is not paying any attention to our cry or desire. But the real object in our life should be to follow the Truth. When we follow the Truth, Peace is bound to come to us. Peace cannot live in falsehood. So if you want to have peace of mind, tranquillity, calm and silence, then you have to live the Truth and it is in Truth that we can have peace of mind.

XII — QUESTIONS BY SIVASHANKARA

412. Is there any way to overcome karma in one's lifetime?

Sri Chinmoy: Yes, it is possible, Sivashankara. At the same time, it is not possible. If you ask if there is any way to overcome one's karma, I should answer, "Yes, there is one way." But if you ask if it is always possible for a human being to overcome his karma, then I would say that it is not always possible. Every human being on earth cannot overcome the law of karma just by mere desire or by wishful thinking or even by aspiration. Desire is out of the question. If something goes wrong in the family and I cry, "Oh, how I wish I could be the happiest person in the world and my dear ones would have no problems," then nothing will change. Even by praying, we cannot overcome karma. Just by aspiring, we cannot. The necessity of the Grace is required, and this Grace must come from God, from the Divine, from the Supreme. When God's Grace and the seeker's aspiration meet together, then we see that karma can be nullified and at the same time, future karma which the seeker will be creating, will all be done under the guidance and protection of the Divine. Your future karma will be made under His guidance, under His protection, under His knowledge, under His Grace. At that time, karma will not bind you. Karma does not bind you if it is the karma of devotion, dedication and surrender. Only that karma binds us which brings us results or the fruits of action.

We have to know what kind of karma we are creating. Real karma is that which is being done by the inner being within you. Otherwise there is no end of karma and responsibility, obligation and counter-obligation. I will say, "This is your responsibility." You will answer, "No, it is your responsibility." There is no end to human duty and obligation. But the real end we shall get only when we listen to our duty from deep within ourselves or from someone who can study our mind, who can study our heart, who can study our soul. Only he can advise us soulfully of our duty.

So to come back to your question, Sivashankara, it is possible to overcome karma when one has conquered desire and when the Divine Grace descends. Along with these are also required prayer and aspiration, but by themselves, they are not sufficient. When the infinite shower of Divine Grace descends upon us, when God's Compassion flows into us, then in one lifetime – it is not even a matter of one life – in a few days or in a few hours, it can be accomplished.

If you pray to a particular goddess, your own two thousand or four thousand years of karma can be nullified by her, by this Mother, by the Goddess Kali. And your name is Sivashankar. Siva is her consort. So you have already been blessed with this spiritual name, this Indian name. You are happy to have that name, Sivashankara. If you pray to the Goddess Kali, she will do miracles for you.

413. Is getting married asking for more karma?

Sri Chinmoy: In the ordinary life, not only marriage, but every activity in life sets the wheel of karma into motion. Anything that you do – it need not be marriage; for example, if you just walk out of this place and think of something or someone (other than God) then karma is already created. In anything you do, it is the same.

"Marriage" is a very sweet word but most of the time it is made of very bitter experiences. Without being married, one has thousands of problems. Now when you get married, you add to your life another problem. You may say, "I am a hero; I shall conquer her problems." She, on her part, also thinks, "I am a heroine; I shall conquer his problems." So both of you enter marriage determined to solve the problems of the other. This I am saying from the viewpoint of difficulties, since you have asked about the karma entailed in marriage. But of course, there is another side, the side of joy. I mean human joy or human love. You will say, "I have so much love for her." She will say, "I have so much love for him, so let us be joined." Now if this human love is rightly guided by the inner reality or inner being of the couple, then they blend together; otherwise the union breaks into pieces. Immediately the two sides start fighting, this side and that. You start your journey with your possession: sweet love, human love. She also started this way. Then afterwards, everything goes wrong. This is the kind of karma that two people bring on themselves. But if you do not enter into marriage, then you may try to solve your problems alone. There is nothing on your shoulders. Now sometimes in this world, we feel, "If I can take somebody's burden from him, then I will be appreciated and I will feel a sense of pride," but again I tell you that this is all coming from a sense of ego. It is not only ego or marriage which adds to your karma, but anything you do, unless it is done by God's Grace. Then there is no bondage at all.

Normally in marriage, the individual karma of each party become joined into a whole which they naturally share. The woman, for example, offers the man all her soul's capacities and strengths, but she also gives him the effects of her accumulated actions and thoughts – her karma. The reverse is just as true. When they bring down a few more souls in the form of children, the children's karma is added to their own. That is why in India they say that there are three divine moments in a person's earthly sojourn: his birth, his marriage and his death. In India, marriage is extremely important, first because of the many, intricate ties, duties, responsibilities that the person makes, not only to his partner, but to the family of his partner; and second, because it was clearly understood that marriage set the pattern for the remainder of the person's lifetime and, in India, deeply affected the general growth and direction of the individual soul. To a lesser extent, the same is true in the West.

Marriage is certainly an additional form of karma, but if you marry with the idea of progressing spiritually and aspiring for a higher life, and if your spouse also wishes to lead the inner life, then the two of you can march along the path like two pilgrims, side by side. At that time, if you can offer all your joint actions to the Supreme, you do not have to worry about your wife's karma becoming a burden to you or vice-versa, because you will be surrendering your actions to Him. Marriage is a burden in the ordinary life; in the spiritual life, it can be different. The Supreme Himself can take the burden.

414. The people we meet today – are they persons we were related to in our past incarnation?

Sri Chinmoy: Often yes, but not always. We meet people who were in our past lives, but we also meet new people. Since the Supreme wants us to grow and flower, He may place in our path persons who can help us, teach us, inspire us and lead us. And then there are associations that are not important, people who casually pass us as we carry on our normal activities.

415. It is said that when twins are born, it is because they were enemies in a past incarnation and they had to be joined together in that way, I mean as Siamese twins. Then neither one can kill the other since he will be killed as well.

Sri Chinmoy: That is true. Sometimes they come to punish each other. In a past life, they could not tolerate each other, as it happens sometimes, and they were intense enemies. They come back to work out their mutual hatred. If one takes incarnation in a certain family, the other one says, "I, too, will take incarnation there so I can make your life miserable." So they come together, sometimes as identical twins to torture each other and all their lives they quarrel and fight. We often see that identical twins are not happy or harmonious. They were enemies in their past life and by getting the opportunity to be twins they may be able to transform their hatred into love. At least they get a chance to express their enmity. In any case, they don't bother with each other, usually, in the following lifetime.

416. Sometimes we hate somebody without any apparent reason, just for his appearance.

Sri Chinmoy: Hate is often an obverse form of love. You hate someone whom you really wish to love but whom you cannot love. Perhaps he himself prevents you. Hate is a disguised form of love. You can only hate someone that you have the capacity to love because if you are really indifferent, you cannot even get up enough energy to hate him. Hatred is the frustration or blockage of normal, free-flowing love.

417. I was thinking of my mother-in-law. No matter what I do to please her, she hates me.

Sri Chinmoy: Your problem is not your mother-in-law, Sivashankara. It is your wife. If you had not married that wife, you would not have that mother-in-law. You bring me a picture of your mother-in-law and I will tell you what connection you had with her in your past life.

XIII – MR QUIÑONES VIDAL'S PROGRAMME,
RADIO INTERVIEW ON STATION WKAQ

418. Mr Quiñones Vidal introduces the Master

Here with us is a representative of spiritual philosophy from the Orient. Although many great Masters have come from India like Buddha, Ramakrishna and others, I don't want to say that philosophy belongs to India because philosophy, like religion, is universal and does not belong to any particular country.

I greet Sri Chinmoy Kumar Chose with much love in the name of the station WKAQ and in the name of this programme, *Quiñones Vidal*. It is a pleasure to have such a noble person on our programme.

419. I heard the beautiful explanation of your philosophy about life. Really, that is what I understand by philosophy. But there is a word in Spanish, maybe it is because of the translation into Spanish, "to accept life". To accept or discover. Is there not a difference between acceptance without investigation, without doubt and merely discovering life?

Sri Chinmoy: To discover life is different from acceptance. When we say, "discover life", that means to go deep within and discover our own intuitive God-realisation. We speak of self-discovery, but self-discovery and God-realisation are one. When we discover our true self, we realise God, because in our true self is the existence of God. Now, we say life is a short span of time, say forty or fifty or sixty years. But this is not the real life. The real life came into existence and real life will always exist. This is a short span of life: fifty, sixty, seventy years which we call life, but the real life, which was there before the creation, and which transcends the creation, which is in the creation, which goes through death and passes beyond death and becomes the Infinity and Eternity together, that is called the real life.

So "acceptance" is the word I would use here for our day-to-day activities. Very often we get disgusted with the world and curse the world because of our fate. This is in outer life, in our day-to-day existence. Where the inner life is concerned, we call it discovery because we have to discover our true self and that true self is God. Self-discovery and God-discovery are one. When we are speaking of inner spiritual discovery, we call it self-discovery. But when we are speaking about our day-to-day life, people want to commit suicide because they are frustrated, they feel that the world has deserted them, the world has been a curse to them instead of a boon. So in that case I say, "No, face the world, face the problem." When we enter into life, immediately some problem arises. Life is no problem. Life is an opportunity to realise God here on earth but instead of that, we feel life is only thousands and millions of problems. That is life.

Mr Quiñones Vidal: I would like to continue for the whole hour but unfortunately this is a commercial programme and I am bound by time. We appreciate from our heart your holy presence on this programme. Really your philosophy is great and wonderful and certainly in a future talk we shall have more questions and answers.

The AUM Centre where Sri Chinmoy teaches is at 659 Miramar Avenue, Santurce. Thank you very much.

XIV – QUESTIONS AND ANSWERS, AUGUST TO OCTOBER 1968

420. Why could Vivekananda not overcome his doubts about Ramakrishna?

Sri Chinmoy: This is a very significant question. Let us start with doubt. Doubt is a slow poison. If somebody has doubt by nature, it is extremely difficult to remove it from his mind or from his being. Now if one remains most of the time in the heart or in the soul, but not in the mind, then it is easy to remove doubt. A spiritual Master had a disciple who was constantly doubting his Master. The Master had deep affection for that particular disciple. The disciple wanted to know from his Master how to overcome his doubt, so the Master said, "Even if I wrote sixty pages about doubt, even then I would not be able to remove an iota of doubt from your mind, as long as you live in the mind."

Now in Vivekananda's case, there are a few reasons why he doubted Ramakrishna. In the first place, Ramakrishna used to tell Naren [Vivekananda] that he was a great spiritual person: "I see inside you all divinity; I see inside you spiritual Power and at the same time, I see you as the *vibhuti* of Lord Shiva." At that time, Naren was only a college student. He did not take the spiritual life seriously. He had an exuberant and external life. He could not believe Ramakrishna. He simply couldn't take Ramakrishna seriously. "One day you will awaken the whole world," Ramakrishna told him, "for you have all spiritual possibilities." Vivekananda's father had died and the son was an ordinary boy at that time. He could not maintain his family financially. He did not have the means to buy even the simplest necessities and he often starved for days together. Then he hears Ramakrishna say that he is a great spiritual person and that one day he will liberate the entire world. He said, "I cannot feed even my own mother!" He used to come home and say, "Mother,

I have eaten at my friend's place, so you don't have to cook for me." It was all lies; he was starving but he wanted to save the food for his mother and for the elders of the family.

Another reason for Vivekananda's disbelief was that Ramakrishna's actual experience and assessment of Vivekananda were totally different from the boy's own experience of his life. His Master naturally used to see the highest and the deepest. Vivekananda would only see his ordinary life as a student. Ramakrishna had so many disciples, but in front of them, he used to have Naren stand and he would say, "Naren, Naren, Naren." If Naren did not come to Ramakrishna's place, then the Master would go to his place. If other disciples did not come, Ramakrishna did not care. But if Naren didn't come, he was unhappy. In fact, he got angry with his other disciples if they did not bring Vivekananda back to him. So this is the kind of thing that Ramakrishna did for Naren.

Now if you care for someone, there is always the tendency for that person to suspect that there is some ulterior motive in your love. What is behind it? Why are you not running after someone else? The human mind, no matter how pure the person is, tends to be suspicious. But the soul wants to love the person, not for himself and not for the soul's own benefit, but for the divine in the person.

Once Naren told his Master, "You are, all the time, thinking of me. Don't you know the story of King Bharata? He always thought of a deer and then he had to become a deer. Don't you know the story?" The other disciples said, "Naren, you are insulting Ramakrishna. You always ignore Ramakrishna, calling him mad and all that." But Ramakrishna immediately took Naren's rebuke seriously for he was, after all, a serious student of Western philosophy, Eastern philosophy, the Indian scriptures, etc. So he went and told his Divine Mother, Kali, what Naren had said. Kali told him, "No, you are not running after Naren. You are running after the Divinity that you see in Naren. It is for that you are running. But that Divinity will express itself only in years to come." So Ramakrishna went back to Naren and said, "It is not you that I want; it is the Divinity inside you."

All these things had disturbed Naren's mind. He felt that he was nothing and, at the same time, was worshipped by Ramakrishna who adored him. When he heard Ramakrishna say that he was so great spiritually, at the beginning, he had doubted him. "What is it that he sees in me?" he said. However, when the question of Ramakrishna's realisation arose, he used to say, "Ramakrishna is the Highest, he is the Highest." But at that time, he did not realise what he himself was. Ramakrishna used to say, "The day he realises himself fully, he will not stay on earth." Indeed, when Vivekananda came to know what he actually was, his life was nearly over.

So in one sentence, I wish to say to you that Ramakrishna's vision of Vivekananda's spiritual greatness, Vivekananda could not see or understand. That was the cause of the doubt in his mind.

In our spiritual life, there is only one enemy, a mightiest enemy, and that is doubt. We are always doubting. Either we are doubting ourselves or we are doubting God. In both cases, we limit ourselves. If we doubt ourselves, we never realise God and if we doubt God, then there is only frustration and misery in our life. If you have implicit faith in God then this will be complemented by faith in ourselves. If we have faith in ourselves, then when we go deep within, we see that divine love is embracing us. If we have faith in ourselves, we can solve all our problems. This faith is not the arrogant pride of self-attachment but it is the spontaneous light of wisdom which operates in our very existence.

421. In the spiritual life, which way will be best, to arrive at the truth in order to gain freedom, or to try to gain freedom in order to arrive at the truth?

Sri Chinmoy: Now the thing is that truth and freedom go together. We cannot separate freedom from truth. Where there is truth, there is freedom. But this truth is Truth with a capital "T". In our ordinary life, we say, "This is true, this is false." Truth here is measured. But when we think of the highest Truth, the Eternal Truth, we see that it exists in infinite freedom.

Now we have to find out what our soul wants first and needs first, even within our daily existence. If the soul wants Truth and we are not getting the opportunity to obtain it because we are bound by the family or by circumstances, at that time, you have to think of Truth first, and even if you don't have freedom, you have to go to Truth first. Let me make this clearer to you. In your day-to-day life, your soul may make you feel, "This is the Truth; meditation is the Truth; God is the Truth; realisation is the Truth." Now in spite of this inner conviction, if you feel that the family is standing in your way, friends are standing in your way, society is standing in your way, then at that time, do not think of freedom. Just try to go to the Truth first, because this is what your soul wants. Freedom will automatically come.

If your soul's spontaneous urge makes you feel that Truth is the only thing that you need, then outer freedom is bound to come, because outer freedom will automatically come and assist your soul's aspiration. But if you wait for the outer freedom to be offered to you by humanity, then you will never get it. Truth has its own infinite power and when we approach it without caring for the outer circumstances, the Truth itself will pave the way so that we can live in the Truth, feel the Truth and become the Truth.

So freedom you do not get from other people – from society, from humanity. You should not worry, but you should try to go directly to the Truth. Then Truth will automatically bring freedom to your life. If you wait to be given freedom from friends, relatives, humanity, then you will never get it. Truth will always remain a far cry. You yourself have to approach the Truth and then the Truth is bound to come to you.

Let us run towards the Truth without looking to the right or left, forward or backward. Run towards the Truth, the Golden Shore. Then you will see that God's Truth will create freedom for you because Truth has infinite Power, the Power to make you free.

422. You have explained how to remember. Now what is the best method of rejecting thoughts that you do not want to have?

Sri Chinmoy: There are two kinds of thoughts: one kind comes from outside and strikes the forehead here. The other kind of thought, which we already have inside us, has perhaps been taking shelter there for five years, ten years, twenty years or thirty years. Now the thought that comes from outside is easier to control than the thoughts that are already inside. Some people say, "I did not think of that, so how did that thought come inside me?" It is because the personality, the individuality, or the existence of someone you have already cherished has taken the form of a thought and entered into you.

So we have to know, first of all, if the thought that we are going to control is inside us or coming from outside. You please try, all of you, to distinguish. The one that comes from outside wants to strike us, squeeze inside us, go into our mind, into our brain. The other thought is the one that you have already inside your existence.

So when you want to reject them, you have to understand that it is these silly thoughts that are not productive, the thoughts that are damaging, the thoughts that are not fruitful, the thoughts that are negative, the thoughts that we do not want in our existence.

When you first observe that kind of damaging thought, uncomely thought, first you have to determine whether it is coming into us from outside or actually going out of our existence from inside. If it is coming from outside into our existence, it is easier, infinitely easier to control. Why?

Here right in front of your forehead, you have to feel that you have a shield, right in front of you. It is a protection. Instead of taking it as a part of your body, as a limb or an organ, you have to feel that right on your forehead is a coating, a protection. Try to feel that you are constantly on the lookout here in your mind to see if an attack is coming, if a thought is going to attack you. At the same time, try to feel that here, in the same place, is your shield and protection. If a thought comes to strike you, the shield will control the thought. But if we feel that our forehead is something soft, mellow, very delicate and exposed to anything and everything, then immediately we become victim to all these undesirable and wrong thoughts. Wrong thoughts can never come if we consciously make ourselves feel this forehead is a shield, a solid wall. They cannot come. But what usually happens is that when we think of our head or forehead, we think of them as something vulnerable and easily pierced. On the contrary, we have to consciously make ourselves feel that it is something solid, something very strong, like a solid wall or a fort where there are many soldiers deep inside, ready to fight against an attack. When an attack of wrong forces comes, the strongest soldiers inside us are purity, sincerity and aspiration. Our eagerness for God, for God-realisation – these are all divine forces too, divine soldiers: purity, sincerity, aspiration, concentration and our meditation. Even the very idea of God-realisation is a divine soldier inside us. All these soldiers will immediately be on their guard the moment a wrong thought comes. They will serve as bodyguards and if, by chance, the wrong forces attack here, they will be cast out by the divine soldiers deep within us. This is for the thoughts that are coming from the outside.

Now what about the thoughts that are already inside us, creating problems? It is very difficult, in comparison, to throw *them* out. But we can do it! How? Again it is through the extension of our consciousness. We have a body; inside this body are these wrong forces that have taken the form of ugly, damaging thoughts. If we can extend our physical consciousness as we extend an elastic belt, we will feel that we are extending our whole body through the mind's conscious effort, through aspiration. We are extending, extending, extending the whole body to the infinite. We are extending a sheet of white consciousness. The moment we feel the infinite extension as a sheet of white consciousness, you will see that it is all purity. Each pure thought, each pure drop is poison to ugliness or to wrong thoughts in us. On our part, we are afraid of impure thoughts, but impure thoughts are also afraid of our purity. Why is that?

This is what actually happens. We identify ourselves with impure thoughts, let us say, and do not identify ourselves with pure thoughts. The moment the pure thoughts and our physical existence become one, when we say, "This thought represents me," or, "I represent that pure thought," then impurity inside us immediately dies; it loses its existence. The impurity or the wrong thought inside us exists just because we identify ourselves with it. If we subsequently identify ourselves with something else, the first one has to die. Now I tell people that jealousy, anger, etc. have to leave us the moment we have poise, peace, etc. inside us. Anger feels that it has a legitimate place within us only because we identify ourselves with it and nourish it with our concern and attention. We cherish it within us. But the moment we make friends with peace, poise and tranquillity, anger says, "Why should I stay here; they don't want me." Anger itself will become jealous of peace. You can try it.

So about rejecting thoughts, I wish to tell you that if you can expand your consciousness, then the problem is solved. All you have to do with a negative thought is to fight it with a positive thought. If it is an undivine thought, we have to fight it with a divine thought. Always in this life, we have an opportunity to make a choice, as Anugata has said. Although we have become victims of wrong thoughts, these wrong thoughts cannot exist inside us if we open ourselves to divine thoughts. We have allowed wrong thoughts to exist inside us. New divine thoughts we can create through our love for God. When we create divine thoughts inside ourselves, they will act like powerful dynamic soldiers to fight for us and to give us what we actually seek.

423. Are we to believe literally in the story of Adam and Eve, that we are actually suffering from the consequences of their fall? Or are we the product of evolution from animal life?

Sri Chinmoy: From the pure spiritual point of view I wish to tell you that there is no fall; there is no such thing as a fall. It is only an experience. Who is having that experience? Not you, not me, but God Himself. He is experiencing it. He is the experience and He is the experiencer.

Now there are two viewpoints. One viewpoint is that of evolution which is absolutely true. We are evolving. From the plant life we have come to the animal life and from the animal life, we have come to the human life. This is the theory of evolution. Now again there is another viewpoint, which is equally real, that the Spirit entered into matter and Spirit permeated matter. When Spirit entered into matter it was not the fall of the Spirit, because inert matter had to be accepted by Spirit, a divine reality; Spirit likewise had to accept matter in order to have a divine life inside matter. So Spirit entered into matter, but people now say, "Oh, it is a fall; you were at the top of the tree and now you have descended!" No. Spirit descended there in order to create palpable life. Where there is creation there should be life and there should be manifestation. For that, Spirit is required to permeate and animate matter.

You say that according to the Bible there was the fall. I must say that from the strict spiritual point of view there is no such thing as a fall. It was an experience; at that time, Divinity was going to express itself through humanity and it was Adam and Eve, the representatives of the Supreme here on earth, who embodied humanity. The Supreme wanted to have that experience through these two human beings, Adam and Eve.

There is no fall; there is only one track, one single way towards the goal. But sometimes we take a rest, sometimes we halt. We can tread awkwardly, we can walk, we can march, we can run. This is the path of evolution. If we go unconsciously we will go slowly; if we go consciously we will go faster. Now when we speak of falling, it means that we are going back towards self-destruction, towards annihilation, where there is no existence, where it is all death. But it is not like that. So to come back to your question, there is no such thing as a fall. It is the experience that the Supreme had in Adam and Eve and it is the same experience that He is having in us, with us, through us – to fulfil His dream, to transform His dream into reality.

424. A neighbour of mine often swears very loudly to the Supreme against Him and when he does that, I always say, Dios te bendiga. *["May God bless you."] Is this the right thing to do?*

Sri Chinmoy: The thing is – in such cases – I wish to tell you that the best thing will be on your part not to say anything to him. If you feel that you really want to help him, then you can spend five minutes of your most precious time in inner prayer to the Supreme, asking the Supreme to give him some illumination. He is ignorant, but if you tell him that he is ignorant, he will be your worst enemy and he will make no progress. But you can pray to the Supreme if you want to, if you feel from within that it is your duty. First you should feel inwardly that it is your duty. If so, then do it.

But you have to know one thing: whether basically that man is good or not. If basically he is not good, then I do not want you to spend even five minutes on him. Let him, at God's own Hour, come to some basic understanding of his behaviour towards God. So if basically he is poor quality, then you don't have to waste any time on him because you are not doing him any favour. But if he is basically good, you can offer five minutes of your prayer to the Supreme to change his mind towards God. He is, after all, God's child and God Himself is hearing him. Just as God is hearing your prayer and observing your meditation, so also He is listening to this man's curse. God has enough strength to bear his insult just as He has enormous capacity to observe your meditation and listen to your prayers. But you have to see whether he is a fine man, basically, or whether he is basically of poor quality. If he is bad by nature, then forget about him. If he has many good qualities and just for an immediate shock he is cursing, then if you feel from within that you would like to help him, then from the very depths of your heart offer your prayer to the Supreme for five minutes, in order to change his heart and mind.

XV — QUESTIONS FROM STUDENTS AT YALE UNIVERSITY

[Sri Chinmoy had answered a question in which he said, "You will grow with the one thought, 'God wants me and I need God.' There should be no other thought around you. Then you will see that slowly, steadily and gradually, God's divine thoughts are entering into you and permeating your whole inner and outer existence. Then you will have tranquillity in your body, in your vital, in your mind. Please try." The following question referred to this answer.]

425. *It seems that mystical experience cannot be forced in this way, in that manner. And I would think that if one thought that he could reason himself completely into religious awareness or experience, he might never really get there.*

Sri Chinmoy: Why not? One grows into one's own thought, when one is aspiring. One of our greatest spiritual Masters, named Sri Ramakrishna, used to say, "If you say, 'I am a sinner, I have committed so many sins, I must be a sinner', then you will always feel like a sinner and you will always be a sinner. You will be earthbound. But if you say, 'My Father is God; I am free, eternally free,' then you will become free." This is the positive way. God has created me in His Image. I have to be consciously one with Him. He is one with me. Of this, I am consciously aware. You grow into these divine thoughts. You are not forcing experience; you are entering into the consciousness of a true devoted servitor of God and when this devotion and union become an integral and natural part of your everyday life, the higher mystical experiences will come by themselves.

If you really want to have Divine Oneness as your goal and if you say, "This is my goal," either you have to reach your goal with your aspiring inner cry or by asserting your own inner will and revealing what is already within you. You know you are God's Son; either you have to cry for that realisation or you have to feel that you already, in fact, have it within you and you just have to uncover it. There are two ways. One way is to go, like a beggar to your Father, saying, "Father, give me, give me Yourself." The other way is to feel that the Father has kept everything inside you in a box and inside the box is a jewel. The key is also inside you. Now if you have a spiritual teacher as your guide, the teacher can show you where the box is, where the key is and how to open the box. But if you don't have a spiritual teacher as your guide, then you have to cry for this inner experience of oneness. Crying does not mean shedding tears, but it means the inner cry of intense aspiration. This is the way to uncover your inner divinity. This is how our thoughts help us to enter into true, mystical experiences.

426. Would you please explain the difference in some words you used? "Physically", "vitally", "mentally" and "psychically" .... I don't understand the difference between "vitally" and "physically".

Sri Chinmoy: You know that we have a body, this gross physical body. But inside the physical, we have a subtle physical body, which is the counterpart, on the subtler planes, of the physical body. Now inside or behind the subtle physical body is the vital sheath. Now where in our spiritual life does the vital come in? We know that when the soul comes to earth, it takes a physical form. We are inclined to think that this physical world is the only world. But there are many worlds. There are seven superior worlds and seven inferior worlds. The vital plane is one of these worlds. There is a mental world and there is a psychic or soul's world. According to our Indian philosophy there are seven higher worlds and seven lower worlds. The vital world is inside or behind the physical world and it is from the vital world that we get this vital sheath. The vital sheath is responsible for our ordinary desires and human emotions. When I use the word "vitally" I refer to the dynamic, emotional part of our nature. When I speak of the "lower vital", I am referring to the unillumined and untransformed parts of our desire nature. Often I refer directly to the physical sex-life when I say "lower vital". The ordinary vital comprises those emotions and passions which are not touched by the divine light, such as ordinary joy and sorrow, anger, excitement, etc.

The vital sheath came from the vital world and it will return to the vital world and be dissolved there when the soul leaves the body. Where will the mind go? It will go back to the mental world. It is from the vital world that we get the vital being. "Vitally" refers to the dynamic, emotional nature and "physically" of course refers to the physical nature.

427. Do you mean that the vital body is a less dense form of matter than the physical body and it interpenetrates or gets within the physical body?

Sri Chinmoy: The vital body is undoubtedly less dense than the physical body. The mental body is still lighter. The deeper you go within, the more subtle these bodies become: subtle, subtler, subtlest. But on the physical plane, we have this gross body. We have three main bodies and each body has a different substance. There is the *sthula sharira,* the gross physical body, inside it is the *sukshma sharira,* the subtle body. Then inside the subtle body is another body called the *karana sharira,* the causal body. The causal body contains everything in the being in seed form. Everything that is going to be manifested outwardly is contained in the karana sharira. When we go from the causal body to the subtle body, a manifestation actually takes place on the subtle planes of the physical. This manifestation is very ethereal in substance and cannot usually be seen with the outer eyes. However, people who have inner vision often see things happening on the subtle planes, where the manifestation begins. Then from the subtle body, the manifestation enters into the dense, material plane. Here the experiences, the realities, the realisations take their external and outer form. So this is how the manifestation of everything takes place: from the causal to the subtle to the gross physical plane.

428. Which of these bodies is involved in extra-sensory perception and other psychic experiences?

Sri Chinmoy: All of them. All three bodies participate in the experiences. And once one gets the Real Experience, by which I mean Realisation, one sees the experience in all the three bodies, the physical, the subtle and the causal all at once and also in the three worlds to which these three bodies belong: the physical, world, the subtle physical world and the causal world. When it is a matter of realisation, one will see, feel and become that realisation in all three planes of consciousness.

But this is not the case with minor experiences. Some ordinary unimportant experiences only the physical body will receive. And for people who do not have a strong hold on the material world, but who have an opening to the subtle world, they may receive certain experiences only in the subtle body. If it is not at all important, the experience may be received only in one body.... just ordinary, minor happenings. But if something serious is experienced, then it must be recorded in all three bodies.

429. Can you say something about past lives?

Sri Chinmoy: One has to be very careful when one deals with reincarnation. Suppose you are extremely eager to know about your past and you go to someone who claims to be able to tell you about your past lives. There are many clairvoyants, mediums, card-readers, etc. Ninety-nine per cent of them are simply fabricating interesting stories. Most of these people are fakes. Some people claim to know about their own past incarnations and there are dozens of pocket books on the bookstands full of fascinating accounts of what people claim to have experienced in their past lives. But to a spiritual person, one of the signs that these accounts are totally untrue is that very frequently the person who claims to remember his past incarnation claims that he or she was a person of the opposite sex. Now a genuine spiritual Master knows that a woman will reincarnate as a woman and a man will always be a man in every lifetime. The exceptions are so rare that they can be left aside for the purposes of this discussion. So here is the first sign that their truth is no truth. Secondly, their past lives as they describe them are often very bizarre or flamboyant or most extraordinary. These people almost never have past lives that are quiet or ordinary or modest. And there are many more things I could say about the consciousness of people who claim to remember their past lives. It is not easy to see your past lives. It is very hard to know one's past incarnations. Except for rare glimpses and flashes, you have to be an advanced seeker before your soul will give you the knowledge of what it did before.

Now there are some spiritual Masters who have the capacity to tell you anything about your past incarnations. They can easily tell. But what will it accomplish for you? Suppose a Master tells you that in your past incarnation, you were a thief .... a dacoit. What will be your immediate reaction? You will say, "I was a thief. Then it is useless for me to think of God in this life. In my last life, I was so low. I was such an unspiritual soul." So you feel that in this life also you will be doomed to disappointment. Now the Master has told you about your past life. He has played his part. But who is the sufferer? You, yourself. If, on the other hand, he tells you that you were the President of the United States, you will immediately think, "Now in this present incarnation, where am I? I am nowhere near that." Immediately you will be disheartened. You will feel, "O God, in my last life, I was so great, but in this life I am nothing. So I see that it is useless. I will not aspire because I can never be what I was." So knowing that you were someone very high only created disappointment in you.

Now here is another possibility. If someone tells you that in your past incarnation, you started your inner journey, your spiritual journey, that you cried inwardly, you meditated, then that is a different story. You did not complete your task. You did not come to the end of the road; you did not reach your Goal. When you learn this, you get true inspiration. You say, "There is a Goal and I started my journey. Let me go forward. Let me aspire to reach the Goal. This is the purpose of my life."

430. Will you give me an opportunity to have a private talk with you?

Sri Chinmoy: You have to forgive me. This time it is impossible. I will be coming back in January and at that time, I shall stay for about a month. If you care to stay with the Centre, until I come back, certainly I will give you an interview. So if you can stay for another month, I will be coming back again in January and remaining here another month. At that time, I will give you a very satisfactory interview, if you stay. This time, unfortunately, I will not be able to give any interviews because tomorrow I have much work.

If you want to come the day after tomorrow, on Thursday morning at 10:00 a.m. you are most welcome, all of you. And if you want to feel the highest Peace, Light and Bliss, you are most welcome at ten o'clock. Please come a few minutes early. On New Year's Day, we have to forget the past.

According to our philosophy, the past is dust precisely because the past has not given us what we wanted. Yesterday did not give us realisation. That is why today we are crying for realisation. If yesterday did not give us what we want, tomorrow has to give it to us. So we have to come out of the past, although what was good in the past, we will take. But what happens, very often, is that we enter into the world of depression. "Yesterday I did not get realisation. Am I a fool? How is it that I may get it today? Since yesterday, I did not get realisation, today also I will not get it." This is our human understanding. So I wish to tell all of you that if yesterday, you did not realise God, that does not mean that today you are not going to realise Him. Today, with your aspiration, you are bound to realise Him. And if you cannot do it today, then tomorrow. You cannot say that God is not going to give it to you today.

1969

I

431. Upon bringing a man born blind to be cured by Jesus Christ, his apostles asked him, "Who sinned, that this man was born blind? Did he sin or did his parents sin?" Christ answered, "No, it is so the works of God may be shown through him."

Sri Chinmoy: Christ was absolutely right. Nobody had done anything wrong, but it was God who was acting through him. God has experiences in and through every individual. It is true that as you sow, so you reap. If we do something wrong, we meet with punishment. This we see in the outer world. But at the same time, when we go deep within, we see that it is God who is the Doer and God is also the Action. In such cases, if one is very spiritual, one transcends the law of karma.

Now I wish to tell you something. The law of karma is limited but the Grace of God is unlimited. Again, inside the Grace, what do we see? It is God's experience. Within His Infinite Grace and in His cosmic law, God is having the experience. When He is in His cosmic law, He follows the principle, "As you sow, so you reap." But when He goes beyond His cosmic law, beyond the universal phenomena, there He is boundless, He is infinite, He is limitless. There He does not follow any law or orderly principle. He is above, far above. He is owner of all His laws.

In connection with your question, I wish to say that the Christ was absolutely right. It was not the karma of that particular person; it is God who wanted to have a particular experience, a significant experience in and through that particular human being.

The thing is that one can go beyond the cosmic law. Even here on earth, when there is Grace, this Divine Grace can easily nullify the cosmic law. I think I have told you here a few times that there is an analogy. Suppose right in front of you there are two children, five years old. One is standing with his father and the other is all alone. The one who is standing with his father suddenly comes running and strikes the other one. Now the poor little fellow, the one who was struck, comes back to strike the first one, but the father is standing there and does not allow his child to be beaten. Similarly, although the cosmic law says that if you strike, you will be stricken, as you sow, so you reap, why is it that the one who committed the crime was not beaten? Just because he had the father. Who was the father? Someone who had more power. He was only a human being, but the father had more power than the little child. Similarly in our life, when you do something wrong, if we know how to aspire, how to pray, how to cry, immediately we approach the Highest Power, the Strongest Power, the Mightiest Power. That Mightiest Power comes to our rescue. It is inside us and at the same time, it is Beyond. It operates in this world: at the same time, it transcends this world if you know how to cry, if you know how to pray, that Infinite Power, that Highest Power is bound to come to your aid, even though you made a mistake. You have made a mistake and the results are due to come in the form of painful punishment. But this punishment can be easily nullified by the intervention of a third power, the Highest Power. So here you can see, even in this world, that the cosmic law, "As you sow, so you reap," cannot be applied all the time.

432. Visitor: There are persons who pray and still are suffering!

Sri Chinmoy: How do you know that they have not received the Grace of God? Someone is suffering here, let us say; somebody has been suffering for a couple of months. At the same time, he prays to God most soulfully. I wish to say that this particular person who is suffering would have suffered for perhaps ten years. We do not know how long a person is destined to suffer by his own karma. Even during the suffering if one prays, meditates, contemplates, he will see that the suffering is bound to diminish or the duration of the suffering is being diminished.

The law of karma right now is beyond human comprehension, but if one lives all the time in God's infinite grace, then God will not only perfect that particular devotee and aspirant, but will show him the process of the Divine Grace: how it operates, when it operates and where it operates in a particular disciple.

433. Why did Sri Ramakrishna not cure himself if he had the power?

Sri Chinmoy: In Ramakrishna's case, he himself knew and we definitely know that his disease was not due to his own karma. It was the karma of his disciples that he accepted and embraced. Sri Ramakrishna accepted very few disciples as his very own, when he was in the land of the living. When sixteen or seventeen true disciples had come to him, he said, "Stop now....I don't want to have any more." Although the number of disciples was very few, their sincerity was so genuine and pure, that he really accepted the consequences of the disciples' wrong actions. He used to enter into the vital world, the lowest vital world, and almost every day he cleaned them and purified his disciples. Then, the ignorance that was about to attack them he would invite to himself, saying, "Don't touch my children, touch me." Not only the punishment for the wrong actions of the disciples did he accept gladly, but also the ignorance that would have threatened the disciples in future years. So on the strength of his intuitive oneness with his disciples, Ramakrishna accepted all his sufferings.

Now once it happened that Vivekananda, his dearest disciple, asked him, "Why don't you go and tell Mother Kali to cure you? You have the power to cure yourself, but if you don't want to, go and ask Mother to cure you." He said, "Why?" Vivekananda said, "If you are cured, you will be able to eat. Now you cannot eat anything; you are in such pain. You cannot put anything inside you." So Ramakrishna went to Mother Kali and said, "Mother, Naren is telling me to ask you to cure me, so that I can eat." he Mother said, "What is wrong with you? You are eating perfectly." Ramakrishna said, "When? I am not eating." She replied, "You are not eating? You are eating through your hundreds of devotees and admirers and disciples. When they eat, are you not eating? Do you have to eat separately? In their eating, you are eating." Immediately he fell silent and went back to Vivekananda and told him, "I will never listen to you again. My Mother has told me that I am eating through you and eating through all my disciples. I am one with you."

So on the strength of his oneness, he became fully one with the suffering of his disciples. That is how and why Sri Ramakrishna took upon himself the suffering of the disciples. Otherwise he could easily have avoided this. But on the other hand, from the ultimate point of view, we can say that Mother Kali gave him the most significant experience of true oneness through his dearest disciples.

434. What is the difference between the soul and the Spirit?

Sri Chinmoy: The Soul is the direct representative of the Supreme in each human being. The Supreme manifests Himself in each individual, as well as in every other form of life. He comes down as a living form when the individual soul begins its journey, its divine pilgrimage. When the animal enters into the human evolution, when one becomes human for the first time, his soul starts its divine journey proper. At the beginning, the human is partly animal and partly divine; his soul is like a small jewel implanted in clay. In each incarnation the jewel becomes more evident and more luminous. As the human grows and evolves spiritually, the divine jewel inside him shines more powerfully, until at the very end of his pilgrimage the person is full of radiance and the divine jewel, the soul, illumines his whole being. He himself becomes the Soul. So the soul is the divine representative.

The Spirit is something different. It is not really connected directly with the earth. The Spirit is an aspect of the Highest Transcendental Consciousness which plays upon, shines down upon each individual soul, but is itself undifferentiated. The Spirit is eternally one, undifferentiated like the White Light of the Supreme before it is broken up into different colours. The Spirit is higher than the soul. It pours down as a manifesting Divine Power and Protection for humanity directly from the Unmanifest for the manifested cosmos. It is a kind of divine radiation hovering above and influencing the earth. It is a very high and unified Force from the Supreme. The Spirit should not be confused with other divine qualities of the Supreme, such as Peace, Power, Light, etc.

As you know, the soul, although it is a portion of the Supreme, is individualised and differentiated. Each soul possesses its own colour, fragrance, divine attributes and even its own mission and destiny. But the Spirit is eternally undifferentiated. The Spirit has a direct connection with the Supreme and also an exalted connection with the creation. When the Supreme breaks Himself up into small individual entities, you have the individual souls. When His Force is sent down as a pure and unified power, in direct touch with the Supreme, but hovering over humanity, high above, that is the Spirit. Normally we do not have the same direct connection with the Spirit that we do with the Soul. The Spirit is there above us and only when we are in the highest meditation or in contemplation, can we reach it or be in touch with it. It silently advises the Soul, elevates the Soul or can illumine or console the Soul.

We are speaking about the Spirit with a capital "S". In English we also use the term "spirit" for a multitude of small entities like ghosts, elves, gnomes, hostile elementals used in black magic, etc. These beings are small and insignificant and are not to be confused with the Spirit, the Transcendent Force coming from the Unmanifest. The Soul is individualised; the Spirit is unindividualised.

435. Does evil have a real existence?

Sri Chinmoy: At the highest level of spiritual consciousness, there is no such thing as evil, but in the lower manifestation of divinity here on earth, there is something which we call ignorance. This ignorance has been interpreted in the Western world as evil, sin and so forth.

Now if you say that by losing contact with the Divine, we have allowed evil to take birth inside us or in the world atmosphere, I say it is true to some extent, but let us not use the world "evil". We should rather use the word "ignorance" here because in this world we human beings are not in direct contact or in conscious union with God. We are one in God; that is one thing. But conscious union is altogether a different matter. So when most of us are not in conscious oneness with God, we are away from the Highest, from the deepest Truth or the Transcendental Reality. So you can call it "evil" if you like, but I would like to call it ignorance.

In India there is a philosophy called Vedanta philosophy. The followers or practitioners of that philosophy are not satisfied even with calling it ignorance; they will say that it is a mere obstacle in our path. What you call evil, what I call ignorance, they call an impediment, an obstacle in our way to absolute oneness with God.

So if you take evil in the sense of ignorance or an obstruction on earth, it does exist. But if you say that evil is something very dark or dangerous, like a roaring lion wanting to devour us at every moment, standing right against the Divine Will, a demon or a hostile force incarnate, it is not like that. It is only the play of ignorance in the lower planes of consciousness that we see. We use various terms to describe it. In the highest world, the spiritual world, there is no evil and God Himself has not created any evil. God had created only Good, Light, Peace and Bliss.

436. Is it acceptable to offer the joy that one derives from one's outer life to God? For instance, my music, my songs – although they are not religious songs – or is it an offence?

Sri Chinmoy: It is not at all an offence; on the contrary, you can please God most through your music. The songs need not be particularly spiritual. If you can sing spiritual songs, well and good, but if you sing ordinary songs with a soulful voice, then your soul will come to the fore at that time and your joy, the joy that you get when you are singing the song, if you offer it to God, God will be most pleased with you.

Now in your eyes, you are an infinitesimal portion of God. Each human being thinks that he is only the tiniest portion of the Infinite Ocean, a bubble. But in God's sight, it is not like that. You may think of yourself as one individual. You may think that God has on earth infinite children but that you are not really one of His children. That is your idea. But God takes you as His very image, as His chosen instrument on earth. God takes you as His representative here on earth. Each individual God takes as His own representative, conscious or unconscious.

God is conscious that He has sent you into the world as His representative, but you are not conscious. In order to become conscious, you have to realise God consciously, like me.

This is the difference between a realised person and an unrealised person. But in the case of God, He is most pleased with you because you have offered to Him what you have. God has given you a most remarkable voice, a soulful voice and you are offering God what He has given to you.

We cannot give to God anything more than He has given us. If He has given me a voice to sing, I will give Him my voice. If He has given me the dancing capacity, I will dance and please Him; if He has given me the capacity to write poems, then through poems, I shall please Him. He has given me this divine gift; it is I who have to offer what I have back to Him. He gives and I have to return it to Him. Nothing do we create on our own. He gave us everything and with our deepest gratitude, we are offering Him what He first gave. So what we have and what we are, what you are and what you have, if you can consciously give to God, God will be most pleased.

So in your case, I wish to say that with each song, each line you sing, if you can feel it as a dedication to God, no matter what song you are singing (it may not be spiritual; it may be romantic or anything else) but the very act of dedication purifies your song, illumines your inner life and your outer life. Then you become one with God. While singing on the radio, feel that you are singing to please God inside your admirers, inside the audience. Those who are seeing you or listening to you.... please try to feel that you are pleasing the divinity in them, but that you are pleasing God at the same time in that way, you are killing two birds with one stone. You are pleasing your admirers and the audience, but you are pleasing the One who is dearest to you, who is God.

The most important thing in your life is to please Him in humanity. Then God is most pleased and each time you sing, please try to feel that you are offering each song, each line, as a flower or a garland of flowers to God, placing it at His feet. Then God will be most pleased. Now also He is pleased because your singing is the capacity, the talent He has given you and you are offering it back to Him. You surely are doing the absolutely right thing. Please continue it. And if you follow the spiritual path, you will develop an infinitely better voice, the inner voice, and you will please God infinitely more. I wish you to concentrate here, on this Centre, the throat. This Centre is called, in Sanskrit, the *Vishuddha* or *Kanta Chakra*. The Chakra is right here in the centre of the throat. If you can concentrate daily on it for about five minutes or ten minutes, you will notice an improvement in your voice.

437. What should be the approach of the aspirant to the concept of the Supreme?

Sri Chinmoy: There should be no mental approach, first of all. The Supreme has infinite aspects. If the aspirant gets inspiration or aspiration to see the Supreme, let us say, in a human body, in human form, there is nothing wrong with it. Again, if the aspirant wants to feel the supreme concept as that of infinite Consciousness or infinite Light or infinite Power, he can meditate on that. But it has to come from within.

Some spiritual Masters say that God should be realised in a human form; then the seeker will be more convinced. Experiencing Him in His infinite aspect and infinite consciousness, they say, makes it difficult for the aspirant to even believe in the personal God. But I wish to say that the personal Supreme and the impersonal Supreme, we all know, are One. So each aspirant must realise the Supreme, both in His personal aspect and in His impersonal aspect. In His personal aspect, there is a form which we can see – golden; you cannot describe it. It is beyond description, the colour of the Supreme! It is dazzling and divinely luminous. It is all golden, beyond human description. That is the personal aspect of the Supreme when you see Him in a form. And again, when He is formless, it is all Consciousness or Energy or Power.

So there should be no approach. If from within, you get an inner urge to see the Supreme as a personal Being, try to approach Him or try to meditate on Him in the personal aspect. Again, if you feel you will be happy to see Him in His impersonal aspect, then meditate on the impersonal aspect. But the inner urge of the aspirant will make the aspirant run towards a particular goal. And once he reaches the Goal, there the personal and the impersonal become totally one.

438. When I meditate on you, I feel that I enter into you as a personal God. Is there anything higher than that?

Sri Chinmoy: In my picture, my transcendental picture, I am totally one with the Supreme. There I fully represent the Supreme and I am totally one with the Supreme in His Transcendental Consciousness. I personally look at my own transcendental picture when I am not in my highest; there I am like a beggar. At times I look at my picture for two or three seconds and I enter into it. When I am in my normal consciousness, I see the difference between my highest and my lowest. There it is the top of the Himalayan peak and here, when I am cutting jokes and all that, it is lower than the foothills of the Himalayas.

But again, inside me, the divine consciousness and the infinite consciousness are very vigilant. It is not that I drop from Heaven into hell. No. My highest is always accessible to me when I need it.

When you are concentrating on me, meditating on me, you are absolutely right in feeling that you enter into my Infinite Consciousness which is totally one with the Supreme. At that time, there is no difference between the Supreme and my Infinite Consciousness. At the time when I meditate right in front of you, in front of the disciples, here and in New York, I become everything that one can think of and aspire for. Even in the physical body, which you see inside the frame of the picture, the soul and the physical existence become totally one and there I see and I become the entire universe. At the same time, the entire universe is inside me.

And this experience of yours – I am so happy that you have it. In New York also, there are two or three who have told us about this. If the closest, dearest disciples feel that they can get everything from their Guru, from their Master, there is no mistake in it. It is absolutely true. For the disciple, the Guru represents the Supreme here on earth.

439. *What are the ways that we can expand our receptivity to the Supreme?*

Sri Chinmoy: You can expand your receptivity, you can enlarge yourself in receiving the Supreme in your inner life as well as your outer life just by feeling that you are extremely helpless. You are a babe in the woods without the Supreme. Again with the Supreme, you are everything. Without the Supreme, you are nothing, nothing, nothing. With the Supreme, you are everything. This thought, this idea, this truth must be implanted on the tablet of your heart all the time. You are nothing without the Supreme; you are everything with Him. In this way, your receptivity automatically increases because you have already realised the real Truth in your inner life as well as in your outer life. You know that your entire existence depends on Him, your inner existence as well as your outer existence. Your outer existence depends on Him; your inner existence also depends on Him. If you feel that your entire existence is meaningless, useless, absurd if He is not inside you and within you to guide you, to mould you, to shape you, and at the same time to fulfil Himself in you and through you, then your receptivity will expand. Receptivity is bound to come the moment you feel that the Supreme is the only object of your life and it is He who is meaningful, essential, and inevitable in your life, both the inner and the outer life.

Always try to see, from now on please, that you are the chosen child of the Supreme just because He is utilising you. But if you feel that you are utilising yourself with your own ego and pride, then you are thousands of miles away. The moment you are away from Him, you have to feel that you are nothing, you are useless. The moment you are one with Him with your dedication, devotion and surrender you will feel that you are everything. When you feel that you are everything, automatically your receptivity expands.

Then there is another way to expand your receptivity. During your meditation, try consciously to have inner joy. Suppose the inner joy does not come to you all at once, then try to imagine for a few seconds or a few minutes that you have it. This will not be something false. You can take it as pure imagination but this imagination will help you to some extent in the long run, perhaps a few weeks later, to bring forth the true inner joy. Why? Because you are sincerely aspiring to get true inner joy. You are not going to stop with imagination, far from it. You have intense aspiration; however, at the same time, you don't have inner joy right in front of you. But you are crying for inner joy and this inner joy does not come. But your aspiration is so intense that it is going to bring you true inner joy in a few minutes' time. But before this, you can imagine. Imagination helps the aspirant to some extent and it intensifies the power of aspiration. Gradually, in the course of time you get genuine inner joy.

So to come back to your question, to expand your receptivity to the Supreme, you first need to feel helpless without the Supreme. Then you need to feel inner joy, for its very nature is to expand. You cannot bind inner joy. The very nature of inner joy is expansion, expansion, expansion. When you expand, your receptivity will automatically expand like a vessel that keeps getting larger. This is the way in which you can expand your receptivity in order to receive the Supreme in infinite measure.

440. *Does the factor of having spiritual experiences make you closer to the Supreme?*

Sri Chinmoy: Now here I wish to say both Yes and No. Sometimes you may get experiences, inner experiences, higher experiences and then, what do you feel from them? You get inner joy, inner zeal, but this inner joy and inner zeal are not enough to bring you closer to the Supreme. When you get inner experiences, it inspires you. Your very joy does take you nearer to your Goal. But you have to know that these experiences have been given to you by the Supreme. There are other persons to whom the Supreme has not given these experiences. So the experience is not the most important thing.

Another person has not been given a particular experience. The Supreme has not given it to him, but the Supreme wants that particular person to come to Him without the experience. So it depends on the Supreme. The Supreme can bring you to Him by giving experiences and He can bring you to Him without experiences. But I wish to say that each person has to have a few major experiences, a few higher experiences. If you say that he needs hundreds of higher experiences in order to realise the Supreme, that would be foolishness. There are people who have had only three, four or five major experiences and then, in the process of their meditation, they realise God. Again there are others who have had hundreds and thousands of experiences before they realise God. So what is important? Aspiration. Then the rest we must leave to the Will of the Supreme. If He wants to take you to Him with innumerable experiences, well and good. If He wants to take you with just a few experiences, well and good. But one thing is that when you get experiences, you get inspiration, you get joy, you feel that you are fed. So that gives you inspiration to meditate again and again. But a real spiritual farmer goes on digging the ground. He does not care for the immediate crop. His very nature is to plough the field and he knows that at God's Hour, he will get the bumper crop. So a real aspirant will continuously dig the inner soil and at God's Hour, he will get a bumper crop. If you get experiences, wonderful; if you don't get experiences, do not feel that God is displeased or that it is an indication that you are not marching towards God, that you are not getting closer to God. That is wrong. Is it clear?

441. I want to ask about the meaning of the gods. What powers do they represent?

Sri Chinmoy: You have Ganesha, so I wish to speak only on Ganesha because there are so many gods that it would take a very long time. So I will speak only on the god Ganesha.

Ganesha is the son of Lord Shiva. Lord Shiva had two sons and Ganesha is the elder. The younger one is Kartikeya. Ganesha destroys all human darkness and he is worshipped or invoked by all Indians without exception. At the time of ceremonies, before we perform any rituals, we have to pronounce the name of Ganesha or offer obeisance to him. Ganesha is also called Siddhidada, one who gives *siddhi,* spiritual powers and realisation, one who fulfils our aspiration. So no matter what we aspire for, we have to please Ganesha first. When he is pleased, we can rest assured that we can have victory in our inner life as well as in our outer life.

One thing I would like to say is that the functioning of Ganesha is slow and steady. Slow and steady wins the race. Some gods, like the cosmic gods, work very fast through their aspirants, through their disciples and devotees, whereas Ganesha works slowly, steadily, and at the same time most confidently. When Ganesha achieves success in and through a devotee, this success remains. This success lasts forever. This is all I can say about Ganesha right now.

442. I would like to know in which way to invoke Ganesha.

Sri Chinmoy: First of all, if you have a picture of Ganesha, you should place it in your room, in one of the southern corners or on the south wall. Facing the south, you should pray to Ganesha. In India, we invoke this god thus: "AUM. Dakshine Ganeshaya namah." Now AUM you understand from all that we have said about it. *Dakshine Ganeshaya namah* means, "I bow to Ganesha who abides in the south." This way you can start.

Now if you don't care for the southern part of the room, no harm. You can repeat the name Ganesha most soulfully one hundred and eight times. Either you take your rosary beads and with them say "Ganesha, Ganesha, Ganesha," etc. or on your finger tips you count "Ganesha" one hundred and eight times. In India, we are always advised to repeat the names of the spiritual Masters or deities or cosmic gods one hundred and eight times at least, and this, three times a day. Early in the morning is the best time and four o'clock is the hour of God. We call it the Brahma Muhurta. At that time, the cosmic gods start functioning; that is, the actual day dawns. So the best time for meditation is four o'clock in the early morning. But in the West, it is simply impossible. To most Westerners, we say that the moment they get up is the hour of God! If it is five o'clock, if it is seven o'clock, even if it is ten o'clock, that is the hour of God. That will be your first time of day. Then at noon, by which time everybody is up, you can meditate again. Then in the evening, at the twilight hour, it is again the best time for repeating the name of Ganesha and meditating. So you can do this.

443. They are all the same, Ganesha and the other gods?

Sri Chinmoy: They are all the branches. The Tree is one. You have studied Indian Scriptures? Yes? Oh, I am happy. *Ganesha: AUM Dakshina Ganesha.* That is what they say. "Oh, Lord Ganesh, please grant me your help and blessings."
Disciple: Also Lakshmi, Kali, and Saraswati?
Sri Chinmoy: Yes, but there are also symbolic names for these deities. What are their symbolic names, please? Do you know? Each one has a secret name. Each god has a symbolic, secret name. They don't use the name Lakshmi, for example. When a spiritual figure, an aspirant, prays to Lakshmi, he will not say, "Lakshmi, Lakshmi." There is a secret way of praying to Lakshmi, uttering her secret name. It is possible to use the ordinary name but here is a great secret term, which is the word, *Shring.* For Kali, you have to say *Kring.* For Krishna there is one; we call it *Kling.*

What do they do when they want to have some spiritual power, psychic power? They don't say "Lakshmi, Lakshmi." What they do is very rapidly they repeat this name: "Shring, Shring, Shring, Shring." And if it is Kali, who is the bestower of power, it is "Kring, Kring, Kring, Kring, Kring, Kring, Kring."

And within ten minutes you will feel a kind of power all over you. If it is done in the proper manner, you will get the results. These are the secret names, we call them the seed terms for each god.

444. The question of responsibility has puzzled me for a long time. I have heard that the law of Karma is inexorable, that each action has its reaction; that any transgression of the law brings forth the corresponding reaction in the form of punishment or whatever it may be.

Now for example, a tyrant arises to power in a country and starts committing murders, imposing his will through the most brutal means. He stays in power for many years and causes suffering and bloodshed to millions of people. The prisons are full of innocent people. Why is it that he stands so long in power, doing so much harm. Is he responsible for his actions or is he not? If his actions cause such destruction, with holocausts of persecution and crimes, how is he going to pay to the Supreme for the many horrors that he has caused, the many crimes he has committed through his subordinates? Who is really responsible to the Cosmic Will? If not even the tiniest leaf of a tree moves without the Will of God, and God is All-Love and All-Justice, is the Supreme in all things absolutely perfect and absolutely loving? Why do those things happen and who is responsible?.

Sri Chinmoy: Now who is actually responsible? This man is a tyrant. He is destroying the country and has been doing it for one year, three years, six years, and years beyond. Now let us see who is the tyrant and who is destroying the world. The tyrant is actually an instrument. Just as we are instruments of the divine force, he is an instrument of an undivine force, a dark force. Now there is a cosmic law. True. You say that nothing can be done on earth without God's approval. If God is all kindness, all love, how is it that God is tolerating this kind of injustice on earth?

Now I wish to say that God has given us very limited freedom. He Himself has limitless freedom but when we enter into the physical world, we have very limited freedom. This limited freedom we start to misuse. When an individual starts misusing this power, that power enters into the cosmic vibrations, or let us say, the Cosmos. There it vibrates in a wrong way. Then it spreads into the atmosphere of the world.

Now who is responsible? Undoubtedly the person who is destroying and torturing the world, but behind him there is a destructive force. Where did that force come from? It came from ignorance. Where did ignorance start? It started from matter. Now why did matter allow ignorance to abide inside itself? When Spirit entered into matter, in the beginning matter did not like Spirit, and matter did not respond to Spirit's action. Spirit is all Light, all perfection. But matter found it difficult to be totally identified with Spirit. So matter began to have its own life. Life is existence; and matter wanted its own existence which was, and is, based on pure inconscience. So you see, Spirit came and touched matter, but matter refused to respond. Inside matter dwells ignorance, and inside ignorance, can be found powerfully destructive forces. The destructive force is waiting to be channelled. How? It is waiting for a person who is ready to be an agent of its power.

Let us speak of responsibility again. Now if you see the Supreme as ultimately the Highest, then we also have to say that since He has approved our limited freedom, or since He has given us our limited freedom, He also has the capacity to withdraw this limited freedom. Now in the case of the tyrant you have spoken of, he has now been in power for ten years, twenty years, let us say. But in God's eyes, since He deals with

Infinity and Eternity, these twenty years are not even a particle of a second, not even an infinitesimal portion of a second.

Then His Heart: we see the battlefield. The heart of the Supreme on the one hand is flooded with infinite Peace, infinite Harmony, infinite Joy, infinite Delight, but again on His Heart we see nothing but a battlefield of dark forces constantly fighting with divine forces; fighting, fighting. But the ultimate Victory will be His because He wants Light to prevail on earth.

So when He wants Light to prevail on earth, it means that He has taken responsibility. Right now we do not know the outcome of the battle. He is playing with a football, kicking it to this side and that side. Here is the goal post. He is pretending to kick the ball, pass the ball through. But instead of doing this, He changes His play, and using His left foot, He kicks the ball. There He secures His goal, His object. Similarly, in the beginning we feel that the dark forces that we see will eventually touch the goal, in the sense that they will destroy the entire world. For them that is the goal. But I tell you that the dark forces cannot destroy the world because the Light is God. Atom bombs will not be able to destroy God's creation because God's creation is God's body. If God wants to keep His body safe, He is fully responsible. How can he be separated from His body? Let us take God as the Soul and creation as His body. We know that without the soul, the body is useless. Again, without the body, the soul cannot manifest anything. So God's creation is God's body. How can they be separated? If God wants to fulfil His Vision and Reality together, if He wants His body and soul to go together, then naturally He will be responsible for both His soul and for His body.

So to come back to your question, Sanjivan. God is responsible. Ultimately He will be responsible both for His soul and His body. He is inside everything and finally responsible for everything.

But getting back to the tyrant. When we open our eyes, we see that there is a conflict right in front of us. The tyrant is misusing his limited freedom, but the responsibility goes to the Supreme. The Supreme, through His divine instruments, through His forces of Light, will eventually cause the destruction of the tyrant. Every tyrant is eventually overcome. Even if his brutal system remains, it is significantly weakened by the tyrant's own annihilation. Tyranny lasts only as long as we are in ignorance. Ignorance is temporary; conscious knowledge and perfection are permanent. Tyranny is only a temporary manifestation of darkness, ignorance and misuse of freedom. Since this is God's creation, eventually He is responsible for everything. He is so kind. He is infinitely Great, infinitely Compassionate. He says, "It is My fault".

445. The consciousness of the self is a handicap in the path towards God-realisation and complete surrender. This self-consciousness will limit you in the world of plurality, differentiation and phenomena. Now, this is what we want to transcend because we are searching for that oneness of the Absolute. If we are searching for that oneness, where all differentiation ends and where you will integrate with the universal consciousness, you must try to pull away from these forces that will limit you in the sphere of personality or the ego, that will give you a distorted view of what humanity is, of what the purpose of life is and many causes of differentiation. You are dealing with phenomena that take place in space and time. But you are not dealing with true values, the eternal values of the real Self. What I mean to say is that when I say that you have to transcend that self-consciousness, it is that you have to destroy this consciousness of the individuality as the "I" or the personality as the "I". You will have to live in a broader consciousness, in a broader vision, otherwise you cannot attain that goal. To reach that goal, we need the Master because the Master will be like a catalytic agent who will bring up those forces that are hidden in the inner Self so that they will flow into view.

Sri Chinmoy: So now, the part of the Master is the part of a private tutor. The Master is not the examiner. The Master is the tutor who constantly inspires you, teaches the aspirant inwardly. Then, who examines? God does not examine us. It is ignorance that stands in front of us. Doubt says: "Where are you going?" I am still, pass me, go beyond me. Doubt comes and stands in front of me. Fear stands in front of me. They are like solid blocks. So Master inspires and teaches the disciple how he can go, pass through fear and doubt and so forth.

Now you were speaking about self-consciousness. A spiritual aspirant must feel that his individuality and personality must be merged in his Master's or in God's individuality. Individuality is not the physical height, not that you are five feet, eleven inches, standing there full of aggression and lecturing to me. It is not that you are separate from the rest of the world. No. Divine individuality is the highest individual divinity in a person, not showing off how much power a person can exercise or how much knowledge he has attained. No. Individuality means the highest divinity which you have achieved as your own. When I say, *Aham Brahman,* "I am the Brahman," then your personality is full of Light. Your personality is the lantern-breadth of the universe. Your height is your divine individuality, your luminous breadth is your personality. If you can think that your breadth is your personality and height is your divine individuality, if you can concentrate on it, meditate on it, then the limited individuality and the limited personality which you see in your life is bound to go. You don't have to be conscious at each moment what your defects are. This is a very bad way of making progress in the spiritual life. Try to think what good qualities you have, not what bad qualities. By concentrating more and more on your good qualities, that means by concentrating more on light, you expand your light. Then that expansion automatically covers, envelops the darkness, doubt, fear in front of you. So, how can you expand? You see the positive side which is aspiration, purity, divine beauty, concentration, meditation. If you try the positive side, automatically you are going to the highest and that is your individuality. And when you are looking at this side, it is all your personality-covering. So I wish to tell you that to conquer self-consciousness, feel that you want to be, and say that you are God's child, that God-realisation is your birthright instead of saying that you are in darkness. How can I get rid of darkness? Darkness is all around me, inside me, inside the world. Let us see only the positive way. Then in that case it is not that we are ignoring the fact, the phenomenal world which is full of darkness, no. We are seeing what the reality is inside the phenomenal world and that reality is Light, that reality is Truth.

When we consciously see Reality and Truth, then we expand. In the field of expansion, we expand and in the field of realisation, we go to the Highest. That is how it is done.

Always try, during your meditation, during your conscious life, to feel that you are God's chosen child, God's pride. You are not the pride of ignorance. You are the pride of God. God wants you. God needs you to fulfil Him, to manifest Him. Then, how are you going to think of this human world here on earth if you are only thinking of one individual and this and that? Say instead, "God needs me; thus I have surrendered. I have to fulfil God on earth because God wants it. Not that I want it, God wants me to realise Him, to fulfil Him on earth. What more do I need?" That is what the only concern should be for a spiritual aspirant. And in that concern everything is covered, everything in sight. All problems are solved, all answers are given when one feels that God wants him, God needs him for His manifestation on earth; and just because God wants him, not because he wants this thing from God. Here is the mistake. If he wants from God this and that, he will be frustrated, but God wants him and he wants to be consciously one with God's decision. So we can do all this. Right?

1970

I

446. How can we teach ourselves to love people who hurt us? People who are bad?

Sri Chinmoy: Now here is the question. You say that in this world, you feel that some people are bad, really very bad. In this world, all people are not nice. Now by feeling that a person is very bad or by hating that person, are you gaining anything? Alright, you think someone is very bad. But either you will love him, or the opposite thing, you will hate him. Usually it is very difficult to be indifferent to someone when he has done something very hateful to you. Your immediate reaction will be to hate that person. But you will see what you have gained by hating that person, whether in fact, you have gained something or lost something. That particular person has not gained anything from your hatred. But what have you done? By hating that person, you have lost something very sweet in you. You have lost something. Why should one lose something very precious of her own, just because she wants to correct someone by hating him? In this world, we have to be very wise. You will say that he is very bad and that you have to do something. But hating is not the right instrument. If you want to use the right weapon, the most effective weapon will be love.

You may think that love is not a strong enough weapon, whereas hatred is just like a sharp knife. No. The power of love is infinitely more powerful than the power of hatred, because when you love someone, at that time his divine qualities have to come forward. Someone has done something nasty to you. Alright, but now what do you want? You want to punish him and strike him? After striking him, what will happen? In you, there is something called a conscience. That conscience will prick you. You will say, "What have I done? He has done something wrong, true, but now I have done something worse. Then in which way am I superior to him?"

447. Can one develop this love?

Sri Chinmoy: Yes, you can develop it daily, if early in the morning, when you get up, you say your prayer to God, "Oh, God, in your creation I only want to see good qualities in others. If bad qualities are around me, or if people are bothering me, then please try to give me the necessary patience so that I can remain full of peace in my outer life. They have done wrong things to me but let me offer them my patience."

448. Will God help me if I ask Him for help in that way?

Sri Chinmoy: Now look, this child of yours in the bedroom cries for food. You are in the kitchen, but you run when you hear the cry of your child. The child may be anywhere, but why do you come running from the kitchen? Because you have heard his cry. We are God's children and when He hears our cry, He comes to us. He comes to help us. He cherishes us because we are helpless and because we need Him. When we have a true need and when we cry most sincerely, God will certainly come. He will give you compassion, strength and the power to forgive and love the person who hurt you. God will change that person because when you yourself change, the other person is changed, also.

449. *I have read that one has to help oneself, too. If one does not help oneself, God will not help us.*

Sri Chinmoy: But in the spiritual life, God gives us the capacity to do what He wants. Our surrender to Him is our way of helping ourselves, because He gives us the right attitude and tells us the kind of action that should take place in the outer world. God's Power and God's Light give us the capacity to help ourselves. We have to make an effort, but we must all the time remember that God is our Source. It is He who is giving us the capacity to help ourselves. We have to be His instruments. We do the work, but we have to do it for God. You are God's child and He will fulfil all your needs. Just as you fulfil your own child's needs, God will fulfil your needs.

450. *In each era God manifests in a different way. We are entering into the Aquarian Age. I was thinking that since energy changes her form of manifestation in each era, even psychic energy changes. There is a complete transformation of the creation in each era. I would like to know how true my argument is now.*

Sri Chinmoy: Each era signifies a significant promise, but each era has been unsuccessful in a sense because it has not completed (it has not been able to complete) the whole drama in the way God wanted it to be completed or fulfilled. We are trying, in this era, to raise our consciousness to the Highest and bring down the Highest into the lowest.

When we think of transformation in the terms of an era, we have to be conscious of one thing and that is evolution. We are in the process of evolution. This process will find its proper satisfaction or complete satisfaction only when our human nature is completely transformed. You have heard of the eras of the past and there will be a few more eras in the future. We have to know whether the changes or the transformations that we have made up until now are really noticeable, whether these eras have brought any progress.

The transformation that we are crying for is the transformation of our human nature and human propensities. At the same time, we cannot deny that the ordinary person is making some kind of progress. He is getting a better life, a more fulfilling life. He may be transforming or changing himself but this change need not be actually for the better, even though we are all proceeding towards a higher life. But if one is not aspiring, you will see that he will be caught in his ignorance-sea even though while living there, he may start learning how to swim. In the beginning he was sinking all the time in ignorance-sea, drowning; now he knows how to swim and slowly, steadily, in God's own infinite time – God Himself knows when – one day he will be able to swim across the sea of ignorance and enter into the sea of knowledge.

So here we see again the play of an era. Human consciousness started to run towards the Light. Each era offers that opportunity to aspiring human souls, but what happens? That ignorance does not allow human consciousness to reach the Highest. Now we are marking time: one hour, two hours, three hours, four hours, but when we think of one hour, immediately we feel that in this one hour, we have to accomplish what we thought of accomplishing from the beginning. That is, we are standing still and yet we feel that in this era, we should accomplish everything that was not accomplished in all the past eras. Each era embodies a new hope, a new energy, a new will to accomplish the thing that has not yet been accomplished. But what happens? The promise is one thing, the fulfilment is another. There are various factors that do not allow the era to be fulfilled or to fulfil itself.

Now if you think of all the eras, according to our Hindu *shastras,* there are a great many, but right now we are in the Iron

Age, they say. According to spiritual figures, this is the worst period. In this age, the world is going to be destroyed, it is said. When? Some say next month or next year. Some say tomorrow. But it is not true. What they call "destruction" will eventually be proved to be the transformation of human nature.

You were saying that each era is a promise towards a better understanding of Truth, but not even one era has fulfilled or has been able to fulfil its purpose. Here we are trying, but God knows how far we will succeed.

But what is going to happen? Ultimately, it may take a hundred years or two hundred, four hundred years or six hundred. It may take even thousands of years, but the Truth has to be fulfilled. Nobody, no hostile force, no undivine force can prevent Truth from being established. That is to say, Truth has to be established on earth and for that end, what is required from the earth's consciousness is the total transformation of human consciousness. Unless and until our human nature is completely and totally transformed, the Truth may touch the earth-consciousness, but it will not be able to stay there permanently, because the earth-consciousness is not wide enough to hold the Truth. The vessel is not big enough.

So, to come back to your question, Pratyay. In this era, we are trying to raise the aspiring consciousness into the Highest and bring the Highest into the lowest of our nature, so the Highest and the lowest can have a meeting-ground where the lowest totally transforms itself and becomes fully illumined by the Highest. Then they will work together inseparably.

451. What is the quickest way to achieve self-control?

Sri Chinmoy: There are two major ways to achieve self-control. These are faster than other ways. First you have to have tremendous will-power. Determined will-power, you try to cultivate. Then you have to feel the necessity of the Grace. While you are feeling the necessity of the Grace, you have to feel that determined will-power is coming from the Divine Grace. First you can see them separately, your will-power, your determination, and God's Divine Grace. Now you will feel that it is your will-power that is causing the miracle in you, that you are controlling yourself. This is what you will feel, but this is not fully true. What is actually true is that the miracle-power which we call the Divine Grace is operating through you, through your determined will-power. Otherwise what happens is that the human will-power which people use is very limited. Today I say, "I won't do this; I won't eat that." This is my will-power, this is my determination. But tomorrow, I do the same wrong thing. I do that very thing. Though I said, "I won't eat it," I eat it. Though I said, "I won't do it," I do it.

Now the ordinary human determination that I had was also sincere. There are many people who have a sincere determination, but inside the determination, there was a lack of the Divine Grace. That is why they cannot continue their determination for a sustained period. So when you feel the necessity of the Divine Grace inside your will-power and when you feel that your will-power is operating so heartfully precisely because of the boundless power of God, which is manifesting itself in and through your limited will-power, then only can self-control be achieved very quickly and very completely.

452. What changes do we have to make, when, as seekers, we have to work and eat with other persons who don't feel what we feel? Sometimes I have harsh reactions in my relations with the ordinary world.

Sri Chinmoy: It is true that you are superior to a street urchin because you are consciously praying to God and an ordinary person in the street is not thinking of God, is not praying to God, is not concentrating or meditating on God. In that way, naturally you are superior. But if you yourself consciously cherish the idea that you are a superior individual, then naturally you create a barrier between your existence and the existence of the people around you.

Now let us use an analogy. The mother is naturally superior to the child. But the mother does not consciously feel, twenty-four hours a day, that she is superior. What she feels is that she is absolutely one with the child. Hers is a feeling of oneness and not a feeling of superiority. It is we who say that the Mother has more knowledge, wisdom, more capacity, than the child. But if the mother consciously harbours the idea that she is superior to her child, then she won't be able to show affection or concern or be able to do anything for the child.

So if you consider the world around you and feel that you are superior because they are acting in an animal way, you won't be able to become one with them and enter into them. It is we, the witnesses, who will make the comparison, that you are superior to others who are not aspiring, who are still sleeping.

Now how can we mix with people who are not aspiring, who are destructive in their relationship with us? You lose your patience and you lose your temper, it is true.

Now every day, I am sure, you try to meditate. You not only try, you do meditate every day. Now when you go out, try to feel that your wallet is your spiritual bank. Early in the morning you meditated for five minutes and you gathered Peace, Light, Bliss and Power, etc. This is all your money, your wealth. Just like nickels, dimes and dollar bills, you are putting all this money into your wallet. This is inner wealth, however. In the morning you meditated and you collected the money, this spiritual wealth, which you are putting into your wallet.

Now in your outer life, the moment you are displeased with someone, and you are about to fly into a rage, always when you are about to burst into fury, immediately try to open your inner wallet where you have kept the inner peace. These are the pennies, nickels, dimes, quarters and bills that you have saved. If you can use your inner wealth, which is inside your wallet, then you will not be attacked by the wrong forces; at the same time, the Peace and Poise that you get from your inner wealth will prevent you from attacking them with your human power. What you will do while they are attacking you is to show your money, your Light, Bliss, Peace, Joy, etc. Just open your inner wallet and show them the solid protection that you have. They will not be able to enter into your inner sanctum when you have placed right in front of you a solid wall which is composed of your inner wealth.

Now every day when you meditate, try to feel that the result of your meditation will be in the form of spiritual currency and this currency you are putting into your wallet for later use. Then you will see that the rest of the world will not be able to torture you. At the same time, you will have no occasion to attack them.

453. In one of your poems you say, "Hope lost.... destruction close." What can one do if that person is losing hope? What can an aspirant do?

Why does a person lose hope? First of all, I wish to tell you *why* a person loses hope, not what he can do. Why does one lose hope? One loses hope because one feels that there is a certain period, a given time in which to achieve something. You have fixed the time, deciding that, for example, in two days you are going to achieve some specific thing. Now frequently in our hopes, we have inwardly fixed or recorded some particular time for the accomplishment of something. Outwardly we may say that in the near future, we hope to get something or to do something. But it is not entirely true. For if we go deep within ourselves, we see that our minds have already projected a particular date by which to finish something. Inside yourself, if you turn within, you will see that your mind has set the fifteenth of November, for example, as the date. Now when that date arrives, your outer mind may not know that this was the last date given or recorded in your inner mind's calendar. But on that day you will feel that everything has collapsed because you did not achieve and receive the hoped-for result. And when you don't see the result on that day, you feel miserable. You thought that hope was the instrument that would bring the result. On the given day, therefore, you lose hope; you lose the strength of hope even though your physical mind was not even aware of the day that was given by the inner mind. There you are lost. You lose hope.

Now what can you do to regain hope? Here we have to know that hope is not something weak. Very often our conception of hope is something very delicate; a sweet, smooth, soothing feeling which is a kind of balm to our outer minds. But this is not an adequate definition of hope. We have to know that hope is something very solid. It is something strong. It has seen the Truth, only it is unable to bring the Truth into its world. Hope is not something that is crying for the world beyond or crying for a truth which it has not seen. No. Hope has seen the Truth but it cannot and does not yet possess it.

So what can you do when you lose hope? If you know what it is, first of all, you will not lose it. If you know that hope is something that has already seen the Truth which you are ultimately going to achieve, then you will get strength from this knowledge. The time has not come; hope has not yet been able to bring the Truth in front of you. The real time which has been planned by God has not yet come.

Now again, what can you do to get back your hope? Try to cast aside all expectations from your desiring mind. It is the desiring mind that feeds our outer hope. If we can be above the desiring mind, and remain all the time in the spontaneity of our heart, we will have a constant feeling of divine possession, of possessing the Truth. We shall know then that hope is the vision that sees the reality and finally becomes the Reality itself in the Supreme's own Hour.

Our inner heart is always full and complete, requiring nothing. It is our outer mind which feels that it needs something, wants something. Then hope comes into play. When you need something, hope begins to play its part, but when you need nothing, hope does not enter the picture, for it is not at all necessary.

Now I would like to point out that ordinary human hope can never be fulfilled because inside it there is no determination; there is no sincerity, there is no conscious willingness to accept the highest Truth. If, with our human hope, we want to achieve the Highest, the Ultimate, we will see that when the Highest is descending and descending, approaching our own human physical being, this human hope will be terrified and try to escape at the very moment that it sees the enormity of the reality that it was aspiring to possess.

Now let us look at the fulfilment, in boundless measure, of our ordinary human hope. Hope expected something, say five dollars. When fulfilment came, it came as five million dollars; immediately this human hope was overjoyed. Immediately also it loses its inner poise. When spiritual receptivity is lacking, we always lose our inner balance and poise. But if you started with Divine Hope, where Truth is already seen in its highest aspect, it needs only to be embodied. Your hope is only to bring that Truth into manifestation. There you do not lose your inner balance. Then when hope's fulfilment comes into you, you do not become unbalanced because you knew about it. You knew what was bound to happen. You remain poised.

Now your question was, "What can you do when you lose hope?" When you lose hope, you have to feel that the reality is bound to come to you precisely because you are in the world of aspiration. You are aspiring most sincerely, most devotedly, most uniquely. You are doing the right thing. Now if the Truth or the Fulfilment that your hope has envisioned has not yet been able to manifest, do not worry. It is only when you lose your aspiration that you can feel that you are lost. When I said in my aphorism, "Hope lost, destruction close," it is because the ordinary man will not aspire when there is no hope. It is hope that keeps him alive on earth. Hope plays a great part on earth. For example, some people say that they are doing disinterested work, and so on. Only aspirants and truly spiritual people really do this. Ninety-nine per cent of human beings, in working, are only feeding their own human hopes and desires. That is why they are living, working, existing. Otherwise they would not budge an inch.

Now in a spiritual person, this aphorism "Hope lost, destruction close" does not apply. Where is destruction for a spiritual person? For him, there is no destruction. He acts only to fulfil God's Will. We tend to judge the fulfilment of God's Will in two ways, in the form of success or in the form of failure. But God Himself is above both success and failure. So if you want to become identified totally and inseparably with God's Will, then think neither of success nor of failure. Think only of pleasing the Supreme. According to our human eyes, the fulfilment of hope is success. But according to our divine vision, the fulfilment of God's Will is far above and infinitely higher than the achievement of failure or success.

So if you remain with your burning aspiration, you are constantly identified with God's Will. And when you are one with God's Will, this earthly hope has no value. It will be impossible for earthly hope to knock at your door of aspiration because your divine hope is already self-sufficient. It is already one with God's Will. In God's Will there is everything, the Vision and the Reality. If the Reality is success, well and good. It is the fulfilment of God's Will which is of paramount importance, not success or failure. Fulfilment is always beyond results. We see the results best and we derive the utmost benefit from the results only when we are one with God's Will unreservedly. When we are identified with His Will unreservedly, we know that we are fulfilled.

So what can you do when you lose hope? Only feel the necessity of burning the flame of your aspiration more brightly and more intensely. Then you get the Highest. Hope you don't need. For an ordinary person, (not you) but an unaspiring person – when he loses hope, it is destruction, because he won't make any move forward. For him life becomes a stagnant pool. Self-destruction starts when there is no forward movement. But not you. You have aspiration. You will get everything.

454. I want to know the relationship between maya *and creation.*

Sri Chinmoy: Only you want to know what *maya* is. Maya is a Sanskrit word. It means measure. When we measure something we bind it. I gave a talk on maya a few minutes ago on the definition of the word. In the word maya, commonly translated as "illusion", the root meaning is to bind, is to measure something, to measure. Now in our day-to-day activity we are binding, we are trying to bind the Infinite which cannot be bound. Maya exists in us because we are afraid of something vast, something deep. On the one hand, we say that we want everything, but the moment a little thing is offered to us, our vessel is so small that we feel that it will break us totally. At that time we cry aloud, "We don't want it." Maya exists because we consciously and very often want to wallow in the pleasure of ignorance. That is, only when we aspire do we come to realise that very often, consciously we want the joy of inconscience and foolish emptiness. And when we wallow in the pleasure of ignorance, maya says, "Oh, you are my friend, you are my eternal friend."

Now, how can you get rid of maya, illusion? You have to feel that God the Creator wants something from you and this something is unique. It is only you who will perform God's Will in a unique way. Somebody else will perform God's Will in his own unique way. The moment you feel the necessity of fulfilling God in God's own Way you can rest assured that maya, the illusion, or maya, the limitation cannot stand in front of your way. To fulfil God in God's own Way is to fulfil, is to achieve Infinity in us. So when you are receiving and fulfilling Infinity in your inner and outer nature, there can be no measurement, no mental illusion, no hallucination of the mental life. In your aspiration, illusion will lose its existence and finally it will disappear for good.

455. In the third chapter of the Gita, Arjuna asks Sri Krishna about action and inaction. I would like to know something more about it.

Sri Chinmoy: I will tell you about action and inaction but not from the Bhagavad-Gita. If a specific question is put to me from that chapter, then I can deal with it later. Right now I shall speak generally.

There are two kinds of action. One is disinterested action and the other is the action of desire. Now most of us act only when we feel that we will get a satisfying result. Before we actually act, we think of the result and if we feel that it will be satisfactory and fruitful then we enter into the field of action. If we know beforehand that the result will be unfavourable, usually we do not enter into the action at all.

Now here, the disinterested action, which is the real action, is what we have to do. We have to act for the sake of God and not for the sake of the result, which is what the Gita calls "the fruit of action". Success is not our goal. Failure is not our goal. But the fulfilment of God's Will is our goal.

Now let us speak about action. Normally, we feel that we have acted when we use our limbs, our hands or at least our brains. We feel we must move and be dynamic. But spiritually speaking, when we act, we must feel that it is God who is acting in us and through us. It is God Himself who is acting and we are His instruments. We can feel that it is the Divine Play: our inaction but God's action. We are used by Him for His Purpose. We are consciously moving and working, but the inner Force and the source of the action is coming from Him. This is what "inaction" means here.

On the other hand, if we feel that it is we who are working and God the Witness, the Silent Purusha, is merely watching, then naturally, we will feel that the action is done by us. We call this silent, withdrawn aspect of the Supreme the *Sakshi Purusha,* the Witness Being. He is watching; we are working and earning our daily bread by the sweat of our brow. If this is our feeling and experience, we say that we are working and God is observing. I cannot say that if we have this feeling, then we are totally mistaken. It is a valid experience. It is also much better than being totally unaware of God's existence. But there is a higher Truth about God's relationship with us when we act. I shall speak about this another time.

I wish to tell you that whatever we do must be done only because He, the Inner Pilot within us, commands us. This is called real action. Unreal action is when we cry for the result and when we feel that we are responsible for what we say or do.

From now on, try always to aspire and in your aspiration, pray to God, "Oh God, speak through me, act through me, feel through me." This is real action.

II – QUESTIONS AND ANSWERS FOLLOWING THE LECTURE "THE INNER FREEDOM"

456. Does the inner world affect the outer world?

Sri Chinmoy: Certainly. It is through the inner world that our outer world can be fulfilled. As you sow within, so shall you reap without. If, early in the morning I offer to God one divine thought, one spiritual thought, I will see that during the day I receive the fruits of that divine thought. If I pray for, or meditate on, Divine Love, or Joy, or Peace, during the day I will enjoy the fruits of my prayer and meditation in the form of Love, or Joy, or Peace or whatever I am crying for.

So, to come back to your question, the inner world can and must affect the outer world – for the better.

457. What is the purpose of life?

Sri Chinmoy: The purpose of life is to realise the highest Truth, to reveal the highest Truth, and to manifest the highest Truth.

Our earthly existence is the opportunity to grow and develop both within and without. Inwardly, we grow in our realisation of Truth, and outwardly, we grow into the manifestation of our realisation.

458. How do we reach the inner worlds?

Sri Chinmoy: It is through our aspiration, our real inner cry. As in the outer world we cry for name and fame and all that, so in the inmost recesses of our heart we must cry to realise the highest Truth.

On the strength of our aspiration we can easily enter into the inner worlds.

459. How can one achieve this realisation of Truth?

Sri Chinmoy: To start with, what you need is inspiration. This inspiration you can get by reading sacred, spiritual books, preferably written by real spiritual Masters. Then you must try to live the wisdom of the books. From books you can get inspiration; then when inspiration has played its role, you must enter into the world of aspiration. This aspiration can be expressed through concentration, meditation, and contemplation. Once you are consciously aspiring, if you have a friend who is a very advanced seeker, he may be able to give you some help. And if you are absolutely sincere in your life of aspiration, then you will come into contact with a real spiritual Master who can really help you and guide you towards your own realisation.

460. Have you attained to realisation, or are you still a seeker?

Sri Chinmoy: No, I am not a seeker. To be quite frank, I am a realised soul. At my will I can, at any moment, enter into my highest trance where I am totally one with the Transcendental Consciousness.

But God the Infinite is constantly transcending His own Transcendental Consciousness and creating new worlds of Infinite Peace, Joy and Delight. So although I am fully God-realised, I am still a seeker in the sense that I seek with God His ever-transcending and ever-unfolding Creation. In this sense, I am an eternal seeker.

461. What will happen to you when you die, being a realised soul? Will you be absorbed in God and not take incarnation again?

Sri Chinmoy: The thing is, we have not to feel that God is there in Heaven and we are here in hell. God is all-pervading, so I have not to leave the earth to go to Him.

At the end of this lifetime, when I pass through the tunnel of death, I will shed the five *sthulas* or sheaths and pass through the physical world, the vital world, mental world, and psychic world and then to the region of the soul's consciousness, where I will take rest in my own highest consciousness for as long as the Supreme needs. Then, when the Supreme wants, I will again enter into the manifestation to serve Him.

For all of us, this is not our first incarnation, nor can it be our last.

462. Since you are a realised soul, will your next incarnation be different from that of an ordinary person?

Sri Chinmoy: Certainly. In each incarnation we are given more opportunity and a better situation for our spiritual development. In the case of a spiritual person, he will be born into a spiritual family where he will be inspired and encouraged to live the spiritual life from his very birth.

Each incarnation is a stepping stone towards our ultimate God-realisation. When one has consciously aspired in his last incarnation, his future birth will hold more opportunities for his spiritual progress.

463. Why do we need a spiritual Master? Can't we find Truth by ourselves?

Sri Chinmoy: Why do you go to the university? To learn anything, we need the help of a teacher. If we want to learn to sing, we go to a singer; if we want to learn to dance, we go to a dancer. Similarly, if we want inner knowledge, we need the help and guidance of a spiritual teacher. For everything we need a teacher but not for the spiritual life – it is absurd!

If the mother does not teach the child, how will he learn the alphabet? So when we launch into the spiritual life, we need the blessings and concern of a spiritual Master, and then when we have got our degree – when we are on the verge of realisation or we have achieved realisation – then we graduate and no longer need his help.

True, the Light is within you, but unless someone shows you where to find the Light, you cannot see it. The treasure is inside you, but you need someone to lead you to the treasure box and show you how to unlock it.

464. You said before that each incarnation is a stepping stone towards our God-realisation. Does that mean that we can't reach God in this life?

Sri Chinmoy: No, not at all. It is a matter of previous background and development. If one has been aspiring and meditating in previous lifetimes, then there is no reason why he cannot attain realisation on the strength of his aspiration in his present incarnation. Since we are all progressing towards realisation, in one incarnation or another, this realisation is bound to take place. As I said, it is a matter of the aspirant's spiritual development.

465. How do you define God? I try to define Him as an animate Force, but this just confuses me more.

Sri Chinmoy: We define something. We try to limit and bind it, but God the Infinite is limitless; thus we can never define Him. One minute the mind may think that God is this, then we see that God is also something else. You are absolutely right when you say that God is an animate Force, Infinite Energy, if the lady sitting next to you feels that God is Infinite Joy, then I must say that she, too, is correct. Another may feel that God is Infinite Light. Still another may want to see God as an absolutely divinised human form with two arms, two legs and all. They are all correct. God is everything. God is both personal and impersonal, with form and formless. God is beyond the limitations of the mind. The Vedic Seers said of God [Guru recites in Sanskrit]: "That moves and that moves not. That is far and the same is near. That is within and at the same time, without." Our human mind cannot understand it.

So, to come back to your question, each individual must go deep within where his inner being will tell him which aspect of God is most inspiring to him.

466. You said that we are all evolving and progressing. But where did this whole process start? Was there a beginning?

Sri Chinmoy: We came into existence from God's Delight. When we entered the creation, we evolved through the lower stages: mineral life, plant life, animal life. It is true that we are constantly progressing. Now we have entered into the human life – I beg to be excused, we are still half-animal! There are people who want to kill others, stab others, and do all kinds of violent and destructive things.

But in the case of a spiritual aspirant, it is different. He tries to drop all the lower animal parts of his nature and tries to be aware of and live in his true Divine nature where it is all Peace and Joy and Love.

In the beginning we came from Delight, we are now growing in Delight, and we shall consciously return to Delight.

467. Is the realisation you speak of achieved through a certain kind of Yoga?

Sri Chinmoy: It is only through Yoga that man can realise God. Yoga means "union" – man's conscious union with God.

There are three major kinds of Yoga: *Bhakti Yoga,* the path of love and devotion, *Karma Yoga,* the path of selfless service and *Jnana Yoga,* the path of wisdom and knowledge.

Now, all paths lead to Rome, but one may get us there a little quicker or easier. My path, which we call the Sunlit Path, is the path of Love, Devotion, and Surrender.

It is up to the individual aspirant which path he feels best suited for. One has to be careful, however, not to follow a false teacher. A false teacher can bring your life to ruin.

But again, I must say, if one follows a real spiritual path, he will eventually reach the goal. All paths lead ultimately to the same goal.

468. Is there a difference between man and God?

Sri Chinmoy: No. Today's imperfect and unfulfilled man is tomorrow's perfect and fulfilled God. God and Man are eternally one. God needs man to manifest Himself; man needs God to realise his true Self.

You have a soul, I have a soul, the Christ had a soul. The soul is consciously one with God. On the strength of his highest realisation, the Christ said: "I and my Father are one." How can anyone dare to say differently? In India we say *Tat twam asi,* "That thou art" and *Soham Brahman,* "I am the Brahman."

There is no yawning gulf between man and God. Through his aspiration and meditation, Man can become conscious of his oneness with God.

III – QUESTIONS AND ANSWERS IN MAY AND JULY 1970

469. Is there any relationship between imagination and faith?

Sri Chinmoy: There is no direct relationship between imagination and faith; in fact, there is a great difference between the two. Imagination plays mostly in the mind; in the mental region we imagine. Imagination can be of help to faith and faith can be of help to imagination. The mind imagines. It imagines things according to its own fancy. When something is finite, imagination can make you feel that it is infinite. Imagination in this way can very often mislead us or misguide us. While standing on this side of a river, we may feel that the other side of the river is very beautiful while this side is disappointing us. This is what we feel on the strength of our wishful imagination. Then when we take a boat and go to the other side, we see that it is no better than the first side. But our imagination made us feel that the other side was infinitely better.

Again, inside imagination reality can be found. Some scientific truth or poetic truth or any other type of truth may emerge. When a poet, for example, creates something, he may see the truth through his imagination's light. Then when he expresses it, it is all reality, all truth.

Now to come to faith: faith comes from the heart. Actually it comes from the soul. The soul does not have to imagine anything. The soul lives in reality. When one lives in reality and sees reality all around, then one need not imagine. You are sitting right in front of me; I don't have to imagine that I am seeing you. You are the reality right in front of me. Faith, the expression of the inner reality, makes us one with the object or the subject. That is why faith does not need any kind of imagination. Faith is our inner awareness of oneness. Awareness of oneness is faith. The finite is becoming aware of the Infinite. This awareness comes first, then comes oneness. Faith has the capacity to start with awareness and end in oneness.

How can faith and imagination help each other? When faith shows the truth and wants to expand, imagination can supply the fuel. Imagination can help faith expand. Faith has seen the truth. Faith knows that this is the truth, that we have come this far. Faith feels the truth but faith does not have the inner capacity, the immediate capacity to expand it. Now if behind or inside imagination, we can seize upon the divine intention or the divine will, then faith will be expanded and our vision will certainly be no mental hallucination. Otherwise we expand the consciousness of faith through imagination; and if, inside imagination, there is no trace of God's Will or of God's intention, the purpose is missing and then the result will always be fiction or hallucination.

Very often, our faith is shattered into pieces because when imagination comes to feed faith, imagination does not have God's approval or His Will-Power. It does not have His Concern or Blessing-Light. But if imagination comes with God's Blessing-Light, Concern and Love, then faith can be expanded. In this expansion, faith makes us feel that the finite has infinite possibility to be one with the Infinite.

And then how does faith help imagination? When we imagine something, we may be wrong, we may be right. But when faith comes and enters into imagination, faith gives living breath to imagination. This moment we imagine something and next moment our imagination is frustrated because we cannot go beyond it. We imagine and then, although it is imagination, we come to a halt. If we close our eyes now, we can go to Berlin with our imagination. Then we are unable to go further and there we are caught. Or we can go to some other place and we will be caught there. We cannot go further. But if faith is inside imagination, faith will give us its living breath. A living breath means dynamic movement. Now if Berlin exists, then there should be something farther than Berlin also. Then when imagination feeds us with its living breath, our imagination gets real divine strength to go farther and deeper. Otherwise, what happens is this: imagination loses its own strength to go any further. It comes to a point and then it stops because it feels that there, either it is all achievement or else all frustration. But when faith comes to help imagination, then there is constant movement in imagination, which does not stop. It feels that there is something higher, something further, something deeper. This is how faith and imagination help each other. But it does not happen always. On rare occasions it happens.

So if we say that there is a direct link connecting faith and imagination, we will be mistaken. Faith is something spontaneous. Imagination is not so spontaneous. When faith comes, there is reality flowing there. In imagination, truth can grow if so is the Will of God. If it is the Will of God, then Truth will grow there in imagination. But in faith, Truth is growing all the time because faith embodies truth, reveals truth and manifests truth.

470. A disciple from Arecibo told me one night that he felt the necessity to meditate while he was driving his car at night and that he went out of his normal, physical mind. I told him not to do it and that I was going to ask you about that.

Sri Chinmoy: No, it is not advisable, especially for the beginners to meditate or concentrate while driving. When one becomes an expert in the spiritual life, one can do anything. Right now he is touching the wheel, he is touching the gas, he has to look around and be alert. But a day can come when he has more capacity; at that time he can concentrate, he can meditate. But right now he can repeat the name of the Supreme. "Supreme,

Supreme," he can say slowly and quietly. While repeating this, he won't lose so much of his outer consciousness.

But if he enters into deep meditation and he does not have the capacity to keep a balance between his inner consciousness or his inner aspiration and his outer situation, then he can have a serious accident. At the beginning it is always advisable to meditate at home in one corner of a room. Here he is dealing with life. Here he is taking a tremendous risk and he is also involved with others. He is driving and if he enters into deep meditation and if he takes somebody's life, what right has he? If he is at home at the time of meditation, if he wants to sleep, he can lie down. He can do anything he wants, anything which will suit him. But when you are in a car, when others are involved, you have to be very, very careful. When others are involved in the street, you always have to be very careful. So for the seekers, especially for the beginners, it is inadvisable to meditate in the car. You have twenty-four hours. Right now the beginner need not, cannot, cannot is the right word, cannot meditate for more than an hour. Impossible. You can meditate for fifteen minutes, four times a day. If you can meditate four times for fifteen minutes each day, sincerely, then that is one hour. More than that if he wants to do, he will only count hours, saying that he has meditated ten hours, twenty hours, etc. Out of twenty hours, perhaps ten minutes he will have really meditated and the rest of the time he will have slept or enjoyed all kinds of earthly thoughts, activities, every thing except meditation.

So for my new disciples, from the beginner disciples, I don't expect more than one hour meditation. Then it is like a muscle that is being developed. One hour and ten minutes, one hour and a half, two hours, three hours. But while he is meditating at home or in a group, he has to feel that this is something that can be developed, slowly, steadily and gradually. And this is something right now that has to be done almost secretly.

Ramakrishna and other spiritual Masters said it. If you are doing something which creates a sensation in others or which is drawing attention from others and if you are a beginner, then all of your meditation, all your progress will be in vain. Once you become expert and you are meditating most deeply, no matter how many people are looking at you or mocking at you, are appreciating you or flattering you, you won't listen. While they are flattering you, you will remain unperturbed. But at the beginning you will meditate at home or in the Centre. Otherwise, if you meditate in the street while you are walking, or during your driving, you will run into trouble.

471. Master, please tell me, if I have to come back here in another incarnation, who is going to take care of my soul? You? If you don't want to come to this world again, will you name someone to take care of me?

Sri Chinmoy: Very good. First of all it is true that I will not come back any more. I have played my role. When the game is over, you don't play again. When you are playing your part in a game, sometimes you lose the game, sometimes you win. You only know that you have played your part. You have done what God asked you to do.

You are thinking of your next incarnation. I wish to say that in this incarnation you have to know whether or not you have achieved an inseparable oneness with my soul or not. In ordinary human life we see the bond between mother and son. You are here. Now your son may be in New York. When you are working with your other children, you may be working in the kitchen, but your heart is inside your son. And your son may be studying in New York in the University, but his heart is inside the mother. It is human love, the human bond, and even then it has crossed thousands of miles. This is the human way. Your human body will perhaps stay on earth seventy or eighty years. But in these years, you have developed something which is called a heart. How it is crossing the distance of thousands of miles! Your son is in New York and from New York message is coming to your heart of all his affection, love, concern. This is your offering and his offering. Now you must ask yourself if you have made this heart's connection with me, with my soul, with your Master's soul. Now on the spiritual plane, the teacher himself represents God and his soul is infinitely more illumined than the disciple's soul. Your soul wants to be illumined as my soul and it knows that everyone has to realise God. We can deceive everyone, but not God. We can say that we won't do something or eat something. But one thing we will have to eat is the fruit of the realisation-tree. Realisation-food we won't be able to deny. God will say, "Alright, if you don't want to do this, don't do it; if you don't want to eat, don't eat, but this food, the realisation-food you have to eat sooner or later, in this incarnation or ten incarnations later.

Now it is I, your eternal friend and your eternal Guru, who has to give you this realisation-food. If I am unable to do it during my lifetime, I shall continue to feed your soul after I return to my heavenly Home. I do not need to name someone to take care of you, Vijaya, for it is I who promised the Supreme that I would take care of you eternally. I made this promise to Him when I first accepted you as my disciple.

Even while remaining in the physical, which is a real bondage, a spiritual Master can help his disciples in different parts of the world. But when he leaves the body, he is totally free. From the other shore, the spiritual Master works through the soul's Light or will-power. The soul's Light can be offered from any plane of consciousness, from the highest plane right down to the earth plane. So from the higher worlds, the Master can easily make contact with the disciple's aspiring soul, and the disciple can respond to the Master's Light. In this way, the Master can and does and must help the disciple.

When a Master accepts someone as a real disciple, a true disciple, he makes a promise to God, the Supreme, and to the soul of the individual seeker that he will be eternally responsible for that soul.

When great Masters come to earth, they greatly expedite the progress of their disciples. But how far can they expedite it when the disciples themselves have made so little progress? Still, the Masters try to make a very brave fight; they challenge ignorance. They say, "Let us see how far we can go."

On the part of the disciple, there has to be a real feeling, a radiant feeling, a feeling of oneness with the Master. Then, if the person does not get realisation in this incarnation, the Master, when he has left his body, will make a definite, direct contact, an express connection with that disciple's soul. During the disciple's remaining earthly life and also in the soul's world, where she will go to rest, she will feel the Master helping and guiding her so that in her next incarnation or in one or two future incarnations, she can reach the Highest, the Absolute.

So when the Master is in the physical, it is the greatest opportunity because at that time, the physical mind is bound to be convinced of the value of the spiritual help the disciple is receiving. The soul always feels this help and never needs to be convinced. You get the greatest opportunity when a spiritual Master descends on earth. Ramakrishna used to say, "The cow is standing before you. The cow has milk. Where does the milk lie? Only in the udders. So milk the cow! You should not try to get milk from the tail of a cow, for there is no milk there." So here also, Divine Bliss is standing before you. The whole universe embodies his Bliss, but there is a place, a particular place where constantly Infinite Grace and Compassion are descending in bountiful streams. And that is where the spiritual Avatar has descended on earth.

At the end of the game, everybody will be judged as to where he lies, where she lies, whether or not it is in the Heart of the Master. Everybody is given a chance. Everybody will be given a chance. The Supreme will see the result.

472. What does the human in us want? What does the divine in us want?

The human in us wants constant satisfaction. The divine in us wants everlasting fulfilment.

473. What is the difference between the divine Lover and the Divine Beloved?

God is the Divine Beloved and we are the Divine Lovers. That is the only difference. The Divine Lover smiles; the Divine Beloved cries. The moment the Divine Beloved cries, the Divine Lover smiles because the Beloved is won. The Beloved cries because the game between the Lover and the Beloved has at last ended and the two have become inseparably One.

474. What is life and what is death?

Life is man's present bewilderment and future fulfilment. Death is man's present necessity and future impossibility.

475. What is ego?

Ego is today's destroying gain and tomorrow's liberating loss.

476. What kind of loss and what kind of gain?

The loss of the ego, for then you are liberated. The gain of destroying it, for then you are free.

477. God means what?

God means existence.

478. Truth means what?

Truth means discovery.

479. Man means what?

Man means the eternal pilgrim.

480. The past means what?

The past means unfulfilled intention.

481. The present means what?

The present means determination.

482. The future means what?

The future means liberation.

483. What is God's contribution?

God's contribution is Creation.

484. What is man's contribution?

Man's contribution is his realisation.

485. What is aspiration?

Aspiration is Self-searching.

486. What is realisation?

Realisation is Self-finding.

487. What is revelation?

Revelation is Self-transformation.

488. What is manifestation?

Manifestation is Self-perfection.

489. What does my mind say?

My mind says that its goal is spirituality.

490. What does my heart say?

My heart says that its goal is spirituality.

491. What does my soul say?

My soul says that its goal is yoga.

492. What does my goal say?

My goal says that I am its fondest choice.

493. What is the difference between humanity and divinity?

Humanity is God's compassionate investment in Himself. Divinity is God's constant compensation to Himself.

494. What is the difference between inner and outer education?

Outer education explains everything outwardly, but constantly complains inwardly. Inner education feeds us inwardly and liberates us outwardly.

495. Who is the fool?

He is the real fool who thinks that there can be a compromise between the aspiring life and the unaspiring life. He who thinks the aspiring life and the unaspiring life can go together is a fool. An aspiring life must go with another aspiring life and an unaspiring life must go with another unaspiring life.

496. *Who is the wisest of all?*

He is the wisest of all who realises and who feels that God or the Master is infinitely more important than his human loves.

497. *What does God do when I concentrate on Him?*

When I concentrate on God, He proudly roars because His child is concentrating on Him.

498. *What do I do when God concentrates on me?*

When God concentrates on me, I powerfully snore and sleep.

499. *What does God do when I meditate on Him?*

When I meditate on God, He triumphantly sings.

500. *What do I do when God meditates on me?*

When God meditates on me, I fear Him and hide myself.

501. *What do I do when I contemplate on Him?*

When I contemplate on Him, God unreservedly embraces me.

502. *What do I do when God contemplates on me?*

I consciously, deliberately and wilfully invite ignorance, and lust with ignorance unendingly.

1971

503. How can we tell which is our ego's will and which is the Divine Will?

Sri Chinmoy: When it is our ego's will, we try to achieve something by hook or by crook. That is to say, we don't hesitate to employ foul means. We want something to be done and then, if we see that it is not done, then immediately we try to get it or achieve it by any means: through trickery.... or bribing or by adopting some kind of foul means. That is our ego's will. And then if we don't get it, we curse the person from whom we expected the thing or we curse the thing which we wanted to have and couldn't get. But when it is God's Will, we will see it as a Force coming directly from the heart. It has infinitely more intense power than the ego's will, but this Force only uses its Power because God is inspiring it. It is the soul's will to achieve something for God. Now, when it is the soul's will, when we bring the soul's will to the fore, the first thing we feel is a kind of inner conviction. Whether it is something we are saying or something we want to achieve, we will have the inner conviction that it is something our Inner Pilot wants from us.

The ego's will is not like that. You are not convinced, but you are convincing yourself that you are doing the right thing. You are doing the wrong thing because you are adopting foul means, acting by hook or by crook. You are not doing the right thing, but you are trying to convince yourself that you are.

When it is your soul's will, you are automatically convinced because the ringing conviction comes from deep within. In the ego's will, you are convincing yourself through your mind, through your vital, through your physical. But, when it is your soul's will, you will feel a kind of inner confidence. This inner confidence is accompanied by joy, by an inner ecstasy. In the case of the ego, this does not happen. In the case of the ego, while you are exercising your ego's will, there will be some fear in it. "Perhaps I will lose the battle. Perhaps I will be smashed. I feel that I am going to be defeated by the other party." A constant battle is going on. "Although I feel that I am stronger, superior, more powerful, more dynamic, I have no security inside me, no confidence. I am afraid that the other party will defeat me and I will lose the battle". But in the soul's will, it is definite that we are going to win, not by any kind of foul means but just because God wants the soul to win, because God wants to conquer ignorance, because God wants that particular soul to gain victory over ignorance. That is why God is giving indomitable will to the soul to conquer ignorance.

Now, when the soul's will-power is expressed, it is expressed the way we see a huge wave moving in the sea. Immediately it inundates the whole consciousness. Once the soul's will is expressed, you are bound to feel that your inner consciousness is inundated with inner energy, inner joy, inner delight, inner power, inner confidence. Everything is inundated there. But when you use your ego's will-power, you are thinking that you are building a palace. Again you have enormous fear inside you that while you are building, your palace is going to crack, the building is going to collapse. With that kind of fear, finally it really does collapse because where there is fear, there cannot be any Light or Strength. Light cannot exist in fear. In fear only doubt comes. Our fear and doubt go together and there we see vexation looming large. In the soul's will, we see only confidence, inner assurance, inner oneness with the soul which is Divinity.

504. Could a creature of the Supreme Omnipotent, Omniscient, obtain a temporary suspension of his karma so that he can obtain worthy progress? What are the requisites thereof?

Sri Chinmoy: Spiritually it does not happen in that way. Suppose an individual has done something wrong. Then what will happen is that the cosmic forces, the cosmic law, we can say, offer him the results of it. Now if something wrong has been done and for five or six months the result is suspended although the punishment is due, it may be that for a few months, the cosmic forces are observing him and seeing if he is trying to turn over a new leaf and if he is praying and meditating and all that. You have to know that it is not actually that the result is being suspended. No. The forces are operating which are going to offer him the result of his action. But the divine forces that enter into the particular person, the seeker, here fight with him against these forces of karma. It is not that for five or six months the cosmic punishment is suspended. No, these karmic forces have already inwardly acted. As the result is coming, what is happening meanwhile is that the Divine Compassion is operating in and through that particular person. The Divine Compassion is acting like a divine hero, inside that particular man. So he feels, "Alright, I have done something wrong but now I am doing something right to nullify it. If I am doing something right to nullify it, if I have the capacity to do something good, in the inner life I also have the capacity in the inner life to draw to myself the Compassion of God in the form of forgiveness." Forgiveness is a divine soldier. So that divine soldier is fighting against the undivine result of the undivine soldier.

So I wish to tell you that it is not actually a suspension of karma. The cosmic law is operating. If you have made a mistake you are going to reap the fruit, but at that moment Compassion comes, falls downward to your aspiring heart and fights against outer desire. Your aspiration comes and fights against your outer desire. If a spiritual Master is involved, your own inner, higher deity is involved. Then what will the Master do? If he sees that somebody is about to be punished for his wrong karma and he sees that this punishment will last for only six months, if the spiritual Master wants, if it is the Will of God, immediately he will take the pain inside himself. But he will not suffer for six months. He will suffer for ten days or fifteen days or even only three days if he wants.

Or what he can do is to take the pain and immediately throw it into the universe. That he can do. Now, here, for my dearest disciples, I can do this. About a month ago .... you know today is Monday. Today they offer meditation at the Connecticut Centre where Akuti is president. About a month ago, Alo was not coming down; she was in Vancouver in our Centre there. That Monday, one of our very close disciples was suffering from an abdominal pain for the whole day. Her husband takes me to the Connecticut Centre and she was coming from her place with her husband to take me up there. Now it is a matter of two minutes from their place to our place. She was about to vomit, her pain was so unbearable. Then what did I do? I entered into the car and I was eating something. I was eating peanuts. So I said, "I am eating now, I can't do anything." She was suffering like anything. Then her husband needed gas for the car so he went three or four blocks to a gas station. While the man was filling the tank, I told her husband, "I am very hungry. Bring me a sandwich." He went to the cafeteria and brought me a sandwich. So I was sitting in the front seat and she was in the back. Unbearable, excruciating pain she was suffering. I told her, "Now look, place your hands on the affected area, wherever it is." I looked at her and the pain was gone. She could not believe it! Her husband came back. She smiled and told her husband, "The pain is gone." Now this pain that I took away would have lasted in her at least for four or five hours. At least four or five hours she would have suffered and when I took it, I suffered for three or four minutes. But the pain I suffered for her was a real pain and with the pain I was still eating and smiling. Inside I was suffering, outside I was eating and smiling. I knew that in four or five minutes the pain would be gone. This was done with my own conscious awareness.

Last week you saw Suparna here. She was suffering terribly from a headache, an unbearable headache. She started meditating at nine o'clock. She said to my transcendental picture, "Take it, take it, take it. I cannot bear it any more." Her Master took it. So here I wish to say that the actual karma was for her to suffer. If I had not taken the karma, it would have lasted for a few hours. We can take it away but we can take it only when it is God's Will.

The other day Sevananda and others were saying that their parents are against me because I am exploiting their children. So I told them, "Please tell your parents that either this Indian fellow is very clever, more clever than you are or he has more love for us than you have. Either one of these two qualities he has. Either I am cleverer than your parents, or I have more love for you, and therefore you listen to me."

The law of karma, when you enter into the real spiritual path, is already nullified to some extent. The very fact that one has entered into the spiritual life has opened the person to some higher forces. The spiritual life means the acceptance of a higher force. When one has accepted the higher force, then the higher force tries to enter according to the person's own capacity. The child consciously runs towards his father. The child knows that his father has more power, more love, more wisdom, more capacity than he and that is why the child is running towards the father. Now, the spiritual life is the life of the Father, and the ordinary human life is the life of the child. So when in ordinary life we are running towards the spiritual life, and have accepted the spiritual life, that means we are running towards the Father. So the spiritual life has more power, the Father has more power than the son. When one enters into the more powerful, that means the more powerful has the capacity to help the child. The child is the ordinary human life and the Father is spiritual life, the life of aspiration.

II — TALK AND QUESTIONS AND ANSWERS AT THE SAGRADO CORAZÓN COLLEGE IN SAN JUAN

505. Discourse

Your teacher, our sweet Kimo, has performed something entirely unique. Today we have learned quite a few things from him. The most important thing we have learned is that his combined concentration in the physical, in the vital, in the mental, in the psychic and in the spiritual were all directed in a superb way for his purpose. You all know that karate is primarily for self-defence, but again I wish to tell you, and I am sure that your teacher has already taught you, that it is not for self-defence alone, as such. It is for something deeper. Self-protection is necessary, but along with self-protection, what is necessary is self-Realisation. What are you going to protect if you do not know what you are? In order to know the highest and the deepest and the inmost, we have to concentrate and meditate.

While he was performing this unique and extraordinary set of movements that we saw a few minutes ago, we observed, along with his superb skill, a power of concentration that ran from the sole of his foot to the crown of his head. Every part of his being was surcharged with a dynamic will. Now this will comes from the soul, not from the body. His physical body became the conscious instrument of his soul's dynamic will. Now where did he, how did he, learn this so-called technique, which is actually the concentration of a spiritual Master? He learned it from his soul's inner will.

So what you are getting here is a great opportunity; and this is not the end. You will be taught by him for a few months or a few years and that is just the beginning. The very essence of everything you do is meditation. Kimo's performance was the result of inner concentration and meditation. So, this is my sincere request to each of you, that every day in the morning, you will please try to concentrate for a few minutes or meditate for a few minutes. Meditation is a vast subject. If I speak about it, it would take hours and hours and there would be no end. I have spoken considerably on meditation at various places: spiritual Centres, churches, synagogues, American universities, Puerto Rican universities, European universities. I just came back from a tour on the Continent. There I spoke on meditation.

What I feel would be best for you here is to ask me a few questions on meditation. Otherwise if I give a talk on meditation, it may not serve your immediate purpose, because each one here has a different problem. Your problem need not and cannot be the same as someone else's problem. In your inner life, you have a problem of your own, or you want Light in a different way from your neighbour. You want to grow into the Light, the Light divine. For real growth, your way of approaching the Truth has to be different from the one who is sitting right beside you.

Now, in the spiritual life, we always say that we must grow and become. Now some people will say that unless you have become something yourself, you cannot give anything to others. Yes, it is true. If you don't know something and you try to teach others, it is a matter of the blind leading the blind. But I also wish to say that if you know something better than I do, then you are perfectly entitled to teach me that particular thing. And if I know something which you do not know, you should learn it from me. Now here is the golden opportunity to co-ordinate your knowledge of the physical, the vital, the mental and the psychic with the spiritual. The spiritual life teaches us the unification of all the members of the family: the physical, the vital and the mental must run abreast and inside the physical, the physic and the soul must predominate. Otherwise if you just become an expert in karate, if you learn it mechanically, you are serving no purpose. But if you exercise your inner will through karate, while you are performing, you are not only learning the technique of self-defence, but you are discovering your inner reality which is God-realisation. Everything you do when you study or when you speak to a person should have the soul's will coming to the fore from deep within; then your life will have a purpose. Otherwise you will achieve success, the so-called success, but if the spiritual part of your life is lagging behind, if meditation is missing, your joy will be limited, fleeting, and your achievement will be very insignificant. But if you meditate, you will see an abiding Peace, abiding Light, abiding Joy deep within you.

Now I wish to invite a few questions from those who are interested in the inner life, the spiritual life.

506. Please explain your system, so we can know how to go about meditation.

Sri Chinmoy: There are various systems, but when one is approaching the spiritual life or the life of meditation, one has to adopt only one system. If one says that one will be able to reach God through selfless service, loving humanity and offering oneself, then that is the perfect path for that person. But if one feels that he will follow the spiritual life through mental discipline, that he will meditate on the mind and offer mental wisdom to others after having discovered Peace, Light and Bliss, then that is another system. Then if a third person feels that he can offer love and joy to mankind, then he has to follow the path of Love and Devotion. So when we meditate, we have to know what we are going to be or what we are going to offer to mankind. Now if you wish to give any of these divine qualities – Peace, Joy, Bliss, Love and so forth, to others – then I wish you to meditate on the heart, here. The heart is the most important place in our spiritual discipline, because the heart represents identification. If you want to help someone or to grow into something, then you have to identify yourself with that person or thing. You look at a flower; you appreciate its beauty and fragrance. Then you try to grow into the very same consciousness that the flower embodies, its purity and beauty. First, for a few minutes you observe the beauty and then you try to grow into that beauty. In the spiritual life also, when we enter into the heart, our heart identifies immediately with spiritual Light, Peace, Bliss and Power and so forth. On the strength of our identification, we grow into divine Reality.

Now each individual has to learn how to meditate from a teacher, from a spiritual Master. Here you have a teacher, a karate teacher who is teaching you that art. So also in the spiritual life, you need a teacher. It is the teacher who will be able to direct you personally. Otherwise you will feel miserable that your way of understanding the truth will differ widely from the person sitting beside you. If you want to learn how to meditate, you have to follow a specific path. For that, you have to know if there is a spiritual Master like me. I am not the only Master; there are many Masters on earth. As soon as you see a spiritual Master, you have to feel the necessity of entering into him to see if his path suits you or not. If it does, then you should try to be in his boat. Then he is bound to teach you how to meditate. Why to meditate? Because you want to be divine, you want to be perfect. But how to meditate, unfortunately, a seeker does not know. He has to learn it from an adept, from a spiritual Master. So, for that, one goes to visit spiritual Masters, goes to spiritual places, and then, if one is interested, and inspired to follow the spiritual life, then one asks a Master to accept him. The Master gives a short interview and meditates with that particular disciple.

He tells the new seeker that he has to meditate regularly, daily, devotedly and faithfully. We cannot say in public that there is a certain way to meditate. Yes, there are general rules. You have to keep your mind calm and quiet. You should not allow any thought to enter into your mind because thoughts create disturbances in your mind. These are general rules. Everybody will tell you that when you want to meditate, the first thing is to make your mind calm and quiet. That we all know. But how to do it? That answer has to be given individually. Everyone has a different type of mind and each person has to be dealt with in a different way, because everyone has a different nature. The goal is the same. From here I have to go to New York. New York is my destination. But I can take a plane or I can take a boat. The destination remains the same, but the vehicles are different. Similarly in the spiritual life you have to know that God-realisation is one, but your vehicle to reach it need not be the same as someone else's vehicle.

So in answering your question, I must say that if you are deeply interested in meditation, please read a few spiritual books written by genuine spiritual Masters and then start to meditate on them, then you will have the real need for a guide, a spiritual Master. Then the spiritual Master will give individual attention to your personal spiritual needs and teach you how to meditate.

507. How are our actions in life connected with the spiritual life?

Sri Chinmoy: If you are speaking about the material life that is being led, then I wish you to know that it is a half-animal life; not a full-animal life, but a half-animal life. The complete- or full-animal life we can see all around us – the monkeys, donkeys, dogs and cats and the destructive animals like the foxes and wolves. But we ourselves are half-animals. How? Every day, consciously or unconsciously, we are cherishing jealousy, doubt and destructive forces in our minds. This makes us half-animal from the spiritual point of view. An ordinary man, in comparison to a spiritual man, is a half-animal. When an animal stands in front of a human being, the man feels that he is far superior to the animal because he has a developed mind and a developed soul. That is why he feels superior. Similarly when a spiritual man stands in front of an ordinary man, he feels himself to be superior because he is crying for Light, Peace and Bliss, he is crying for inseparable Oneness, conscious Oneness with God.

When ordinary persons are constantly fighting in their minds and when jealousy, doubt, obscurity (which is darkness), impurity and imperfection loom large in their everyday life, day in and day out, then they are half-animal, from the spiritual point of view.

But again, when a spiritual person sees someone quarrelling and fighting all the time, he does not look down upon that person. An ordinary person when he sees a real animal, like an elephant or a tiger will immediately think, "Oh, here is a real animal! Thank goodness that I am a human being. You remain in your own life. I am so proud that I am not acting like you!" But a spiritual person, when he sees someone below his standard of consciousness, does not lord it over that person. On the contrary, he tries to help that person to kindle the flame of aspiration inside him.

Now in answering your question, if you are following the inner or spiritual life, then your activities can be motivated from this inner life. Each thought gives rise to action. If you are leading a spiritual life, then at every moment, God comes first in your life. To an ordinary person, God does not come first. Prosperity, power, importance, fame and other things come first. But a spiritual person immediately says, "God has to come first; the inner life has to come first." From within we come without.

An ordinary person usually feels that we should go from outside to inside. But this is impossible. "As we sow, so we reap." We sow a seed and it germinates. Then it grows into a huge Banyan tree. So our inner life must come first because everything in our outer life, whether or not it is spiritual, is a result and an embodiment of whatever is in the inner life. A spiritual person feels that the inner life is of paramount importance and that it has to come first. An ordinary person feels, "No, the spiritual life is vague and meaningless. Let us enjoy life. Let us possess and be possessed. Let us enjoy the world and let the world enjoy us. There is no bridge between the spiritual life and the ordinary life." But a spiritual person sincerely cries and says, "Let me realise the Truth in its own way and then bring down the Truth into my outer life." The Truth is within, and then it has to be felt and expressed outwardly also. Truth is universal, it is true, but only if we go deep within do we first get a glimpse of it.

So in our day-to-day life, if we can meditate for ten or fifteen minutes a day, we can enter into the Source of life, Eternal life. From there, we have to enter into the fleeting life of fifty, sixty or seventy years, which is our life-span. Every day, consciously, let us offer our spiritual breath, our divine breath, to the Inner Pilot. Then let us try to grow into the perfect image of God in our inner life. Then from this inner life, we have to come forward to the outer life.

Let us not attempt to govern our inner life only with outer capacity. Outer capacity means possession. By possessing something or someone, if we feel that we will be able to govern our inner existence, it is impossible. Inner existence is always flooded with Light, Delight and inseparable Oneness with the Cosmos, with the Universe, and with the transcendental Supreme.

Coming back to your question, I wish to say that the more we follow the inner life, the more meaningful will be the outer life. Otherwise the outer achievement without the core, that is to say, without the inner life, will have no meaning. Nothing will satisfy you or me or anybody on earth except the inner life. The inner life is the life of the soul, where reality and divinity are constantly growing. So please follow the inner life and the inner life will guide you, inspire you, instruct you on how you can be divinely and supremely successful in your outer life.

508. Is meditation a way of having absolute freedom from all attachments which cause us to be separated from Delight which is our inheritance on earth, spiritual Delight?

Sri Chinmoy: Delight is a spiritual term that I know you understand. The term we use for outer enjoyment is "pleasure". Pleasure and Delight are two different things. Delight is infinitely stronger and more powerful than pleasure. Certainly meditation will take you far beyond the boundaries of pleasure, which is immediately followed by frustration. In the ordinary human life, we know what pleasure is. We get pleasure from satisfying the senses. As I said, this fulfilment is immediately followed by frustration and inside frustration, destruction looms large. First pleasure, which comes from temptation; then frustration immediately standing in wait for it; then destruction.

But in meditation we get Joy, inner Peace, inner Light and inner Delight. And about the freedom that you are speaking of, you are absolutely right, meditation will give you eternal freedom.

Now let us speak about freedom in the outer life. We see children who leave their parents and they feel that they are free. Right; they are free from their parents because they are living elsewhere. They are not staying with their parents. But there are hundreds and thousands of problems that they still have. Only since they are not staying with their parents, this is the freedom they feel they are getting. Yet there are other obligations all around them that loom large in their day-to-day existence. So where is freedom? First their mind is a constant victim to ugly and venomous thoughts. They cannot get rid of their thoughts. Now, from the spiritual point of view, if one cannot get rid of ugly, undivine, hostile thoughts, then one is still subject to ignorance. Inner freedom comes from within. It does not come from freeing oneself from outer restrictions and obligations No. You may be free from your parents for a day or a month or a year, but this is no freedom. Real freedom is the feeling of universal oneness. This you can get from a life of meditation.

Meditation will free you from the sea of ignorance. Meditation will give you everlasting freedom. And this freedom is the freedom of oneness. Right now you cannot unite yourself even with another person right beside you. You feel with your ego that you are yourself and she is somebody else. So where is the freedom? Your freedom is so limited that even with your very limited capacity and limited knowledge you are trying to exercise your will and utilise your human power to lord it over others. That is what you call freedom. This is not freedom. Real freedom is the inseparable oneness with the universe. There you are growing together. You are achieving something and you are seeing that the entire world is achieving it at the same time. When you are sorrowful, immediately you feel that the whole world is suffering with you, sympathising with your cause, growing with you.

God is One and He multiplies Himself into many. Now God says, "I am a tree. Since I am a tree, I want to become also the branches, the leaves, the flowers and the fruits." Freedom lies in becoming the many while maintaining the oneness. The leaves, flowers and fruit see the same consciousness flowing through them as flows through the trunk. A spiritual person, when he stands in front of a tree and meditates on it, sees the one consciousness which is flowing through the root, the trunk, the branches, flowers and fruit. This kind of oneness is the real freedom.

So if you want inner freedom, spiritual freedom, then I wish to say that it is in becoming one with the rest of humanity. Otherwise the freedom that you cherish in the West by separating yourself from others, what are you gaining? Yes, we should separate ourselves from ignorance, imperfection, limitation, bondage and so forth, but we should not, and we must not, separate ourselves from our soul, from the reality which is Light and Delight. So when we are following the spiritual life, we have to know that our real freedom is in identifying ourselves with the rest of the world, with humanity at large. By becoming one, we stand united, we march united towards the Highest, united we shall fulfil our Goal.

509. During meditation, can one enter into the level of unconscious thought?

Sri Chinmoy: One can enter into the level of unconsciousness, but it should be done with a view of transforming the unconsciousness into consciousness. While meditating, the very aim of the person is to climb to the Highest. When I have gone up to the Highest, if I see that my toe is bothering me, that there is some pain there, naturally I have to come down and cure it. I have to be perfect from my toe up to my head. I need total perfection. So if you enter into the unconscious level of your mind – let us call it inconscience – what for? To transform the inconscience that is in you; otherwise you will be limited. The body will be transformed, the heart will be transformed, but the mind will remain imperfect. Now if a member of my family is not progressing, is not perfect, I cannot be happy. So in your meditation, you have to take your whole existence as a unit, as a complete totality. If you enter into your unconscious level, you have to know that you are entering there to spread the inner Light, to infuse the unconscious level and transform it into Light, the Light that is inside the heart and the soul. This is the soul's own Light. With that purpose only you can go; not to show off that you have the capacity to go into your unconscious part or that you are far better off there, but only to transform the very face of the unconscious level. You want to be integral. You want to be perfect. You have to be perfect. If your unconscious mind is imperfect, I cannot call you perfect. You have to be perfect everywhere, both in the conscious and the subconscious. Subconsciousness is inside you. As you have the overmind, the higher mind, the illumined mind and all these higher dimensions, you also have lower qualities. Your higher qualities are that you pray to God, you want to be good, divine and spiritual. These are your higher qualities. Again you have undivine qualities which quarrel with the divine ones. These are doubt, jealousy, hypocrisy and so forth. These are undivine qualities within us. So with our divine qualities, our love for God, our feeling of universal oneness, our real concern for mankind, we have to enter into our undivine qualities that we cherish: fear, doubt, worry and so on. We have to transform fear into strength, doubt into certainty, jealousy into sympathy, separation into universal brotherhood and oneness. That is why we enter into the lower parts: to transform them.

510. Is this done through a mental process?

Sri Chinmoy: No, it is done through an inner, psychic process. It is not through the mind, it is through feeling. When we aspire, we stop the functioning of the mind. It is from here, from the heart. When we think, for one minute we will think a good thought, cherish it, and then the next moment, we will think an ordinary uncomely, or undivine thought. But when we do it from here, from the heart, we don't think at all; we just go into the reality through inspiration. We discover that there is a burning flame within us. The burning flame helps us to become divine and spiritual. So when we kindle the flame of aspiration, we transform ignorance into light. The higher the flame of aspiration goes, the farther the light spreads. You go up, up, up and you see it spreading its light all around. It is a conscious awareness of one's inner Divinity within us. It is here; in the heart.

511. How does a person become a Guru?

Sri Chinmoy: The word "Guru" means spiritual teacher. Kimo has become a teacher by practising karate for fifteen years or so. He has acquired wisdom, knowledge and capacity from that particular field. In the spiritual life also, there is a kind of knowledge, an inner knowledge. One has to practise concentration, meditation, contemplation and a few other things in order to become a Guru.

When you go to school, you start your lessons from the kindergarten and then you complete your journey when you get your university degree. From kindergarten you go to elementary school, then to high school, then to college and then to university. In the spiritual life also, one has to start at the beginning.

In my case, right from my childhood I took up the spiritual life. When I was two months old, my parents took me to a spiritual shrine, a very well-known spiritual place in India. Then when I was three years old, four, seven and eight years old, I was taken to another place. Unconsciously, I was going with my parents to a spiritual Master. When I was twelve years old, I became conscious of the inner life, the spiritual life. Then from twelve right up to thirty-two, I spent five hours, eight hours, ten hours, twelve hours a day in rigorous meditation.

Now you know that when you study something, you spend an hour or two, or three or four hours, according to the necessity of your study. So spending all those hours in meditation is nothing unusual if one wants to achieve a high standard in the spiritual life.

When I was twelve years old, I said, "Now is my time to be conscious." And I started meditating one hour, two hours, three hours. But not for the sake of counting the hours. If you just count the hours, you are not doing real meditation. But if you can develop the inner capacity to meditate, your capacity becomes greater. When you take exercise every day, you gradually develop muscles. Then instead of five minutes, you can exercise for an hour. Then you develop your capacity to two, three hours.

In the spiritual life also, we start with five minutes, then we increase it to ten minutes, fifteen minutes; then slowly it goes up to six hours, eight hours, nine hours a day. At that time, one has become an expert. One gets inner illumination; one becomes consciously one with the universal soul, with the Highest Absolute. At this point the person becomes a spiritual Master because he has achieved and received the Inner Illumination.

The spiritual Master at this point will not grow two horns or a tail. No, he is still a man. My spirituality is inside me, inside my heart, inside my consciousness. My disciples feel it, those who are my disciples.

Then when a spiritual Master meditates on his disciples, he offers them his Light, inner Peace, inner Bliss. He meditates on each individual and he spreads the inner Light. When he gets his own illumination, then and then only, can he offer his Light to others, to the seekers of the world.

Now you are apt to say, "How does he know he is illumined?" He knows on the strength of his absolute oneness with the Transcendental Truth. Those who are following the same path as he will see, inside him, the real Light.

If you are a doctor, you will have a very good idea of whether another person is a genuine doctor or not. Immediately you will ask him some questions and if he is not a doctor, he will be totally lost. In the spiritual life also, when a seeker comes to a spiritual Master, he asks a few questions, inner questions. If the Master is really spiritual, he will be able to answer them. If not, he will not be able to answer.

In the spiritual life, the Guru's answer is an immediate psychic response; it comes directly from the soul. It does not come from the mind. Many seekers come to me. Some of them don't ask questions, but others ask hundreds of questions during the hours they spend at the Centre. Sometimes these are questions that nobody has been able to answer for them, but when I answer their questions, they are convinced that this person has inner illumination.

It is not by answering questions alone, that you convince others that you are a spiritual Master. Thousands and millions of books, containing answers to questions, have been written on the spiritual life. From books you cannot get illumination. Books can give you inspiration.

There are books about realisation, but you cannot get realisation from reading them. Inspiration you can get. Realisation is inside you, inside everyone. But it has to be brought to the fore. And for that, a spiritual Master is needed. And when he has grown in inner illumination, it is the seeker who sees in his Master and feels in Him, the Illumination of the Supreme.

1972

512. In your article "New Creation", you say that the best way to use our life, every moment of our life, is through inspiration and aspiration. My question is: how can we, in what way can we put forth our utmost effort to bring to the fore our highest inspiration and aspiration?

Sri Chinmoy: As an individual disciple, as a seeker, as a child of your spiritual parents, you have to feel that you have a most significant task to perform. Each individual has to feel this. Then when you feel that you have something to do, you will go one step within. What is the message that you will receive from within? From within yourself, the answer will come that you have to become a most perfect instrument, a divine soldier and a unique messenger of Light and Truth.

Now this is not the end of the answer. Once you know what you have to become you will get inspiration and aspiration. But you have to ask yourself, at each moment, when you do something or say something, whether it can be utilised for a divine purpose or can be added to your own dedication or to your surrender to the Will of the Supreme. You have said something, for example. You have spoken for a few minutes. Then you have to ask yourself, "Will this, in any way, help in realising God or in serving God?" For five minutes you have spoken to someone. Now you have to ascertain whether this talking will in any way help you or help him or help anybody else. Then if you feel, "Yes, it has helped me; it is helping my friend; it is helping others," then I wish to say that everyday you should try to do that kind of thing. It can be used as a service to you and to the one whom you speak to and to others who are around you.

This is all done on the physical plane. It is outer action. When you do something, everybody notices you. But in the mental plane again, you will be the observer and we will be the observers.

The Supreme Himself will be the Observer. In the mental plane, when you are seeing someone or saying something, talking to someone inwardly, you have to feel that the action is taking place in the mind. Is it going to be of help to you or is it going to be a hindrance to your spiritual progress? So at each moment, when thought tries to knock at your mental door, you have to be careful, very conscious and alert. Will you allow that particular thought to enter into your mental room or not? If it is a good thought, open wide the mental door. If it is a bad thought, do not allow it in. Just act like a soldier standing at the mental door.

So.... action on the mental plane, action on the physical plane can make each person inspire and aspire most soulfully and most profoundly. Each action is responsible either to make you realise God or to take you away from your Goal and to delay you in realising God. Each action, whether on the physical plane or on the mental plane can do that. This is why I say that each thought, each idea is equally responsible, equally important in the spiritual life if one wants to be a man of knowledge or if one wants to do something extraordinary on earth. Each second is most important in the spiritual life.

When you value the breath of a second, the capacity or the gift of a second, then inspiration and aspiration automatically come to you. They have to come because action compels inspiration and aspiration to increase. They are within, but when you throw yourself into the sea of divine activity, they come forward and you can climb to the Highest. Inspiration will take you as high as it can. Then aspiration will come to take you to the Ultimate Goal of the Beyond. These are two friends. The first one takes you quite high but it cannot take you to the Highest. Then the second one takes you to the Ultimate Goal. But the second one also was there all along with the first one. But there comes a time when the first one, inspiration, has played its role and merges into aspiration. At that time, we don't see inspiration as such because it has lost its identity in aspiration. Then aspiration goes high, higher, highest and there it reaches its Ultimate Height which we call Realisation. After reaching this Height, it merges into realisation itself; they become one. So the three become one: inspiration, aspiration and realisation. And then after they have become one, they try to do something jointly. To do that, they come back here again from where they started. But this time, it is not with imperfection. This time it is with Perfection-Light. They try to manifest Divinity and Immortality here on earth.

513. It is very easy for us to conceive of God in the Infinite and the Ultimate. But how can we see God in our everyday life, in our relations with people, in our activities with people? How can we see God here, the Divine here?

Sri Chinmoy: When you look at others, you feel that they are all monkeys and all imperfect. True. The idea is coming to you that you want to see God in Sevananda, but when you speak to Sevananda, he says something nasty to you. At that time, you say, "How can I see or realise God in him?" This is wrong, but the very idea which has come to you, that you want to see God in Sevananda is the first step. Then what do you see? When you speak to Sevananda, you may use your outer eyes. You see him, his features. But try to feel and try to do one thing. Do not give any importance to your eyes catching his eyes; that is to say, do not allow the eyes to meet together. But feel that there is something which will really connect both of you. If the physical eyes meet together, immediately there will be some confusion. If you want to appreciate something of his physical nature, immediately you will be disappointed because you will see perhaps that he has not combed his hair properly or he has not taken a shower. Something, something will bother you because you are trying to see perfection in him. Poor fellow, he is not perfect, according to your judgement or according to your standard. So how can you see God in him? Don't try to see God. Only use your heart to identify yourself with him. When we stand in front of someone, we never think that we ourselves are imperfect. Always the other one is imperfect and "I am perfect". This is our constant feeling.

You stand in front of twenty persons. When humility comes forward for a second, you may feel that you are imperfect; otherwise twenty-three or twenty-four hours a day at least, you will think that you are perfect and others are imperfect. Why? Because the mind is playing its role. But if the heart plays its role, immediately it will see only oneness. The heart does not see defects. In oneness we do not see any defects. No. No matter how ugly my nose is, because I am one with it. I will feel that it is as fine as any other part of me. My eyes, my hands, my nose have all become part and parcel of my existence. I represent my nose and my nose represents me. This way, I cannot separate myself from it. When I use the heart, I see that even my little finger is equally important in my body. Here and everywhere I feel the message of oneness.

So use your heart and you will see God in all human beings. Sevananda is your friend, but there may be some people who are your enemies. You will see even in them the living presence of God because you are using an instrument within you which is bound to act like a magnet and that is your heart. Use the heart and you will see, you will feel, that God is in everyone; in addition, you will feel something more, that you are all the time for them and of them. When you use the heart, first feel your oneness with them. Then as soon as you have established your oneness, you are bound to feel that you are no different from them. When you establish your oneness with God, you are bound to feel that you are of God. If you have not created or established your oneness with God, you can never feel that you are of God. Somebody else is of God, but you are not of God. You are of something undivine; this kind of ignorance will come to your mind. But once you have established your oneness with God, you will know that you are of God. That means that you are of Light. And once you feel that you are of Light, the next moment you have to feel that you are for Light. The reason for this is that in this world, as soon as we know the Source, we try to fulfil the Source in its own way.

Always try to identify with something vast that God has already given us. The sky He has given us. The ocean He has given us. Cosmic nature He has given us. Anything that immediately gives us the feeling of vastness must be brought to our physical consciousness. Then I assure you that your heart will become large, magnanimous, boundless and supremely fruitful.

514. In one meditation you say that if anybody strikes me on the right cheek, I shall not turn my left cheek to him because I love him and I don't want him to commit the same mistake again. Do you mean that one can get mad at that person?

Sri Chinmoy: No, it is not that. Let us say that somebody strikes me or does something wrong. Now if I allow that person to do the thing once again, my theory is that in no way will I be helping to perfect him. On the contrary, I am increasing his ignorance. One thing is to forgive and not to take revenge. The saying of Christ from the Bible we all know. I do not want to enter into any controversy. I am only justifying what I have previously written.

Suppose I see that someone has consciously done something wrong and it is damaging him. By doing this wrong thing, he is not in any way, expediting his spiritual progress or inner progress. On the contrary, I am seeing clearly that he is descending in the scale of evolution. Then what shall I do? In me also is the living God. Now my living God here is acting like a Transcendental Being who is just. It is very easy to forgive someone. But by forgiving him, we have to know whether that person is really going to change his nature. If I just go on saying, "You have done something wrong; you can do more; you are exercising my compassion," yes, I will exercise my compassion, but in the eyes of God, I will not be allowing him to come to the right path and at the same time, I am wasting my precious life by indulging someone else's wrong action.

So we have to be very careful when somebody does something wrong to us. It is not that we are threatening them. Far from it. Only we have to feel that by allowing him to do the same thing again, or indulge in the same wrong action, we are taking him away from his own divinity.

At each moment, just as we should always try not to do anything wrong ourselves, consciously or unconsciously, we should also not allow another person to do anything wrong. We know that our encouragement of his mistake is in no way serving as a kind of compassion. No. If we encourage him to do the wrong thing again and again, then this is not compassion. This is our self-imposed weakness in the name of compassion. We shall not attack anybody, consciously or unconsciously. If somebody attacks, then we have to defend ourselves because in this self-defence, he will realise that he is striking someone who is innocent, who is crying for Light, for Reality, for Truth. Since we are crying for Light, Truth, Reality and Divinity, we have also to make the other person feel that only in Light will he receive his satisfaction. By striking me, he will not get satisfaction. I tell you because a day will come when his soul will come forward and make him feel that he has done something extremely wrong. So if we know that he has done something wrong, then we have to make him understand this, the sooner the better. Then he can enter into the soul's Light and be guided all the time. So this is how I explain this aphorism of mine.

During Christ's time, the average man lived in a very undeveloped semi-animal consciousness. When Christ instructed them to turn the other cheek, it was in line with His entire teaching of brotherly love, and compassionate kindness. He was trying to teach them mildness and harmlessness which was very necessary at the time. If he had given them the same instruction that I have given you now, they would not have been able to understand it. They were not sufficiently evolved. Since the average person has evolved considerably in the last two thousand years, we have come to a point where a higher level of teaching can be applied. What Christ said was divinely and supremely necessary for the people in His day. I am not saying anything against the Christ or contrary to Him. Each spiritual Master teaches according to the level of consciousness of his devotees. Each Avatar is bringing humanity one step higher up the ladder of evolution.

My view was never tit for tat, that if somebody strikes me, I have to strike him back. Only since we are marching in the process of evolution, each individual has evolved. Each aspiring human being has evolved. We are saying that we can also help others in evolving. If you have evolved, if you have come five steps higher on the rungs of evolution and if we see someone who has not yet climbed up at all, we feel that it is our bounden duty to stretch out our hand and lift him up and not allow him to stay all the time in the clay and mud. Unless we pull him up, he will go and throw mud and clay at us. If we pull him up, that action itself may be punishment to his unlit vital, but it is a reward to his soul.

515. About two weeks ago, we were talking here about attachment and detachment. We think that we are attached only to somebody whom we like. But Sudhha told us that we can be attached to somebody we dislike. How can we detach ourselves from a person whom we dislike?

Sri Chinmoy: First let us speak about attachment in the positive way. You like someone and you are constantly trying to please him. You are trying also to be pleased by that person. This is the positive way. The other way is that you have an enemy. He is jealous of you; you are jealous of him. In spite of this, your mind is constantly on that person. You are all the time thinking of how you can surpass him, how you can make him feel that you are superior to him. In that way there is a kind of challenging attitude you have. You are thinking in a negative way, but all the time that person is on your mind.

Either you are thinking of your friend or you are thinking of your enemy. When you think of your friend, at least it is in a positive way. You are trying to bind him or you are allowing him to bind you. In the negative way, you are hurting the person, but at the same time, you do not want to be hurt. In the previous way you are binding someone and you get joy that the person is also thinking of you. But here in the negative way, you only try to hurt the person whom you decry and at the same time, you want that person to remain silent. You don't want him or her to strike you back. It is one-sided. You will strike him, for you know better, but you won't allow him to come near you. You will put a solid block in front of you the moment that person wants to attack you back. Only you want to attack.

In every possible way, you want to stay on the top of the tree and you want your enemy to remain at the foot of the tree. But the very fact that you want to be something and you want him to be something else shows that this is a negative attitude. In the positive way, when you want to be something, you want your friend to be that also.

But again you have to know what you want and what that person wants. If you want anything from that person, on the physical plane, you are only binding him. And if that particular person wants something from you, he is binding you. On the physical plane, it is always like that. On the spiritual plane, on the other hand, it is all a devoted feeling. You may ask, "When I think of the Master, then is it not attachment?" Far from it. Why? When you deal with a spiritual person, it is not attachment but a devoted feeling of your inseparable oneness. When you deal with ordinary, unaspiring, unrealised people, it is total attachment. You are binding them with your desire and they are binding you with their hearts' desire. It is all attachment. But in the spiritual life, you are not binding. Here you are trying to throw yourself into the vast consciousness which your soul feels. In your aspiring moments, you feel that this consciousness is boundless. So when you throw yourself into it, that means that you are going to be free. But when you are ready to throw yourself into someone who is unillumined and you want the other party to throw his or her existence into you, since both of you are unillumined, naturally there is only a sense of limitation. Where there is darkness, there is limitation. Wherever there is Light, it is limitless and infinite.

So you have to know, all of you, that when you devote yourselves to the spiritual life, to your Master, it is not attachment; it is your devoted feeling of inseparable oneness, where you can be in the Vast, with the Vast and for the Vast. That is to say, you can consciously dive into the Infinite and act with the Infinite and for the Infinite.

The positive type of attachment is binding because there you are entering into darkness consciously or unconsciously, since that person is not illumined and you yourself are not illumined as an individual. Two blind persons going together can never offer light to each other. But one who is strong, powerful and mighty stands in front of both of you and he strengthens both persons.

In the spiritual life, when it is a matter of unaspiring beings, unillumined beings, unrealised human beings, then you are bound to be fettered. This is in the positive type of attachment. And in the negative type, it is always destruction. You want to destroy and at the same time, you don't want to be destroyed. You want to attack everybody and make them feel that they are no good; they are useless. This is when you have an enemy. Then at the same time you are well protected, shielded and guarded so that the enemy cannot come. But the mind is all the time thinking: sometimes how to attack and the next moment how to escape, because you are afraid that you yourself will be attacked. You are playing a game of tit for tat.

In the positive kind of attachment, you are thinking of someone and you want him to think of you. If he does not think of you, you are miserable. So both the positive and negative attachments are both useless when the attachment is directed towards an unaspiring and unillumined person. But you can direct your thoughts, ideas, ideals and aspiration, your sense of inner duty, towards your Mission, your Goal, towards your Master. Then I wish to say that you are safe, you are illumined, you are fulfilled.

1973

I

516. Besides meditating, if you have confusion, say someone has told you something that confuses you in your own spiritual life, how can you clear that up?

Sri Chinmoy: Your name: I have given you the spiritual name Mita, friend, eternal friend, universal friend, friend to the aspiring world, friend to the illumining world. You are the friend to everybody. Friendship you have. Now we have confusion!

When somebody creates confusion, what does he say? He says something which is unreal, and only an unreal thing creates confusion, not a real thing. Somebody says to you, "Your name is not Mita," now what will happen? Either you have to believe or disbelieve. You know your name is Mita. I have given you that name and whether others know it or not, you know. Even if there is no second person on earth to confirm it, you know that your name is Mita. So here in the spiritual life, you have to know that your name is also Aspiration. If somebody comes and tells you that, "no, no, no, your name is not Aspiration," then what will you do? Will you believe that person? As your name is Mita, so in the spiritual life your name is Aspiration. Now, if somebody tells you something which creates confusion, that means you are denying your own name. It is like this: who can create confusion in you if you do not allow it? Confusion is an unreal statement, an unreal reality, it is not real. Now, if you are real, who can create confusion in you? If you have faith in yourself, if you have faith in me, if you have faith in God, who can create confusion in you?

Suppose this is your building and somebody comes and says, "No, no, this is not your building. This is my building," what will you do? He can stay for twenty-four hours saying it is his building. It is not yours, it is his building. How will you believe him? No, you simply will say, "No, this is my building." So if your building is aspiration, there can be no confusion. But if your building is not aspiration, if your building is doubt, or curiosity or an unsettled state of things in your spiritual life, then I tell you, confusion can get in any moment. You must be firm in your aspiration and feel that your name is Aspiration. Who can tell you otherwise, who can deny it? But if you are not sure of your own name, which is Aspiration, you see that at this moment you have many names: your names may be fear, doubt, insecurity, uncertainty. If you have four or five names, naturally you will lose the game. But if your name is only one, one name you have which is Aspiration, I tell you, nobody can confuse you, nobody. Your aspiration is infinitely stronger than others' capacity. Their capacity is doubt, their capacity is fear, their capacity is undivine gossip, that is all. But if you think that you have only one name, Aspiration, and one capacity, divine capacity, absolute capacity, supreme capacity, nobody can destroy you. Not even an iota of your aspiration can be destroyed if you feel that your name is nothing but illumined Aspiration.

People say, "He has confused me." How can he confuse you? That means you have opened your heart's door. You will open your heart's door only to God, only to Truth, only to Light, only to Purity, only to Divinity. Do you open your door to your enemy? Do you open your door to the stranger? No. Who brings confusion? He who is a stranger, he who is your enemy. No, a real friend of yours will not bring confusion into your life. A real friend will only bring messages about God, messages of aspiration, love, joy, concern, all the divine messages, divine gifts he will bring forth. But he who is not your friend will bring only undivine gifts, fear, doubt, anxiety, worry. No human being on earth who has aspiration can be confused. Where aspiration lags, confusion starts. It is like that. Otherwise there is no confusion.

Aspiration is a flame, a burning flame which is our divine property, our real divine gift. Constantly it is illumining us, illumining and fulfilling us. And how is it possible that Grace which is aspiration can be confused with something else? It is impossible. Here it is all light now. No matter what you bring in, it is all illumined. But instead of bringing obscurity into light, what we do is that we feel that in darkness there is some joy, some pleasure. That darkness here is gossip, darkness here is lack of faith.

So, instead of keeping ourselves all the time in light, for the sake of pleasure we go to others who tell us gossip and all kinds of things, undivine things. Then we are confused. I wish to tell you that nobody, nobody can take your faith away, nobody, unless you feel that your faith is of secondary importance. If you feel that your faith is of paramount importance, that there is nothing greater than, or superior to your faith, then this imperturbable, unshakeable faith you already have, everybody has, will remain adamantine. But we allow ourselves to waver. We feel that we have been in light for ten hours, now let us go and be in darkness for five minutes. I meditated here for a long time for half an hour; it is a long experience, now let me lie down in the back room. While lying down in the back room all undivine forces come to attack. No, while lying down also I have to continue keeping the vibration of my meditation inside me during my sleep. Twenty-four hours we have to be vigilant. Then there can be no confusion. Always we have to be vigilant.

517. What can we do with the hostile forces when they attack us and try to separate the Centre or the members, instead of feeling as one group? What can we do?

Sri Chinmoy: What can you do? First of all you have to know that the hostile forces do exist. If we say they don't exist, it will be wrong. If we say there is only day, there is no night, it is wrong. Day is followed by night, night is followed by day. This is absolutely true right now. This is the physical world, the planet earth. But again we see that when consciousness is awakened, when the consciousness is illumined with the inner light, one only sees light and delight. There one does not see the night at all. Here we have a few hours of day, a few hours of night. Again on the physical plane, there are places where you can get sunlight for nineteen, twenty hours out of twenty-four. When I was in Stockholm and other places, for practically nineteen hours or twenty hours a day there was light. When it was around twelve o'clock midnight, twelve thirty, it began to get dark. And at 3:00 a.m. it started to get light again. It was all light. I saw this for the first time because in India for eleven or twelve hours we had light. But in Scandinavia, for seventeen, eighteen, nineteen hours, sometimes for twenty hours, I was seeing sunlight. How vast is God's creation!

But let us not think about this light and night. Let us think of our inner light which is spiritual. First of all we have to accept the fact that hostile forces do exist. Then our next step is to challenge them. How do we challenge them? We challenge them not by standing in front of them. No, we challenge them by going to somebody else. We go to Light. The moment we go to Light, the hostile forces will say, "What kind of audacity do you have, that you go to Light and not to me?" And the hostile forces will come and attack you while you are in the Light. Then Light will immediately say, "What right have you if she is taking shelter in my heart? I will not allow you to stab or to take my child from my heart." Then immediately Light will fight. But if one wants to go to night and fight, thinking that if night is very bad, the hostile forces are bound to be very weak, you will find that they are very strong. They will attack you more. But the very moment one goes to Light, the hostile forces feel that it is a defeat on their part and they feel that you have the audacity to go to Light without going to them. These hostile forces are all from ignorance. For years and years we have fed ignorance and ignorance has fed us. So ignorance feels that it is its bounden duty to keep us under its jurisdiction. Light feels that once you take shelter in it, it is the duty of Light to guide you, to protect you, to help you in your full illumination, salvation and liberation.

Then every day, consciously, during meditation, first offer your gratitude to the Supreme that you are praying and meditating well, that God has given you the capacity, the opportunity to meditate whereas there are millions of people on earth who are not praying and meditating. So God has given you this opportunity and capacity. First you offer your gratitude to God, then you pray to God for protection, always for protection. Then, how will you receive God's protection? It is through gratitude. If you have gratitude, then God offers you protection. Then if you ask for protection, immediately God feels grateful to you that you are asking Him to do something. Here, on the contrary, in this world, in the human world, when we ask someone to do us a favour, we feel that that person should offer us his gratitude. I ask somebody to do something for me; why should he be grateful to me? If you ask me to do something, you should be grateful to me; why should I be grateful to you? This is on the earth plane. You have asked me for a favour. Naturally I am the benefactor and you become an object of compassion. This is our human understanding.

In the spiritual life it is different. In the spiritual life, you ask me questions, I invite questions. Now here I am ready to offer you light. I beg you to ask me questions. Now when you are asking me questions, I feel that you have given me the opportunity to reveal the Supreme's Light which I have. Here in the case of God, God also is like that. When you ask God, beg God, "Give me illumination, give me liberation and give me strength and give me the capacity to save the world," immediately God becomes so happy and full of gratitude that you have asked Him, and not Satan, not the devil, not an undivine force, to be of service to you.

So God always appreciates those who ask Him for the right things. You are asking Him to give you Light, illumination and not millions of dollars and not power to destroy the world. You are asking him to give you the power to love the world, to illumine the world, to fulfil the world. So each time you pray to God to give you something, God becomes really happy, really grateful, really proud of you because you are asking Him to do something significant. And when you ask Him for His service, He becomes extremely grateful. You could have asked somebody else to do the service, somebody else who is called ignorance. There are two teachers on earth, either God or ignorance. So you take the teacher God. Naturally, if you select a teacher to teach you, that teacher will be most pleased with you. The other teacher, ignorance, whom you have not selected to teach, naturally will be displeased with you. So here, we will care only for the teacher you need and that teacher is God. So when you offer gratitude, God protects you and when you ask for protection, which is a kind of Light, God will be grateful to you.

And if you are in between the two shores, the shore of gratitude and the shore of protection, then I wish to say there can be no obstacle in your way and no problems in your life of aspiration.

518. I would like to know if detachment is in humility or if humility is in detachment and which one comes first.

Sri Chinmoy: First things have to come first. If there is no humility then one cannot make any progress. And if we cannot make any progress, how can we achieve detachment? Detachment is very difficult to achieve. So if one wants to make a choice between humility and detachment, humility should come first and humility should always remain. Otherwise if you start with detachment, today you will be detached and tomorrow you will be full of attachment. But if you start with humility, then one gets an inner knowledge, inner wisdom.

These are two divine qualities, humility and detachment. There are people who are very good seekers, the best seekers, but who are attached. They can be humble but they are very attached. Humility and detachment are in the same room. Both are absolutely necessary. My hand is necessary; my legs are necessary. They need not come together. Sometimes when I am working, I use my hand. Sometimes while I am here sitting, I may use my leg and not my hand. But you have to know that my hands and my legs are equally important, especially when the time comes for them to work together. So in this case, these are two divine qualities, but we must know that humility should come first.

519. How can we best tell the difference between true humility and when our ego thinks it is humble?

Sri Chinmoy: How can you know whether it is true humility or false humility? When it is true humility, you will get tremendous joy and you will feel that the person to whom you are bowing down is in no way superior to you. It is only that you see the Supreme in him. That is why you are bowing down to him. And while you are bowing down, you have to feel that it is like your hand touching your feet. You should not be ashamed of your hand touching your feet.

Now there are two ways. One way is touching your feet. We are not ashamed of touching our feet, no. But if we feel that the feet are something inferior to the hand, naturally we will feel that it is beneath the dignity of our hand to touch our feet. But when it is necessary, our hands do touch our feet.

Now, in touching my feet, I am getting joy. It is my foot; part of my body is touching another part. There is nothing wrong in it. I am getting joy. But when it is false humility, the moment you express your false humility, there is no joy at all, no joy. You don't get joy in your heart, you don't get joy in your mind. When you are offering insincere humility, your mind will be cursing you because it is all false. The mind will not get any joy and the vital will mock at you saying, "What kind of humility are you showing?" But when it is true humility, the physical, vital, mental, heart and soul all will participate in your action. And at that time you get tremendous joy. When you get real joy, it is true humility. When you are getting no joy or you are criticised by your own inner being or the members of your family, the vital, the mind and the physical, then you can rest assured that it is false humility.

520. How can you obtain a love for humanity in a true, practical sense? That is easy to speak about but difficult to practise.

Sri Chinmoy: It is true that it is easy to say that we love humanity. In reality we do not love; it is all a self-deception. But how can we acquire the true love of humanity? In order to love humanity, we have to go to the Source. The Source is not humanity, the Source is Divinity. And if we really can go to the Source and love Divinity, then Divinity is not something apart from our real existence. First you have to love God who is Divinity Himself. If you can love God, then you will feel that your inner existence is not separate, and cannot be separated, from God. Your existence, your true divine existence and God are one. Then you will see that your existence, which is your divine personality, is the entire humanity.

Your inner existence and God's outer reality are one thing. So when you divinely love yourself, not emotionally or egotistically, you are loving yourself just because God is breathing inside you, a God who wants to fulfil Himself through you. If you love yourself egotistically, you are killing yourself. If you love yourself undivinely, you are binding yourself. But when you love yourself divinely, you love yourself just because inside you is God. That is why you are loving yourself. You and God are one.

If you are fully aware of this truth, you will see, inside you, all of humanity. Humanity is not around you or outside you. It is inside you. If you become one with your divine existence, then you will see that inside you is humanity. Whatever is inside you is yours. Whatever is outside you is not yours. You can help to fulfil, illumine only that which is inside you. So you have to feel that humanity is inside you. Then you will be able to help humanity truly and effectively.

But first you have to realise God. Philanthropy is a very good practice, but real philanthropy begins inside. Just as it is said, "Charity begins at home," so also in spirituality, philanthropy and everything like it starts deep inside yourself. And what is the reality there? Only God inside you who is also the real humanity. So if you realise God, then God will show you how to love humanity. First things first. God-realisation is first for a spiritual seeker and not philanthropy; far from it. Realise God and then you will see that the world is inside you. If you don't realise God, you will see humanity around you as a world apart from you. The moment you realise God, you will feel that humanity is yours and the rest of the world is only yourself.

[This ends the transcription of talks and answers offered by the Master in Puerto Rico and the New York area, over a span of seven years, from 20 July 1966 to 23 July 1973.]

NOTES TO BOOK 3

257. *(p. 269)* Ahana (Mrs Blanca Bueso), San Juan, Puerto Rico, 21 August 1968.

258–265. *(p. 272)* These questions were answered on 20 July 1966, during Sri Chinmoy's first week in San Juan, Puerto Rico.

266–272. *(p. 276)* Remainder of material referred to.

276. *(p. 283)* Questioned asked by a seeker, after a disciple mentioned, "On that table is a display of the magazine that Sri Chinmoy is publishing. It is his way of spreading the Truth. When we finish here, you have the opportunity of looking at it and deciding if you are interested."

277–28. *(p. 284)* and 283. These questions were answered by Kalipada (Mr Harold Wong), when the first few disciples of the AUM Centre met at Sri Chinmoy's home at 3817 Fort Hamilton Parkway in Brooklyn, New York, on 10 September 1966.

. *(p. 286)* 279,4. Present at the meeting, in order of their duration with the Centre, were: Kalipada (Mr Harold Wong), Turiyananda (Mr Isidore Friedman), Maheshwari (Mrs Esther Sherman), Lakshmi (Mrs Lillian Gerber), Durga (Mrs Irene Silver), Priyta (Miss Priyta Lakini), Karuna (Mrs Ruth Moseley), Asim (Mr Virgil Gant), Dulal (Mr Sol Montlack), Indrani (Miss Barbara Callen).

284. *(p. 292)* Devadas (Dr Ventura Anselmi), San Juan, Puerto Rico, 10 January 1967.

285. *(p. 292)* Lakshmi (Mrs Esther Elvira), San Juan, Puerto Rico, 10 January 1967.

286. *(p. 293)* Madhuri (Mrs Nancy Ruiz), 504 East 84th Street, New York, 10 January 1967.

287. *(p. 295)* Ahana (Mrs Blanca Bueso), San Juan, Puerto Rico, 5 July 1967.

288–289. *(p. 297)* Ahana (Mrs Blanca Bueso), San Juan, Puerto Rico, 7 July 1967.

290. *(p. 299)* Mrs Aida Feliciano, San Juan, Puerto Rico, 7 July 1967.

291–292. *(p. 301)* Sita (Mrs María Teresa González), 13 July 1967.

293. *(p. 303)* Agni (Mr José Luis Casanova), San Juan, Puerto Rico, 17 July 1967.

294. *(p. 307)* Prajna (Mrs Haydee Casellas), San Juan, Puerto Rico, 26 July 1967.

295. *(p. 308)* Prajna (Mrs Haydee Casellas), San Juan, Puerto Rico, 26 July 1967.

296. *(p. 310)* Anugata (Mr Gustavo López Muñoz), San Juan, Puerto Rico, 26 July 1967.

297. *(p. 316)* Arati (Mrs Esther Marcano de Torado), San Juan, Puerto Rico, 26 July 1967.

298. *(p. 318)* Sudha (Miss Carmen Suro), San Juan, Puerto Rico, 31 July 1967.

299. *(p. 319)* Agni (Mr José Luis Casanova), San Juan, Puerto Rico, 31 July 1967.

300–301. *(p. 320)* Akuti (Miss Dorothy Eisamann), San Juan, Puerto Rico, 16 August 1967.

302–304. *(p. 323)* Devadas (Dr Ventura Anselmi), San Juan, Puerto Rico, 17 August 1967.

305. *(p. 329)* Sonia Cabanillas, San Juan, Puerto Rico, 1 October 1967.

306. *(p. 330)* Visitor, a young girl, 504 East 84th Street, 1 October 1967.

307–309. *(p. 332)* Barbara Callen, 504 East 84th Street, 1 October 1967.

310. *(p. 334)* Shobhana (Mrs Fay vom Saal), 504 East 84th Street, 1 October 1967.

311. *(p. 337)* A visitor, a gentleman of about thirty-five.

312–313. *(p.339)* Corina Torres.

314. *(p.339)* Dorothy (visitor), 504 East 84th Street, New York, N.Y.

315. *(p.341)* Abhaya (Miss Lotti Wolff), San Juan, Puerto Rico, 1 October 1967.

316. *(p.343)* Abhaya (Miss Lotti Wolff), San Juan, Puerto Rico, 10 December 1967.

317–324. *(p.344)* San Juan, Puerto Rico, 27 December 1967. Moderator: Sudha (Miss Carmen Suro). Panel: Vijaya (Mrs Sarah Casanova), Agni (Mr José Luis Casanova), Prajna (Mrs Haydee Casellas), Mr Pedro Dacosta. The TV Program was conducted on a bilingual basis. Sudha translated into Spanish all the questions while the person who asked the question translated into Spanish Sri Chinmoy's answer to him or her.

318. *(p.344)* Vijaya (Mrs Sara Casanova).

319. *(p.345)* Agni.

320–321. *(p.346)* Sudha (Miss Carmen Suro).

322. *(p.347)* Prajna (Mrs Haydee Casellas).

323. *(p.348)* Mr Pedro Dacosta.

324. *(p.348)* Sudha (Miss Carmen Suro).

325–326. *(p.350)* Gauri (Mrs Graciela Todd), San Juan, Puerto Rico, 4 January 1968.

327. *(p.352)* Miss Marín, San Juan, Puerto Rico, 7 January 1968.

328. *(p.354)* Talk at the Retailers' Centre in Hato Rey, Puerto Rico, 15 July 1968.

329–330. *(p.357)* Questions and answers following Sri Chinmoy's talk at the Retailers' Centre in Hato Rey, Santurce, Puerto Rico, 15 July 1968.

329. *(p.357)* Mr Cándido Rosado.

330. *(p.357)* Mr Manuel Borrero.

331–343. *(p.360)* TV Programme *Temas del momento*, "Themes of the moment", director: Mr Evelio Otero, 16 July 1968.

344. *(p.364)* Abhaya (Miss Lotti Wolff), San Juan, Puerto Rico, 25 July 1968.

345–349. *(p.366)* La Voz Del Figaro, Colegio De Barberos, Villa Palmeras, radio programme "The barber's voice", 26 July 1968.

346. *(p.366)* Mrs Eneida Cruz, lady barber.

347. *(p.367)* Mr Manuel Aponte, barber from Cayey.

348. *(p.368)* Agni (Mr José Luis Casanova), San Juan, Puerto Rico, 28 July 1968.

349. *(p.369)* Visitor, San Juan, Puerto Rico, 28 July 1968.

350–383. *(p.371)* Sri Chinmoy was interviewed by Mr Roberto García from *Bohemia,* a Spanish magazine, at the AUM Centre, Santurce on 29 July 1968. Translated from the Spanish text by Mr José Luis Casanova.

384. *(p.383)* Talk to members of the finance department of the government of Puerto Rico, 1 August 1968.

385. *(p.384)* Mr Pedro De Jesús Escobar.

386. *(p.385)* Mr Tiburcio Rosario.

387–391. *(p.387)* TV Programme on Channel 2, Telemundo, *Foro de la Comunidad (Community Forum),* San Juan, Puerto Rico, 3 August 1968. Moderator: Agni (Mr José Luis Casanova(.

388. *(p.388)* Ananta (Mr Ramón Torres Peña).

389. *(p.388)* Miss Petrita Hernández.

390. *(p.389)* Abhaya (Miss Wolff).

391. *(p.390)* Agni (Mr José Luis Casanova).

392. *(p.391)* TV Channel 6, WIPR interview, 9 August 1968. Host: Hector Campos Parsi.

393–403. *(p.393)* Interview at radio station WKYN, San Juan, 13 August 1968.

404. *(p.397)* Akuti (Miss Dorothy Eisamann), San Juan, Puerto Rico, 17 August 1968.

405. *(p.399)* Abhaya (Miss Lotti Wolff), San Juan, Puerto Rico, 17 August 1968.

406–409. *(p.400)* Chaitanya (Mr Juan Marina), San Juan, Puerto Rico, 17 August 1968.

410. *(p.404)* Savita (Miss Mae Arostegui), San Juan, Puerto Rico, 17 August 1968.

411. *(p.406)* Marilú Escobar, San Juan, Puerto Rico, 17 August 1968.

412–417. *(p.408)* These questions were asked by Sivashankara (Mr Tirso Mattai), San Juan, Puerto Rico, 17 August 1968.

418–419. *(p.413)* Mr Quiñones Vidal's programme, radio interview on station WKAQ, 17 August 1968, Saturday, 8:30 a.m.

420. *(p.415)* Chaitanya (Mr Juan Marina), San Juan, Puerto Rico, 21 August 1968.

421. *(p.418)* Ahana (Mrs Blanca Bueso), San Juan, Puerto Rico, 21 August 1968.

422. *(p.419)* Mrs Miña Calbazana, San Juan, Puerto Rico, 1 September 1968.

423. *(p.422)* Mr Hollen Harris, 504 East 84th Street, 15 October 1968.

424. *(p.424)* Shanti (Mrs Blanca Maldonado Mijón), San Juan, Puerto Rico, 16 October 1968.

425–429. *(p.426)* Questions from students at Yale University, following a talk given on 4 December 1968.

430. *(p.431)* José Padilla, San Juan, 30 December 1968.

431. *(p.434)* Abhaya (Miss Lotti Wolff), San Juan, Puerto Rico, 23 May 1969.

434. *(p.437)* Mrs Quiñones, San Juan, Puerto Rico, 25 May 1969.

435. *(p.439)* Ahana (Mrs Blanca Bueso), San Juan, Puerto Rico, 26 May 1969.

436. *(p.440)* Well-known singer, San Juan, Puerto Rico, 26 May 1969.

437. *(p.442)* Sudha (Miss Carmen Suro), San Juan, Puerto Rico, 30 May 1969.

438. *(p.443)* Akuti (Mrs Dorothy Eisamann), San Juan, Puerto Rico, 17 August 1968. The date could be 1969, but it is not sure at this point.

439. *(p.444)* Chaitanya (Mr Juan Marina), San Juan, Puerto Rico, 30 May 1969.

440. *(p.446)* Hlandini (Katherine Wood Marina), San Juan, Puerto Rico, 30 May 1969.

441–442. *(p.447)* Abhaya (Miss Lotti Wolff), San Juan, Puerto Rico, 4 June 1969.

444. *(p.450)* Sanjivan (Mr Samuel Medina), San Juan, Puerto Rico, 6 September 1969.

445. *(p.453)* Anugata (Gustavo López Muñoz), San Juan, Puerto Rico, 9 September 1969.

446–449. *(p.458)* Linda López, San Juan, Puerto Rico, 20 January 1970.

450. *(p.460)* Pratyay (Juan Alvarez), San Juan, Puerto Rico, 9 February 1970.

451. *(p.463)* Louis Byron, Inter American University, San Juan, Puerto Rico, 17 February 1970.

452. *(p.464)* Shanti (Mrs Blanca Maldonado Mijón), San Juan, Puerto Rico, 23 February 1970.

453. *(p.465)* Chaitanya (Mr Juan Marina), San Juan, Puerto Rico, 25 February 1970.

454. *(p.469)* Jorge Fuentes, San Juan, Puerto Rico, 27 February 1970.

455. *(p.470)* Shanti (Mrs Blanca Maldonado Mijón), San Juan, Puerto Rico, 27 February 1970.

456–468. *(p.473)* Questions and answers following the lecture "The inner freedom", Fairfield University, Fairfield, Connecticut, 8 April 1970.

469. *(p.480)* Sevananda (Mr José Padilla), San Juan, Puerto Rico, 7 May 1970.

470. *(p.482)* Agni (Mr José Luis Casanova), San Juan, Puerto Rico, 23 July 1970.

471. *(p.484)* Vijaya (Mrs Sara Casanova).

472–502. *(p.488)* Sri Chinmoy asked himself and then answered these questions on an Eastern Airlines flight to Puerto Rico on 27 October 1970.

503. *(p.494)* Mohini (Miss Jennifer Napoli), San Juan, Puerto Rico, 18 January 1971.

504. *(p.496)* Sanjivan (Mr Samuel Medina), San Juan, Puerto Rico, 18 January 1971.

505. *(p.500)* This is a talk given by Sri Chinmoy to the students of Karate Teacher, Mr Kimo Wall of Honolulu, Hawaii, at the Sagrado Corazón College in San Juan, at 2:00 p.m. on 19 January 1971, after Kimo and his students had given a lengthy and extraordinarily skilful performance of karate for the Master and the disciples of the San Juan Centre.

506. *(p.502)* Miss Rebecca Delgado.

507. *(p.504)* Pedro González.

508. *(p.507)* Jaime Sifre.

509–510. *(p.509)* Rebecca Delgado.

511. *(p.511)* Coralia Polanco.

512. *(p.516)* Charles Medeiros, San Juan, Puerto Rico, 23 June 1972.

513. *(p.518)* Ashpriha (Louis Byron), San Juan, Puerto Rico, 23 June 1972.

514. *(p.520)* Suniti (Mrs Luz María Dávila), San Juan, Puerto Rico, 23 June 1972.

515. *(p.523)* Miss Sylvia Torres, San Juan, Puerto Rico, 25 June 1972.

516. *(p.528)* Mita (Miss Wanda Caballero), San Juan, Puerto Rico, 23 July 1973.

517. *(p.531)* Vijaya (Mrs Sara Casanova), San Juan, Puerto Rico, 23 July 1973.

518. *(p.534)* Gauri (Mrs Graciela Todd), San Juan, Puerto Rico, 23 July 1973.

519. *(p.535)* Eulogio García III, San Juan, Puerto Rico, 23 July 1973.

520. *(p.536)* Devadas (Dr Ventura Anselmi), San Juan, Puerto Rico, 23 July 1973.

APPENDIX

FOREWORD TO FIRST EDITION

FOREWORD TO FIRST EDITION OF
EARTH'S CRY MEETS HEAVEN'S SMILE, BOOK I

I

Sri Chinmoy needs no introduction to the world-wide community of spiritual seekers. He has been enshrined in the souls of thousands of aspirants as a *Mahayogi*, a great Being merged in ineffable Union with the Absolute.

His Public Meditations, held in many countries of the world, have provided an incomparable inner experience to followers of all paths and persuasions. Here seekers are offered the opportunity to bask in the descent of the Master's Golden Light. Like a torrential rain it descends, Heaven's Infinite Light on earth, re-awakening and renewing each soul with the universal assurance of Heaven's boundless Compassion and Concern.

Twice a week at the U.N. Headquarters in New York City, the Master offers to the soul and body of the United Nations his rare and unparalleled Prayer-Height and Meditation-Light.

Crying earth's supreme need for Heaven's Compassionate Smile can be clearly seen and felt in the thousands of questions and answers being prepared for this continuing series of books.

Sri Chinmoy's immortal replies represent the capacity of the Mahayogi to embrace the *particular* and then transmute it into the *universal*. The Master first enters into the consciousness of the seeker, and without losing his own loftiest height raises the question from its limited scope. Even the most mundane question is dignified by the Guru's rarefied consciousness. While widening and heightening the scope of the question, Sri Chinmoy elevates the consciousness of the seeker and often reveals, within the isolated question, a deep, universal significance. Responding to this larger unvoiced cry, the Master offers us in his inimitable and spiritually enchanting answers, a truly immortal glimpse of the Infinite Truth.

2

Since Sri Chinmoy formally began his mission on 27 August 1965, he has answered literally thousands of questions and answers, on subjects pertaining to the spiritual life. Most of these questions and answers, though recorded and transcribed, are still unpublished.

After many years' delay, we are now bringing out this new series, *Earth's cry meets Heaven's Smile*. This set will draw together not only the unpublished material, which will be of great interest to the Master's own disciples, but also the previously printed questions and answers which were scattered in dozens of successive issues of magazines or pamphlets.

Because of the staggering number of questions and answers that we have on hand, we are deliberately making no effort at this time to publish them under headings of subject matter. Rather, we are approaching the material in a chronological way and one which will distinguish between questions and answers that are very familiar to many disciples and those that have never been seen. When all the questions and answers have finally been published, our plan is to organise and categorise them into spiritual topics for the benefit of future aspirants and students.

Book I, this present volume, begins at the beginning. Here, we have reprinted all the questions and answers which appeared in *AUM* magazine from 27 August 1965 to 27 July 1969.

Book II will present all the questions and answers from *Sri Chinmoy Answers*, a series published in 1970.

Book III, beginning with new material, will publish Guru's answers to questions asked by Puerto Rican disciples at the San Juan Sri Chinmoy Centre from 20 July 1966 extending through the present time. These are entirely the work of Agni, who transcribed and recorded in longhand thousands of pages of these spiritual discourses.

Book IV will print unpublished questions and answers from the Connecticut and New York Centres from 1968 to 1972.

Several more books in this series are planned after book IV.

This present volume is a joint effort of the New York and San Juan Centres. It was beautifully typed in New York, and the rest of the work was done at the AUM Press in San Juan under the most devoted supervision of Nivedan. We offer our gratitude to Kanti, who has been raising funds with great care and concern for the publishing of recent books. We also offer our gratitude to Euloglo and Bansidhar for making negatives, Kalyan, for developing plates, Daisy, for masking, Ashpriha, Victor and Lester for printing, Bishwas for binding and many others, including our eternally faithful Ananta, who have been participating in all the other operations needed to bring this book to its successful birth.

FOREWORD TO FIRST EDITION OF
EARTH'S CRY MEETS HEAVEN'S SMILE, BOOK 2

1

Here is the second book of Questions and Answers, reprinted from the 1970 pamphlet-series entitled *Sri Chinmoy Answers*.

Once again the Great Yogi illumines our faint and groping light. He strengthens our dawning spiritual convictions and reassures us in our faltering march to the goal of God-Realisation. If there is a key-word to describe these teachings, then it is Power. Sri Chinmoy's compelling certitude and his simple but inexorable Knowledge Supreme feeds life to our aspiration and Power to our souls.

2

While most of the questions of book 1 of *Earth's cry meets Heaven's Smile* were posed by seekers attending Centre meditations or public talks in the New York or San Juan areas where Sri Chinmoy's major Centres were located, those in book 2 reflect the steady expansion of the Master's spiritual mission. Questions from all parts of the United Kingdom and some from continental Europe now make their appearance. Onwards from 1969, public lectures were given by Sri Chinmoy in various European countries. Each talk was followed by a Question-and-Answer period, samples of which first appeared in the series *Sri Chinmoy Answers*, reprinted here.

A number of Sri Chinmoy Centres, established as early as 1968, will be represented in later books of this series.

The thanks offered to the disciples who produce these books are never adequate acknowledgement for the long hours of tedious and exacting labour that go into every publication. In the final stages, the disciples often work around the clock without rest or sleep, and in Puerto Rico, in intense humid heat, with very little food. Therefore each outer line of gratitude comes with Sri Chinmoy's deepest inner Blessings and his Eternal Love.

We offer our grateful thanks to Nilima of the New York Centre for her beautiful and accurate typing of both books One and Two. Assisting her were a number of excellent proofreaders from the Connecticut and New York Centres who worked extremely hard to eliminate the inevitable typographical errors.

The printing of the book was again done at the San Juan Centre in Puerto Rico. Ashpriha, Bansidhar, Bishwas, Drona, Kalyan and Nivedan deserve very special praise and gratitude for their conscientious leadership and high sense of responsibility.

Working very hard and selflessly for long hours on various aspects of the publication were Ananta, Daisy, Dhananjaya, Lester, Madhavi and Shubhra.

We also wish to thank Aidita, Anna, Dulce, Eddie, Eshana, Kanti, Mangal, Mita, Victor and Zulma who offered us their services when they were free from their other duties.

Shubhra's mother, Mrs Millie Jackson, gave us her generous assistance on many occasions and Edward Robertson, the new proprietor of Suniti Bhavan was kind enough to help us in laminating the books. We thank Nivedan's father, Mr José Hidalgo and the General Binding Corporation for their kindness in allowing us to use their laminating machine.

*

[*Note: first edition of book 3 was published with no foreword.*]

BIBLIOGRAPHY

SRI CHINMOY:

EARTH'S CRY MEETS HEAVEN'S SMILE (3 VOLUMES)

–*Earth's cry meets Heaven's Smile, book 1*, New York, Agni Press, 1974.
–*Earth's cry meets Heaven's Smile, book 2*, New York, Agni Press, 1974.
–*Earth's cry meets Heaven's Smile, book 3*, New York, Agni Press, 1978.

Suggested citation key: EH.

Bibliographical notes

The full title of book one and two was: *Earth's cry meets Heaven's Smile, countless spiritual questions answered by Mahayogi Sri Chinmoy.*

First edition of book 3 included several photographs of Sri Chinmoy (pages xx, 4, 26, 238, 274), of Sri Chinmoy with Pope Paul VI (page 260), of disciples–at times with Sri Chinmoy or with Alo Devi (pages 90, 176, 202, 286, 287, 288).

POSTFACE

Publishing principles

The works of Sri Chinmoy series aims to obey the Author's wish: scrupulous fidelity to his original words, use of typographical style by him selected, specific spelling choices, end placement of any editorial content (i.e. not written by Sri Chinmoy himself), particular treatment of some personal nouns in special cases, etc.

Textual accuracy

The series has been checked to ensure faithful accuracy to the originals. Although much effort has been put in proofreading and comparing different versions of the text, this print may still present lingering errors. The Publisher would be grateful to be apprised of any mistypes via postal mail or facsimile, possibly with scan of the original page where the text is different. Please use original books only, specifying the year of publication, as no online version can be considered authoritative.

Ongoing reprints will include any revised text from these errata.

Acknowledgements

The Publisher is very grateful to the late Professor Lambert and his équipe for his invaluable advice. For many decades Prof. Lambert conducted a small publishing house specialising in hand-made prints of philological edition of the classics. The standard of this edition would not have been the same without his scholarly advice.

The Publisher is also grateful to the international team of collaborators that spent countless hours proofreading and checking the current text against the originals.

Our deepest gratitude to Sri Chinmoy. His living presence can be felt breathing throughout his writings. It is a privilege to be involved with his works, in any form.

Citation keys

Citation keys can be used throughout *The works of Sri Chinmoy* to allow accurate cross-reference of texts across titles and editions. Examples: EA 13, ST 50000, UPA 7. Suggested citation keys can be found in the bibliography at the end of each volume.

Sri Chinmoy Canon

We could not use better words than Professor Lambert's, who kindly offered the name *Sri Chinmoy Canon*:

> «By defining Sri Chinmoy's first editions as *editio princeps* we chose to follow classical scholarship criteria, not because we consider Sri Chinmoy's work antique, but because we believe it is among the few post ‹classical antiquity› works to rightly deserve to be considered a *classicus*, designating by that term *superiority, authority* and *perfection*.
> «The monumental work Sri Chinmoy is offering to mankind is awe-inspiring and supremely pre-eminent in proportions and quality. It is manifest that Sri Chinmoy's work — which we feel right to call *The Sri Chinmoy Canon* — will be of profound help and source of enlightenment to anyone seeking a higher wisdom, truth and reality supreme.»

[Translated from French by M. G.S.]

TABLE OF CONTENTS

BOOK 1	3
I – QUESTIONS AND ANSWERS	3
II – SRI CHINMOY'S FIRST TELEVISION INTERVIEW	9
III – QUESTIONS AND ANSWERS	14
IV – QUESTIONS AND ANSWERS AT THE PUERTO RICO CENTRE	16
V – INTERVIEW ON WHOA RADIO STATION	21
VI – QUESTIONS ASKED AT THE UNIVERSITY OF PUERTO RICO	38
VII – QUESTIONS ASKED AT THE INTER-AMERICAN UNIVERSITY, SAN JUAN, PUERTO RICO	44
VIII – QUESTIONS ASKED AT YALE UNIVERSITY	51
IX – QUESTIONS ASKED AT YOGA OF WESTCHESTER, NEW ROCHELLE, NEW YORK	55
X – QUESTIONS ASKED IN 1969	65
XI – QUESTIONS ON SURRENDER	73
BOOK 2	85
I – QUESTIONS AND ANSWERS, UNITED KINGDOM AND CONTINENTAL EUROPE	85
II – MEDITATION	106
III – QUESTIONS AND ANSWERS, AMERICAN INTERNATIONAL SCHOOL, ZURICH, SWITZERLAND	146
IV – QUESTIONS AND ANSWERS, UNIVERSITY OF BRISTOL	157
V – QUESTIONS AND ANSWERS, ST. DAVID'S COLLEGE, UNIVERSITY OF LAMPETER, WALES	167
VI – QUESTIONS AND ANSWERS, THE AMERICAN CENTRE FOR STUDENTS AND ARTISTS, PARIS, FRANCE	172
VII – QUESTIONS AND ANSWERS, CONWAY HALL, LONDON, ENGLAND	178
VIII – QUESTIONS AND ANSWERS, UNIVERSITY OF GLASGOW	188
IX – QUESTIONS AND ANSWERS, UNIVERSITY OF LEEDS	196
X – QUESTIONS AND ANSWERS, UNIVERSITY OF ESSEX, COLCHESTER, ENGLAND	206
XI – QUESTIONS AND ANSWERS, UNIVERSITY OF NOTTINGHAM	214

XII – QUESTIONS AND ANSWERS, AMERICAN COLLEGE, PARIS	223
XIII – QUESTIONS AND ANSWERS, UNIVERSITY OF LONDON	233
XIV – QUESTIONS AND ANSWERS, KEBLE COLLEGE, OXFORD UNIVERSITY	244
XV – QUESTIONS AND ANSWERS, KINGS COLLEGE, CAMBRIDGE UNIVERSITY	255
BOOK 3	269
I	269
1966	
I – QUESTIONS AND ANSWERS ON 20 JULY 1966	272
II – WEEK OF 20 JULY 1966	276
III – 20 JULY 1966	281
IV – AT SRI CHINMOY'S HOME	284
1967	
I	292
II – TV PROGRAMME, WKAQ, CHANNEL 2	344
1968	
I	350
II – TALK AT THE RETAILERS' CENTRE IN HATO REY	354
III – QUESTIONS AND ANSWERS FOLLOWING SRI CHINMOY'S TALK AT THE RETAILERS' CENTRE	357
IV – TV PROGRAMME "TEMAS DEL MOMENTO"	360
V – RADIO PROGRAMME "THE BARBER'S VOICE"	366
VI – INTERVIEW WITH	371
VII – TALK TO AND QUESTIONS FROM THE FINANCE DEPARTMENT STAFF, PUERTO RICO	383
VIII – TV PROGRAMME ON CHANNEL 2, TELEMUNDO	387
VIX – TV CHANNEL 6, WIPR INTERVIEW	391
X – INTERVIEW AT RADIO STATION WKYN, SAN JUAN	393
XI – QUESTIONS AND ANSWERS ON 17 AUGUST 1968	397
XII – QUESTIONS BY SIVASHANKARA	408
XIII – MR QUIÑONES VIDAL'S PROGRAMME, RADIO INTERVIEW ON STATION WKAQ	413

XIV – QUESTIONS AND ANSWERS, AUGUST TO OCTOBER 1968 415
XV – QUESTIONS FROM STUDENTS AT YALE UNIVERSITY   426
1969
I   434
1970
I   458
II – QUESTIONS AND ANSWERS FOLLOWING THE LECTURE
"THE INNER FREEDOM"   473
III – QUESTIONS AND ANSWERS IN MAY AND JULY 1970 480
IV – QUESTIONS ASKED BY SRI CHINMOY HIMSELF   488
1971
I   494
II – TALK AND QUESTIONS AND ANSWERS AT THE SAGRADO
CORAZÓN COLLEGE IN SAN JUAN   500
1972
I   516
1973
I   528
APPENDIX
FOREWORD TO FIRST EDITION
FOREWORD TO FIRST EDITION OF
EARTH'S CRY MEETS HEAVEN'S SMILE, BOOK 1   551
FOREWORD TO FIRST EDITION OF
EARTH'S CRY MEETS HEAVEN'S SMILE, BOOK 2   554
BIBLIOGRAPHY
POSTFACE
TABLE OF CONTENTS

*Composition typographique par imprimerie
Ab Academia Aoidon, Paris & Lyon.*

*Un grand merci à Prof Knuth pour
l'utilisation avancée de* T_EX.

A LYON, LE 13 MAI LXXXIX Æ.G.

www.ingramcontent.com/pod-product-compliance
Lightning Source LLC
Chambersburg PA
CBHW030110240426
43661CB00031B/1362/J